The Anti-Samuelson

BY MARC LINDER

VOLUME TWO

Microeconomics:

BASIC PROBLEMS OF THE CAPITALIST ECONOMY

URIZEN BOOKS / NEW YORK

Library of Congress Cataloging in Publication Data

Linder, Marc.
　　Anti-Samuelson.

　　　Bibliography.
　　　Includes index.
　　　1. Samuelson, Paul Anthony, 1915-　　Economics.
　　I. Sensat, Julius, 1947-　　joint author. II. Title.
　　HB119.S25L5　　　330　　　76-20796
　　ISBN 0-916354-16-4 (v. 2)
　　ISBN 0-916354-17-2 (v. 2) pbk.

Second Printing

Copyright © 1977 by Marc Linder

All rights reserved

Manufactured in the United States of America

Contents

10	Money	1
11	Banks and Credit	33
12	Central Banks and Fiscal Policy	53
13	Supply and Demand—An Empirical Approach	87
14	The Failure of Supply and Demand as Applied to Agriculture	101
15	Marginal-Utility Theory	117
16	Price Theory	147
17	Monopoly Theory	169
18	Marginal Productivity Theory	181
19	The Theory of Ground Rent	201
20	Wages	211
21	Interest	227
22	Theories of Profit	241

IMPERIALISM AND THE WORLD MARKET

	Introduction to Chapters 23-27	249
23	The World Market and World Money: Theoretical and Historical Outline	257
24	World-Trade Theories	299
25	The Development of Imperialist Trade Policy	323
26	Aspects of the World Market and International Currency Crises	339
27	"Underdevelopment	389
	Notes and References	425

Chapter 10: Money (S's Chapter 15)

This chapter in S is intended as a link between the income analysis of Chapters 10-14 and the anticyclical measures of the Fed in the subsequent chapters. It repeats and embellishes previous material on price and money amidst a selection of statistics with no theoretical bridge to the text. In order to provide an introduction to what is rather difficult theoretical material we have decided to begin with S's remarks on inflation.

INFLATION

Although S has not defined price for us (all we know is that "everything has a price"—43), he nonetheless proceeds to measure it and tell us how it has changed over the years in the U.S. Then we are told that "some definitions will be useful. By *inflation* we mean *a time* [? !] *of generally rising prices* for goods and factors of production—rising prices for bread, cars, haircuts; rising wages, rents, etc. By *deflation* we mean a time when most prices and costs are falling" (270). Even though we just "discovered" that inflation represents "generally rising prices," S suddenly shifts to "changes in relative prices"; "Unforeseen inflation tends to favor debtors and profit receivers at the expense of creditors and fixed-income receivers" (*ibid.*). But when it comes to a concrete historical analysis of inflation, S sacrifices this differentiated view in favor of a good guys–bad guys description:

> Nothing good can be said for a rapid rise of prices such as took place in Germany in 1920-1923 and more recently in China and Hungary. Production and even [!] the social order are then disorganized. The total wealth of large groups of the population is wiped out as money becomes worthless. Debtors ruthlessly pursue creditors in order to pay off their obligations in valueless money. Speculators profiteer [273].

S contradicts himself here. First we are told that "nothing good" can be said about the matter, and then we are informed that large groups were wiped out. Thus small groups who benefited from this operation must have found the whole business "good." An economist with a semiofficial position in Germany, who was the author of a standard history of that inflation, wrote:

> There is no doubt that the paper inflation would not have assumed such vast proportions if it had not been favoured in many ways from the people who drew a large profit from it. It is clear from the discussions held in 1922 and 1923 in the "Economic Council of the Reich" that representatives of those classes used their influence on the Government to impede the reform of the public finances and to sabotage all proposals for the stabilization of the German exchange, which they accepted only when, at last, an economic catastrophe threatened Germany and it was evident that the consequences of the inflation would rebound against their authors. . . . It may be said that on the whole the inflation generally favoured the entrepreneurs and the owners of the material means of productions, especially strengthening the positions of industrial capitalists; that it caused a lowering of the real wages; that it decimated or destroyed altogether the old middle class of investors. . . .[1]

Let us look at some of the methods used to exploit the proletariat. The income tax then constituted one-third of Germany's state budget; of this, 90 percent was paid by the working class. The workers' income taxes were deducted from their wages, while the capitalists did not pay taxes for more than a year after the taxable income was "earned." And because the inflation from 1921 to 1923 was so severe they paid their taxes in relatively worthless money. Thus the capitalists were supposed to pay $70 million in taxes in the first quarter of 1923, (from 1921 income); by this time that sum was worth only $1.333 million. Moreover, the capitalists did not immediately hand over the taxes deducted from the workers' wages: they held them for two weeks, during which time they used the money to buy means of production, and sold their newly produced commodities at their reproduction price, which, because of the inflation, was of course higher than the production price. Handing over the money to the state in depreciated form, they kept the difference.

Next we come to the effect of inflation on total production. S asserts that "an increase in prices is usually associated with high employment. In mild inflation . . . output is near capacity. Private investment is brisk. . . . In deflation . . . the growing unemployment of labor and capital causes the community's total well-being to be less . . ." (272). On an empirical level, contemporary stagflation of course, gives the lie to this. S, however, fails to provide the missing theoretical links. "Mild" inflation is often accompanied by, or rather accompanies, "well-lubricated wheels of industry" precisely because wages rise more slowly than other commodity prices, thereby allowing capitalists to realize superprofits by buying labor power below its value; as a result there is in the short run increased capital formation and also increased or relatively higher employment.

S would have us believe that the contemporary preference for inflation over deflation is the result of some sort of marginal-utility calculus poll that found inflation to be "the lesser of the two evils" because the "losses to fixed income groups are usually less than the gains to the rest of the community" (272). To the extent that inflation is planned, it is done so for and by capital.

It would however be erroneous to believe that things are much better under conditions of stagflation than deflation-depression, for the enormity of contemporary underutilization of industrial capacity must be put into perspective: given utilization of between 70 and 75 percent, and a GNP of, say, at least 600 or 700 billion dollars in terms of 1929 purchasing power, the total value of output represented by underutilization exceeds that of total GNP at the end of the boom of the 1920s (1929 GNP-103 billion dollars). It is necessary to place this development in a theoretical context. Permanent underutilization (only the Korean and Vietnam wars were able to nudge the percentage even to 90) means permanent capital overproduction; it is no longer only during the periodic crisis and depression phases that capital is idled and depreciated: since World War II the conditions of surplus-value expansion have been so altered that a large part of the total social product is maneuvered into investment and government consumption and there made idle, which from the point of view of capital expansion is tantamount to capital destruction.

This development is closely related to "planned" inflation. To begin with, a significant part of capitalized surplus value is neatly tucked away under the rubric "rapid early depreciation allowances"; the ability to do this rests upon the monopoly situation of the largest capitals. Since prices must compensate for these "costs," the consumers bear the brunt. For nonmilitary capital this means that the monopolies, independent of the state, have the power to bring about depreciation of money and redistribution of income. (It must be noted, however, that an increase in monopoly prices need not necessarily lead to inflation in the sense of "flooding the conduits with paper." To begin with, monopoly pricing refers to wholesale prices—that is, transactions among capitalists [either within Department I or between I and II]; such commodity exchange is not normally carried on with paper money but rather by increasing bank money in the form of deposits [increased credit]. This in part explains the large increase in commercial bank deposits. There is also a limit to this credit-deposit creation. Deposits can be created to the extent that moneyless, reciprocal liquidation of claims takes place, in which transactions money functions as means of payment and claims compensate one another. But deposit inflation is also possible when deposits exceed the needs of moneyless transactions; if loan capital as money capital exceeds the needs of the turnover of total capital, then a part of it can no longer function as industrial capital. But loan capital is interest-bearing capital: if its mass is increased without a corresponding increase in the mass of surplus value, then the portion of surplus value going to the industrial capitalist [entrepreneurial profit] decreases relative to the portion appropriated by the money capitalists, or the share appropriated by each lender is diminished [equaling a declining rate of interest]. In the former case there is of course a limit to the drop in the rate of entrepreneurial profit below which industrial capital will not employ any more loan capital; similarly, in the latter case, there is an interest rate limit below which the money capitalists will *not* lend. A resolution of the conflict between loan and real capital as expressed in the inflation of the former is sought in the annulment of part of the deposits or in the equal devaluation of all deposits.)[2]

On the other hand, rising monopoly prices do not necessarily result in an increased supply in retail business; for if wage increases do not correspond to the increase in monopoly prices, then the volume of retail sales remains the same, while the physical volume decreases; thus inflation takes place without an increase in the money supply. An analogous process takes place in the state-military-industrial sphere.

As far as practical pricing is concerned, S informs us that there are three possibilities: (1) stable prices, with money and real wages rising; (2) rising prices, with real wages lagging behind money wages; (3) falling prices, with stable money wages and rising real wages. The third possibility is immediately ruled out on the grounds that we do not live in an "ideal frictionless society" (274); in the appendix to Chapter 18, S implies that this "friction" is in reality monopoly: "If business generally can set its prices so as to keep labor's share of total NNP at about the same fraction of three-fourths, then the resulting pattern of prices is determined" (7th ed, p. 332). Perhaps we are given a historical taste of what S has in mind with the notion that "most vigorous periods of healthy capitalist development without political unrest came during periods of stable or gently rising prices. Capitalism itself developed during the centuries when Spanish New World gold was raising prices" (274). This is how M. Dobb describes the time:

> To the extent that money-wages failed to rise as the commodity price-level rose, all employers and owners of capital were abnormally enriched at the expense of the standard of life of the labouring class; the price revolution generated that "profit inflation" of which Lord Keynes has spoken as being responsible for those "golden years" when "modern Capitalism was born" and as "the fountain and origin of British Foreign Investment." . . . In France and Britain real wages continued to fall throughout the sixteenth century and remained throughout the seventeenth century below the level at which they had stood in 1500. . . . Real wages in 1600 in England were less than a half what they had been a century before.[3]

Are these the halcyon days the American worker is destined to bring about through wage moderation and profit inflation? As this last historical example shows, it is confusing and misleading to "define" inflation as a general rise in the price level, as is commonly done by bourgeois economists. The rise in prices set off by the discovery of gold in gold-currency economies is clearly an anarchic process characteristic of capitalist commodity production and exchange. The inflation that "plagues" capitalism today is not to the same *degree* an anarchic process, inasmuch as various manipulations can lead through the sphere of circulation to a subsequent redistribution of income between bourgeoisie and proletariat. On the other hand, the historical process of the sixteenth and seventeenth centuries depended on more than the discovery of gold. If that had been the only factor, then all commodity prices would have been affected equally and no class changes would have resulted. However, because of the stage of capital accumulation of those affected, the effects in different countries differed. In Britain and France a reserve army of unemployed had already developed which depressed wages; in Spain "the process of primitive accumulation in this still-feudal country had not begun"; various other historically conditioned factors (the expulsion of Moors, colonization, pestilence) also made the labor market "tight," and thus by 1620, wages were higher than they had been in 1500.[4]

This excursion into the past makes clear that inflation unlike, for example, Marx's theory of money, is not an abstract theory. Insofar as inflation is a differentiated and "class-conscious" process, it is in large measure determined by concrete and, viewed from the level of abstraction, say, in *Capital*, historically accidental phenomena. Unless the term inflation is to become a formal classification bereft of all meaning, it appears necessary to deny that inflation has anything to do with (1) a decrease in the value of gold, (2) an increase in the value of commodities, or (3) a deviation of market prices from value as determined by supply and demand; for as a concept existing on a level much closer to concrete reality than, say, value, inflation must be explained in terms of concrete phenomena, and it "just so happens" that today none of these three factors has anything to do with rising prices: (1) productivity in the gold industry has not advanced faster than that in other industries; (2) productivity in the bulk of commodity-producing industries has not decreased absolutely; and (3) the gap between supply and effective demand that characterized World War II and the postwar periods has been closed by the usual overproduction. Now we know some of the things inflation is *not*.

The distinguishing characteristic of inflation is not so much the flooding of the conduits with paper money as the depreciation of that paper vis-à-vis gold. This is not to say that flooding does not also take place; in wartime, for example, "civilian production" drops: "the excess purchasing power can be used to bid up the prices of goods and not to obtain additional goods. Under these conditions, consumers can only pay more for goods; they cannot get more goods."[5] But wars can also be financed without increasing the supply of paper money; the state can tax away the "excess" effective demand; this is in fact what happened during World War II in the U.S.: taxes increased faster than money depreciated.

If all this is true, *then our attention should be fixed on the phenomenon of paper money depreciation relative to gold.* Thus we must develop a theory of paper money, which in turn presupposes the development of a theory of money. S fails to do this.

CRITIQUE OF S'S THEORY OF MONEY

To begin with, S is prepared to go back to an era predating commodity production, a time free of the contradictions inherent in the creation and appropriation of surplus value, and when commodities themselves disappear in favor of "goods"; we are told in effect that there is little if any difference between the exchanges conducted by "the first two ape men" and those using money; for although the latter "at first glance . . . seems to complicate rather than simplify matters," "actually the reverse is the case: the two transactions [viz.: commodity-money-commodity] are simpler than one" (275). Not content with his performance thus far, S makes the "obscuring layer of money" even denser: "The essence of money, its intrinsic nature, is typified by paper currency. *Money, as money rather than a commodity, is wanted not for its own sake but for the things it will buy*: We do not wish to use up money directly, but rather to use it by getting rid of it; even when we choose to use it by holding it, its value comes from the fact that we can spend it later on" (276). This passage is an excellent example of the "essence, the intrinsic nature" of S's approach. There is no such thing as "money as money rather than a commodity": the point is that both are forms of value, forms that value and surplus value must assume in the never-ending process of value self-expansion called successful capitalism. The "essence" of money cannot be "typified" by gold, paper, or any other use value, because the essence of money is a social relation.

"Money is an artificial, social convention" (276). Only the use-value form of money, whether it be shells, gold, silver, or paper, is a social convention; money itself as an abstract embodiment of social labor cannot possibly be a social convention, because it is a social relation which developed over the heads and behind the backs of man: nobody ever sat down and said: "Let's produce a value." This is why "the public neither knows nor cares—and need not know or care" (276) what natural body money acquires. "Paradox: money is accepted because it is accepted" (276). Nonsense. Money is "accepted" because it is the only "acceptable" way of exchanging commodities (including labor power) in capitalism. The point is not which natural form of money is in use, not that at a given time (e.g., Germany in 1923) the system of exchange may break down, but rather that in every "naturally" functioning capitalist economy money as the universal equivalent must exist and the members of that society must "use" money, whether they know what the "essence" of money is or not.

Although S likes to talk about "modern" students and money as the "modern medium of exchange," his theory of money is in fact very old. In fact, it goes back two hundred years, to Hume, whose theory Marx criticized in his *Contribution to the Critique of Political Economy*. (Hume dealt with gold and silver; Ricardo was primarily concerned with paper; but as Marx points out, although Ricardo and his contemporaries claimed to derive the laws of circulation of paper money from those governing gold and silver, they in fact derived the laws of gold money from the phenomenon of paper-money circulation. Thus, from our point of view it is irrelevant that Hume talks about the precious metals since he confused them with paper. What is of paramount importance here is that Hume is more or less the father of the "crude" quantity theory of money for which S has nothing but contempt.)

Both the quantity equation of exchange and the crude quantity theory contain a rational kernel. But the entire discussion in this part of Chapter 15, as well as S's ruminations in the following chapters, suffers from a fundamental defect: this attempt at theory construction here is an attempt to have money supply play a causal role which, owing to the requirements of the circulation process, it cannot play. The roots of this error lie in the material and social process of simple circulation, and since S makes no attempt at serious analysis of this process, it is understandable that he should fall victim to the fetishism produced there.

Let us go into this matter a little more deeply. Contrary to what S says, money is not a mere technical device to facilitate barter, because commodity exchange is not barter, and money arises out of the contradictory requirements of commodity exchange. Commodity exchange is a process both private and social—private, because it appropriates use values to satisfy individual needs, and social, because it proves the social character of the labor of independent producers. Money is required to provide a form in which these contradictory aspects of commodity exchange can exist side by side. In other words, in commodity exchange two producers cannot simply directly exchange their products with each other, for this, the appropriation of use values, is only one of its contradictory elements. The realization of value must be present as well. Another way of saying this is as follows: Commodities cannot remain unchanged while passing through the circulation process (exchange considered as a process of transferring commodities from hands in which they are non-use-values to hands in which they become use-values). For if they did remain the same, they would only show their use-value, as is the case with bartered products. In order to show their value, commodities must undergo a change of form in circulation. The outcome of commodities seeking a value-form in which to express their value is the differentiation of commodities into commodities and money, and thereby the splitting of the circulation process into two antithetical phases—purchase (appropriation of use value) and sale (realization of value)—which exist side by side (every purchase is a sale and every sale a purchase). The producer can no longer simply "trade" his product for that of another producer (barter); now he must *sell in order to buy*, and his commodity must first be *transformed* into money and then *transformed* into another commodity. This change of form can be schematically represented as C-M-C.

In Chapter III of *Capital*, Marx makes the following comments:

> The comprehension of this change of form is, as a rule, very imperfect. The cause of this imperfection is, apart from indistinct notions of value itself, that every change of form in a commodity results from the exchange of two commodities, an ordinary one and the money-commodity. If we keep in view the material fact alone that a commodity has been exchanged for gold, we overlook the very thing that we ought to observe—namely, what has happened to the form of the commodity. We overlook the facts that gold, when a mere commodity, is not money, and that when other commodities express their prices in gold, this gold is but the money-form of those commodities themselves.[6]

This gives material and social basis to the confusion of commodity exchange with barter. But we were looking for the basis of another error of S, one which perhaps contradicts his reducing commodity exchange to barter; namely, his attempt to assign a causal role to money which it cannot play. This is a complex and manysided error; it involves the assertion of impossible causal connections between money and spending, prices, investment, employment, and production. The error therefore cannot be explained solely by looking at the sphere of simple circulation. But the reason for the error, at least with regard to the connection between money and spending, can be seen as lurking there, in the following way:

> The change of form, C-M-C, by which the circulation of the material products of labor is brought about, requires that a given value in the shape of a commodity shall begin the process, and shall, also in the shape of a commodity, end it. The movement of the commodity is therefore a circuit. On the other hand, the form of this movement precludes a circuit from being made by the money. The result is not the return of the money. . . . The movement directly imparted to money by the circulation of commodities takes the form of a constant motion away from its starting point, of a course from the hands of one

commodity-owner into those of another. This course constitutes its currency (*cours de la monnaie*). The currency of money is the constant and monotonous repetition of the same process . . . .That this one-sided character of the money's motion arises out of the two-sided character of the commodities motion, is a circumstance that is veiled over. The very nature of the circulation of commodities begets the opposite appearance. The first metamorphosis of a commodity is visibly, not only the money's movement, but also that of the commodity itself; in the second metamorphosis, on the contrary, the movement appears to us as the movement of the money alone. In the first phase of its circulation the commodity changes place with the money. Thereupon the commodity, under its aspect of a useful object, falls out of circulation into consumption. In its stead we have its value-shape—the money. It then goes through the second phase of its circulation, not under its own natural shape, but under the shape of money. The continuity of the movement is therefore kept up by the money alone, and the same movement that as regards the commodity consists of two processes of an antithetical character, is, when considered as the movement of the money, always one and the same process, a continued change of places with ever fresh commodities. Hence the result brought about by the circulation of commodities, namely, the replacing of one commodity by another, takes the appearance of having been effected not by means of the change of form of commodities, but rather by the money acting as a medium of circulation, by an action that circulates commodities, to all appearance motionless in themselves, and transfers them from hands in which they are non-use-values, to hands in which they are use-values; and that in a direction constantly opposed to the direction of the money. The latter is continually withdrawing commodities from circulation and stepping into their places, and in this way continually moving further and further from its starting-point. Hence although the movement of the money is merely the expression of the circulation of commodities, yet the contrary appears to be the actual fact, and the circulation of commodities seems to be the result of the movement of the money.[7]

According to Hume,

> Gold and silver are . . . worthless things, but within the process of circulation they receive a fictitious magnitude of value

as representatives of the commodities. They are through the process transformed not into money, but into value. Thus their value is determined by the proportion between their own mass and the mass of the commodities, inasmuch as both masses must coincide. Whereas therefore Hume has gold and silver enter into the world of commodities as non-commodities, he transforms them on the contrary, as soon as they appear in the form determinateness of the coin, into mere commodities which are exchanged through simple barter with other commodities.[8]

There are several sources for this notion in Hume. First, Hume confuses money as ideal reckoner (measure of value) and money as means of circulation. He does not understand that a change in the value of gold as measure of value causes the commodity prices to change and for that reason also the mass of circulating money. In other words, he does not see that a decrease in the value of gold leads to a rise of commodity prices and increase in the means of circulation given a constant velocity; instead he sees only the dependency of prices on quantity of money.

The confusion of these two functions of money had the further untoward consequence that, because money as means of circulation can exist in the form of a less valuable material which only represents the value of the full-value gold, it was also assumed that money is per se merely a symbol. This is the basis for having money enter into circulation without value. The end result of the Humean condition is of course the disappearance of the contradictions inherent in the commodity; since Hume does not see the abstract form of money in the exchange of commodities themselves as resulting from the impossibility of resolving the contradiction between use value and value *within* the individual commodity itself—that is, the doubling of the commodity into commodity and money—he does not understand that it is a complete perversion of commodity reality to imagine one camp of commodities and one of money marching off to meet and be matched up in some arbitrary proportions. This is at bottom Say's (or Mill's) metaphysical law of equilibrium: all crises of overproduction are from the start ruled out because in fact commodities are no longer being exchanged—on the contrary, we have retreated to barter: every sale is a purchase: in the Humean version every commodity must get sold too.

Thus one fundamental confusion still permeates modern-day bourgeois economics: that between the functions of money as measure of value and means of circulation. Because paper can replace gold in the latter function, it is supposed that the measure of value itself need not have any value, that it may be purely "conventional." S apparently sees no relation among the various functions of money he *lists* (283); we are told for example that money is a "unit of account in which we express prices." It is here that the second fundamental confusion enters: that between money as measure of value and money as standard of price. Once gold has become the measure of value and exchange value has become price, commodities in their prices are compared and measured as certain quantums of gold; thus once commodities are no longer exchange values measured by their labor-time, but rather relate to one another as specified quantities of gold, the weight measure of gold becomes the standard of price. But it must be remembered that money as measure of value and as standard of price has an entirely different form determination: as the former, gold is objectified labor-time, as the latter, a certain weight of metal.

The weight system is arbitrary (though it must be fixed and unchanging) and is subject to human will; the value measurement is not. By confusing the two, bourgeois economists have fallen victim to the delusion that a given quantity of gold can be set in a fixed relation to the exchange values of commodities. By failing to see the transformation of the measure of value into the standard of price, they believe that quantities of gold are set in relation directly to values and not to other quantities of gold: that is to say, they are not aware of the quality of the measure that previously transformed the values into prices.

This leads us to another problem: S talks of money as a unit of account expressing price (283). He sees money as a technical device that improved upon the barter system but did not essentially change anything: just as barter is more complicated than monetary exchange but can still be effected if need be, so money also presumably makes it "easier" to compare commodities, though in the absence of this kind of thermometer we could still get by. In other words, we are only interested in measuring prices, not in the necessary *expression* of value as a social relation. One might almost say that there is no difference here between value and price: but this is only true for the vulgar economists of Marx's day: today price has supplanted value. Thus in this version the immediate comparison of the commodities among themselves without the intervention of money is a possibility. But is it?

MARX'S THEORY OF VALUE AND MONEY

For S, as we recall, commodities are use values, mere products.

Marx, in *Capital*, remarks that Aristotle recognized that exchange presupposes equality, which in turn presupposes commensurability; since Aristotle believed this commensurability to be inherently impossible, money was introduced as an external expedient. Marx sees the societal roots of Aristotle's exchange conception in the factual absence of abstract human labor: slave society excluded this.[9]

What is S's excuse? He has none, and therefore we will have to furnish an answer to the question of why commodity production contains within itself the seeds of money, why labor-time cannot be expressed immediately.

In order to answer this question and to provide a correct understanding of paper money, it will be necessary to develop Marx's theory of value.

All commodity-producing societies are characterized by the atomistic structural relations between the various producers: the total labor of the society is not precalculated and then distributed among the various branches of production in accordance with the needs of the members of that society. In other words, the producers are private producers carrying on their activities independently of one another. In the absence of social planning, these producers can only be connected with one another through the objectified results of their labor. But one would be wrong to say that they relate to one another on the basis of the use values they produce. For such a society does not produce only use values: in fact, every producer must, while producing a use-value for someone else, produce a non-use-value for himself (if it were a use-value for himself he would use it). But what is this strange non-use-value that he simultaneously produces for himself? Inherent in the use-value itself is the specific type of skill or labor activity required to produce such a thing. The producer is therefore not interested in this aspect insofar as his non-use-value is concerned. What sort of labor produced the non-use-value?

So far we know that the specific or concrete labor of a private producer brought forth a useful object. We also know that when two producers exchange their useful objects, they are interested in the useful aspects of the things they are getting, but not at all in this feature of the things they are producing and exchanging. We also know that as a result of the planlessness of this society, producers do not relate to one another on the basis of their activities but only on the basis of the results of those activities. But as Aristotle pointed out, exchange cannot take place on the basis of incommensurability. The equality and commensurability is established by the human labor expended on the exchanged commodities. Here we do not refer to labor as concrete, for this would make the labor activities as incommensurable as the use-values, but as general human labor, the mere expenditure of labor, but in the *form* it assumes in a social structure in which there is no conscious social planning. Labor does not assume this form in every society, but it must assume it in this type of society so as to establish the commensurability necessary for exchange.

However, even this is not enough; for although *we* know that in fact society is based on labor, such a society cannot be directly based on labor, or more precisely, it cannot appear so to the members of that society, because they cannot regulate these activities directly. Production relations must form on the basis of the results of the activity. But what are these things that producers must, so to speak, manipulate in order to relate to one another? They are not the use-values. Neither are they "general human labor," because that is not a thing. We must now recall that other "thing"—the non-use-value that every producer produces for himself while producing use-values. These non-use-values represent the "thing"-form of the general human labor; the non-use-values are the means by which commensurability is established. But what is being measured? The expenditure of human labor. How do we measure that? Through time. The qualitative equality of labor in this society—or its consubstantiality—provides the basis for exchange; its objectification in things provides the necessary thing-form for exchange. The non-use-values represent the time in which general human labor was expended.

Therefore exchange can only take place on the basis of the equating of the non-use-values as representatives of general human labor-time. Thus when five chairs are exchanged for one bed, what is being exchanged is the equal non-use-value of each—that is, the equality of general labor-time spent on them. This means that Jones exchanges x units of non-use-value contained in his bed for five chairs; and Gray exchanges x units of non-use-value contained in his five chairs for the bed. The producers do not directly equate their non-use-values: obviously, for they are qualitatively and quantitatively equal, and that would not make sense in an exchange. What they do is to exchange their non-use-value for the use-value produced by the other. Thus, they *express* their non-use-value in the use-value of the other producer.

But now something very interesting has taken place. We originally said that commodity producers are private producers and independent of one another as producers. But obviously *some* sort of connection must exist among them, unless they are all mythical Robinson Crusoes. The point is, what kind of connection? And since we already know that all societies are based on labor, the question can now be formulated more precisely: In this society, what *form* does this connection of labors assume? Our answer is, the form of things—but not just things: these "things" are things and yet some"thing" else too, namely non-use-values. In fact we can say that in such a society the social connection—sociality per se—is expressed in these strange non-use-values.

What has happened is that our private and independent producers have discovered that they are connected after all—but only in an indirect and "thing-ified" way. Thus these producers do three contradictory "things" simultaneously: they produce use-values and non-use-values; they work in a concrete and in a general manner, abstracted from any particular labor; and they produce privately and socially. We saw this when the units of abstract labor of the bed were exchanged (previously they were equated) for five chairs. By exchanging in non-use-value for a use-value the producers committed a social act.

In the individual commodity the use-value and the non-use value were easy enough to keep separate. But in exchange this is no longer so. The producer of the beds says that his x-units of non-use value are worth five chairs; here the use-value and non-use-value, instead of being kept apart, are reflected in each other. This is not only not strange, it is also necessary, for the commodity is two-in-one; in order to prove itself as such in society—that is, in order for it to be a non-use-value to its producer and a use-value to its recipient—it itself must, so to speak, double itself, and this it does by creating a new form in which its own non-use-value can appear: namely, in the use-value of the other commodity.

The non-use-value is, of course, the "famous" and now "obsolete" value (just as obsolete as the business cycle). But the non-use-value as labor-time cannot express itself in itself; it can only express itself in the use-value of the commodity for which it is exchanged. In this way, the use value of the one commodity becomes the *value-form* of the other commodity (i.e., the form the commodity value must assume, if it is to appear at all). In principle we have just explained the origin of money and the reason why labor-time cannot be expressed directly. Let us look at it more closely.

The value of the commodity as expressed in the use-value of another commodity is called its exchange-value; although value as labor-time is an objective magnitude, it cannot be expressed directly. Once one particular commodity has been transformed into the use-value in which all other values are expressed—in other words, once it has become the universal value-form—it is called money. Thus, we can say that the value of one bed is one ounce of gold. At some point, the state gives the gold-weight measures different names, so that one ounce might be called a dollar, or a franc, etc. In the essentials, nothing has happened: we are still expressing value in use-value.

Now we have discovered what money is. It is the universal value form. This means that when we exchange five chairs for a bed, we no longer say that the bed is worth five chairs, but rather that it is worth one ounce of gold. Now in all these three commodities there are, say, x units of value; each was produced in ten hours of general-abstract labor-time. The price of the bed is one ounce of gold. However, money is sociality, whereas the commodity was produced by a private producer. The whole point of commodity-production is that the two are not by "nature" equal but are *equated*—and sometimes through very violent and painful processes. If the gold producers become twice as productive, that is produce one ounce in five hours, then the value of one bed becomes two ounces of gold. If, on the other hand, other bed producers become twice as productive while Jones continues to plod along as usual, Jones' labor will not count as ten hours but only as five. When the time for exchange comes around, Jones will learn the difference between social and private labor the hard way. He may have worked ten hours, but the price represents only five. Thus we see that price is not always equal to value, because labor is not directly social in this society, but rather must be *socialized*.

This leads us to the question why products cannot be measured directly in labor-time:

> That in commodity production social labor is performed only as *social* labor of *private* producers—this fundamental contradiction expresses itself in the derivative contradiction that the exchange of activities and products must be mediated by a product that is simultaneously particular and universal.[10]

Or as Marx himself says:

> Because price does not equal value, the value-determining element—labor-time—cannot be the element in which the prices are expressed, because the labor-time would have to express itself as the determining element and non-determining element, as the equal and non-equal of itself. Because labor-time as measure of value exists only ideally, it cannot serve as the material of the comparison of the prices.[11]

> Labor-time cannot itself immediately be money . . . precisely because it in fact exists only in particular products (as object): as universal object it can exist only symbolically, indeed precisely in a particular commodity which is posited as money. Labor-time does not exist as a universal object of exchange, independent and separated (detached) from the natural particularities of the commodities. It would have to exist as such in order to fulfill directly the conditions of money.[12]

Let us now proceed to Marx's theory of money, or precisely to his development of the other functions of money. So far we know money as a measure of value and a standard of price. Since the distinction between money as measure of value and standard of price is not easy to comprehend, we present an explanation to supplement the earlier discussion.

Once gold becomes money as measure of value, the various commodity values can be compared and measured among themselves as certain quantities of gold. At this point a technical necessity arises to relate them to fixed quantities of gold as a measuring *unit*. Once this unit is subdivided, it becomes a standard—and since value measured in money is price, it becomes a price standard. But before gold ever became money it already had such a standard—in metal weights. We now can express prices in ounces of gold. But Hegel knew that a measure is an arbitrary, conventional standard.[13]

Therefore the measuring unit, its subdivision, and its designation (e.g., one dollar is the name given to .888671 grams of gold) can and must be determined by the state: can, because it is arbitrary; must, because it requires constancy, and in bourgeois society the state represents society as a collective compulsive force.

But measure of value and standard of price are two entirely different functions.

Measure of Value
1) social embodiment of human labor
2) transforms commodity values into prices—i.e., ideal quantities of gold
3) measures commodity values against its own value
4) its own value must be changeable since it is a commodity

Standard of Price
1) fixed weight of metal
2) measures quantities of gold
3) measures quantities of gold against a quantity of gold
4) must be unchanging

Since money as a measure of value can function ideally—that is, one need not have gold in one's hand to determine commodity prices—and since the subdivisions of the standard are given names such as dollar, pound, etc., the notion arose that these are not names for certain quantities of gold, but merely arbitrary points of comparison expressing no value; from here the conclusion was drawn that a specified quantity of gold—which we know to have a variable value—could be *set* in relation to commodity values; this fails to take into account that money as standard of price merely compares quantities of gold and does not measure the value of a given quantity of gold against the weight of another, and it also fails to consider that this standard presupposes money as measure of value which previously established the qualitative sameness of the commodities.

Gold is standardizable in its material form, which is not true, say, of cows, wheat, etc.; it can be easily subdivided and put together again in its physical state; it has high specific weight, thus allowing for the representation of a relatively large amount of labor-time. This favors its mobility and transportability; it is immune to most acids and to air; its use as jewelry makes it a form of hoard; being soft, it is not suitable for industrial uses and therefore its use-value will not deprive it of its function within the sphere of circulation; it can be melted down and can move between the sphere of circulation and the sphere of consumption.

But these are all *ideal* processes; money can act in these functions without any actual circulation of commodities. As we all know, commodities do in fact change hands. We might say that commodity A is exchanged for money, and then this money is exchanged for commodity B. S would say that money has acted as a medium of exchange, while in fact all it has done is mediate the exchange of the two commodities: the money is not wanted for itself, but only for what it can buy.

Thus in this process of circulation S sees only barter: one commodity exchanged for another, as soon as we "peel off the obscuring layer of money" (55). But is this really so? As we know, money is not some sort of external thing, but is generated by the commodities themselves: it is the general form of the value of commodities. This means that the value of commodity A takes the form of money before it reassumes the commodity form in B.

But where did the money come from? Obviously from a prior form change of another commodity. Thus while commodity A is being exchanged for money, the money is reassuming the commodity form, or rather the value is reassuming the commodity form which it already possessed prior to its transformation into money. Thus what for A is the transformation of commodity into money (C-M), is M-C for the possessor of the money. Although the process of circulation is in reality one gigantic process of form changes, it does not *appear* that way: it appears as a mess of isolated and unconnected individual acts of exchange.

But here, as opposed to barter, the money does not fall out of the process: whereas in barter the commodities definitively leave the sphere of "circulation" (we abstract here from resale), "circulation constantly sweats out money"; thus because someone has sold a commodity, that person is in no way obligated to reappear on the market as a buyer. This is the telling blow to the theory of the metaphysical equilibrium of buying and selling: and at the same time it is the elementary form, or abstract possibility, of crisis. And of course it is no coincidence that S would like us all to believe that commodity circulation is really barter, so that there is no reason to believe that crisis is inherent in capitalism.

We posed the question where the money comes from. If we are talking of gold-money, it comes from the ground. But when it is exchanged by the gold producer for, say, coal or shovels or clothes, it is being exchanged not as money but merely as another commodity. But once the gold has become monetized, this is no longer true. It is of the utmost importance that these two processes not be confused; for, as we established above, commodities have prices and money has value prior to entering into the process of circulation. The failure to understand this results in depicting the commodities as entering the circulation process "priceless" and money as "worthless"; it results in a vicious circle of presuppositions that underlie the quantity theory of money (crude or refined):

> If we consider M in C-M not as metamorphosis of another commodity, then we take the act of exchange out of the circula-

tion process. Outside of the latter however the form C-M disappears, and merely two different C, say iron and gold, confront each other, the exchange of which is no particular act of circulation, but rather one of barter. Gold is a commodity like every other commodity at the source of its production. Its relative value and that of the iron . . . is represented here in the quantities, in which they exchange for each other. But in the process of circulation this operation is presupposed, in the commodity prices its own value is already given. There can therefore be nothing more erroneous than the notion that *within the circulation process* gold and the commodity enter into the relation of barter, and that therefore their relative value is ascertained through their exchange as simple commodities. . . . However the quantity of gold for which the commodity is exchanged within the circulation process is not determined by the exchange, but rather the exchange is determined by the price of the commodity, i.e., by its exchange-value estimated in gold.[15]

In this constant form change of C-M-C the independent representation of exchange-value is only a "fleeting moment"; for another commodity soon appears to replace the money. Moreover, at any one time a certain quantity of gold constantly remains in circulation. Given these two conditions it is theoretically possible for objects which have little or no value (which in any case do not have the value of gold) to be placed into circulation by the makeshift of society—the state—to represent the gold symbolically.

If this theory should not prove persuasive, we can look at the actual practice. And here we find two examples. If a gold coin is involved in ten transactions per day, then it has in fact performed the duty of a gold coin with ten times the weight that performs only one such operation. In other words, the coin assumes an ideal existence in circulation apart from its real existence—although it is only the real existence that appears at every single operation.

Our second practical example is that of a coin which has been worn down or intentionally clipped: it remains within circulation as long as no one notices, a mere symbol of itself. In this case of gold as means of circulation and gold as standard of price diverge, and the gold is no longer the real equivalent of the commodities whose prices it realizes. Since gold is a cost of circulation, i.e., it has no use-value other than that of money, it makes dollars and sense to replace it as means of circulation with some material that has as little value as possible and will therefore cause the smallest possible circulation cost.

As long as the state circulates paper money representing the quantity of gold that should be circulating, everything is okay, except for the theory of paper-money à la S, which asserts that paper-money is the essence of money. In fact, paper-money turns all the laws of monetary circulation upside-down.

It is essential to remember that paper replaces gold only as a means of circulation—not as the measure of value. The value of paper money is not determined directly through the commodities, but rather circuitously through gold. The sum of the prices of the commodities determines the value of the paper money; but this price sum presupposes the value of gold money. To ignore this is to fall into the quantity theory of money with its vicious circle of presuppositions and its identification of price and value.

What happens if the amount of paper-money issued exceeds the amount of circulating gold? If a million ounces of gold were circulating, and paper with a face value corresponding to this has been in circulation (for the sake of simplicity one ounce of gold equals 1 dollar), and if now 9 million more paper dollars were issued, then these 10 million paper dollars would still be the representative of 1 million ounces of gold. Since the same dollar now would represent only 1/10 as much gold as before, all commodity prices would rise ten-fold, and then ten times as much paper would in fact be needed (given constant velocity). All that has happened is that the name of the standard of price has been changed; the rise of prices is only the mode in which the circulation process forces the paper to be the symbol of the gold necessary for circulation of the commodities.

MONEY AS MEANS OF PAYMENT AND CREDIT

Before continuing the discussion of paper money and inflation let us look at another function of money important in connection with credit. With the development of "market production" the length of time required to produce a commodity often varies; in any case the various lengths of time need not coincide. Thus A may sell his commodity, a plow, to B, before the latter's harvest has been reaped. Since B has not yet realized the money form of the value of the commodity he produces, he cannot pay immediately. Or it may happen that someone may "buy" a commodity before he can receive the commodity (whereby under these primitive conditions he can do this only if he has previously sold a commodity—i.e., realized its value in money—without subsequently having bought another commodity). Thus the commodity will change hands without the "help" of money. Money may be said to function here ideally as means of buying—i.e., the promise to pay causes the commodity to change hands. When the money is in fact later handed over, it is no longer functioning as means of circulation, because the commodity has already been transferred; instead of mediating the transaction, the money concludes the transaction. Whereas in the previous function of money as means of circulation the exchange-value really never attains an independent existence inasmuch as the commodities and money are constantly changing places, here it does: Money here becomes *means of payment*.

This new relation in its elementary of abstract form embodies the credit relation of debtor-creditor. Here we have another latent aspect of crisis: for as long as claims compensate one another, money need function only as a measure of value; but once the time comes for "the bills to be paid," money ceases to be a mere mediator, a representative of commodity, but rather becomes the incarnation of social labor. At this point—which may be a crisis period—the shallowness of S's remarks on money stands revealed; for no one wants money now for what it can buy because nobody is buying anything in the crisis: the debtors have already "bought" without paying; they are not buying now, but paying debts; and the creditors have no intention of expanding production at such a time—they merely want the money equivalent of the commodities they had "sold" previously. This would seem to indicate that money did after all have some non-"conventional" value in capitalism.

Hoarding.
Here it is also possible to see the outlines of capitalism in an abstract *form*, since producers will sell without buying—in fact, that they will do this quite often until they have *accumulated* a *hoard*. Here one buys in order to sell, that is, the acquisition of money becomes a goal in itself: M-C-M replaces C-M-C as the motive force. Of course, not even capitalists are such fetishists that they would really execute a M-C-M; the second M must, as we know, be larger than the first (or at least that is the purpose of retention).

In S's "list" of money functions the hoarding of money ("safe way of holding wealth," "precaution"—283) is somehow oriented at future consumption. His wisdom here seems very strange. Money, we are told, provides safety "against the ups and downs inherent in stocks, land, homes, and bonds. When all these are going down in price, the canny hoarder of money is the most successful speculator in the community" (283). The only ups and downs inherent in lands and homes come from earthquakes. (A parenthetical remark added by S negates his previous praise of money: rising prices make the money holder "suffer.") In his final summation, he informs us that all the functions of money are "worth paying for. And we each do incur a cost in holding a coin, a bill, or a demand deposit—namely, the *sacrificed interest and profit yield* that might be obtained from purchase of earning assets" (283). Well, that's very nice that someone is willing to pay $100 so that he can "make" $200—but he in the end can pay the 100 only if he can make the 200; but S has still not told us how 100 is transformed into 200.

PAPER MONEY AND INFLATION REVISITED

We couple paper with inflation because there is little sense in speaking of inflation as being related to a rise in prices resulting from a change in the value of gold. Marx states that as long as paper money receives its denomination from gold (or, in his time, silver), convertibility into gold remains the practical measure of value of every paper money, that convertibility is an economic law for the paper money, whether this convertibility is politically possible or not. Marx then lists three possible reasons for the depreciation of paper money (that is, the drop of its real value below its nominal value): loss of faith in the government, excessive issue of paper money (i.e., in relation to the gold it is supposed to represent), or a particular demand for gold which would create a privilege for gold for export against paper money.[16]

It is clear that these three factors can arise independently of one another; it is also clear that the inflation, or more accurately the depreciation will take on different forms according to the circumstances involved. In the case of too much paper, the result is higher prices. If it is the gold "privilege" (which can arise for instance under an unfavorable balance of payments), then the depreciation appears as a lower exchange rate of the currency vis-à-vis other national currencies.

These results can also influence each other. Thus a rise in prices can bring about a special need for gold and lead to a lowering of the exchange rate; similarly, a lowering of the exchange rate can lead to rising prices.

But these factors are not the causes of inflation. What then are they? According to Varga, the contemporary inflation has been brought about by the "contradictory movement of the real and nominal national wealth and national income," in other words by the militarization of the capitalist economies in the post-World War II period. But he adds:

> Present-day methods of financing wars, and peace-time military expenditure make it possible to cover the enormous state budget deficit without a large issue of additional paper money. At present it is not a direct issue of paper money that corresponds to the inflated post-war sum of prices but the increase in deposits, used in the wholesale commodity circulation turnover instead of paper money, and the issue of war loans and other substitutes for paper money.[17]

This explanation is consistent with those of other Marxists to determine the nature of inflation.

We have thus discovered some concrete mechanisms by which inflation serves its goals. The massive use of paper money, or more accurately the complete replacement of gold by paper in internal circulation, formally gives the capitalist state elbow room for maneuvering with respect to its traditional role as enemy of the working class. Monopoly pricing on the other hand gives the monopoly capitalists the possibility to seize extra booty from "consumers" via higher prices, and from smaller capitalists via a redistribution of surplus value. Taxation on the other hand enables the state to withdraw part of the workers wages and redistribute it to the needs of the state as national and international protector of capital.

But as was pointed out, inflation in the sense of the reducing of the purchasing power of paper money (and it is not yet clear what this means until we examine the question of gold more closely) is also possible without an increase in the supply of paper money.

It must be stressed, however, that the redistribution of income from labor to capital and/or unproductive government utilization of capital made possible by inflation is not the basic enemy of the working people in capitalist countries. Although it is an obvious tool of class oppression it is merely a supplement to the basic exploitation embodied in surplus value.

Excursus on Inflation and the So-called Wage-Price Spiral The myth of the wage-price spiral is based on the assertion that the laborer gets the full value he produces; that therefore a rise in wages conditions a rise in prices; and that in the end all remains the same—so why increase wages?

As we know, the wage is the value and/or price of labor power: labor itself has no value; it only creates value. And we also know it was Adam Smith's erroneous notion that the value of a commodity was made up of wages, profit, and rent. But the value of a commodity is derived solely from living labor and frozen labor transferred from the means of production. The worker's wage is a cost item to the capitalist; but the whole "value-added" is not, for the capitalist gets the surplus-value free of charge. Thus if wages increase, the value of the commodity remains the same, as long as the surplus value decreases by the same amount. Capitalists producing means of subsistence will get more "play," those producing or pandering to the "needs" of the bourgeoisie will get correspondingly less. The general rate of profit will fall.

As Marx illustrates in Chapter 11 of the third volume of *Capital*, since the value of the commodities is not affected by a general rise of wages, the price of production of commodities produced with a capital of average organic composition (i.e., a capital whose relation between c and v is equal to the average of the total social capital) would also not change, although its rate of profit would drop. Now in order that the average rate of profit be reestablished (this is not to be understood mechanically as taking place overnight) for all capitals, the prices of production of capitals with above- and below-average organic composition would have to change; those capitals with above-average composition—i.e., with relatively less labor—would result in lower prices of production; those with relatively more labor would result in higher prices of production.

The explanation for this is as follows: Since the capitals with lower organic composition are as it were hit harder by the wage increases, their rate of profit would drop below the new average if they continued selling at the old production price. Conversely, for capitals with higher compositions, being relatively less affected by the wage increases, continued sales at the old price of production would result in above-average rates of profit.

Now all this presupposes free flow of capital between branches. Has monopoly capital changed this mechanism? Monopoly results in a redistribution of surplus-value: it does not produce more value and cannot therefore redistribute more value than already exists. Thus in our case, it is likely that those branches with the highest organic composition would also be the most heavily monopolized. This would mean that they could keep their prices of production above the level portrayed above: they would not lower their prices and therefore their rates of profit would not average out but would remain higher (they were already, but they would probably rise even more). Through their monopoly they could stop the free flow of capital, and therefore the averaging-out of the rate of profit.

For the other capitalists there are two possibilities. Either they pay monopoly prices to the first capitalists, and therefore do with an abnormally low rate of profit (even below their previously below-average rate), which would lead to bankruptcy and further concentration of capital, or they would pass off some or all of their added costs to consumers. This latter case, inflation, we have discussed above. It is tantamount to a lowering of real wages. But the general principle remains as Marx formulated it: the rise in wages brought about the price rise only because the capitalists were powerful enough to negate the wage increase by increasing prices and thus maintaining the ratio between wages and surplus-value.

Chapter 11: Banks and Credit (S's Chapter 16)

> We small bourgeois artisans, we who work on the nickel cash registers of the small store-owners with the honest crowbar, are devoured by the large entrepreneurs behind whom the banks stand. What is a skeleton key compared to a stock? What is the burglary of a bank compared to the founding of a bank? What is the murder of a man compared to the hiring of a man?—Mackie Messer, in Bertold Brecht, *Die Dreigroschenoper*

The objective function this chapter is to surround capital credit operations with a mystique to convince the reader that the Fed is omnipotent and that We the People need no longer fear that *our* economy can get out of hand. It is our purpose to demystify this sphere, to show the rational kernel and limits of these manipulations.

THE MODERN BANKING SYSTEM

In this section, S intends to serve up some "superficial but useful history" much in the manner of Chapter 5 on "business organization" (294). First we are "informed" that the "primary economic function of commercial banks is *to hold demand deposits and to honor checks drawn upon them*—in short to provide us, the economy, with the largest component of the money supply. A second important function . . . is to lend money to local merchants, homeowners, farmers, and industrialists" (292).

From this we might get the impression that all that is happening in these banks is that money or titles to money keep being transferred about, that we are dealing with a society of hoarders, and more particularly with a society made up exclusively of a sphere of circulation. What possible sense is there in talking about shifting and holding all this paper if do not have any idea how all this is connected with social production?

From the bourgeoisie's point of view it makes a good deal of sense. As Marx notes (in the first chapter of the second volume of *Capital*), the circulation of capital as money capital is the most abstract, most onesided form of the circulation of capital. For here we have money capital buying means of production and labor power, applying them in production, selling the finished commodities, and realizing surplus value: $M-C \ldots P \ldots C'-M'$. But here the beginning and the end is the money capital, with production a mere necessary intermediary (which is the abstract expression of capitalism as surplus-value production); on the other hand the source of surplus value is extinguished in the process, and thus this aspect of the circulation of capital makes it the most fetishistic.

Now from the viewpoint of bank capital, production is an isolated act of the capitalists' advancing money capital. Thus the magic powers formerly attributed to money are now transferred to, or at least shared by, credit. The credit form becomes isolated from material production; it loses its social content and becomes magic.[1]

The bank function of supplying money is also not very clear. Money of course means demand deposits in commercial banks. But what sort of money is this? R. S. Sayers contributes the following on the matter:

> Banks are institutions whose debts . . . are commonly accepted in final settlement of other people's debts. . . . The cheque itself cannot reasonably be described as money; but the deposit that can be so transferred does serve as money, "money" being the word we apply to anything ordinarily used in settlement of debts. . . . The word "debts" is here used in the broad sense of any obligation fixed in terms of money. . . .

Very neat! First we get money defined in terms of debts and then debts in terms of money. Then to confuse the matter further, we get this: "When a child buys an ice-cream from the ice-cream van in the street, the child incurs a debt which has to be settled by the immediate payment of six-pence." . . .[2]

Here Sayers has neatly transformed money as means of circulation into money as means of payment, and thereby confused the logical derivation of debt from the latter. Credit relations are inextricably bound up with money as means of payment.

At this point we can summarize the main functions as follows: (1) the mediation of loan capital between industrial capitalists and money capitalists; (2) the transformation of income into loan capital; (3) the creation of means of payment and means of circulation which become loan capital. Marx generalizes:

> . . . The banking business consists in concentrating the loanable capital in its hand in great masses so that instead of the individual money lender the bankers as the representatives of all money lenders confront the industrial and commercial capitalists. They become the general administrators of money capital. On the other hand they concentrate the borrowers vis a vis all the lenders inasmuch as they borrow for the whole commercial world.[3]

Banking represents a capitalist division of labor. Instead of individual capitalists each taking care of the technical details—keeping reserves, cashing checks, etc.—this is done jointly for many capitals by the bank and in this—socialized—way the capital that must be "wasted," i.e., used unproductively in this sphere, is minimized. Thus, instead of each capital taking care of the purely technical movements that money goes through in the circulation process of industrial capital, a part of the total social capital is set aside to take care of nothing but these operations.[4]

Further, S tells us that "Banking is a business much like any other. . . . A bank provides certain services for its customers and in return receives payments from them in one form or another. It tries to earn a profit for its stock owners" (294).

Banking is much like any other business only if you approach it as S does: i.e., through its ledgers. You do certain things for some people and they pay you, and then in the end you see whether you got more than you gave. This is what was meant above by saying that S approaches capitalism via M-D . . . P . . . C'-M'. All he sees is the top surface: the money difference between cost and revenue.

Unfortunately banking is not like any other "business"; for banking produces nothing: it is, as just mentioned, exclusively taken up with mediating the form changes in the sphere of circulation; it expedites money along its merry way from capital to capital. All the "costs" here are those of circulation: instead of each individual capitalist having to put aside part of his capital for the unproductive tasks of accounting, etc., one segment of social capital is set aside (not consciously: like everything else in capitalism, this division of labor also arose spontaneously). Bank profits result from the difference between the interest they pay out and the interest they receive on loans. Interest is a part of surplus value created in the factories, mines, and farms of society. Banking is as much a cost of circulation as printing dollar bills: as such its "productivity" consists in taking up as little of productive social capital as possible. To equate it with productive capital is pure mystification.

The subtlest dose of apologetics is proffered with this little gem: "Unlike England and Canada, where a few large banks with hundreds of branches are dominant, the US has tended to rely upon many independent, relatively small, localized units ' (291). What is the nature of "the old American distrust of 'big finance' " (292 n. 2)?

As usual, S is operating in a socio-historical vacuum. We just have these innocuous banks rendering "services." Does their role ever change? No answer.

Monopoly capitalism is based on the concentration of capital: those capitalists who have accumulated the most capital can raise the productivity of their workers most, thus driving their competitors to the wall, which results in the latter's being eaten up by the former (this is called the centralization of capital). This process is accompanied by the monopolization of the sphere of banking, and the merging of the two results in the rule of finance capital.

Based on S's remarks on industrial concentration we can expect him to deny similar trends within "banking." Although here too there is "something" to S's delineation of the differences between the banking structure in the U.S. and, say, Canada or the U.K., S neglects several essential points. First of all, in absolute size the U.S. banks are clearly the international leaders. Thus at the end of 1972, the three largest U.S. banks were also the three largest in the capitalist world; their deposits (in billions of dollars) ran as follows: Bank of America—35.428; First National City—27.750; Chase Manhattan—24.998. The largest British Bank (National Westminster) ranked sixth, with deposits of 18-.889 billion, whereas the largest Canadian Bank (Royal Bank of Canada) ranked seventeenth, with deposits of 14-.284 billion.[5]

These absolute magnitudes do not accurately reflect the imperialistic power and national capitals of the various banks; thus, for instance, the Bank of America cannot compete with the two other U.S. banks with respect to international loans.

Secondly, although it is true that the U.S. has erected some legal obstacles to nationwide branch offices—in contrast to European practice—this prohibition has had no effect on large commercial loans, since only the large banks are in a position to mediate this capital. In this respect the existence of so many small ("independent") banks is statistically misleading. And finally, there is a trend—in large part brought about by foreign bank competition in the U.S.—to eliminate these last legal restrictions so that the near future will probably see many mergers, etc.[6]

Similarly, if we look at the development of the banking structure during this century, we note a very definite trend toward centralization of finance capital. Thus in 1912, that is, prior to the birth of the Fed and the end of "anarchy of unstable private banking" (292), thirty-four banks controlled one-eighth of all banking resources.[7] In 1960, the

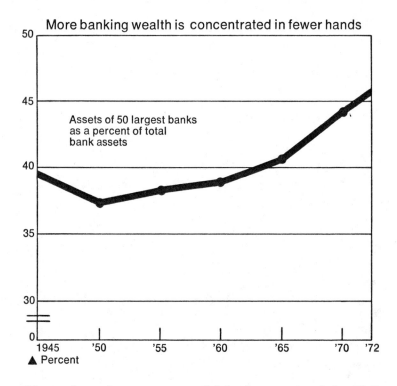

fifty and ten largest commercial banks accounted for 38.9 percent and 21.5 percent respectively of total bank assets; by 1971, these respective shares had risen to 48.5 percent and 26.6 percent.[8] In 1967, the three above-mentioned U.S. banks alone accounted for one-eighth of total commercial bank deposits.[9] Another measure we may point to is the tight control over the world's largest pool of investable funds"; here ten banks control about 40 percent, and four (Morgan Guaranty, Bankers Trust, First National City, and Chase Manhattan) about one-quarter of these funds. This led Wright Patman, the then chairman of the House Committee on Banking and Currency, to state that these data "show that the American economy of today is in the greatest danger of being dominated by a handful of corporations in a single industry as it has been since the great money trusts of the early 1900's."[10] These bank trust departments have come to control very large blocks of the total outstanding shares of the largest U.S. corporations. When we further take into consideration that many of the largest banks are not separate entities, but rather united into finance capital groups, the degree of centralization becomes ever more apparent.

In other words, we are dealing with finance capital groupings whose "resources" rival the Fed in magnitude—and yet they receive no mention from S.

INTRODUCTION TO CREDIT

In the previous chapter S claimed that "by controlling the behavior of money and credit, the government and its Federal Reserve System can hope to affect the balance of saving and investment expenditure" (277). On the one hand, such a "balance" is not fundamental, and on the other, we must now examine the validity of the claim that capitalism can "manage" its money.

Karl Kautsky has provided a clear view of the limits of circulation-sphere "rationality" which will be a useful introduction to our discussion of credit. Kautsky notes that money can enter circulation only through the purchase of commodities, not through banks issuing money. He asks ironically whether the bank could not perhaps give people money so that they can buy commodities.

> Unfortunately no one has yet come up with this sort of social regulation of circulation. Now as ever it is still the individuals who through their purchases bring about circulation, either with their own or with borrowed money. The only change lies in the fact that a part of their own money is deposited in the bank and must first be given out by it, on the other hand that it is primarily the banks that serve their credit needs. And only through credit and loans to individuals—physical or legal persons—does the bank put money into circulation. . . .
>
> Because of their vast mechanism . . . banks are in a better position to handle the granting of credits than isolated money capitalists. But the circulation process of the commodities is only a part of the production process, is determined by the latter's needs and results, and as long as the private ownership of the means of production determines the total process, there can be no social regulation of even a part of that process.[11]

Kautsky has touched upon a fundamental relation by referring to the sphere of circulation; yet he too remains on the surface insofar as he fails to spell out the real significance of the control over money and credit. We know that money is not a primary phenomenon, but rather a peculiar reflection of the uses to which labor is put in capitalist society. This does not mean, however, that monetary movements are totally dependent on, that they stand in a one-to-one relationship to, the "real" material results of labor. On the contrary: Marx takes great pains to show how monetary phenomena assume an autonomous existence which in part is responsible for lending superficial credence to the fetishistic belief in the primacy of money.

To what extent does this autonomous existence entail an independent power to influence the process of surplus-value creation and accumulation? A major Marxist study of state-monopoly capitalism suggests that because the results of profit production appear in money "through manipulations with money and money-capital, the fundamental categories of property and income of the capitalist mode of production can be influenced, and consequently also the distribution of social total-labor." This, of course, involves a tautology. The individual capitalist is tendentially the absolute ruler within his factory or group of factories (tendentially because the workers oppose this authority): his capital is his castle; he can directly control the labor activities of "his" workers. However, that does not obtain when he wants something from workers not directly subject to his capital. Here he must enter into exchange and wheel and deal with money and commodities. In other words, labor as social labor *appears* as value; as long as labor is private (i.e., within the control of one capitalist) it appears as what it is: capitalists and workers within one unit are involved in the creation of use-values. On the social plane, however, labor can be "commanded" only indirectly by the purchase of commodities.

Therefore by "definition" all *social* exchange of labor must be mediated by money. The state is no exception: to the extent that it acts socially, it too must have recourse to the indirect road of money. In this sense money is not only the suitable mechanism for such control but the only mechanism.

The state can of course also directly command labor; but to the extent that it does, private capital has ceased to exist, profit is no longer the immediate goal, but rather the improvement of conditions of profitability for the remaining total capital.

CREDIT

Before we can study a phenomenon as concrete as "deposit creation" it will be necessary to establish the prerequisites of credit in general—a task which S unfortunately does not tackle.

In the previous chapter the abstract possibility of credit relations was discovered during the discussion of money as a means of payment. But that discussion was abstract precisely because it dealt with the sphere of commodity circulation. What does credit mean in the capitalist mode of production?

Once capitalism develops, every sum of money has the potential of being transformed into capital; this means that it is transformed from a given value into a value that can expand itself by allowing the capitalist to extract surplus-value from his workers. For example, a worker's $100, when lent to a capitalist and exchanged for means of production and labor power, can help the capitalist expand this sum into $200:

> Therewith it obtains, aside from the use-value which it possesses as money, an additional use-value, namely that of functioning as capital. Its use-value consists here precisely in the profit which it, once it is transformed into capital, produces. In this quality as latent capital, as means of producing profit, it becomes a commodity, but a commodity sui generis. Or what is the same, capital as capital becomes a commodity.[13]

It might be expected that Marx's renewed interest in

use-value will lead to strange results; for it was another peculiar use-value, labor-power, that lies at the base of surplus-value. And, indeed, the transaction between the lender and the borrower turns out to be extraordinary, for here there is no form change of the value (C-M-C or M-C-M); neither does the lender get a commodity for the money he gives the borrower, nor, if his sum of value happens to be in commodity form, does he sell it for money. Lending in fact is the way in which money is alienated not as money and not as commodity, but rather as capital. The lender gives the borrower the *power* of producing an even greater sum of money. The lender is then paid back the original sum plus a fraction of the expanded sum, which in fact was the use-value of that which he lent.

But fetishism runs rampant here, inasmuch as no change of value-form appears in this transaction: all we have is M-M'; i.e., a sum of money is given away in return for an even bigger sum. The return of this sum apparently no longer depends on an economic process but rather seems to be an arbitrary legal agreement. Such a semblance is given ideological stability by the fact that loans can be made to people who will not use the money to expand the value but merely to buy use-values. Nevertheless, these people must also in the end fork over the principal plus delta x, regardless of where this extra amount comes from (even if it is another loan).

The name of the increment that has to be paid back is called interest; and as bourgeois economists never tire of telling us, it is the price of money, or alternatively, the price of capital. But this is an irrational expression (on a par, however, with the price of labor) since money-capital thus becomes a commodity with a double value: a value and also a price different from this value, although price is the money form of value. Thus although price is the value of a commodity, in contradistinction to its use-value, here we have a price qualitatively different from value. The problem here is that the value of money or commodity as capital is not determined by its value as money or commodity, but rather by the surplus-value it produces for its owner; and in this sense the interest expresses the self-expansion of the money-capital, and therefore it constitutes the price paid the lender.

There is one other important aspect that evolves from this relation. Interest is a part of surplus value, or more concretely, of profit. In this sense a quantitative division is made between the two, and the difference becomes the entrepreneurial profit (the profit made by the user of the borrowed capital). But the lender and the borrower, or the money and industrial capitalist, are not merely legally different individuals; they also fulfill different roles in the reproduction process because lender and borrower subject the same capital to two entirely different processes—one lends it, the other employs it productively.

In this way, the quantitative division has given rise to a new qualitative division. The fact that a part of total profit has been transformed into interest automatically transforms the remaining portion into entrepreneurial profit, whether or not any particular individual capitalist *borrows*. This in turn means that as soon as the average rate of profit has been established, entrepreneurial profit appears to be determined not by the wages paid to the workers (for this has already been "calculated" before the surplus-value is distributed among various capitalists), but rather by the rate of interest. The industrial capitalist thereby seems to "earn" his profit just as much by labor as does the worker his wage. Thus the industrial capitalist can tell the workers that they are allied against the real hogs—the money capitalists who take profits (interest) without doing any work. Interest then expresses the means of production as capital, as means of appropriating surplus-labor.

But with the stabilization of money and industrial capitalism, the reference to the "suitability" of money manipulation by the capitalist state becomes easier to understand. For in the "money market," the specific qualitative applications of capital, as they are manifested in competition, disappear: here money-capital appears as the common capital of the class of capitalists as a whole unrelated to any and every particular employment, ready to be disseminated to every production need. With the development of large-scale industry, money capital appears as a concentrated, organized mass which "quite otherwise than the real production is placed under the control of the bankers representing the societal capital."[14]

Marx is saying here that in this centralized form money-capital can be distributed in accordance with the "production needs" of each sphere. But what does he mean by "needs"? Certainly not the needs of the workers. "Needs" here refers to the needs of surplus-value production and accumulation. It means that vast industrial undertakings can be initiated without regard to the capital owned by the manipulators in that sphere. The bankers do not have the power to redistribute more surplus-value than has already been produced. But they do have the power to redistribute it in such a fashion that the largest amount of surplus-value will be produced in the next round.

This new-found strength also shows the contradiction in capital insofar as it indicates that the privateness of capital is running into conflict with its inherent sociality. The power of the "collective" money-capital grew out of the powerlessness of the individual capitals to carry on production on the scale dictated by the demands of competition.

The question arises whether with the transfer of this centralization and the control thereof from the banks to the state, a similar augmentation of power takes place. It is within this framework that the basic functions of the Federal Reserve System must be viewed.

How does *commercial credit* operate? A coal-mining capitalist, for example, may receive a bill of exchange from his customer, an iron-producing capitalist, for already delivered coal, because the latter cannot yet pay since he has not yet realized the value of the iron he has sold. These bills of exchange can continue to circulate until they are paid in cash, and then retired. Now two aspects are of importance here: first, this process has nothing to do with lending unemployed capital; rather, it is a method to hasten the value-form metamorphoses of capital from the commodity to the money form and from money to commodity form; secondly, all these obligations become mutual: a general entanglement of debts develops. Now the clearing of these debts depends on the fluidity of the return flows, that is, whether the reproduction process is running smoothly. Here we are involved with credits within Department I (producers of means of production) and/or between Department I and Department II (producers of means of consumption).

But once the fluidity turns into stagnation as a result of flooded markets and falling prices, the above-mentioned nexus of mutual debts asserts itself. In fact, there develops an excess of productive capital and of commodity capital that cannot be employed or sold. Thus credit contracts because capital is unemployed, and capital cannot continue its metamorphosis.

The amount of money in society has not changed, nor was it the determining factor. As we saw, as long as things were going well credit was enough: there was no critical shortage of money. But as Marx points out, money as means of payment (the abstract form or possibility of credit) contains an "unmediated contradiction": as long as claims compensate one another, money functions merely ideally as a measure of value; but when the moment of truth arrives and hard cash must be forked over, money becomes the absolute commodity, and no substitute will do. At this point capitalists want to borrow money as means of payment to pay off their debts: everyone must pay and no one wants to buy. So who would be willing to make loans at a time when the fluidity of the reproduction process has touched bottom?

Aside from this commercial credit there is also *bank credit*, i.e., credit that banks can "grant" on the basis of "unemployed" capital deposited with them by capitalists, or of income deposited by any class. The former represents accumulated surplus-value that is not immediately employable either because this particular capitalist's investment sphere is sated or because the amount of capital necessary for his prospective investment has not yet been reached. Capital can also be released if the production process has been interrupted. The depositing of income (mainly by the bourgeoisie but also by the working class) merely expresses the fact that in capitalism every sum of money can take the form of interest-bearing and loan capital. In any event, the accumulation of money capital obviously can exceed the real accumulation of capital.

What exactly is this "deposit creation"? S's presentation, aside from not having bothered to establish the theoretical framework which first makes all this material about banks and loans comprehensible, under the guise of "avoid[ing] ambiguity" by (8th ed., p. 281) complicated matters supposes that new deposits stem from the government's having printed money. Now this may well be the case—but it is clearly not the base on which the essence of credit can be explained. If paper money were just hurled into circulation by the state without any regard to the actual needs of circulation, the market would soon react by raising prices correspondingly. Unless a differential effect on class-income redistribution took place (which S of course does not mention), such a procedure cannot help the U.S. out of its periodic recessions. Secondly, S is not at all specific as to what is done with the money that is borrowed, although we just know that this will have serious effects.

Let us return to the fount of bourgeois economics—Adam Smith. He wisely noted that if the borrower uses his money on consumption, "he acts the part of a prodigal, and dissipated in the maintenance of the idle, what was destined for the support of the industrious. He can, in this case, neither restore the capital nor pay the interest, without either alienating or encroaching upon some other source of revenue. . . ."[15]

But what generally happens in such transactions between lender and borrower? (Smith here is speaking of loans for productive ends—to buy means of production, not to pay debts):

> By means of the loan, the lender, as it were, assigns to the borrower his right to a certain portion of the annual produce of the land and labour of the country. . . . The quantity of stock, therefore, or, as it is commonly expressed, of money which can be lent at interest in any country, is not regulated by the value of the money . . . which serves as the instrument of the different loans made in that country, but by the value of that part of

the annual produce which . . . is destined not only for replacing a capital, but such a capital as the owner does not care to be at the trouble of employing himself. . . . The money is, as it were, but the deed of assignment, which conveys from one hand to another those capitals which . . . may be greater in almost any proportion, than the amount of the money which serves as the instrument of their conveyance: the same pieces of money successively serving for many different loans, as well as for many different purchases. A, for example, lends to W a thousand pounds, with which W immediately purchases of B a thousand pounds worth of goods. B, having no occasion for the money himself, lends the identical pieces to X, with which X immediately purchases of C another thousand pounds worth of goods. C in the same manner, and for the same reason, lends them to Y, who again purchases goods with them of D. In this manner the same pieces, either of coin or of paper, may, in the course of a few days, serve as the instrument of three different loans, and of three different purchases, each of which is, in value, equal to the whole amount of those pieces . . . . And . . . the same pieces of money . . . may likewise successively serve as the instrument of repayment.[16]

Now, as Marx points out, if A had lent the money to B, and B to C directly, without the mediation of purchases, the same money would have represented not three capitals but only one capital value:

> How many capitals it really represents depends on how often it functions as the value-form of different commodity-capitals. The same thing that A. Smith says about loans in general is valid for deposits, which are after all only a particular name for the loans which the public makes to the bankers. The same pieces of money can serve as instruments for any number of deposits whatsoever.[17]

Thus, the possibility of large amounts of deposits on the basis of a relatively small amount of means of circulation is given as long as each unit of money executes multiple transactions and as long as the reflux of the money to the bank in the form of renewed deposits is guaranteed by some mechanism. For example, a supermarket may deposit $10,000 a week in the bank; with this money the bank can pay out a part of another deposit of the local dress manufacturer, who pays his workers' wages with this money; the workers buy their means of subsistence from the supermarket, which redeposits it in the bank.

The deposits have a twofold function: (1) they are lent out at interest, and are therefore not in the bank but merely credited to the depositors; (2) they serve to compensate the mutual credits and debits of the depositors, who pay each other by writing checks against their accounts (this mechanism is not essentially affected if the accounts happen to be in different banks).

With respect to credit creation, we must distinguish between credit and money capital. If a bank grants a capitalist credit and the latter offers nothing in return but his "good name," then it has given him money-capital. If, however, the capitalist in exchange must pledge stocks or securities, he may possibly have to put up greater value than he is getting from the bank. Since securities already are capital, what he wants from the bank is money, not capital. The same is obviously true if he has the bank discount bills of exchange he is holding.

The creation of new buying power is "semblance" only from the standpoint of the individual relation between the bank and the client. This disappears, however, as soon as we look at the phenomenon from the standpoint of capitalist society as a whole. Now let us assume that the bank grants credit to capitalist X without the latter's having had to pledge any values. The credit takes the form of an account which the bank opens for X. Now X, no prodigal, wants to buy some means of production. So he writes out a check against his account to capitalist Y who produces the machines and materials X needs. If Y demands that the bank pay out the value of the commodity he has sold to X in cash, then the fiction of the *new* buying power is evident. If instead Y opens an account (or merely has it added to an already existing account), that is, if deposits the check, then the bank creating the deposit in the first place becomes a debtor of Y for this sum either directly if the account is in the same bank, or of his bank. The imaginary account which the bank had opened for X has thus been transformed into a real account of Y.

In this manner the credit system can influence the velocity of circulation, since there is no need to wait until a sale is actually made; rather, the money can be deposited in the bank, lent out again to effect a transaction, and so forth.

This is considered a mark of "progress" in that it permits the extension of production beyond narrow "personal" limits. But this expansion also proves to be the downfall in the event of crisis, when it becomes manifest that the credit system has allowed an increase of production beyond the needs of the consumers as solvent demanders.

Thus credit is one of the clearest manifestations of the contradictions inherent in capitalist relations, expressing private relations of capitalist commodity producers which at the same time must attain a certain sociality.

SUMMARY OF CREDIT

Credit is a sphere in which rational kernels abound. There is good materialistic reason for this. As Marx observed, credit contains within it a further, that is, more concrete, expression of the contradictory nature of capitalism: credit can accelerate and intensify the exploitation of living labor, but at the same time it inevitably and periodically leads to overproduction, a situation in which the use-value production exceeds the "needs" of value and surplus-value production, which can be resolved only by a destruction or depreciation of capital itself (this is the rational kernel of the frequently dogmatic Marxist assertion on the contradiction between the forces and relations of production).

Since this contradiction is inherent in the credit relation, bourgeois credit theorists, not aware of this connection, come on as mixtures of "swindler and prophet."[18] We must keep this in mind as a guide in our further exposition.

At this point, let us summarize the results of our discussion of credit. Credit becomes necessary to mediate the equalization of the rates of profit among capitalists. Without the possibility of the flow of capital from one branch to another in the search for the highest rate of profit, the driving force of capitalism would disappear. Once capital has assumed its money form, it is in a position to reappear as any particular use-value, namely any particular means of production (productive capital) capable of extracting surplus value from labor. Thus we might say that credit is immanent in the concept of capital itself. This should not seem strange inasmuch as the abstract possibility of credit already existed in the sphere of simple commodity circulation in money as means of payment.

Aside from this necessity of profit-rate equalization, there is the following consideration: surplus value can arise only in the sphere of production; however, each productive phase is separated by a circulation time; if each capitalist had to wait until he realized his commodity capital in order to begin his cycle all over again, he would "waste" the entire circulation time, during which his capital in the form of means of production would lie "idle" and thus be factually depreciated as capital. One way of avoiding such a situation is via commercial credit, whereby the customer, who has already realized his commodity capital, advances the necessary capital to his supplier, who can then carry on his production without interruption.

A third factor is involved in the development of credit: the increasing socialization of production, in the sense that enterprises are begun which exceed the capital capacity of any individual capitalist. To undertake this capital investment, the capitalist must obtain control over other people's capital. Even though this pooling of capital represents a socialization, the profits continue to remain private. The only difference here is that the lenders, the money capitalists, receive a portion of the surplus value "produced" by the industrial capitalist. The important point here is that the industrial capitalist, aside from retaining the lion's share of the surplus value, also reinvests it, that is, accumulates it. This means concentration of capital on the basis of the economic control and utilization of the capital belonging to others.

It is only one step from this lending mechanism to the formation of joint-stock companies or corporations that issue stock. In the previous case, one capitalist lent money-capital, and at the end of a stipulated period got back his principal plus interest. In the joint-stock corporation, a capitalist buys a share and thereby permanently channels a certain amount of capital into the productive concern; this capital in money form is transformed into productive capital and, as far as that money-capitalist is concerned, it is gone. He has received title to a certain portion of the yearly profit produced in that company. In order to get back his principal, he must seek a buyer on the market, whereby the ups and downs of the market may bring him either gains or losses, but in any event are no longer directly dependent on the productive operations of the corporation.

The joint-stock corporation is thus a necessity of capitalism; at the same time it is a powerful lever for the further centralization of capital. The point here is that this centralization takes place, at least on the surface, in the form of fictitious capital. (Fictitious capital is formed through the capitalization of the yield; thus an "investment" that yields $10 a year when the average interest rate equals 5 percent is said to represent a capital of $200.) The fictitious capital formed on the basis of shares in productive concerns is divorced from the actual production of surplus value; yet this corresponds to a relatively low level of fetishism when compared to similar calculations performed for investments in, say, government securities. Here the original capital no longer exists: it has been spent on B-52s or White House luxuries; furthermore, it was never borrowed with the intention of being spent as capital, nor was it in fact so used: it was employed unproductively. These securities yield returns because the state in the last analysis still has the power to tax, and as long as the state appears to remain in control of this respect (provided the economy is producing something that can be taxed), people will continue to buy these bonds.

Chapter 12: Central Banks and Fiscal Policy (S's Chapters 17-19)

There is in general only one expression of bourgeois confidence in any form of the state: *the latter's quotation on the Exchange.*

—Marx-Engels: "Revue: Mai bis Oktober," in *Marx-Engels Werke, VII*, 434.

INTRODUCTION

We finally find ourselves approaching the seemingly ubiquitous, omniscient Fed. It is hardly accidental that the elevation of the state to the status of *deus ex machina* remains inextricably bound up with another "convention"—money. For money and the state, as bourgeois social philosophers since Locke have been telling us, are creatures of man—having made them, we make them serve us.

We have established in previous chapters that money is not an "invention" but the result of a social process: the working out of the contradiction inherent in the commodity. The thesis according to which money is a mere convention must be seen as a moral, nonscientific, ideological approach to reclaim for capitalism society's *forces propres* which the latter has lost to the *things* of its own creation.

S has not undertaken to analyze the specific qualities of money in capitalism; where he does refer to monetary and credit phenomena peculiar to developed capitalism, he does not establish the link to simple commodity circulation but merely grabs from the surface of the present-day United States the most obvious "concrete" phenomena. Nor does he draw any logical connection between any of his categories. The only connections we are shown are those arbitrarily arrived at on the basis of "functions," graphs, "definitions," "conventions" (e.g., criteria for GNP "accounting," etc.).

HISTORICAL ORIGINS OF THE FEDERAL RESERVE SYSTEM

This brings us to that august institution which owes its existence to "the panic of 1907, with its alarming epidemic of bank failures: the country was fed up once and for all with the anarchy of unstable private banking. . . . The Federal Reserve System was formed—in face of strong banker opposition" (292). Was that really the way it happened?

Having gotten to know S's free and easy way with truth, we would guess not. Gustavus Myers describes the background thus:

> The panic of 1907, like previous panics, supplied the propitious opportunity to the great magnates to crush out lesser magnates and seize control of their property.
>
> The requirements of industrial centralization demanded the effacement of certain minor magnate groups which, from the point of view of the great magnates, had possessed themselves of a rather dangerous degree of industrial and financial power.[1]

Morgan and Rockefeller were interested in "getting" the Heinze-Morse group that controlled certain competing copper and steamship companies. To this end the stock prices of these companies were driven down until the owners were driven out. Then Morgan and Rockefeller went after banks and trusts associated with this group, which in turn led to runs on several banks. At this point J. P. Morgan entered the public stage as the nation's savior by organizing a "pool" to stem the tide of falling share prices—to buy them dirt-cheap.

It so happened that one of the affected trusts was controlled by Morgan's major competitor, The Tennessee Coal and Iron Company—the only other steel producer with an independent source of iron ore. The only hitch was that the antitrust laws prohibited such a combination (524); by the way, S conveniently fails to mention this little ploy. Morgan sent his representatives, Gary and Frick, to Theodore Roosevelt to inform him that if the takeover were thwarted, he would unleash the worst panic in the history of the country, leading to the closing of every bank. Roosevelt caved in and did just as Morgan bade him.[1a]

Now S asserts that this made *the* country fed up. Again we have good reason for being suspicious. In Chapter 6 S found it necessary to indulge in a little apologetics for old J. P. Morgan (127 f.), by informing us that no one was "hurt" by the issuance of watered-down stock after the formation of the Steel Trust. In fact, Morgan persuaded and coerced his own steel workers into buying the common stock; his skillful manipulations forced the price down from 44 to $8\frac{3}{4}$, at which point Morgan "saved the day" again by buying back the shares and repeating the whole process over again ad infinitum.[2]

What about the Fed? How was the alleged "banker opposition" structured? The point here is that Morgan's dictatorship at the end of the nineteenth and beginning of the twentieth centuries was under attack both from within and without the banking sphere. Rockefeller in particular had capitalized a bank from the profits reaped from Standard Oil. The Fed in part was established to undermine J. P. Morgan's special position of the *bankers' banker*.

> A helping hand in creating this system was lent by Senator Nelson W. Aldrich, who was related by marriage to the Rockefellers, the banker Paul Warburg of Kuhn, Loeb, and other opponents of the Morgan dictatorship. Their efforts did not bring immediate victory. In its "infancy" (up to the beginning of the 1930s) the system greatly depended on the Morgans, because, first, it did not as yet work with the provincial bankers who were natural enemies of Wall Street and, second, its main link, the Federal Reserve Bank of New York, was headed by Morgan men.[3]

But by the end of the 1930s the Fed had served its purpose of breaking up the Morgan hegemony.

Allegedly the Fed will do away with this sort of chicanery and skull-duggery. But can it? It is dealing with a system composed of private banks dedicated to make the transformation of money capital into commodity capital and productive capital and back again as smooth as possible. To the extent that this technical operation is vested in a central bank it can doubtless be made more efficient: i.e., it can waste less productive capital in the sphere of circulation; it can gather "idle" money and money capital from all social classes and geographic areas in order to lend it out to capitals more in "need" of it at a given time; it can, and in fact does, represent a higher stage of capitalist socialization of the process of production inasmuch as it allows capitalists to function with capital that does not "belong" to them; *but*, while accelerating the "material development of the productive forces and the establishment of the world market," credit, as the greatest feeder of overproduction, also accelerates the violent explosions of crises.[4]

Can a central bank prevent the blatant capitalist infighting à la Morgan? To the extent that a capitalist central bank functions, it can do so only as a link in the production and accumulation of surplus value. This greatly restricts the scope of the bourgeois state as ideal aggregate capitalist, for it can act only as the representative of certain individual capital or capitals (capitalist faction). Which capitals will gain and which lose must be determined empirically in each case. This becomes obvious particularly in the U.S., where the central bank is a non-state capitalist enterprise: it is literally a union of private banks in which the largest ones (in fact, only a few banks and/or bank monopoly combinations bulk large) fight for preeminence.

This is not to say that the state cannot intervene at all. But there are limits to its power. Thus, it can make laws that forbid the watering of stocks; it can "insure" banks, etc.; but it cannot create more surplus-value than has already been produced—it cannot insure total social profitability. But in general, it cannot intervene in the essential processes of value and capital.

FED—INTRODUCTION TO THE REALITY IT IS MEANT TO DEAL WITH

What then are the miracles that the Fed hath wrought? Although S in typical fashion points out that there is "nothing automatic" about deposit-creation, still his description of Fed interventions lead one to believe that our fates rest in good and wise hands that know how to tame the excessive swings of the business cycle. This confidence derives from the superficial theories of Keynes and the monetarists who talk about spending in an undifferentiated manner with respect to profitability.

The U.S. economy as measured by bourgeois statistics began declining and/or stagnating in 1969. A "mix" of Fed measures to expand the money supply and to keep interest rates low did not put an end to this phase of the cycle. This is another one of those ironies that beset contemporary capitalism. On the one hand, the bourgeoisie allegedly wants to see the excesses of this cycle tamed, and on the other, the cycle is doubly necessary for capitalism: it expresses the contradictions of that mode of production in periodic overproduction (of commodities and of capital); and it provides for the periodic mastering of this overproduction. The method consists in the depreciation of capital, which "kills off" enough capital so that the level of surplus-value production is sufficient for this new, reduced total capital (this is a cyclical barrier to the falling rate of profit, as well as an aspect of that tendency). This depreciation of capital can take different forms, such as idling (excess capacity), waste (nonprofitable government utilization thereof), and partial or complete destruction of its value. All these forms, however, mean the same as far as capital is concerned: it is prevented from, or interrupted in, the process of self-expansion.

To the extent that the state through taxation, credit, money, etc., is in a position to redistribute income and to affect the losses each capital must bear in this process, the state, at least on the surface, is able to "dampen" the cycle.

(By "surface" we mean GNP and unemployment: production and unemployment are maintained at levels corresponding to political needs of stability precisely because profit-making capital can no longer "deliver the goods.") The obverse side consists in the unpleasant circumstance for this best of all possible societies that capital is stagnating. Given the extra-economic forces at work in preventing a deep downswing, the very mechanism which allowed for restored conditions of profitability is put out of action. Therefore the upswing (by which we mean the profitability of capital, not the above-mentioned surface phenomena) will be similarly curtailed.

As pointed out before, the crisis of the 1930s marked a turning-point in the development of capitalism. This crisis is instructive for it showed the forces at work that lead to the overproduction of capital and the falling rate of profit on a world-wide capitalist scale; at the same time it proved that capitalism will not collapse spontaneously: only class struggle can deal capital the death blow. But class struggle is a two-sided affair. The bourgeoisie did not stand by passively waiting for its quantum leap into oblivion. It too resorted to political forms of struggle—against the proletariat, against other national capitalist classes, and among itself. The so-called perverted priorities of modern capitalism are a spontaneous result of the forms taken by this struggle.

In Chapter 8, we attempted to analyze some of the connections between Keynesian theory and fascist-capitalist reality. Contrary to Keynes' babble about increasing the propensity to consume, the Nazi economy escaped the more blatant aspects of the depression by increasing the military sphere at the expense of personal consumption. U.S. military-industrial reality is no different. Here is a statistical presentation using bourgeois rubrics:

(C) Consumption, (I) Investment and (G) Government Spending as a Percentage of GNP.[5]

	1929	1933	1940	1945	1950	1955	1960	1965	1970
C	75.5%	83.0%	72.3%	56%	67.5%	64%	65%	64%	63.5%
I	16	2.5	13.4	5	19.1	17	15	16	14.0
G	8.5	14.5	14.3	39	13.4	19	20	20	22.5
	100	100	100	100	100	100	100	100	100

Thus between 1929, the last predepression year, and the beginning of World War II, the state doubled its share; by the end of the war this share had risen another 50 percent, thus attaining a level approximately three times higher than that of 1929.

Since great significance is attributed to G's alleged ability to jump in for "slumping" C or I, it must be stressed that G's share has leveled off since the Korean War. But beyond this quantitative determination of the bounds of state economic activity, it is also necessary to break down this activity. Approximately 25 percent of the Federal budget is devoted to social-security and other "trust"-fund payments. This can scarcely be termed intervention. It is merely a delayed payment of wages. Similar objections can be raised with respect to education and health expenditures, which also must be considered as part of total social variable capital, whether it be received and consumed by the worker individually or collectively. A hefty portion of the remainder of the budget is accounted for by the redistribution of already created surplus value and the deduction from workers' taxes rechanneled to the capitalist class (in the form of interest payments on the national debt or Lockheed subsidies or subsidies to large capitalist farmers, etc.).

The differential effects of this redistribution appear to be much more the reaction to developments in the capitalist sphere than autonomous interventions by a neutral state; for these subsidies reflect the increasing inability of profitable capitalism to "deliver the goods" (railroad, electronics, airplanes, etc.). To the extent that individual capitals profit from this mechanism, the concrete situation of competition among them has been changed. However, this is not the result of neutral intervention but of intracapitalist class struggle.

One of the major tendencies, already referred to earlier, is the decline in the proportion of the total social product falling into the sphere of personal consumption. For as S never ceases to tell us, the goal of capitalism—yes, of every economic formation—is consumption. If this were true, then capitalism has been missing its mark for the last forty years, as the following table makes clear:

INDUSTRIAL PRODUCTION

	1939	1947	1959	1969
Total	100%	100%	100%	100%
Consumption	39	36	29	28
Equipment (of which)	9	12	18	20
Business	(9)	(11)	(12)	(13)
Military	—	(1)	(6)	(7)
Intermediate products and materials	52	53	53	52

As the commentary to this table laconically observes, "the share available for consumer use has fallen over each of the periods since 1939."[6] Now in general, a rise in Department I vis-à-vis Department II would indicate increased capital accumulation and a "healthy" capitalist accumulation; this is however only partially true of the period in question, since even a large segment of the categories business equipment, intermediates, and materials is devoted to subsidized, nonprofitable production. On the other hand, if we look more closely at particular cyclical developments we gain some insight into the workings of the capitalist economy: namely, we see that far from being the goal of capitalism, consumption is the chief burden. The following is a tabular presentation of growth rates for total industrial production, and for each department:[7]

	1948-1953	1954-1961	1962-1966	1967-1968
total	5.6%	2.3%	7.3%	2.8%
Dept. I	10.4%	0.9%	9.7%	2.9%
Dept. II	4%	3.6%	5.5%	3%

A similar trend prevails in the present period of stagflation. With 1957-59 as the base year (=100), we find the following development:[8]

	1968	1969	Dec. 1970	June 1971
total	165.5	172.8	164.4	167.9
consump.	156.9	162.5	162.4	169.5
equipment	182.6	188.6	164.2	156.2
matls.	165.8	174.6	166.0	170.6

Several observations are in order here. First of all, we are apparently confronted with a regularity of capitalist industrial cycles: during "upswings," Department I grows more rapidly. This should not come as a surprise, since capitalism's goal is the production and appropriation of surplus value. But this surplus value is not for the purpose of the capitalists' consumption (whatever they might subjectively believe), for that is precisely the historical distinction between capitalism and previous class societies: productive accumulation. Accumulation is equal to that part of the social product which is consumed neither by workers nor capitalists. Consumption is therefore a drag on capital accumulation (it is here of course that subjectivity assumed significance, since the capitalists have no trouble consuming during crises and depressions). Increasing consumption, as we saw in the tables, is an expression of the downs of capitalism.

But here too a dialectic is at work. Increasing capital accumulation cannot go on forever, for at some point it brings about such a low level of worker consumption that

Department I has exceeded the limits within which it can operate without causing overproduction of itself—namely, capital.

Increasing consumption will not do the trick at this point; in fact, it is merely an expression of the decreasing accumulation: Department I is cut back. Increasing consumption is just as much a part of the self-healing industrial cycle as the destruction of capital; for in its most general sense, the destruction or depreciation of capital is the same as preventing its appreciation of self-expansion—and this is what the relative increase of Department II also means.

THE FED—WHAT IT IS

Trying to determine what the Fed can achieve is not an easy task; bourgeois economists tend to clothe the system of banking and credit in an air of mystery.

Before we can proceed to an analysis of what the Reserve banks do, we must study what they are. One hundred years ago Marx asserted that for the most part bank capital is composed of what he called fictitious capital: claims (commercial paper), government securities (which represent past capital), and stocks (titles to future profit).[9] Is the situation any different today?

As of December 31, 1971, member commercial banks of the Fed had approximately $366 billion outstanding in loans and investments. Of this total, $111 billion were invested in U.S. government, state, and local securities; $50 billion were lent to individuals, largely for consumer credit; $55 billion went toward real-estate loans; $9 billion were lent for the purchase of private securities; $17 billion were lent to banks and other financial institutions; and approximately $105 billion were lent for commercial, industrial, and agricultural purposes. Thus, approximately 28 percent of total loans and investments found their way into productive reinvestment; for the most part, these represented commercial paper. A slightly larger proportion (30 percent) was held in various state securities; the balance rested in speculative or consumptive hands.

During the early years of the century, before the founding of the Fed, government securities averaged about 10 percent of commercial bank loans and investments; this percentage rose slightly during the period between World War I and the Depression. Although this conclusion is based upon extrapolations, it would appear that during these two periods commercial-industrial loans comprised as much as half of total loans and investments.

What is the significance of this change in the direction of commercial bank-credit policies? A recent essay by a Federal Reserve Bank economist does a rather poor job of putting this trend into its proper perspective:

> U.S. Government securities have occupied a major role in the asset structure of the Nation's commercial banks since the depression years of the 1930's. During that time, a contraction in private credit demand coincident with an expansion in Treasury borrowing to finance Federal expenditures induced banks to acquire a sizeable amount of Government obligations. . . . In the years since World War II, however, U.S. Government securities have declined in importance relative to other commercial bank assets. . . . Accompanying the diminishing importance of Government securities in bank portfolios during the past decade, the share of bank-held Governments relative to the total amount of public debt outstanding also has declined sharply. . . . Notwithstanding the marked decline in bank holdings of Governments relative to other bank assets, and relative to the public debt outstanding, the absence of an absolute decline in these holdings over the past decade underscores the force of the traditional motives banks have to hold Government securities. Principal among these motives is that Government securities . . . provide a valuable source of liquidity to banks because they are the most readily marketable of all fixed income securities. With bank loan demand subject to cyclical variations, Government securities are generally considered an investment vehicle from which banks can escape with a minimum of loss to accommodate an upswing in loan demand. Conversely, these securities serve as a temporary haven for bank funds when loan demand is low. . . . Government securities also provide income to banks, although this function is secondary relative to liquidity protection.[10]

Well, one might object, this doesn't seem very serious; a bit of private-credit contraction here, a bit of Treasury financing there. So what if banks *are* induced to buy more government securities? After all, didn't Marx say that bank capital was largely fictitious? What's the difference between holding a state security or holding stock or commercial bills of exchange? Anyway, government securities are more liquid and they're backed by the Nation.

Have the Marxists been outwitted? Let us look at this entire complex in somewhat greater detail.

Is it true that banks were *induced* to acquire government securities? And what was the role of the almighty Fed in this matter? Although the trend toward greater commercial-bank involvement in financing various federal government "projects" experienced a sharp relative increase during the Depression (as a percentage of commercial bank loans and investments, government securities rose from 14 to 50), in absolute amount the increase was not very significant (approximately from $5 billion to $15 billion). (The percentages in the table on page eleven refer to federal, state and local government holdings; before the late 1950s the non-federal securities did not bulk very large and hence are not treated separately; the structural change that took place in the 1960s will be discussed below). In this context it must be remembered that the New Deal was not very radical; on the whole it merely brought the U.S. to the level of "anti-laissez-faire social interventionism" of pre-depression capitalist Europe.

World War II became the Great Divide. Between 1939 and 1946, total Federal Reserve Bank ownership of the national debt rose from $2.5 to $23.4 billion; during this period total commercial bank ownership of the national debt rose from $12.7 to $74.5 billion.[11]

Although it is true that the World War II period presented an "abnormally" state-oriented economy, and that therefore any judgments based on absolutizing this historical experience without taking into account the further postwar development would be distorted, certain basic structural changes in late capitalism do receive clear expression in these relations between state and private capitalism.

THE FEDERAL RESERVE SYSTEM AND PAPER MONEY

To what extent is it true that the U.S. is on a "low yield government security standard," and to what extent has the public debt become monetized?

Let us first look at so-called currency in circulation. This is one component of "M_1" which, aside from demand deposits, includes coins and Federal Reserve Notes. At the end of 1971 there were about $54 billion of Federal Reserve Notes (and $6.5 billion in coins) in existence. In 1939 Federal Reserve Notes amounted to about $7 billion; by 1945 this sum had quadrupled to $28 billion; the 1945–1960 period saw a relatively insignificant increase ($2 billion), whereas between 1960 and 1971 the amount doubled.[12]

It must be understood that we are not dealing with what is ordinarily meant by paper money. With respect to the immediate goal of paper money we may distinguish two main types: the first is directed at covering state deficits but is not compensated for by any withdrawals from the economy. In this sense no limits are imposed on its issue and it can therefore lead to the sort of hyperinflation Germany experienced in the early 1920s. The second kind is based on government credit and taxation; it is therefore subject to limits; it is the proper tool for what has become known as controlled inflation. For example, the state needs money to pay the military-capitalists for "services rendered," but the "people" from whom it is to collect the taxes cannot pay since they have not yet realized their commodities. And these people happen to be the suppliers of the selfsame military-capitalists. Instead of taking a bank loan, the state issues paper money to pay the military-capitalists. These in turn pay off their suppliers, who are then able to pay their taxes by returning the paper money to the state, which can then retire the money without having increased the money supply above that which was needed. The state has thus issued what we may designate as state credit money.

This, however, is not the mode of operation of the advanced capitalist countries. For the most part contemporary capitalist money takes the form of bank notes, but the content of paper money is of the second type described above. Bank notes were credit money issued by banks on the basis of commercial credit:

> Until goods reach the final consumer, banks grant commercial credit secured by bills of exchange. These bills were discounted by emission banks which issued banknotes on their basis. . . . When a commodity reached its final consumer, it was sold for cash which passed from the retailer to the wholesaler, then to the manufacturer, and finally to the bank in redemption of the commercial bill of exchange, whence it was returned to the emission bank issuing banknotes.[13]

The important point here is that such banknotes, since they automatically return to the issuing bank, cannot exceed the need for them and thus become surplus in circulation.

Instead of being guaranteed by commercial bills of exchange, contemporary "banknotes" are guaranteed by state securities. As we will have occasion to develop in greater detail below, paper money is issued by the Fed on the basis of the securities it has "bought" from the Treasury. In other words, the Fed Notes must be backed up by government securities. But since this mechanism is tightly bound up with the Fed's relation to the commercial banking system, it would be correct to state that government credit rests on bank credit while bank credit rests on government credit. This cannot serve "liquidity protection"; on the contrary, it is bound to weaken the liquidity situation of the banks. In the past the ability of banks to pay off their depositors depended on their ability to realize their outstanding loans—in other words, on the ability of the industrial capitalists to appropriate enough surplus-value to pay their loans. Now this ability of the banks would appear to be dependent on the Federal budget. The fact that government securities form the backing for these Fed Notes justifies our claim that these notes have the content of paper money.

As mentioned above, the second type of paper money is similar to nonconvertible banknotes in that neither can be converted to gold and both are instruments of controlled or planned inflation. The main difference of course is that whereas the former functions through a fiscal-budgetary mechanism, the latter operates on the basis of bank credit. Another essential difference must be seen in the fact that pure paper money is used for purely unproductive purposes—covering government expenses; state banknotes, though issued for the same purpose, do not necessarily limit the credit destined for industrial investment; on the contrary, this issue is used as a resource for such credit.

We have established that present-day capitalist money is not ordinary paper money, or at least that it does not take that form. What then is the purpose of giving paper money the form of banknotes? And beyond that, what is the mechanism through which this concealment is realized? The answer, or at least a partial answer, is furnished by Backman, who points out that with respect to armaments budgets, the "use of loans obscures the situation"; for "when future generations repay those loans there is a transfer of funds from taxpayers to bondholders which involves a redistribution of the national income."[14] The problem of the debt is indissolubly connected with the system of Federal Reserve Notes and reflects class relations in the U.S. today (albeit from the more superficial distribution side). As Backman discloses, the advantage of the government securities (loans)–Federal Reserve Notes mechanism over printing more paper money is that the bourgeoisie can more easily shift the burden of the expenses of militarization on to the working class while making a supplementary profit through its "loans" to the state.

What happens in financing state ventures into domestic and international repression can be summed up thus: for the capitalists, investment in state securities appears very profitable. By subscribing to these loans, they are in fact engaging in a rather common practice: they are, at least formally, extending credit to their customer: they are financing the purchase of their commodities by the state. With these loans the state can then purchase the needed commodities from them. Subsequently, taxes will have to be raised in order to pay off the loans. Somewhere along the line more Federal Reserve Notes will also be issued on the basis of the open-market purchases of these securities. This mechanism should be kept in mind while reading S's story about Peter and Paul (376). For these capitalists are never taxed as much as they gain, otherwise they would not engage in the business to begin with. Here the bourgeoisie has a decided advantage over the proletariat: it decides which wars to fight and how to finance them.

We can now focus on the essence of contemporary money in the U.S. We have established that Federal Reserve Notes are banknotes in form and paper money in content. How does this compare with S's teachings? "Federal Reserve notes are the Fed's principal liabilities. These are the various dollar bills we all [!?] carry in our wallets. These IOU's cost the Fed no interest, and it is highly privileged to have been granted by Congress this power to issue currency" (7th ed., p. 301). This is literally all that S deems fit to tell us about these slips of paper.

Is it true that the Notes do not cost the Fed any interest? Do they "cost" anyone interest? They must, since contemporary banknote-paper money is based on government securities, which are of course interest-bearing. And, in fact, in 1972 the Fed paid the Treasury approximately $3.2 billion as "interest on F.R. notes"; since 1947 these payments have exceeded $29 billion.[15]

The Fed, in order to maintain its façade of independence, does not directly purchase government securities in "exchange" for printing notes at the Treasury's request. The printing of money takes place indirectly through the open-market operations of the Fed. However, the sham becomes evident when we recognize that the aim of the open-market operations is the regulation of the money supply. The Fed in large part returns the interest it receives on the government securities it holds to the Treasury; but it has already printed up new notes (or created deposits) in order to pay off those from whom it buys the Government securities; these latter payments of course must also include the interest due on the securities.

The departure from the gold standard which took place about the time of World War I was connected with certain developments in international capitalist relations, and although both the international and national contradictions of capital are obviously tied to the general crisis of capitalism, this disintegration of the gold standard was a happy coincidence on the national level, for it provided the *technical* means for the institutionalization of inflation.

In the U.S. this transition was effected even before the country went off the gold standard. The passage of the Glass-Steagall Act in February, 1932, amended the original Federal Reserve Act (1913) so that Federal Reserve Notes, instead of having to be guaranteed by gold and commercial paper (and the latter category did not include loans for speculation), could now be "guaranteed" up to 60 percent by government securities.

The following interchange between a Congressman and the Vice-Chairman of the Federal Reserve Bank is informative:

> Mr. Johnson [Congressman Albert Johnson of Pennsylvania]: I notice in this Federal Reserve bulletin that as the currency outstanding in the U.S. increases, the amount of Government bonds held by the Federal Reserve System almost equals the amount of currency you issue. Maybe this is a coincidence.
> Mr. Robertson [J. L. Robertson, Vice-Chairman FRS]: Pure coincidence. We buy or sell Government bonds for the purpose of increasing or decreasing the availability of money and credit in the country, and how it will jibe with any other particular statistics is coincidental.[16]

From this it is clear that although FR Notes may not cost the Fed anything, they do in fact cost the taxpayer "something," since this banknote form of paper money is the mechanism by which the capitalist state finances its "business" of militarism and subsidizes capitals unable to self-expand.

This points up the patent absurdity of the contention that the Fed and the Treasury almost never use the authority to issue currency "except to satisfy the currency-using habits of the public"; behind this notion lies the current bourgeois classification of money. Money, in the strictest sense of these classifications, called M_1, comprehends currency plus demand deposits (checking accounts). The criteria for adopting this or any other classification are deemed purely arbitrary:

> The user or analyst may take his pick. Or, he may wish to devise a definition of his own, offering it not necessarily as a definition of money as such, but rather as the definition of a financial or monetary magnitude he deems to be significant. . . . With a definition in hand, whichever one it may be, the analyst may proceed to measure the size of the money supply and to monitor changes in it that take place over time.[17]

Such a do-your-own-thing methodology represents another step in the progressive degradation of science by bourgeois society. Nor is this approach unfamiliar, for we have seen S apply it repeatedly (e.g., GNP criteria). What is S's criterion for including checking accounts in the money supply?

> Because it is difficult to draw a fast and hard line at any point in the chain of things that do have a direct bearing on spending, the exact definition of M, the money supply, is partly a matter of taste rather than scientific necessity. . . . A century ago, demand deposits would not have been included in M. Today economists would include demand deposits, since even the most stubborn adherent of the old narrow concept has to admit that the existence of checking accounts does economize on the use of currency and thus acts much like an increase in the effective amount of currency [281].

The basic reason for emphasizing M_1 appears to be the fact that its components can be "spent directly," whereas other "near monies" must first be converted into M_1 elements before they can be spent. Since government bonds are "highly liquid," they also share "many of the properties of money." In this sense one might say that any commodity is a "near money" since its function is to be exchanged for money; its actual "nearness" to money does not depend on the subjective definitions of bourgeois economists but on the very objective conditions of the market. In any case, no matter how close a commodity may be to becoming money, it "shares" none of the properties of money (except those common to money and commodity as value forms) until it is "completely" money.

The argument that checking accounts economize on the use of currency merely emphasizes the bourgeois economists' neglect of the two-sided nature of credit. As Marx pointed out, one of the main functions of credit is to reduce the essentially unproductive circulation costs; the use of credit increases the velocity of money directly insofar as a smaller amount of money in circulation can serve the same number and volume of commodity transactions, and indirectly insofar as it accelerates the velocity of the commodity metamorphoses and through this the velocity of money circulation. In fact, this mechanism was known to us in its abstract form in simple commodity circulation as money qua means of payment.

Thus Marx would personify the "stubborn adherent" of the "old" definition of money even though he was the first to conceptualize the process of economizing on money. What then is S's rationale? No one would deny that credit can expand the process of production beyond the limits set by "cash." In fact, as Marx observed, to the extent that credit replaces gold, it increases the wealth of capitalist society (here Marx of course is referring to gold, but it would appear that this is also valid for paper money or banknotes, not insofar as the production of gold can be replaced by the production of "real wealth," but rather to the extent that the velocity of money—that is, the already circulating money—is increased.[18]

S's lack of understanding of the other side of credit finds expression in the identification and/or confusion of currency with checking accounts; for the credit relation, a more concrete expression of the abstract possibility of the separation of selling and buying common to simple commodity circulation must "somehow" also contain the basic contradictions of capitalist commodity production. Although credit is obviously a "socializing" process inasmuch as it extends the power of the individual capitals by intertwining them, the fact that at some point in the great chain of payments some capitalists may find that the private labor of their workers never gained social recognition unfailingly points up the "other" side of credit in every crisis.

Although money owes its existence to anarchic processes uncontrollable by the members of "money economies," still, this money must be uniformly established (after the fact, of course) by the social will capitalism has been able to muster—the state; the credit relation, however, is *in this sense* a private affair, debt that in itself does not affect society. The existence of credit can replace money, as long as mutual debts balance and until the payoff. This became very apparent in the 1930s when thousands of banks lost the confidence and money of their customers; and this was no doubt also a major reason why the currency component of M_1 increased so quickly during World War II: the recent mass bankruptcies made many people hesitant about accepting the essential identity of both components of M_1. In other words, if a commodity is paid for with money, then the transaction has been completed: the commodity form of the capital value has again assumed its money form; if a commodity, however, is paid for by shifting demand accounts about, the transaction may be complete and again it may not, depending on the chain of factors determining the liquidity of that particular bank, which in turn depends on the total social situation of surplus-value production.

The rational kernel behind the M_1 notion might very well be the circumstance that bourgeois economists today tend to view all moneys as more or less arbitrarily created fiat money; although we know this to be false, the notions, or at least the contemporary version of it, is rooted in the military-inflation complex characteristic of the post-World War II U.S. (to some extent). By this we mean that the state can finance its activities by the securities-loans-Federal Reserve Note mechanism.

From the point of view of the budget-induced inflationary processes this difference between Federal Reserve Notes and the deposits created for the state at commercial banks does not appear to be great.

Any scientific understanding of the breakdown between cash and cashless payments must be based on an analysis of the reproduction process of capital; that the greatest number of transactions are effected without cash is nothing new. On the other hand, is it mere coincidence that the proportion of Federal Reserve Notes within total M_1 is roughly equal to the proportion of final ("consumer") consumption within GNP (about ¼)?

THE NATIONAL DEBT

As Marx points out, the national debt, or the sale of the state, is the only part of the "national wealth" that really belongs to all the people. Marx illustrated this with the British development. At the end of the seventeenth century the Bank of England began by lending the government money at 8 percent interest; at the same time it was empowered by Parliament to coin money from the same capital by lending it to the public in the form of banknotes. Soon this credit money created by the Bank became the coin in which the Bank made loans to the state and paid the interest on the national debt for the state. In other words, the Bank was being paid by the state, that is the public, in the form of interest, for the power given it by the state to transform these same banknotes from paper into money and then lend to the state.[19] Compare this to Alvin Hansen's description,[20] which has nothing but praise for this momentous turning point in financial history when "the public debt became a secure investment," "a truly *national* debt; not the debt of a capricious monarch liable to repudiation. It became a debt for which the whole nation was responsible, and in which merchants, traders, capitalists, and property owners in general found a safe and dependable financial investment."

This is actually not a bad description of what the national debt is all about: property owners get a safe investment and the nation "as a whole" pays up. S to be sure waxes apologetic when he speaks of this aspect: "To the degree that the people involved are different and that the interest receivers are wealthier, more thrifty [!], or deemed less in need of income, there will be some (admittedly minor) *redistributional* effects to reckon with" (365). What he means by "reckon with" is not clear—except that the working class can count on getting fleeced. It is instructive to compare this account with that which S was forced to present back in 1948:

> ... The statistical evidence suggests that the people who receive bond interest are *on the average* not in the lower income brackets. Thus interest on the public debt constitutes a regressive (Robin Hood in reverse) element in our fiscal system. "Soaking the poor to pay the rich" tends to reduce purchasing power and runs counter to many modern notions of equity. Nevertheless, it is a necessary evil if past commitments with respect to the public debt are to be scrupulously honored, as they must be [1st ed., p. 429].

Why these past commitments must be "honored" is not clear—unless it has something to do with the marginal propensity of the rich to continue sponging off the poor; as Marx says, with the rise of the public debt, breach of faith with respect to that debt replaces the sin against the Holy Ghost as the forgivable sin.[21]

As we pointed out above, S conveniently separates the debt from the issuance of paper money, alias Federal Reserve Notes. At this point we can look into the interconnections of debt—taxes—paper money. By taking out loans the state is in a position to spend extraordinary amounts without making the taxpayers feel the brunt of it immediately; later of course they will feel it, for the debt must be honored. Since the Federal Government has continued to run budget deficits in the post-World War II period, it has had to borrow more and more, and therefore the interest payments increase as well. This of course means that taxpayers will have to shell out more. In other words, the fiscal system of our wonderful mixed economy, like that serving the repressive class state in Marx's time, contains the "seeds of automatic progression."

Now theoretically the deficit could be financed simply by increasing taxes; however, especially in light of the enormous burden which taxation already puts on the working class, and in light of the fact that many of them remember a time when they paid no income tax, an attempt to increase taxes immediately instead of distributing the burden over time is probably considered politically too risky.

We know that a more complicated mechanism has been established to conceal the fact of "soaking the poor to pay the rich"; this involves the issuance of Federal Reserve Notes "backed" by government securities; in the end the taxpayers still foot the bill for the interest payments.

In connection with costs and profits it is necessary to look at S's extremely apologetic presentation of the "quantitative problem of the debt." To begin with the "problem" of the origin of the debt, S's trump card is that the "bulk" of it arose during World War II "in order to maximize our effectiveness against the enemy" (365), allegedly fascism, so everything seems to be in order. This line of reasoning conceals the contribution of U.S. imperialism in the postwar period to an increasing debt; and this means not only "our" overt aggression in Korea and Southeast Asia, but in general the many billions of dollars "invested" in military services.

In point of fact, however, the Federal public debt rose from 259.1 billion dollars in 1946 to 469.9 billion in 1972.[22] In other words, about 45 percent of the current public debt was created after World War II; if we look merely at the period of the Vietnam War, we see that between 1965 and 1972 the public debt increased by 128.4 billion dollars; thus 28.6 percent of the current debt was accumulated during this time alone.

In an attempt to belittle the significance of the debt, S points out that interest charges on the debt as a percentage of GNP have not increased since the end of World War II (368). However, it is more relevant here to look at the interest charges as a share of total Federal Government expenditures; and here we note that this percentage has more than doubled between 1945 (about 3.8 percent) and 1973 (about 10 percent).[23]

In 1973, these interest payments amounted to approximately 21 billion dollars, representing Federal budget expenditures approximately 50 percent higher than those for education, manpower, community development, and housing.[24]

That S does not understand the interconnections among the national debt, inflation, and the stagnation of capital expansion comes out clearly in his assurance: "So long as continuous deficits *do not result in the public debt growing faster than GNP grows*, good economic health can prevail" (362).

Inflation arises when capital that could not function profitably in the private economy is lent to the state; such state expenditures, however, reduce total profit relative to total capital; in order to attain average profits, prices are raised, which in turn necessitates an increase in the money supply. If this price-money mechanism did not function, then the subsequent drop in profit would of course counteract the purpose of government spending—to "stimulate" the private economy; for with sinking profits, production would be cut back even further. Thus, inflation does not come about as a result of government-induced production causing demand to exceed supply (which would be absurd if the basic problem is lack of effective demand), but rather "as the means by which the non-profitable character of government-induced production by way of deficit-financing finds its partial compensation in higher prices."[25]

S consoles us with this gem: *"We must not forget that the real national product of the United States is an ever-growing thing."* Actually, one might just as well ignore this piece of wisdom since periodically that ever-growing thing just stops growing and even shrinks a bit, as in 1969-70 and 1974, when real production declined.

Despite S's claim to "have looked carefully at the facts about the public debt" (7th ed., p. 351), he omitted the minor detail of the actual distribution of debt-ownership. In order to help form an understanding of the class nature of this distribution and the trends in the past 30 years, we present the following table (the top part gives the absolute amounts in billions of dollars, the lower, the percentages):[26]

	1940	1950	1960	1970
US Gov't investment accounts	$ 7.6	$ 39.2	$ 55.1	$ 97.1
Federal Reserve Banks	2.2	20.8	27.4	62.1
Commercial Banks	17.3	61.8	62.1	63.2
Individuals	10.6	66.3	66.1	81.9
Insurance Companies	6.9	18.7	11.9	7.0
Mutual Savings Banks	3.2	10.9	6.3	2.8

Corporations	2.0	19.7	18.7	10.6
State and local gov'ts	.5	8.8	18.7	22.9
Foreign and international	.2	4.3	13.0	20.6
Other	.5	6.2	11.2	21.1
Total	$ 50.9	$256.7	$290.4	$389.2
US Gov't investment acct.	14.9%	15.3%	19.0%	24.9%
Fed. Res. Banks	4.3	8.1	9.4	16.0
Commercial Banks	34.0	24.1	21.4	16.2
Individuals	20.8	25.8	22.8	21.0
Insurance Companies	13.6	7.3	4.1	1.8
Mutual Savings Banks	6.3	4.2	2.2	.7
Corporations	3.9	7.7	6.4	2.7
State and local gov'ts	1.0	3.4	6.4	5.9
Foreign and international	.4	1.7	4.5	5.3
Other	1.0	2.4	3.9	5.4
Total	100.0%	100.0%	100.0%	100.0%

We must provide an interpretation of the long-run tendencies operating here. In the first place, in the postwar period the share of commercial bank-holdings dropped (although its absolute holdings remained constant). This is in line with our findings that during this period the share of bank loans and investments in U.S. Government securities dropped while that in commercial-industrial enterprises rose, a development easily explained by the higher profits (i.e., interest) to be gotten in the private sphere during this period. Also, commercial banks began to invest more heavily in more profitable state and local bonds.

Another notable feature was the sharp increase in holdings (both relatively and absolutely) by U.S. Government trust funds (various social-security trusts, etc.); that these holdings occupy an ever-growing portion of the national debt indicates that the Federal government is facing increasing difficulties in finding private investors willing to invest in these securities. As a result, the state must increase the yields of its securities in order to "attract" more investors. Moreover, the increased use of social-security trust funds for holding these securities compels U.S. workers to give additional financial support to capitalist state activities.

The increased holdings by the Fed would appear to give it additional latitude on the open market (selling securities in order to lower M_1); as we saw, however, to the extent that commercial banks do not want to buy, this policy backfires. The profits of the commercial banks that have hung on to their holdings are by no means peanuts: in 1969 they amounted to $80 billion, or one-fifth of the Federal debt.

In concluding this section we will touch upon a subject not directly related to the stabilizer–fiscal-policy complex: state and local debt. Although S devotes a few pages to non-Federal government taxation and expenditures in Chapter 9, he does not go into the problem of debt.

State and local debt has been increasing much more rapidly than Federal debt in recent years; thus in the 1960s, while the Federal debt rose 2.1 percent annually (excluding U.S. government accounts), state and local debt rose by $78 billion, or 8.2 percent annually.

Not only are Federal taxes being mortgaged to finance capital, but also those on the state and local levels (where even according to S the principal taxes are "regressive" [172]). Given the fact that a larger portion of state and municipal budgets than of the Federal budget are devoted to activities in one degree or another useful to the mass of people (education, housing, hospitals, etc.), it would be important to see how large banks influence the decisions on these projects: whether or not new hospitals will be built, how great a burden on the taxpayers the profits of the banks will be, whether it will make the projects prohibitively expensive.[26a]

During the 1960s state and local debt doubled while commercial bank ownership of this debt rose more than threefold.

THE LIMITATIONS OF THE FED

S is so busy giving us a blow-by-blow description of how the Fed works that he has no time to explain exactly how limited its power is. However, before we embark on an analysis of certain of these limitations, we wish to point out that since Marx locates the central contradictions of capitalism in the sphere of production (crisis as overproduction of capital as a result of too little surplus value)—that is, since he generously grants capitalism a smoothly running sphere of circulation—nothing the central bank can do will ward off cyclical crises. To the extent that a central banking system and a fully developed credit system have been created, the smooth functioning of these operations becomes a *technical* matter; at times policy will fail, at other times, not. When they work, they have provided capitalism not with a breathing spell but with the fullest possibilities it can ideally attain.

The point is that even when the central bank helps realize the ideal conditions for the sphere of circulation, and, by channeling capital, also affects production and therefore the conditions of self-expansion, even then all it has done is to help create a situation in which the basic contradictions will still surface. Up until now, central bank policy has called for working within the capitalist framework, and as long as it does, it will continue to preserve capitalism (along with its crises).

It is in this connection that we can perhaps best examine the relation between ideology (as false theory) and seemingly successful practice. The Fed may work out some very long equations for dealing with M_1, and they may or may not know how to control these "magnitudes," but they still have no understanding of the real relations between money, credit, and profit.

In order for the deposit multiplier (or divider)—the Fed's most powerful "tool"—to work, the following conditions (not meant to be exhaustive) must be met: (1) that the Fed effectively control member-bank reserves; (2) that banks (and other capitalists) react passively; (3) that there exists an unsatisfied demand for bank credit; (4) that there is no "breakthrough" into cash transactions; (5) that the size of the reserve multiplier is stable. Since S explicitly or implicitly concedes some of these points we will concentrate on a few.

Let us take a closer look at some of the big "anticyclical" moves the Fed has allegedly undertaken in the post-World

War II period. What did it do to head off the "recession" of 1954? It went to work like the proverbial early bird: from May to December, 1953, it bought $1.5 billion in government securities on the open market; it lowered the FRS interest rate; reduced reserve requirements; and in a burst of activity, industrial production sank 10 percent between August, 1953, and April, 1954.

What happened during our next "recession"—1957-58? In order to dampen a dangerous-looking upswing (characterized by heavy speculation), the Fed sold $677 million of government securities during the second half of 1957; interest rates were raised, as were margin requirements; nevertheless industrial production, prices, stock issues, and speculation mounted. What did our friends at Chase Manhattan et al. do? Not only did they not "cooperate," but in general they paralyzed the moves of the Fed. From 1955 to 1957 the commercial banks sold $6.7 billion of government securities while increasing other private operations by $15.8 billion. Once the crisis came, the Fed made an about face: it bought about $2 billion in government securities, lowered the interest rate, lowered margin requirements, etc. But, as might have been expected, the crisis still ran its course, and production dropped 14 percent compared with the precrisis level. As to the 1969-72 crisis, the Fed itself has more or less admitted that it is powerless to improve the situation.

The trouble with the Fed-government securities "anticyclical" mechanism is that it reverses cause and effect; for in fact the supply and demand of bank credits is determined by the objective conditions of the reproduction process; and in no lesser measure are operations with government securities determined.

During the crisis phase of the cycle, capitalists sell their government securities to raise money to pay off debts; at the same time, the demand accounts of banks are being depleted for the same reason. Thus they too are selling government securities, because they guarantee a certain income˙ which may not only be higher than that deriving from their usual capitalist investment but also more certain. As S himself admits, under such circumstances the Fed cannot "encourage" private investment, even at a zero interest rate (336).

And, finally, in the period of the upswing, capitalists will sell their government securities to invest the proceeds more profitably. Under such conditions nothing will "induce" them to buy less profitable government securities.

Having presented this basic theoretical objection, let us look at the five-step jig the Fed performs to "control spending": (1) it cuts bank reserves, which (2) leads to multiplier contractions in deposits, which (3) makes interest rates rise, which (4) depresses investment, which (5) "puts a multiplier damper" on income and prices (314 f., 331). But as we have just seen, the Fed does not exercise such strict control over reserves—in other words, the profit motives of the commercial banks override the alleged national interests pursued by the bank.

Step 3 is based on a fundamental misconception of the monetary theory of cycles: namely, an identification of money and loan capital. However, the quantity of money in circulation is much smaller than the amount of loan capital, since one "piece" of money in the course of a certain period of time can complete several circuits as loan capital (velocity of money applied to capital). Moreover, at different points in the cycle the mass of circulating money and the mass of loan capital can change in opposite directions. Thus, for example, during the crisis phase the amount of loan capital may decrease, while the quantity of money in circulation may rise.

In general, the absolute quantity of money does not determine the rate of interest. During a period of expansion, abundant money can still be accompanied by a relatively high rate of interest as a result of increasing demand for loan capital; a period of business contraction can also mean a relatively low rate. Except at the time of the extreme crunch, the absolute mass of circulating money does not influence the rate of interest, because the former is determined by commodity prices and volume ($P \times Q$) and by the state of credit, but it does not determine credit.

Step 4, the influence of the interest rate on investment,

will be discussed more fully. But we should like to advance some important arguments at this point. First of all, S lends his assertion an air of plausibility by mixing up capital investment with consumer spending on "durables" ("people's decisions as to whether it is profitable to build a new house or plant . . . usually depend upon how they can finance such investment spending" [315]); this is so particularly because interest rates (installment buying, etc.) and mortgage rates are so high and the incomes of most consumers so low that added interest costs may in fact be a major factor in determining whether one buys a house or not. But this sort of consumer "rationality" does not play an important role in investment decisions, for here high interest rates in periods of high profits do not deter increased investment, while low interest rates in depressions do not spur such investment.

(On a biographical level, it is also curious that S places so much stress on this element, since in an earlier article he granted that the interest rate "is less important than Keynes himself believed.")[27] Although interest "costs" have been rising, they have never represented more than 3 percent of the gross product of nonfinancial corporations during the post-World War II period.[27a]

THE INFLUENCE OF THE INTEREST RATE ON INVESTMENT: THE ALLEGED SYNTHESIS OF MONETARY AND INCOME ANALYSIS

Chapter 18 pretends to be a synthesis of monetary and income analysis with a view toward integrating government monetary and fiscal policy to achieve the goal of a progressive economy: one that enjoys reasonable price stability and lives up to its production potential (334). This is the chapter which supposedly demonstrates that "more sophisticated quantity theory" promised in Chapter 15 and the "modern" (Keynesian) theory of income determination. But this combination is nothing but a dialectical fraud; for even on a bourgeois level it offers only the form, not the content, of a synthesis. Keynesians have never had any qualms about urging the Fed through its manipulations with the money supply to affect interest rates, and therefore "investment," while such tinkerings are vehemently opposed by "modern" quantity theorists such as Friedman. In the appendix to Chapter 18, S admits that the differences between these two groups are not merely terminological, and that a synthesis has *not* yet been achieved:

> At a deeper level, however, those who prefer one terminology usually think that certain hypotheses about the real world are more fruitful then certain others. . . . If the day ever arrives when the proponents of the velocity approach can prove by their researches that theirs is the more convenient tool, pragmatic scholars will welcome all its help [347].

Such an admission, of course, coming as it does in the fine print of an appendix, is right in line with S's practice of sneaking in a "not-A" whenever he feels that he may be challenged on his previous assertion of A.

At the risk of being nitpicking and repetitive, we must ask where this "goal of a progressive economy" comes from both in a supposedly value-free science and in a class society which lacks the collective rationality necessary to formulate such a goal, much less carry it out.

The pseudo-scientific superficiality of S's explanations and pedagogy is particularly apparent in the first few paragraphs of Chapter 18, where he "presents" the monetary side of his "synthesis." The causal chain is supposed to run as follows:

$$M \text{ up} \rightarrow i \text{ down} \rightarrow I \text{ up} \rightarrow NNP \text{ up, up}$$

This schema, and the graphs (335), which are nothing but a fancier, more colorful representation of the schema, are worthless without some theoretical foundation establishing and expaining the alleged connections among the entities involved. S obviously believes that the graphs explain the schema: "The blue so-called "liquidity-preference schedule" of Fig. 18-1 (a) *summarizes how* an increase in M resulting from monetary policy (open-market purchases, etc.) leads initially to a reduced interest rate. . . . Fig. 18-1 (b) picks up the story to show how reduced interest rates . . . make more investment profitable" (335 f., emphasis added). However, the graphs, being nothing but pictorial equivalents of the schema, cannot "show" how any of the underlying processes indicated by the schema actually work.

S, then, presents his schema without any theoretical backing. But the schema did not spring theoryless from his brain. The concepts of liquidity preference and marginal efficiency of investment are Keynesian, and Keynes postulated them explicitly as psychological concepts, embedded in a fairly explicit psychological theory purporting to explain the behavior of entrepreneurs. The question arises as to why S does not introduce the concepts in this way and why he does not present the Keynesian psychology or more modification of it.

Two possible answers, not mutually exclusive, present themselves. The first is that there is a methodological principle of behaviorism operating here, just as there is in S's first chapter on supply and demand. The fact that he refers not to liquidity preference and marginal efficiency of investment but rather to liquidity preference *schedules* and marginal efficiency *schedules* speaks in favor of this hypothesis. If so, then S probably feels that the graphs contain all the theory one needs, for they tell what the value of one parameter *would be* if the value of the other were such and such. That is, the graphs tell you how one parameter would react to a change in the other. In other words, the graphs tell you what one parameter *would* do, for whatever reason (the fact that the reason is irrelevant explains why no additional theory is needed), in response to a change in the other parameter. Such reasoning seems to be behind the move to the behaviorism of "revealed preference schedules" in the theory of utility, and it may well be operating here. In response we offer the objection that the "would" in the above sentences is not well defined without further theory. An entire schedule of counterfactual conditionals cannot be constructed without a theory to back it.

The second possible reason for S's failure to tie his schema in with a theory is that it makes his "synthesizing" easier. This is what Crosser is getting at when he talks about S's "deconceptualization" and eclecticism, which is not really eclecticism because no opposing *concepts* are brought together. S, both in the chapter and the appendix contends that various graphs, such as the famous Hicks-Hansen Diagram, synthesize various diverse theories. It is indeed no mean feat to synthesize Keynesian economics and its subjective-psychological concepts with classical economics, which relies almost completely on objective, natural-law type concepts. S makes short shrift of it. The strategy is simple: remove the psychological basis from the concepts of liquidity preference and marginal efficiency; then translate some of the theories of classical economics into views about the shape of the graphs of l.p. and m.e. But S apparently does not realize that such deconceptualization leaves one with nothing but a meaningless schema which cannot form the basis for any real synthesis.

Another aspect of S's methology is his ahistoricity, his failure to treat capitalism as a totality, an ensemble of social relations which grew out of specifiable causes and which developed and evolved in certain more or less determinable ways and which simultaneously is continually reproducing itself and tearing itself apart. Perhaps this failure on S's part has reciprocal causal connections with his addiction to graphs, but whether it does or not, it is definitely present in full force in Chapter 18, as is evidenced by the following quote:

> "Satchel" Paige, a great baseball player, once said: "Never look backward; someone may be gaining on you." This is good advice in economics, too. Do not look back to find what caused past layoffs; look forward to see what you have to do to restore high employment. This is more efficient—and more helpful.
>
> Better still, this approach means you do not have to decide whether the pessimists are right who argue that inventions will kill off more jobs than they create. Why care? *In every case we know that high employment without inflation will require monetary and fiscal policies of the correct magnitudes, and mixed economies know what needs doing* [341 f].

What S fails to realize here is that no one can know what needs doing without viewing capitalism as a developing totality or entity with a history, and this means among other things determining whether inherent in this evolving system are tendencies to create and maintain unemployment; and this in turn means that both on a concrete and an abstract level talking about the causes of past layoffs is appropriate and important. Such a procedure may indeed find that tendencies toward unemployment are too fundamental a part of capitalism to be thwarted by monetary and fiscal policies of whatever magnitudes.

Now for the relation to the addiction to graphs. It is worth noting that S himself sees a connection between this part of his methodology and his use of graphs; immediately following the above passage is a section entitled "Graphical Restoration of High-Employment Equilibrium," in which he talks of applying "this fruitful approach" (i.e., the ahistoricity) by using the "consumption plus investment plus government-spending schedule" to find full-employment equilibrium. Unfortunately, given S's "fruitful approach," any restoration of employment that is real as well as graphic will be accidental, or at least not determinable by him.

To the extent that S's graphs "talk about" actual factors or elements of capitalism, they wrench them from the totality and relate them (ideally) to each other, in isolation from the other elements of the system. Almost always when the graph is constructed the other elements of the system are assumed not to change ("all other things being equal"). This is done, as S, says, "because, like any good scientist who wants to isolate the effects of one causal factor, we must try to vary only *one* thing at a time" (66). This type of graphic depiction of the quantitative relations of two phenomena in isolation from "outside interference" is an integral part of bourgeois science.

S, having gotten this far, seems satisfied with himself. Making little or no attempt to relate the plotted phenomena to other factors, he uses his graphs as a basis for policy recommendations concerning manipulations upon or within the totality. To a certain extent this inadequacy can be criticized on the level of bourgeois science. For S himself knows that the "other things" are hardly, if ever, equal, and that one must take into account what the other things are doing before one can determine "what needs doing" (68). And given this admission, it remains a mystery why S does not talk more about relations between the graphic phenomena and the "other things."

The mystery is solved, however, when we realize that on a bourgeois level this inadequacy cannot be remedied. Bourgeois science cannot properly reintegrate its isolated categories precisely because it rejects (as inefficient, arbitrary, metaphysical, or whatever) the *essentially dialectical* requirement of maintaining as the object of investigation a self-reproducing historical totality. Such a rejection has extremely important ramifications, especially within capitalist society. Bourgeois science is left without any adequate basis for determining: (1) what the "other things" are with which the isolated categories must be integrated; and (2) which of these other factors are more important, fundamental, essential. In the absence of such a basis, two criteria usually are followed, sometimes explicitly, sometimes implicitly: (a) The "other things" are selected from the realm of categories which more or less "stand out," i.e., from the manner in which data immediately present themselves; and (b), whatever ranking is done of the "other things" in terms of importance or essence is done on the basis of how these other factors appear to be connected with regard to the achievement of some goal, e.g., full employment and price stability. The latter criterion puts the lie to the alleged value freedom of bourgeois science. And the former criterion goes a long way toward explaining two things—the apologetic character of bourgeois science, and the fact that the achievement of many goals using policies based on the results of bourgeois economics is doomed to be thwarted from the outset.

Graph I

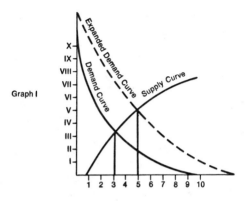

Graph II

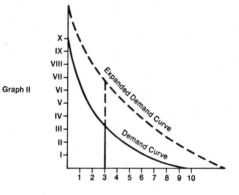

Graph III

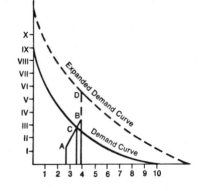

Chapter 13: Supply and Demand—An Empirical Approach (S's Chapter 20)

In this chapter we shall attempt to illustrate the weaknesses of the empirical application of supply and demand by examining some of S's own examples.

I. A FEW METHODOLOGICAL OBSERVATIONS

In this methodologically chaotic section S says about micro and macro: "We cannot even say which comes first: some books begin with one; some with the other." (378) When someone writes chapter after chapter about money, commodities, markets, supply and demand, national income, etc., without having previously discussed the fundamental concept of value, the reader would like a reason for this procedure rather than a "survey" of how many texts begin with one or the other.

The other point we wish to make here has to do with the nature of the supply-demand curves. The following is a summary of the criticism by a Soviet Marxist in the 1920s of the bourgeois depictions of such curves and of an outline of the Marxist rationalization of this procedure.[1] Although a former Menshevik, Isaak Rubin at the time was recognized in the Soviet Union as the greatest expert on Marx's theory of value. A school was formed by his pupils. Toward the end of the 1920s he came under severe attack; in 1931 he was put on trial with other Mensheviks.

As Rubin points out, since the intersection of the two curves changes with a change in either of them, it seems that a change in demand can alter the price even in the absence of any changes in the conditions of production; and since price is identified with value, demand can also alter value (see Graph I). Rubin sees the root of this false result in the construction of the supply curve itself; namely, it is based on the model of the demand curve, except that it runs in the opposite direction (starting at the lowest price). A supply curve running through such extremes as still producing at ridiculously low prices or throwing everything the capitalists have on the market at high prices is possible only when considering the market conjuncture of a given day or moment. But if we want to see what the stable long-run average price is, then we must note that below a certain price production would be interrupted, and that above a certain price additional capital would flow into this branch.

Rubin then constructs two graphs to explain his position: A simplified one shows only a demand curve (see Graph II). There is supply only at the value (or production price). This is a straight line which intersects the demand curve. Above this original demand curve there is another one which represents expanded demand. It is Rubin's contention that such increased demand with the concomitant expectation of a price higher than the previous social average will bring an inflow of capital from other branches; in the long run this can have the effect of tendentially unlimited increases in production (as a result of increased profitability). Thus, compared with demand, one can say that at the price of production supply is limited. Rubin therefore merely extends the old supply line further to intersect the new curve of expanded demand. In this example a change in demand can change the supply but not the price.

A more complicated diagram (Graph III) depicts a situation in which the firms belonging to the group with the highest productivity can only supply a limited amount; the remaining units would have to be supplied by the firms belonging to the groups of average and below-average productivity. Here the supply curve would be a line connecting the highest points of the supply lines aggregated for each price. Thus, for example, if at $2.50, 200,000 units could be supplied, at $3.00, 300,000, and at $3.50, 400,000 (meaning that the average firms can produce 100,000 units at $3, and the least productive another 100,000 at $3.50), then the supply line would run through those latter two points to the point representing the group of most productive producers (200,000 at $2.50).

This means that demand can operate only within very narrow limits, limits determined by the conditions of production in the firms of varying productivity and the quantitative relations among these groups (their specific weights within the total production of the branch).

Actually, much in this section would seem to be true if for supply and demand we substituted the law of value. E.g., we are told that although price is determined by supply and demand, it also depends on other factors, such as gold production and war. However such factors "are not *in addition* to supply and demand, but are included in the numerous forces which determine or *act through* supply and demand" (389). It would seem then that within bourgeois theory, supply and demand, like the law of value, is the fundamental explanatory law of capitalism. Although on the surface it would appear that certain factors also contradict the determination of price by supply and demand, one might think that a good bourgeois economist would want to find the mediating links between essence and appearance.

But we are bound to be disappointed if we harbored such illusions; for shortly thereafter S informs us that in fact supply and demand are "not ultimate explanations of price. They are simply useful catchall categories for analyzing and describing the multitude of forces, causes and factors impinging on price" (390). Supply and demand is thus reduced to a formal classificatory tool, and not even a very precise one.

In this case it would turn out that the above statement was incorrect: the law of value is not a perfect substitute for supply and demand. In the following example it fills that bill more closely. Here, S chastises the neophyte for confusing the state's ability to affect prices with its ability to "repeal the law" of supply and demand: "These governments have not violated the law of supply and demand. They have worked (not always to good purpose) through the law of supply and demand. The state has no secret economic weapons or tricks. What is true for the state is also true for individuals" (390).

Here we could substitute the law of value in the sense that the state can preserve capitalism only with the same capitalist methods that contain contradictions within themselves. And it is also true that the state cannot act vis-à-vis total social capital the way the individual capital agent does vis-à-vis his capital. We have made this point before, but this is the first and probably only time that Samuelson concedes it; for the most part he is too busy extolling the magic powers of state intervention into the anarchic processes of capitalist commodity production.

II. EMPIRICAL APPLICATIONS OF SUPPLY AND DEMAND

A. RATIONING

Now we come to concrete cases of state intervention with respect to price determination. The state decrees that sugar cannot rise above 7¢ per lb. As a result of "prosperity or bad crops let demand be so high and supply so small" that price would have risen to 20¢ had not the state interfered (391). Now this is a strange situation. One could imagine that as a result of a drought or hurricane or whatever, the sugar crop could have been so damaged as to make for a shortage of supply (in physical terms) in relation to the traditional demand. If x pounds are consumed annually, but this year only one-tenth x reaches the market, then the state might well ordain that the price remain at the usual level for this 10 percent that can be salvaged and sold. Otherwise the price would have risen, say, tenfold. (Whether the state would in fact do this is another matter—but it is at least conceivable.) But the case of "prosperity" is a horse of a different color. This is baffling to the reader until it is revealed that S is talking about a war situation. In any case, at best it is a case of increased incomes *and* shortages. This well may mean that there is a shortage even compared to the prewar income (and solvent demand) level (in this case the depression of the 1930s), so that the prosperity part may be irrelevant; or it may be a shortage compared to the new level of income. (In fact, neither per capita sugar production nor consumption rose between 1930 and 1950.)[1a]

In any case, the only rational kernel of this whole discussion could be a situation in which acts of God cause a shortage. But notice what S writes: "Consumers want thousands of pounds of sugar in excess of what producers are willing to supply" (391 f.). The "willing" is misleading. The point is, the producers have no more to sell. If they hold out what they have, then they won't get anything. Although S recognizes that letting prices float will burden the poor, he emphasizes that with the price fixed, someone will drink bitter coffee despite the fact that this someone would "gladly bid the price up to 8 or 9 cents or more." Then "there follows a period of frustration and shortage" (392). This step is needed for the conclusion: that shortage results from government price-fixing. With the price mechanism "stymied," the world has ceased to exist for S, because "Patriotism is more effective in motivating to brief acts of intense heroism than to putting up day after day with an uncomfortable situation" (396).

The solution to the nonmonetary distribution of the sugar is rationing: "Of course there are always a few women and cranks, longer on intuition than brains, who blame their troubles on the mechanism of rationing itself rather than on the shortage" (7 ed., p. 377). But it is S who is apparently longer on dollar votes than brains, for he is the one who saw the shortage only after there were people who would have outbid others for the sugar but were not allowed to. And although he recognizes that in a class society price always means rationing by "rising to choke off excessive consumption" (393), he sees economically relevant "frustration and shortage" only for those who have money but cannot spend it; that there are many who do not have the money and whose nonspending does not therefore result from shortages, S does not recognize as scientifically relevant except in the sense that "there is never enough to give everyone all he wishes" (393).

But what is the "remarkable efficiency" of the price mechanism which we can better appreciate by observing its absence in the "psychiatric ward" of war? (393). It is apparently some sort of super-duper circulation-sphere equality. Not only are owners of money equal in qualitative terms, but each dollar is equal; and apparently a further condition consists in everyone's being able to cast all his dollar votes if he so desires. The efficiency of the market is reflected in the circumstance that where the highest bidders win, those who cannot bid so high ("women") need not spend their time waiting on line. The efficiency of the market allows these women to sit at home since they know there is no point in playing musical chairs at the grocery store.

Next we come to admonitions: state intervention ought not be "squandered on minor peacetime situations" (393). After all, even Adam Smith knew that such mercantilist devices were inefficient. One cannot speak in an undifferentiated manner of monopoly in times of merchant and monopoly capital domination. Nor can one judge the quality, or for that matter the quantity, of state intervention in these different periods in an ahistorical way. That state intervention could have been a positive and necessary force for the formation of merchant capital *and hence* also for industrial capital later, that subsequently it could have hindered the development of industrial capital to the extent that at some point it aided merchant capital when the latter was no longer a precondition but rather a foe of industrial capital, and, finally, that it could be a necessary support for the continued existence of capitalism in our own time and yet hamstring the development of a society that would develop social relations capable of utilizing the forces of production for the good of the working people—all this remains sealed to S.

B. MINIMUM WAGE LAWS

Let us look at some of these "minor peacetime situations." First we get minimum-wage laws. S needs only three lines and a graph to prove that these laws hurt the very people they are supposed to help—the people S is most concerned about too: black youths. (In this he is in agreement with Milton Friedman.) For the higher wage allegedly is the reason for the "youth" unemployment in the first place.

Let us look at this more closely. Richard Lester points out that there is a need for such laws precisely because the marginal-productivity theory does not correspond to capitalist reality because labor markets are imperfect and labor is "exploited." Minimum-wage rates can "eliminate the possibility of employers' keeping the wage rate low by not bidding up the wage in order to hire more workers, or the possibility of depressing wage rates by hiring fewer workers." Lester indicates that after passage of a minimum-wage law capitalists would be likely to hire more workers at that wage because they cannot obtain labor below that wage by cutting down on hiring.[2]

It would perhaps be instructive to view minimum-wage laws in a manner analogous to Marx's treatment of maximum-hours legislation in England in the middle of the nineteenth century. Marx pointed out that although the individual capitalist would have liked to work "his" workers to death since there would always be others to take their place, in the long run such vast exploitation would tend to kill the goose that lays the golden egg. Once individual capitalists acceded to workers' demands in this direction it became in their interest to compel all other capitalists to be similarly constrained so that no "unfair advantages" would result in competition.[3]

It would appear that something like this was also taking place with respect to the minimum wage. A three-volume work on the economics of labor indicates that the problem transcends that of a "minor peacetime situation":

> The widespread attempts, in the last four decades, to regulate wages through the exercise of the coercive power of the state have been an inevitable consequence of industry's failure to pay millions of its [!] workers enough to enable them and their families to live in decency.[4]

But as the authors also point out, this was not a comprehensive undertaking to raise the purchasing power of workers generally, but was mainly directed toward particularly outrageous sweatshop situations and below-average wages for women and minors. (It is interesting that back in the thirties blacks did not even rate mention in social policy of this kind.)

At this point the book becomes somewhat more analytical. It notes that "the health, strength, and morals of workers—especially women workers—depend in part upon wages; industries or enterprises not paying living wages are social parasites...."[4a] This probably means that the large capitalists are sick of paying taxes to support unemployed and down-and-out workers and their families. The capitalists not paying minimum wages are parasites in the sense that they get the advantage from the social overhead expenditures. The large capitalists find it unfair that their competitors can pay lower wages and get away with it.

Millis and Montgomery go even further:

> ... The minimum wage movement has had underlying it the assumption that concentration of production within those firms able to pay decent wages would not be undesirable. In industries where comparatively little capital is necessary to start a small-scale establishment, a large number of irresponsible [!] "fly-by-night" firms are chronically to be found—firms whose chief source of survival capacity is low labor cost. If minimum wage legislation pushes these firms across the marginal line and production is concentrated in a smaller number of larger and more efficient plants, the result to be expected would be a higher wage bill for the entire industry without necessarily—or at least without proportionately higher—costs per unit of product.[5]

If we disregard some of the efficiency and welfare-humanism verbiage, it becomes clear that at some point at least in the history of capitalism minimum wages were a conscious move to drive out the smaller capitals.

The First National City Bank asks why minimum wage laws shouldn't be abolished altogether, and replies that although such laws are a political necessity, the "elimination of this legal floor under wages would ease the transition from school to employment."[6]

One explanation for this turn against "liberal" labor legislation might be connected with the move of large corporations into traditionally nonunionized areas (for instance the South) because of the low wages and "good work discipline," and so they might well oppose such extensions of national legislation. To the extent that the small "feeders" or subcontractors of large monopolists might be destroyed by such legislation, this would disturb the present economic and political allegiance of these groups.

The Keynesians have prided themselves on their ability to avoid "politically and socially unacceptable" rates of unemployment. Now all of a sudden the bourgeoisie tells us "historically, the 4% or less jobless rates have always been associated with war periods, and there is no really solid reason to expect a change from this pattern."[7]

But there was never "really" any reason to expect capitalism to do away with the reserve army. What the bourgeoisie is apparently saying is that: (1) the rate and mass of surplus value is not high enough, so that wages will have to be kept down, whether by "freezes" or by hiring people from the reserve army; and (2) given trade union militancy over bread-and-butter issues, it is perhaps more expedient to "work over" those portions of the proletariat which are less organized and less likely to put up strong resistance (women, teenagers, blacks, Puerto Ricans, Chicanos).

That proportionately more women and teenagers are now working is due in large part to the fact that inflation has so eaten into wages that families can no longer get along with only the income of the traditional bread winner. S himself admits this when he says: "The labor force sometimes tends to grow in recession: when a husband is thrown out of work, his wife and children may seek jobs" (577 n. 2).

This would of course refute the standard bourgeois tenet according to which labor is just like any other factor of production: less is supplied at lower rates; for here the lower the wages become, the larger the sections of the reserve army which must be thrown into the factories in order that the aggregate value of the labor power of the nuclear family be reproduced.

On the basis of these findings we might come to the tentative conclusion that since the capitalist class is in need of a larger number of cheap workers at this stage, it would tend to oppose minimum-wage laws more broadly than before because these laws would tend to include precisely those workers whom the capitalists are counting on.

C. RENT CONTROL

S's major complaint against rent control is that it restricts the construction of new housing. Since he uses France as an example, let us look at some other examples of the effects of the free housing market in Western Europe. In West Germany the gradual abolition of rent control began in 1963. From 1960 until 1967, the number of apartments rose by 20 percent while total rents rose 160 percent (from 12 to 32 billion marks annually). During the same period the rent share of total expenditures of families with four members rose 40 percent.[8]

And a study of that foremost Social Democratic country, Denmark, shows that the result of a free housing market neither reduced the price of new housing nor increased production, but rather brought higher rents for the same quantity of housing. The mechanism works as follows: Capital can be more profitably invested in building new housing, if not to create a housing reserve, then to compete the oldest housing (which is already amortized) out of existence. This is the best case for the free market, but it presupposes that those capitalists who are profiting from the old houses are not the same ones who are investing in the new. And this in one of the most "progressive" capitalist countries, where as of 1965 there was at least a deficit of

5.5 percent in housing, 11.4 percent in rooms, and where 40 percent of all dwellings did not have private baths and toilets.[9]

But what about the U.S. where World War II rent controls were long ago abolished? What miracles hath the free market wrought there? The disparity between needs and production in housing has not narrowed since the war, for as the *Wall Street Journal* of January 11, 1971, remarked: "But wanting a home and being able to buy one are not the same." Why are houses (the same is more or less true for apartments) so expensive? Although the bourgeois press and politicians are screaming about "labor costs," these as a percentage of costs in one-family houses have declined from 1949 to 1969 from 33 to 18 percent, whereas land costs have risen from 11 to 21 percent.[10]

That the free market is really at the root of the problem is admitted by a Commerce Department official, A. Allan Bates, the Director of the Office of Standards Policy, who in Congressional testimony asserted that it is land speculation which "makes truly low-cost housing in significant quantity nearly impossible" in the U.S. He also recognizes that this is not a result of *the* industrial society: "Within a few years—perhaps a decade—it will probably be generally acknowledged internationally that the best housed inhabitants of any large country in the world are those of the USSR. The political impact of this situation will be profound."[11]

But perhaps we have misunderstood S all along; perhaps he has a different sense of what needs the free housing market satisfies. Others seem to lead the way to a better understanding. Thus *Forbes* announces that "wherever there has been a great need in the U.S. business has usually found a way to fill it. . . . But that's what American capitalism is all about: It satisfies needs, especially the needs of the middle class."[12] That is correct—if the middle class is the capitalist class and its needs—profits. And one author, E. Fisher, writing in the depth of the depression outdid *Forbes* by asserting that U.S. slum dwellers had neither solvent nor nonsolvent demand for better housing;

it was his considered opinion that among these people there is "contentment with conditions as they are."[13]

If this is what S means—that in capitalism the workers have neither the purchasing power nor the absolute need for better housing, we agree that the free market can satisfy such nonexistent demand.

D. USURY LAWS

As to S's opposition to usury laws that set ceilings on interest rates below what would be determined by supply and demand: first of all he merely repeats what he already said in the case of sugar when he states that "the cheap money you can't get does you little good" because the funds have "dried up" (394). Here too we must reply that "supply and demand" also is a rationing factor so that the available funds you can't get because you can't afford 8-12 percent interest rates are of just as little use.

As usual, ahistoricity runs rampant. Historically, usury served an important role as a powerful tool of primitive accumulation by destroying many independent producers and helping centralize many splintered means of production. Once capitalism was on its feet, it no longer needed usury—hence the laws were done away with.

As Marx points out, interest-bearing capital retains the form of usurious capital vis-à-vis persons and classes and in relations where the borrowing is not in the sense of the capitalist mode of production, that is to say, where one borrows for the purpose of consumption.[14] Why then does S choose examples—mortgages and student loans—which have little to do with the essence of capitalism?

Chapter 14: The Failure of Supply and Demand as Applied to Agriculture (S's Chapter 21)

> Actually, Marx himself had little to say about agriculture. He was a city boy, primarily interested in diagnosing the social ills of early industrial societies.—Orville L. Freeman, former U.S. Secretary of Agriculture, "Malthus, Marx and the North American Breadbasket," *Foreign Affairs*, XLV, No. 4 (July, 1967), 583.

INTRODUCTION—HISTORICAL OVERVIEW

Although S seems to believe that this chapter will convince the reader how relevant an analysis supply and demand can offer (406), what it in fact shows is that bourgeois economics cannot distinguish between the underlying material processes and the socio-historical forms they assume in particular modes of production.

It is of course true that one of the characteristics of the "general" tendency of the steady increase in human productivity, particularly since the rise of capitalism, has been the relative increase in total labor time expended in industrial as opposed to agricultural enterprises—obviously a "progressive" development inasmuch as it has allowed man to create and satisfy more "civilized" needs. Agricultural production therefore represents more "basic" needs which man has sought to satisfy for thousands of years. One could perhaps say that with increasing agricultural productivity, given the "more basic" aspect of the needs satisfied by food, human society will be able to take care of *absolute* needs in this area sooner than in others.

The suprahistorical factor pointed up in the preceding paragraph forms the rational kernel of the bourgeois economists' assertion that declining relative demand is the root problem in agriculture. But as we well know, demand and absolute need are as contradictory as exchange value and use value. Yet it must be obvious that the latter cannot provide the explanation for the former; for what suprahistorical phenomena there are find but a distorted expression in specific societies.

One must moreover always bear in mind that general tendencies and global figures mask rather divergent movements between social classes. Even if one admits that working-class families have in the course of time reduced the amount of money they spend on food, one should not assume that this complex of needs has been unconditionally sated. Given the capitalist distribution of income, it should not come as a surprise that in absolute terms the rich spend more for food—especially for meat—even though their share of total private consumption is considerably lower than that of working-class families.

If, moreover, we take into consideration the greater divergence between needs and solvent demand in the so-called Third World, then the "applicability" of the demand tool to explain agricultural crises becomes doubtful.

The neglect of the most important societal aspects of contemporary agriculture goes hand in hand with the failure to discuss the peculiar historical development of capitalist agriculture. Although "no one can possibly understand" the issues without supply and demand (406), it is apparently not necessary to know what happened before 1910. Yet the roots of the present-day "problems" of capitalist agriculture do in fact lie in the past.

In the U.S. vast stretches of fertile land were settled by noncapitalists; given the relatively small funds (we are intentionally avoiding the term capital) needed to establish such farms, the production and class structure which arose was not purely capitalist in nature. In the nineteenth century, however, a long-term process of U.S. agricultural capitalization began, a process which has not yet been completed. The elimination (whether through state-sanctioned violence or through "the market"—that is, through higher productivity) of these small farmers represents the twofold process of "primary accumulation": forcing large masses of formerly independent producers on to the labor market by depriving them of their means of production (basically of their land) and the centralization of production on the remaining farms.

What we have just described is a historical tendency. "Pure" class societies composed of workers and capitalists do not exist in reality. Under given historical conditions modifications arise. Thus in the U.S., the destruction of the small farmer, although already an economic fact, has not yet been completed. That is to say, although some 2 to 3 million small farmers still exist, they are no longer the major supplier. These farmers have managed to resist because they can still eke out a livelihood; they can take part-time work elsewhere; and they can work relatively small areas of land intensively. They do this for three reasons: (1) a petit-bourgeois interest in property; (2) a non-petit-bourgeois interest in avoiding the capitalistic horrors of factory work and in enjoying the less "alienated" labor on the land (whether it be theirs or someone else's or everyone's); (3) they cannot find jobs in the cities.

These are some of the main factors counteracting concentration and centralization in U.S. agriculture. But we must be careful not to let statistical ownership block our view of the real economic relations in agriculture. Formerly independent farmers in fact working for usurers, mortgage companies, feed companies, tractor companies can be confusing. Small holdings turn farmers into a source of cheap labor for the large capitalistic farms. What appears as ownership is really a means of pauperization.

"EXCESSING" THE FARMER

With this general theoretical structure in mind, let us examine the Nicholls-Samuelson proposition that in order to solve the agricultural crisis we must "reduce our surplus of farmers. No doubt this has to be done gradually. And it is actually happening all the time: each year there are fewer and fewer people in agriculture" (403). But what are the "problems" to which this is the solution?

The two main ones, according to S, are efficiency and distribution. Supposedly, if we were to get rid of the small farmers, the supply side could not be out of kilter. But, first of all, these farmers furnish only a small portion of the supply, so that eliminating them will not in itself solve the "supply" side of the problem; but more significantly these farmers will not simply disappear—their land will be taken over by the capitalist farmers who, given their more efficient methods, will increase production even more.

Although income distribution in agriculture is not easily determined, largely because the cut-off points for the highest income groups are so low that no homogeneous social class emerges, still the "lower end" share of farm families with income below the poverty level established by the Federal Government is twice as high as the share of all families. On the other hand, there is a tendency toward assimilation in the sense that the share of the poorest farm families is declining.[1] This does not mean, however, that their poverty is diminishing, but merely that they are disappearing from agriculture.

In any case, the large capitalist farmers are making a profit while the small farmers barely subsist. But this is not a problem peculiar to agriculture; it is true of all small businesses in which only minimum capital is needed. The question is why so much attention is paid to the plight of these small "businesses": probably because the bourgeoisie does not want to antagonize unduly a group of people at least formally supportive of private property in the means of production. To the extent that the expanding industrial sector could in the long run absorb those driven from the farms, the destruction of the "family farm" did not involve any great political dangers. Apparently during the Roosevelt administration certain sectors of the bourgeoisie were calling for the destruction of the small farmer (which was well under way during the Depression) in conjunction with other efforts to encourage concentration. A representative of that position stated: "The solution lies in the progressive elimination of the surplus farmer, that is, the submarginal farmer on the submarginal land, and in shifting the unsuccessful farmer into urban production and occupations where their incomes will rise."[2] This is almost identical with several of S's formulations ("many of the remaining family farmers would find their incomes so low in agriculture as to speed them into industry"—417).

Apparently those who won out decided that given the mass unemployment in the cities, "speeding" millions more into bread lines would only exacerbate an already revolutionary situation. Hence it was decided to formulate a farm policy which would, as S puts it, make the transition "gradual." But in any case, government support of the so-called family farm has been more rhetorical than material.

The following table shows the distribution of direct state subsidies according to the size of farms:[3]

FARMS BY VALUE OF SALES CLASSES, 1960-71

Year	\$40,000 and over	\$20,000 to \$39,999	\$10,000 to \$19,999	\$5,000 to \$9,999	\$2,500 to \$4,999	Less than \$2,500	All Farms
Percentage distribution:							
1960	2.9	5.7	12.5	16.7	15.6	46.6	100
1961	3.2	6.3	12.9	16.4	15.1	46.1	100
1962	3.7	6.9	13.4	16.0	14.5	45.5	100
1963	4.0	7.5	13.8	15.7	13.9	45.1	100
1964	4.2	7.8	14.0	15.5	13.6	44.9	100
1965	4.9	8.4	14.0	15.2	13.7	43.8	100
1966	5.9	9.5	13.9	14.8	13.8	42.1	100
1967	6.0	9.7	13.8	14.7	13.8	42.0	100
1968	6.6	10.3	13.8	14.5	13.9	40.9	100
1969	7.7	11.5	13.7	13.9	14.1	39.1	100
1970	8.2	12.1	13.7	13.6	14.1	38.3	100
1971	8.8	12.7	13.6	13.4	14.2	37.3	100
Direct Government Payments: Percentage Distribution by Value of Sales Classes, 1960-71							
Percentage distribution:							
1960	15.2	16.0	22.8	20.7	11.5	13.3	100
1961	16.7	16.8	22.8	19.6	10.9	13.2	100
1962	17.2	17.7	24.2	18.5	9.8	12.6	100
1963	17.6	18.6	25.2	17.5	9.1	12.0	100
1964	17.5	19.0	26.0	17.0	8.7	11.8	100
1965	18.7	19.9	25.5	16.0	8.4	11.5	100
1966	27.3	22.1	21.8	12.3	7.5	9.0	100
1967	27.6	22.3	21.6	12.2	7.4*	8.9	100
1968	29.2	22.9	20.8	11.6	7.2	8.3	100
1969	32.1	23.9	19.4	10.4	6.8	7.4	100
1970	33.3	24.3	18.7	10.0	6.6	7.1	100
1971	34.5	24.8	18.1	9.5	6.5	6.6	100

Thus we see that the largest farms receive the largest—and increasing—share of the subsidies, which also constitute a greater share of the total income of the largest farms—25 percent, versus 4 percent for the smallest farms.

S tries to portray the process as the reverse of what it really is. Thus he asserts that parity programs keep some "inefficient farmers from going to higher-productivity occupations" (411). First of all, this is neither the intent nor the effect of farm policies. And secondly, he is simplifying matters when he depicts, say, 50,000 tobacco pickers being "excessed" by a mechanical harvester as somehow being restrained from entering better-paying jobs by the bone thrown to them by the government.

But according to one of the foremost bourgeois farm experts, Theodore Schultz, the problem lies elsewhere. He notes the paradox that since World War I transfer of labor into and out of agriculture has not followed the pattern of farm-price changes: when these declined, more people stayed in farming; when they rose, more people left (which they also did when farm prices rose relative to industrial prices). He explains this by the job market in industry; for the gap in wages between agriculture and industry is so wide "that the relative prices of the products which each produced have been quite inoperative in bringing about a transfer of the excess labor in agriculture."[4]

EXCURSUS ON THE APPLICATION OF MARGINAL PRODUCTIVITY THEORY TO AGRICULTURE

Schultz also claims that most family farms are unable to get enough capital to establish an optimal farm size; as a result, they expend too much labor relative to the capital they use and hence the returns per labor unit become depressed. Obviously, as Marx says, the larger capital beats the smaller one. Those who cannot reproduce the average conditions of productivity in the branch will, if they fall far enough behind, not even meet their production costs. Since these people cannot buy the new machines, and since for the most part they cannot find jobs elsewhere, the entire family will work more intensively with their limited land

and capital in order to have more to sell. Presto—diminishing returns!

As Blake ironically remarks: "There is a diminishing return on the use of the plow until the tractor is invented. There is a diminishing return on the soil until phosphate and potash are used."[5] The point is that this is the exceptional case of marginal productivity theory being based on stagnant technology.

What sort of capitalist would keep adding units of a "factor" beyond what is efficient? But we are obviously not dealing with a capitalist here, or at least not with a successful one. For this guy does not accumulate—in fact, his inability to accumulate is what got him into a mess to begin with, and even now he is at best trying to subsist and pay off debts.

But as Marx notes, there is a rational kernel to this irrationality: namely, the farmer can appropriate the whole product of his labor instead of delivering up the excess beyond the value of his labor power to a master—this "he owes not to his labor—which does not distinguish him from other workers—but rather to the possession of the means of production. It is thus only through the possession of the latter that he takes possession of his own surplus labor, and in this way he relates as his own capitalist to himself as wage worker."

Marx also notes, however, that retention of such an ambiguous class situation contradicts the tendency of capitalist development: such a producer will either turn into a small capitalist exploiting the labor of others or he will be dispossessed of his means of production, despite his formal retention of property rights, as in the case of mortgage. (The latter alternative accurately describes what has been happening in U.S. agriculture this century.)[6]

This little excursion also points up the objective social relations which form the consciousness of the working poor who support the private ownership of the means of production.

Our little dissection of marginal productivity theory with respect to Schultz finds ample application to S himself. Thus in his discussion of "differential birth rates" he tells us that we are "lucky" that farmers are moving to the cities, for in the absence of such migration, given the higher rural birth rates, cities would shrink and the farm population would grow. "What does the law of diminishing returns tell us such an eventuality would mean? It would mean a great reduction in the productivity of each man-hour spent on the farm. The land would become crowded with many people, each producing little. . . ." (407). We just saw that this does not apply to a developed capitalist society (primitive accumulation has not yet done its work in full); so we are not surprised when S tries to lend credence to the notion by bringing in Asia, where with three-quarters of the population in agriculture, only one-quarter "can be producing the comforts of life." S appears to have his causality confused: it is not because so many are farmers (or really rural unemployed or underemployed) that so few "can" be factory workers, but rather because so few are factory workers that so many must be farmers or rural lumpenproletarians. Especially in countries with limited farm land where the necessary intensive farming requires relatively substantial mechanical and chemical means, a developed chemical and electrical and automative industry are obviously prerequisites. And in fact it is relatively recently that U.S. agricultural productivity has come into its own; only in the post-World War II period has agriculture become truly industrialized. Thus in the 1920s and 1930s U.S. farm productivity on the average was one-quarter that of New Zealand, and just about the same as in much of Western Europe.[7]

Crop yields per acre (for wheat, rye, corn, and hay) remained constant between 1866 and 1940 but have more than doubled since then, while man-hours per bushel in some cases have been cut by more than 90 percent in the last quarter century.[8]

CRISES

S accurately describes this tremendous increase when he says that there will be "financial pressure and hardship on those farmers and rural workers whose efficiency has not undergone tremendous increase" (409). This is correct, but it contradicts the basic error of the entire chapter: *the* farmer.

What is happening in agriculture is no different from "the competitive system" elsewhere, except insofar as there are proportionately more small farmers than other small businessmen.

S's description of the differential effects of productivity increases for agricultural producers also contradicts his claim that "the" farmer is losing because "his" productivity is rising more rapidly than industry's. But it is precisely here that one has to proceed in a differentiated manner since it is mainly the small producers who are forced by competition to abandon production. This is the famous scissors, supposedly the root of all evil. But the scissors is neither the cause nor the essence of the agrarian crisis, as is shown by the fact that crises persist even where the scissors is opening in favor of the farmers.

More important than the relation of agrarian and industrial prices is the absolute level of the former; for we must remember that a large component of farmers' costs is not part of industrial costs: namely rent, taxes, and interest on mortgage. Thus if industrial prices fall more rapidly than agricultural prices, this could still spell disaster for the small farmers if their "overhead" (the three above-mentioned items) eats up their income; and conversely, a more rapid rise of industrial prices could still mean relative prosperity for the small farmer. Both in relative and absolute terms, the crisis has had devastating effects on the small farmers in the twentieth century (as opposed to the nineteenth).

From the pre-World War II period to 1950, taxes, rent, and mortgage payments as a percentage of expenditures declined from approximately 20 percent to 12.3 percent; this declined further to 11.7 percent in 1960; since then, however, the trend has been upward, so that in 1971 these payments already constituted 14.9 percent of expenditures.[9]

Breaking these figures down further, we find that during

the 1960s tax payments doubled, mortgage payments tripled, while rent remained constant.

We have already touched on the assertion that the crisis is largely due to the inelastic demand curves. What agriculture shows in this respect is that any branch producing commodities that are a prime consumption item of the working class is going to be faced with a realization problem in the form of limited working-class purchasing power.

The other part of the problem, according to S & Co., is inelastic supply. This too has a rational kernel; in agriculture capitalism still has to overcome significant natural limits (e.g., a longer production period). Industrial production can be more easily adapted to demand.

In agriculture, instead of—or rather in addition to—idle capital in its productive form, we have the destruction of capital in its commodity form. To the extent that we are speaking of the destruction of capital values, it is not clear what fundamental distinction exists here between agriculture and industry, especially since overproduction of agricultural commodities will eventually lead to a cutback in production (removing land from cultivation, etc.); moreover, if the loss of income due to the destruction of the commodity capital is great enough, the original capital structure cannot be reproduced (at least not without supplementary funds), thus in effect destroying productive capital values (and without replacement of obsolete machinery, etc., capital itself).

It would appear therefore that the basic "problem" in U.S. agriculture lies in the circumstance that it is less monopolized than other branches, and not in its peculiar supply-demand structure.

CONCENTRATION AND CENTRALIZATION PROCESSES IN U.S. AGRICULTURE

As we have already pointed out, the "weakness" of agriculture—superficially reflected in bourgeois discussions of supply and demand—lies in the fact that "the" farmer is not in the same position to pass on losses as are his capitalist brethren in more monopolized branches. This by no means indicates S's competitive model for agriculture, for the latter branch is merely the obverse (or losing) side of monopoly, not its putative competitive negation.

Because concentration in agriculture has not proceeded as far as in many industrial branches, even the largest agricultural capitalists are big fish in a little pond. One of the prime means of raising the profit of monopoly capital is to lower that of nonmonopoly capital. In this process agriculture is a major whipping-boy. The main mechanism for this redistribution of surplus value is the pricing system: the industrial monopolies charge monopoly high prices for their commodities while the nonmonopolists charge monopoly low prices. This is the main reason for the so-called scissors or parity issue: agriculture as whole is a nonmonopoly branch.

This line of reasoning receives indirect support from Schultz, who sees the agricultural crisis as being rooted in a more wide-ranging economic "disequilibrium"; thus he believes that from 1895 to World War I the price system functioned properly, but that since that time the economy has been so unstable that the pricing system has been unable to "guide the allocative process in production efficiently and at the same time keep farm products moving into foreign and domestic markets at a rate consistent with short-run developments." By short-run he means "the kind of commitments that arise when processors and other handlers buy farm products with a view to marketing them to consumers."[10]

A major difficulty faced by all farmers is that they are by and large buying from and selling to monopolized industries. Thus the commodity bought by farmers for use in production which rose most in price in the last fifteen years was farm machinery; between 1954 and 1969, the rise amounted to 66 percent.[11] This cost bulks very large among expenditures (second to feed). This is of course a very concentrated industry.[12]

The same holds true for the selling side. The dairy, the meat packing, and cereal industries, et al., are also very concentrated; a clear case of monopsony: very few large capitals exerting their pressure against a much larger number of smaller capitals.[13]

It is necessary to look for the hidden aspects of concentration (i.e., those other than direct expropriation). A major example of this is vertical integration, agribusiness, contract farming, etc.; this would appear to represent a further socialization of production—within the sphere of immediate production. Traditionally all the commodities were brought to and auctioned off at large markets (such as the stockyards in Chicago). (Of course, S's reference to the auction market [482] is ideological obfuscation, for by and large small farmers were never able to take their cattle, crops, etc., to the big markets because they were not in a position to pay for the costs of transportation and preservation. Instead, they sold them to middlemen at a lower price than they would fetch at the market. Incidentally, one reason for these markets was the fact that, in the absence of government-enforced standards, the food processors wanted to inspect the stuff they were buying. The transfer of this function to the aggregate capitalist—and financially to the taxpayers—is one reason why these central markets are no longer necessary.) This represented a lower stage of socialization—one effected strictly through the sphere of circulation.

The direct intervention of food and feed and machinery companies, etc. in the sphere of production often conceals an economic relation of capital-wage-labor beneath a veneer of formal property ownership on the part of the small farmers. This process, which has turned farmers into raw materials-suppliers of the food industry, is connected on the one hand with the above-mentioned centralization processes in the branches that supply and buy from agriculture, and on the other hand with the apparently insufficient profits of agriculture, which have hindered a massive flow of industrial capital into this branch. An integration of some sort has become necessary because the large producers of farm machinery, etc., need a market which can be supplied more "rationally" than the splintered demand of millions of small farmers permits, while the food industry requires a reliable standardized flow of supplies. By permitting the farmers to remain the formal owners of the means of production, the large industrial corporations avoid the risks involved in a sufficiently productive output to pay ground rent and finance large capital expenditures, while gaining de facto wage-workers who are probably cheaper than organized factory workers.

Although this process is advantageous to small farmers insofar as it can provide a more stable source of income, it must be remembered that this is always the case during the transition from small commodity producer to wage worker.

The following table offers some key data for U.S. commercial farms in 1959 and 1964 grouped according to the value of farm products sold (I—more than $40,000; II—$20,000-40,000; III—$10,000-20,000; IV—$5,000-10,000; V—$2,500-5,000; VI—less than $2,500):[14]

Subject and Year		All Commercial farms	Class I	Class II	Class III	Class IV	Class V	Class VI
Number of farms	1964	100.0	6.6	12.0	21.6	23.3	20.5	16.1
	1959	100.0	4.2	8.7	20.0	27.1	25.6	14.4
Land in farm	1964	100.0	28.0	19.2	22.5	16.4	9.5	4.4
	1959	100.0	25.8	17.0	22.0	19.3	12.1	3.8
Cropland harvested	1964	100.0	21.2	22.3	27.7	18.3	8.3	2.2
	1959	100.0	15.0	17.3	27.9	24.3	12.4	3.0
Regular hired farm workers	1964	100.0	59.2	19.3	13.2	5.7	2.1	0.5
	1959	100.0	48.7	20.4	17.1	9.3	4.0	0.6
Tractors other than garden	1964	100.0	13.9	17.7	26.0	22.5	14.0	5.9
	1959	100.0	10.0	13.8	25.8	27.1	18.1	5.2
Fertilizer used, tons	1964	100.0	34.1	21.9	20.8	13.3	7.2	2.6
	1959	100.0	23.4	17.3	23.5	19.3	12.5	4.2
Expenditures, total	1964	100.0	51.4	18.8	15.6	8.7	4.1	1.3
	1959	100.0	39.3	19.3	19.9	13.5	6.7	1.4
Feed for livestock and poultry	1964	100.0	49.8	20.2	16.7	8.4	3.6	1.3
	1959	100.0	32.2	20.2	23.5	15.7	7.1	1.3
Purchase of livestock and poultry	1964	100.0	61.2	18.0	11.6	5.6	2.7	0.8
	1959	100.0	50.2	20.2	15.9	8.8	4.2	0.7
Hired farm labor	1964	100.0	62.4	16.4	11.6	6.1	2.8	0.7
	1959	100.0	51.7	19.1	15.3	8.9	4.3	0.8
Machine hire and custom work	1964	100.0	40.6	16.9	19.0	14.2	7.6	1.8
	1959	100.0	30.4	16.0	20.2	18.3	12.0	3.1
Purchase of seeds, bulbs, plants and trees	1964	100.0	34.6	20.1	22.0	13.9	7.1	2.3
	1959	100.0	29.4	17.5	23.0	18.1	9.5	2.4
Gasoline and other petroleum fuel	1964	100.0	26.6	20.8	24.2	17.0	8.6	2.7
	1959	100.0	19.5	17.1	25.8	22.6	12.1	2.9
Value of all farm products sold	1964	100.0	43.7	20.7	19.2	10.6	4.7	1.1
	1959	100.0	32.8	19.2	22.8	16.0	7.7	1.6
Value of land and buildings	1964	100.0	29.3	20.6	22.2	15.3	8.7	4.0
	1959	100.0	19.5	18.6	26.1	20.8	11.8	3.1

14. Source: U.S. Census of Agriculture, 1964, Washington, D.C., 1964, II, 604

Here we can detect two very important phenomena. First, it is clear that in all categories the shares of the largest farms (especially of Class I) are increasing, whereas those of the smallest farms are rapidly declining. A slightly different table for the year 1970 shows that this tendency has continued unabated, for by that year farms with annual sales above $40,000 already accounted for 52.6 percent of all farm sales, although they represented only 7.6 percent of all farms:[15]

NUMBER OF FARMS AND INCOME, BY VALUE OF SALES CLASSES, 1970

Item	Total	Less than $5,000	$5,000 to $9,999	Value of Sales $10,000 to $19,999	$20,000 to $39,999	$40,000 to $99,999	$100,000 and over
Number of farms (thousands)	2,924	1,444	370	513	374	169	54
Percent of total	100	50.4	12.7	17.5	12.8	5.8	1.8
Cash receipts from marketings, (millions)	$52,948	$2,457	$3,060	$8,259	$11,346	$10,599	$17,227
Percent of total	100	4.6	5.8	15.6	21.4	20.0	32.6
Realized gross farm income (millions)	$56,580	$3,895	$3,450	$8,952	$12,004	$11,182	$17,097
Percent of total	100	6.9	6.1	15.8	21.2	19.8	30.2
Farm production expenses (millions)	$40,867	$2,108	$2,158	$5,767	$8,278	$8,250	$14,306
Percent of total	100	5.2	5.3	14.1	20.2	20.2	35.0
Realized net income (millions)	$15,713	$1,787	$1,292	$3,185	$3,726	$2,932	$2,791
Percent of total	100	11.4	8.2	20.3	23.7	18.6	17.8
Realized net income per farm from farming	$5,374	$1,238	$3,492	$6,208	$9,962	$17,349	$51,685
Off-farm income per farm	$5,833	$7,506	$4,984	$3,452	$3,503	[2]$5,803	[2]$5,803
Total income per farm, dollars	$11,207	$8,744	$8,476	$9,660	$13,465	$23,152	$57,488

[1]Estimated from totals of farms with sales of $40,000 or more.
[2]Average off-farm income of farms with sales of $40,000 or more.
Source: USDA, Farm Income Situation, July 1971.

The fact that the total-income share of "off-farm income" is so high for the smallest class—about 85 percent, compared with less than 10 percent for the largest farms—indicates that the small farmers are semiproletarianized, that is, they work only part-time in farming. It is estimated that by 1980, farms with annual sales exceeding $40,000 may account for 20 percent of all farms and 75 percent of all sales.[16]

Secondly, the data concerning wage workers provides an important indicator of the class composition of the agricultural producers. In 1964, 50 percent of the farms used no wage labor whatsoever, while an additional 38 percent "used less than one-half man-years of hired labor. Thus 88 percent of all farms—accounting for about 50 percent of all farm commodities—were so-called family farms (although the "owners" themselves may be disguised wage workers).[17]

The capitalist structure becomes even more apparent when we examine those farms with annual sales exceeding $100,000. In 1959, they "employed" 30.1 percent of all agricultural wage workers. By 1964, 31,000 of these farms—now accounting for ca. 1 percent of all farms—"employed" 40.6 percent of all agricultural wage workers.

Looking at the very largest farms, we see their rapidly rising shares of total farm sales[18]:

Size	1959 Number	Sales	1964 Number	Sales	1970 Number	Sales
over $1 million	408	4.2%	919	6.8%		
$500,000-1 mil.	800	1.7%	1674	3.1%		
$200,000-500,000	4570	4.2%	7760	6.4%		
$100,000-200,000	14201	6.2%	21148	8.0%		
Total	19979	16.3%	31401	24.3%	54000	32.6%

Apparently none of these trends warrants S's attention. Instead he refers to "some observers" who think it "odd" that the government is simultaneously helping farmers to produce less food more efficiently (412). What is so "odd" about a capitalist's wanting to bring about an artificial shortage while lowering his costs?

Chapter 15: Marginal-Utility Theory (S's Chapter 22)

1. HISTORY OF THE THEORY

OBJECTIVE AND SUBJECTIVE VALUE

Since modern bourgeois economists tend to pooh-pooh the classical and/or Marxist insistence on the strict separation of objective and subjective moments, it is only appropriate to begin by devoting some attention to the differences. Of course, the historical development of the question of subjective value complicates matters. Since S manages to fill literally hundreds of pages with graphs, charts, anecdotes, and tables of little value, it seems strange that there is no "space" to discuss this "fundamental notion." But even from his paltry description of utility (which he places in quotation marks at its introduction [431], presumably to indicate his distance from it), reveals his attitude toward it.

The two lines devoted to utility are followed by the statement that the "law" of diminishing marginal utility (as always this concept remains unexplained) concerns the "Behavior of psychological utility" (we are never told whether there is another sort of utility).

Such a psychological approach would fit in well with the prior development of "orthodox" theory. Thus Friedrich von Wieser, one of the founders of marginal-utility theory, proclaimed that the "doctrine of value is . . . applied psychology."[1] And C. Menger explicitly relates value to the perception of scarcity: value does not exist outside the human consciousness.[2]

It is extremely interesting to compare this position with

that of the English anti-Ricardian Samuel Bailey (1791-1870). In addition to insisting upon the purely relative nature of value, Bailey introduced subjective criteria. Thus value became definitely disconnected from a specific societal process of production:

> When we consider objects in themselves, without reference to each other; the emotion or pleasure or satisfaction, with which we regard their utility or beauty, can scarcely take the appellation of value. It is only when objects are considered as subjects of preference or exchange, that the specific feeling of value can arise.[3]

For Bailey then an inquiry into the causes of value is, in reality, an inquiry

> into those external circumstances, which operate so steadily upon the minds of men, in the interchange of the necessaries, comforts, and conveniences of life, as to be subjects of interference and calculation. . . . Whatever circumstances . . . act with assignable influence, whether mediately or immediately, on the mind in the interchange of commodities, may be considered as causes of value.[4]

Marx takes up this matter in the third volume of *Theories of Surplus Value*, where he devotes almost fifty pages to Bailey. Marx considers that simply to characterize the value-determining or -causing factors that influence the mind does not at all enlighten us about the nature of those factors. Marx's commentary on the Bailey passage should be quoted in full, because it contains a concise statement of Marx's understanding of the objectivity that characterizes the economic base:

> This means in fact nothing but: The *cause* of the value of a commodity or of the equivalence between two commodities are the circumstances which determine the seller or also the buyer and the seller to consider anything to be the value or the equivalent of a commodity. The "circumstances" which determine the value of a commodity are not any further recognized by qualifying them as circumstances which affect the "mind" of

those who exchange, which as such circumstances lies in the consciousness of those who exchange (or then again perhaps not, or perhaps only falsely perceived).

The same circumstances (independent of the mind, although affecting it) which compel the producers to sell their products as *commodities*—circumstances which distinguish one form of social production from the other—give their products (also for their mind) an exchange value independent of the use value. Their "mind," their consciousness, may well not know . . . through what circumstances in fact the value of their commodities or their products as values are determined. They are set in relations which determine their mind without their having to know it. Everyone can use money as money without knowing what money is. Economic categories are reflected in the consciousness in a very inverted way.[5]

It may sound very democratic to assert that people's preferences determine production, but this stands in contradiction to the workings of the accumulation process.

With respect to causality we can say the following: both in the Austrian school (Menger, Wieser, Boehm-Bawerk) and in the mathematical school (Jevons, Walras, Pareto) we get a theory that sacrifices causal explanations. Although this is more obvious among the mathematicians, the Austrians are no better off; for with them, the various Robinson Crusoe stories play the same role of providing a protective cover for their causalityless theories. Since their theory of "objective" value needs a subjective value not previously influenced by market prices, the Robinson stories fulfill this task. In fact, it would be no exaggeration to state that the theory of supply and demand is the base and the marginal-utility apparatus only a superstructure or ornament. Marginal utility assumes a helping role vis-à-vis a theory of demand: with a given quantity of commodities it determines maximum price; with a given price, it determines maximum demand.

The sham of marginal utility can be seen very clearly in Marshall when he says: "We cannot express a person's demand for a thing by the 'amount he is willing to buy,' or by the 'intensity of his eagerness to buy a certain amount,' without reference to the prices at which he would buy that amount and other amounts."[6] Before that he introduced the "law of satiable wants or of diminishing utility": namely that total utility of a thing does not increase as quickly as the increase of the stock (Gossen's first law). Then he wishes to "translate this law of diminishing utility into terms of price."[7] The translation is quite simple: it is our old friend the "law of downward-sloping demand," which, according to S, "is in accordance with common sense and has been known in at least a vague way since the beginning of recorded history" (61). Marshall can deduce the "law" of downward-sloping demand curve from the "law" of diminishing utility only because he has already introduced the former into the latter: namely his identification of maximum price and utility.

Thus Marshall can "deduce" one law from the other only because he has made the two into one. With S this is somewhat more difficult to prove, since some 350 pages separate his chapter on supply and demand and that on utility. But nevertheless he repeats uncritically that it was only after "hitting upon" the notion of marginal utility that economists "felt able for the first time to derive the demand curve and explain its properties" (431). And in his summary to the chapter, S expresses himself even more clearly: "The concepts of total and marginal utility were introduced to explain the law of downward-sloping demand" (438).

The identification of the two "laws" is incorrect because the main reason for the drop in the demand curve lies in the fact that with increasing purchases the purchasing power at the disposal of the buyer or demander declines. Diminishing utility, though obviously not entirely devoid of a rationality, is not quite so suprahistorical as we are led to believe.

Marginal utility assumes that goods be divisible and succesively supplied. But under such conditions utility comparisons can be made only for homogeneous goods. For the most part such goods belong to the group of subsistence items needed in a rather unchanging quantity; in any event, this quantity is determined by the "total utility" of securing one's existence, not on the basis of marginal considerations. On the whole, goods transcending the subsistence level do not fit into the above two assumptions—divisibility and supply with successive units—and thus a priori are disqualified from marginal treatment.

THE SOCIETAL BACKGROUND OF THE THESIS OF EQUAL MARGINAL UTILITY PER DOLLAR OF EVERY GOOD

Next we are treated to a discussion of "the process of rational choice" or "the fundamental equilibrium condition" necessary to make a consumer "truly best off in terms of utility or well-being," which finally becomes transmuted into "a law of logic itself" (7th ed., pp. 419, 422); this of course is the "proportionality" thesis, namely that the marginal utility per dollar of every good is equal.

This theory has undergone a number of transformations since its first appearance on the bourgeois scene in the middle of the last century. At that time it popped up as what later became known as Gossens second law.[8] Gossen contended that given the choice among various pleasures but not enough time to enjoy all of them fully, a person wishing to attain maximum pleasure would partially enjoy all of them before fully enjoying the greatest pleasures, so that at the time he interrupted his activity the magnitude of pleasure received from each one would be equal (regardless of the absolute differences).

In Jevons we get a similar statement: if a stock of a commodity be capable of two distinct uses, "it is the inevitable tendency of human nature" to choose the combination offering the "greatest advantage."

> Hence, when the person remains satisfied with the distribution he has made, it follows that no alteration would yield him more pleasure; which amounts to saying that an increment of commodity would yield exactly as much utility in one use as in another. . . . We must, in other words, have the *final degrees of utility* in the two uses equal.
>
> The same reasoning which applies to uses of the same commodity will evidently apply to any two uses, and hence to all uses simultaneously. . . . The general result is that commodity,

if consumed by a perfectly wise person, must be consumed with a maximum production of utility.[9]

Now it would appear that such a "law" presupposes at least these two conditions: (1) that there are different commodities and the possibility of substitution or changing of proportions (in the absence of such possibilities the postulate of maximum utility would be undermined); and (2) that there is a limited possibility of full satisfaction (otherwise the question of choice would make no sense).

A close look at these conditions would indicate that Gossen's second law presupposes the existence of commodity production: with money one can buy any commodity, but the amount of money at anyone's disposal is limited.

The unreal nature of this "law of logic" has not been overlooked by some of the more realistic bourgeois economists. Thus Hans Mayer took a critical position. He indicated that there were two modes of "deriving" this law: one empirical and one psychological. As to the former, Mayer objects that empirical study shows that, say, a 10 percent increase in income does not lead to a uniform increment in all consumption items. Some remain unchanged, others rise, and still others drop, and all in different proportions. The same holds true for a drop in income.

As far as the psychological derivation (à la Jevons) is concerned, which allegedly explains the empirical behavior of economic subjects, Mayer points out that the proposition that maximum utility has been attained when the marginal increments bring about equal marginal utilities rests upon a *petitio principii*: "The last increments in all . . . kinds of goods must have equal degrees of marginal utility; *otherwise one would have made other arrangements!*"[10]

Another important unrealistic assumption of the psychological derivation maintains that in all types of needs the same intensities of satisfaction appear simultaneously; only under this assumption could marginal increments lead to equal utility increments. Against this Mayer notes that not only is there a complementarity of needs (intensities of satisfaction for one good can depend on the intensities already reached for other goods), but that such interdependence is not a general mutual dependence but rather a genetic and causal relation, so that some needs become immediate only after other needs have already been satisfied in part or in full. (By this Mayer does not mean the commonplace "dynamic" development of "higher" needs, but rather the "static" course of appearance on the scene of needs that have already been formed and exist; e.g., someone who is starving will not have an immediate need for paintings.) But if the above is true—i.e., if heterogeneous needs do not become "relevant" simultaneously, do not coexist—then the "psychic foundation" of Gossen's second law is destroyed.

In the course of a "digression" on substitution effects, S lets the cat out of the bag as far as his silent assumptions about *the* consumer are concerned. Since *the* consumer will shift to other goods if the customary ones become too expensive, he is doing "only what every businessman does when rises in the price of one productive factor cause him to adjust his production methods so as to substitute cheap inputs for the dear inputs. . . .Similarly do consumers buy satisfaction at least cost" (435).

This is, as it were, a textbook case of what Crosser calls designification, or the removal of social content form political-economic categories.[11] Marginal productivity made a giant step in this direction by placing the "inputs" land, labor, and capital on the same categorical level. Now S comes along and removes the distinction between the motives for production and consumption. We are told that consumer rationality is no different from, is in fact identical with, production rationality.

S does not even have the modesty to suggest that this claim be limited to capitalism; it supposedly characterizes all production and consumption. Let us first look at how this would presumably function in capitalism. On the production side we get as the basic mechanism the equalization of the rate of profit. Increased profits in any sphere of investment will lead to capital inflow there, which in turn will lead to higher production, which in turn will lead to lower prices (supply will out-run demand), and finally to a drop in the rate of profit. Equilibrium will be reached when the rate of profit is equal in all branches and there is no longer motive for further movement.

On the consumption side this would mean that increased consumption of any good would lead to increasing total satisfaction but also to diminishing marginal utility. Equilibrium will be reached when there are equal marginal utilities per dollar, for then there will be no further stimulus to substitution.

There can be no doubt that this identification is a violent one: the principles guiding capitalist producers have been gratuitously ascribed to consumers in general. But even on an empirical level S's chatter is refuted by the existence of classes in our society. It is just not true for vast numbers of the bourgeousie that if the price of tea goes up "it pays . . . to *substitute* other goods for tea in order to maintain one's standard of living most cheaply" (434 f.). This insight is not any major theoretical breakthrough on our part; and if confronted with this, S and Co. would doubtless retreat to some quantitative income line, above which the rules of rational consumption lose their meaning. Still such an admission of the class nature of consumption (that in fact on the market all are not equal) is politically significant. Furthermore, the material preconditions do exist for a society in which the mass of the people would be as concerned with the "price" of tea as is Rockefeller.

One major reason that S can get away with this nonsense derives from the standard Robbins definition of economics which he accepts, and which contains within it the concept of rationality peculiar to equal marginal utilities per dollar. Since economics merely becomes a science studying human behavior as the relation between ends and scarce means having alternative uses, it becomes absorbed into a universal theory of action not allowing for socio-historical differentiation.

In the first edition S appears much more moderate and positivistic: he admits that for example diminishing utility "must stand or fall on the basis of the economic behavior of consumers" (pp. 481 f.). If this is refuted by "observable facts," then economists must "modify" their theory. Although S would like to give the impression that he is strictly common-sensical and firmly rooted in facts, he is really going around in circles: the fictitious preferences (fictitious in the sense that they are drawn up by the economist himself) are devised to churn out the desired answer: namely the equality of marginal utilities per dollar.

"CONSUMER SURPLUS"

Now we come to the paradox of Value and the idiocy of Consumer Surplus. It is here that the thoroughly eclectic and apologetic base of marginal utility finds its fullest expression.

When the orthodox assert that the value (= price) of the marginal good is determined by the marginal utility of that last part of the stock, they are talking about a natural economy without production (the isolated consumer). When they assert that there is "only one price in a competitive market," and that therefore every unit is sold at the same price as the marginal unit, they are clearly speaking of commodity production, and capitalist commodity production at that, in which the regulating role of the value or production price of a given commodity is assumed by a group of producers operating in an average social situation.

Now the second of these elements is not present in pre-commodity-producing societies. In these (we mean natural economies, but the following is also valid for Robinson Crusoe) the community will reckon the "utility" of the whole stock of products and from this deduce the "value" of the individual goods. Now in a producing natural economy the entire stock belongs to one physical or "legal" person; the community will evaluate the stock according to the labor-time expended in producing it. Of course, if all the goods of one kind are produced under the same conditions, there will be no difference between a "primary" evaluation of an individual exemplar and a derived evaluation (= total divided by number of items). But where the products are produced under unequal conditions, the whole stock is primary and the individual item is derivative.

The eclectic approach of the subjective school in general

("mixing" elements of commodity production and natural economies) takes as its starting point a single private-economic unit in a commodity-producing society. Such a unit is characterized by rationality within and anarchy in its relations with other economic monads. But this dualism, or dialectic of autonomy, disappears on the total social level where life is unorganized. The subjectivistic school, however, suffers from an inability to understand this dialectic. It either (1) denies the sociality of commodity production (commodity production becomes a sum of totally autonomous individuals), or (2) denies the anarchy (commodity production is turned into an organized economy).

This confusion also permeates equal marginal utilities per dollar. It is significant that S only looks at one side of the deal; for such an approach can make no sense as far as the seller is concerned, precisely because he does not view the commodity produced by him as having any utility for himself.

Here we have a good example of S's eclecticism. The classical subjectivists like Jevons had a way out. They assumed, wrongly, that the only way the proportionality thesis could be made to "work" on both sides of the deal was to construct a seller who merely sold his surpluses, or perhaps even part of his necessities. Then the goods traded by him will also have utility for him. This is of course a ridiculous assumption, especially in light of the further assumption that consumers can fulfill all their needs on the market; that is to say, the two assumptions, production for the market and production for the needs of the producer contradict each other.

S recognizes the most glaring blunders of his predecessors and wishes to avoid them without, however, renouncing their joint apologetic goals. So he merely drops the seller from the formal analysis, and brings him back in the peripheral discussion of consumer surplus, where he interjects this gem: "In a swap, one party does not lose what the other gains. Unlike energy, which cannot be created or destroyed, the well-being of all participants is increased by trade" (437).

This hints at the real purpose consumer surplus is scheduled to play in S's book. He believes that "the important thing is to see how lucky the citizens of modern efficient communities really are. The *privilege of being able to buy a vast array of goods at low prices cannot be overestimated*. This is a humbling thought" (437).

There is a certain irony here; for although Marshall, who gave the notion of consumer surplus polish and shape, meant it as a partial refutation of certain harmonistic interpretations of capitalism, S on the other hand junks the "scientific" application of the notion, using it exclusively for apologetic purposes. He buries the partly critical content of Marshall's conception by subsuming it under precisely the *sort of* harmonistic nonsense Marshall was attacking.

If the marginal utilitarians wish to fool around with subjective magnitudes, that is their business; but when they attempt to compare such fictitious magnitudes with objective ones, they literally arrive at nothingness. The utility measured by the money is subjective; the money measuring the utility is objective. Thus one sum of money viewed from the value side is made equivalent to another sum of money viewed from the side of useful effect. This is nothing but the preclassical confusion of value and use-value.

II. A CRITIQUE OF THE FOUNDATIONS OF UTILITY THEORY

A. DERIVATION OF DEMAND CURVES AND THE WEBER-FECHNER LAW

S begins Chapter 22, entitled "The Theory of Demand and Utility," as follows: "In a competitive market, price is determined by the schedules of supply and demand. But what principles of economics lie behind the demand schedules? . . . In this chapter we shall investigate briefly the economic principles of *total utility* and *marginal utility* that underlie the market demand schedule" (428). There is indeed a need to derive the demand curve from some more fundamental principles. Probably the most important reason, from a methodological point of view, is to back up the claim that the demand curve expresses a *lawlike* relation between price and quantity demanded. That is to say, the demand curve is allegedly more than a mere graph of observed price-quantity correlations; it is supposed to tell us what correlations *would* occur under certain conditions *even if* these conditions never come to pass. For example, the demand curve for wheat is supposed to tell us what quantities of wheat would be purchased at various prices, even at prices which never actually obtain in any market. And mere observation cannot give us these *counterfactual* correlations in addition to the empirically given ones. This requires more theory from which the demand curves can be derived.

Secondly, the desire of bourgeois economists to provide a justification for capitalist institutions such as the market by establishing such theses as consumer sovereignty and the optimality of free-market allocation of resources requires a correlation between demand and supply schedules and the "satisfaction" accorded the consumer who trades in the market. Thus the demand curves are treated as depending on consumer-preference rankings of commodity combinations on the market.

Thirdly, a theoretical derivation is necessary to provide justification for general assertions about the shape and slope of the demand curve. Both demand curves and supply curves must satisfy some restrictive conditions with respect to shape and slope in order to intersect at a uniquely determined price-quantity point. On the demand side, the most well-known of these conditions is the so-called "law of downward-sloping demand," which asserts that if the price of a good is raised, less of it will be demanded, all other things being equal. In this connection S says the following:

> Return to the law of downward-sloping demand, which is so basic a law that we have to investigate the economic principles operating in the background to justify and explain it. A century ago economists hit upon the fundamental notion of "marginal utility," and it was from this analysis that they felt able for the first time to derive the demand curve and explain its proper-

ties. There is space here only to sketch the basic notions underlying such theories, leaving refinements and developments to specialized treatises and advanced economic theory [431].

He then goes on to state the "law of diminishing marginal utility," which was used to provide a foundation for the downward-sloping demand curve. He then describes an alleged psychological basis for this "law," one which was asserted by the early marginal-utility theorists:

> Suppose you blindfold a man and ask him to hold out his hand, palm up. Now place a weight on his palm; he certainly will notice it. As you add more units of weight, he notices their addition too. But after his palm is carrying a good deal of weight, you can add just as big a weight as you did in the beginning, and yet this time he will reply that he is not conscious of any addition. In other words, the greater the *total* weight he is already carrying, the *less* will be the effect of an extra or *marginal* unit of weight.
>
> When earlier economists learned that perception of sound, light, and other sensations seemed to show a similar *Weber-Fechner* law of decreasing marginal effect, this—rightly or wrongly—gave them even greater confidence in the economic law of diminishing marginal utility [433].

By using the phrase "rightly or wrongly," S withholds his endorsement of this analogy with the Weber-Fechner law. To get his view of the matter, we have to refer to one of his "specialized treatises":

> It is clear that in its early formulation [utility analysis] was thought to have very definite, even revolutionary, consequences for the analysis of price and value. Moreover, even today the instinct of the textbook-writer is methodologically sound in his attempt to deduce the negatively sloping demand curve from the Weber-Fechner law and diminishing marginal utility; this does not alter the fact that the whole demonstration is hopelessly fallacious and illogical.[12]

Here S both asserts that a presentation such as the one in his textbook is fallacious and claims that it is nevertheless justified. A textbook presentation of fallacious theories may be justified from an idea-historical or a motivational point of view; however, we must here keep in mind the avowed purpose for which this presentation was made: "to investigate the economic principles operating in the background to justify and explain [the law of downward-sloping demand]" (431). And another passage from one of S's "advanced" papers reveals his view on the suitability of the Weber-Fechner analogy for this purpose: "The discrediting of *utility* as a psychological concept robbed it of its only possible virtue as an *explanation* of human behavior in other than a circular sense, revealing its emptiness as even a construction."[13]

B. COMPLETENESS, TRANSITIVITY, AND REFLEXIVITY OF PREFERENCES: THE FOUNDATIONS OF UTILITY THEORY

The above-quoted passages from S's *Collected Scientific Papers* show that he would not invoke the analogy of the Weber-Fechner law with one of his colleagues in an attempt to provide a foundation for the "law of downward-sloping demand." Why then does he do so in his introductory textbook? We believe that he considers this appropriate, because the starting point of utility theory is the preference relation that is supposedly revealed by the decisions of agents, in the same way as the perceptual relation of seeming-heavier-than is revealed by perceivers ordering bodies suitably felt in some weight order. It is this analogy to psychophysical relations which led the aforementioned early utility theorists to apply the Weber-Fechner law to explain "diminishing marginal utility." And we feel that, in spite of S's claim (433 n. 3) that a psychological notion of utility is not essential to an adequate theory of consumer preferences, and in spite of his attempts in "advanced treatises" on "revealed preference" to do without a psychological utility concept, the analogy to psychophysical relations persists in modern formulations of utility theory. Furthermore, it is this analogy, however it may be covered over, which is primarily responsible for giving utility theory the appearance of scientific plausibility. Consequently, we hope in what follows to undermine the analogy in detail.

To this end we must begin by elaborating on the analogy more fully. In formulations of utility theory the preference relation is asserted to satisfy certain requirements, each of which has a counterpart in the seeming-heavier-than relation. Thus, just as a person given two material objects—x and y—can decide whether x feels heavier than y or y heavier than x, or both feel equally heavy, in utility theory each consumer must be able to decide with respect to any two combinations of commodities whether he prefers one to the other or whether likes them equally well. This is the requirement of *completeness*. Secondly, just as if x feels as heavy as or heavier than y, and y as heavy as or heavier than z, x feels equally heavy as or heavier than z, then in utility theory if a consumer prefers x to y and y to z, then he prefers x to z, and similarly, if he is indifferent to x and y and to y and z, then he is indifferent to x and z. This is the requirement of *transitivity*. Finally, just as the same object does not feel heavier than itself, the consumer cannot prefer any commodity combination to itself. This is the requirement of *reflexivity*. We may summarize these requirements of utility theory as follows: If x, y, and z are any commodity combination, then

(1) Either xRy or yRx (completeness)
(2) If xRy and yRz, then xRz (transitivity)
(3) xRx (reflexivity).

Here "xRy" is to be read as "x is not preferred to y." There are other ways of formulating these requirements, but for our purposes this is the simplest.

Before going on to a critique of the requirements we shall briefly describe their role in the indifference-curve analysis discussed by S in the Appendix to Chapter 22, which is probably the most popular formulation of utility theory today. According to this geometrical for a given consumer approach, an indifference curve is associated with each commodity combination x. This curve consists of all points representing commodity combinations y such that the consumer is indifferent to x and y. In our notation, the indifference curve of x is the set of all y such that xRy and yRx.

To derive demand curves from indifference curves, the latter must meet certain stringent requirements. We need to know what commodity combination would be chosen at any given set of prices. As S points out, this can be determined, given the consumer's income, by constructing a *budget line* corresponding to the given income and a given set of prices. It is then assumed that the consumer will choose the commodity combination on his budget line which represents maximum satisfaction for him. According to indifference-curve analysis, this optimum point is the point of tangency between the budget line and the highest indifference curve—i.e., the curve "farthest away" from the origin. This unique point of tangency presupposes that the layout of the indifference curves on the graph satisfy the stringent requirements alluded to above: first, movement away from the origin must represent an increase in satisfaction; second, the indifference curves must be shaped so as to allow a unique point of tangency with the budget line.

If the preference relation does not satisfy conditions (1)-(3), then the indifference curves will not satisfy these two requirements. First, if transitivity fails, then the indifference curves could cross each other as in Figure 1. Figure 1 is a graph of the situation in which the consumer is indifferent to x and y and to y and z, but not to x and z, as transitivity would require; rather he prefers x to z. If this situation could occur, then more than one point of tangency would be possible with a budget line (see Figure 2), and there would be no clear sense in which increasing satisfaction could be identified with movement away from the origin, since there is no clear sense in which we can say that curve A is farther from the origin than curve B, or vice versa.

Secondly, if reflexivity fails, and thus x could be preferred to itself, then (assuming transivity) any point y such that the consumer is indifferent to y and x would also be preferred to x ("The consumer is indifferent to y and x" and "The consumer prefers x to x" imply by transitivity "The consumer prefers y to x"). This would mean that every point on x's indifference curve would be preferred to x, and thus there would again be no sense to correlating increasing satisfaction with movement away from the origin.

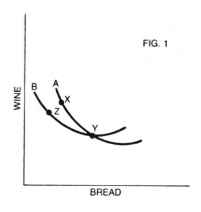

FIG. 1

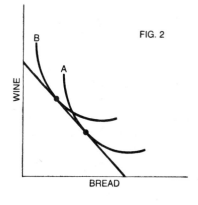

FIG. 2

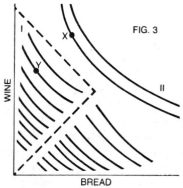

FIG. 3

Finally, suppose completeness fails. This means that some commodity combinations do not even enter into preference or indifference relations with other commodity combinations. Figure 3 depicts one such possible situation. The points in area I do not enter into preference or indifference relations with points in area II. Thus we cannot say that x is preferred to y, and once again movement away from the origin does not necessarily represent increasing satisfaction. Furthermore, it is clear from the graph that there might be two points of tangency to a budget line, one in area I and another in area II.

Thus we see the importance of requirements (1)–(3) for the indifference-curve formulation of utility theory. Furthermore, this importance is not peculiar to the indifference-curve formulation but extends to the other formulations as well. This is easily demonstrated: Requirements (1)–(3) merely say that the R relation is isomorphic to the less-than-or-equal-to relation among the real numbers. And utility theorists need such isomorphism to buttress their claim that utility is a quantity and consequently admits the possibility of maximization (when subject to certain constraints, such as budget limitation). That is to say, it is essential for utility theorists to be able to construct functions h(x), based on the preference relation, with the following property:

(*) $h(x) \leq h(y)$ if and only if xRy,

where h maps commodity combinations into the real numbers. But functions with this property could not exist unless the R relation satisfies (1)–(3), because the less-than or equal-to relation itself satisfies (1)–(3), i.e., is complete, transitive, and reflexive.

A word of clarification on the previous paragraph is in order. We are *not* claiming that utility must have a *cardinal* measure to be viable. The construction of a function such as h above is usually called the construction of a *utility function*. Now, the requirement that the utility function satisfy (*) does not imply that the values of the function represent absolute amounts of utility, or that differences in the values of the function represent definite amounts of utility, as would be required by a function expressing a cardinal measure of utility. The requirement that there be functions satisfying (*) only means that utility be an *ordinal* magnitude; in this case, only *relative* values of the utility function have significance, not its absolute values.

Before going on we wish to note that the "theory of revealed preference" for which S is so well known cannot dispense with the assumption that conditions (1)–(3) obtain. The goal of revealed-preference theory is to dispense with methods such as introspection by making it possible to construct a consumer's utility function from his observed market behavior. But a necessary condition for the possibility of such a construction is that the consumer's behavior conform to certain axioms. And these axioms insure that (1)–(3) hold.[14]

C. CRITIQUE OF THE FOUNDATIONS OF UTILITY THEORY

In Marxist terms, it should be clear that marginal utility theory seeks to give a quantitative expression to the notion of *use-value* and to use this expression to explain *value* categories and relations—i.e., the superficial notions of supply and demand in markets, and behind them the structure of production and consumption in the society. It is our overall goal to show, via a critique of assumptions (1)–(3), that a scientific notion of use-value cannot be used to this end, and that the bourgeois economists' quantitative notion of use-value is really a disguised value notion which presupposes the money form, and thus cannot be used to give a noncircular explanation of capitalist production relations.

C.1. *Empirical Failure of the Basic Assumptions* The first thing that need be said in our critique is that assumptions (1)–(3) do not hold true. This is an empirical fact widely accepted by everyone involved with the theory.[14a] For instance, when confronted with a decision on preferences, people might legitimately claim that it does not make any sense to say that they prefer one object to another *or* that they are indifferent to both (for example, does anyone like a Mercedes and a good night's sleep more than, less than, or equally as well as a house and a walk in the rain?). Such failures of objects to enter into preference relations with each other counter the completeness assumption. Furthermore, it is widely acknowledged that people are not transitive in their preferences; they may prefer wine to roast beef, roast beef to a concert, yet a concert to wine.[14b] And finally, reflexivity is also frequently violated. One might ask how this is possible, for on the face of it it is absurd to prefer x to itself. But when we consider the temporal dimension, the seeming absurdity vanishes; for then the failure of reflexivity may simply indicate a change in judgment over time that is to say, if x_1 is the object x the first time judged and x_2 the second, then it is perfectly conceivable that not $(x_2 R x_1)$, i.e., x, has risen in the agent's preference ranking—he liked x better the second time around.

C.2. *Responses to the Empirical Findings* Such fundamental breakdowns could not be ignored, especially by a theory which touts its scientific adherence to the subjective. Consequently, several responses to the empirical findings have been made by utility theorists, some of them in the form of denials that the findings refute the theory, others in the form of suggested modifications of the theory in light of the findings. Let us examine some of the most typical moves.

C.2.a. *Reflexivity* The most common response to the failure of reflexivity is to impose a temporal condition. The theory is restricted to periods in an agent's life when there are no changes in his preference judgments. Such a restriction turns the theory into a kind of preferential statics. While it is a consistent move on the part of utility theorists, it considerably narrows the scope of the theory.

C.2.b. *Completeness* The reader will recall that people sometimes claim that it just does not make any sense to compare certain objects with respect to preference or indifference. The boldest response to such claims is to deny their validity and say that such people are mistaken. An agent considering a hypothetical choice may *claim* that it makes no sense to compare two dissimilar objects, but his real-life situation shows that he *does* make such comparisons. He must decide on the amount of food and clothing he is to consume, since his income is limited and food and clothing are not free. Thus, so this argument goes, the fact of a limited income and the fact that every commodity has a price *force* all commodities to be comparable.

This argument sounds persuasive; yet, given the functions utility theory is supposed to fulfill in the theory of consumer behavior, it puts the cart before the horse. We would be the last to deny that the value of the most diverse commodities can be compared by means of prices; to make possible such comparisons is the very function of the development of money out of commodity production. And it is certainly true that given a set of prices and incomes, people do buy certain commodity combinations rather than others. What these facts amount to is that in our society products (use-values) are circulated via commodity-money exchange in a market, and at any given time this market has a certain definite price-quantity structure. But these phenomena of the "marketplace" are supposed to be *outcomes* of the theory built on the preference relation, and therefore cannot be presupposed by it if the theory is to be noncircular. In the formulation of utility theory, the consumer's preference ranking is not supposed to depend on prices or income.[14c]

C.2.c. *Transitivity; Further Discussion on the Salvageability of All Three Conditions* We now consider two typical responses to the empirical failures of transitivity. The first is to modify the basic relation of the theory from "x is not preferred to y" to "x is preferred, with lower probability than y." The theory thus weakened allows for occasional failures of transitivity, these being simply racked up to the claim that since we are really only dealing with probabilistic preferences there are bound to be exceptions. (The modified theory is usually called "stochastic" preference theory.) The second response is to impose a rationality condition on the theory. It is claimed that transitivity is a characteristic of *rational* choice, rather than a necessary feature of every actual choice situation. Since it is a truism that people do not always act rationally, some failures in transitivity are to be expected. One might accept the rationality condition if one believed that people make rational choices most of the time, for then the predictions of the theory could be expected not to diverge too radically from empirical phenomena. This seems to be the option preferred by S.

> A consumer is not expected to be a wizard at numbers or graphs, nor need he be, to approximate the demand behavior of this chapter. He can even make most of his decisions unconsciously or out of habit. As long as he is fairly *consistent* in his tastes and actions, all he has to do to make the present analysis relevant is to avoid repeating those mistakes which he found in the past failed to give him the goods and services he most wanted and to avoid making wild and unpredictable changes in his buying behavior. If enough people act in this way, our scientific theory will provide a tolerable approximation to the facts [434].

The argument for the rationality of transitivity is sometimes called the "money-pump argument." In general terms it goes as follows: If agent X has an intransitive choice structure, then given certain presuppositions connecting money with preference he would act in a manner which would force him to lose any amount of money that he starts with. Since the loss of money without any commodity to show for it is obviously irrational, if X is to be rational he must have a transitive preference structure. Let us spell the argument out in more detail. The presumed relation between preference and money is:

(*) If agent X prefers y over z then there is a sum of money $S(y, z)$ depending on y and z such that if X possessed $S(y, z)$ and z, he would exchange them for y.

Further let us assume the following:

(i) X prefers a over b.
(ii) X prefers b over c.
(iii) X prefers c over a.

It should be noted that this is an intransitive preference structure. By (i) and (*), if X possessed b and S(a, b) he would exchange them for a; by (ii) and (*), if he possessed c and S(b, c) he would exchange them for b; and by (iii) and (*), if he possessed a and S(c, a) he would exchange them for c. Let us assume that all these exchanges can be made and that X starts out with c and a sum of money at least equal to S(a, b) + S(b, c) + S(c, a). This situation leads to the following sequence of transactions:

X exchanges c and S(b, c) for b.
Then, X exchanges b and S(a, b) for a.
Finally, X exchanges a and S(c, a) for c.

At the end of this cycle, X is still in possession of c as he was in the beginning; however, he has lost S(a, b) + S(b, c) + S(c, a) in money. Thus a certain amount of money has been pumped out of him while he is no better off in nonmonetary terms. Since the above cycle can be repeated indefinitely if X does not change his preference structure, he will end up with no money after a certain finite number of cycles. Since only a moron or a lunatic would allow this to happen, it is certainly an irrational state of affairs. Intransitivity is irrational, and hence rational choice is transitive choice.

Although this argument seems persuasive, a number of devastating objections can be made. First of all, the absolutistic presentation of the conclusion is not warranted by the rest of the argument. The above argument has a very definite social context qualifying rational choice; the agent is presumed to live in a society which has private possession, exchange, and money. This is not a universal condition of mankind. The agent lives in a commodity-possessing and -exchanging society in which the conditions of production are sufficiently developed to allow value to be treated quantitatively in the form of money. Once we make this essential qualification from rationality per se to commodity-money rationality, then we see that one use of the argument and its implications is invalid. The rationality of capitalism has been defended by showing how the main institutions of capitalism are based on the rules of rational choice which is taken as a transcendent notion. But upon analysis rational choice turns out to be merely commodity-money rational choice, and consequently this defense of the rationality of capitalism is reduced to a tautology: capitalism is rational since capitalism rests upon capitalistic rationality. Or put another way: the institutions of commodity production cannot be justified by the above argument without falling into circularity, since those institutions are presupposed by the argument. The ideological and mystificatory nature of the argument thus becomes clear. It stops us from asking the truly scientific question: Is the commodity-money context of human choice in capitalism at this stage in history rational? Ruling out this very question vitiates the usual arguments for consumer sovereignty and optimal allocation of resources under competitive market conditions.

Thus the above argument for the rationality of transitivity presupposes the commodity form in general and the money form in particular. These social relations must therefore be accepted as given and cannot be derived or explained by any theory of economic behavior based on the argument. This restriction vastly reduces the worth of such a theory, for it is surely legitimate to demand that an adequate theory of economic behavior explain the basic economic institutions in which people act. Yet someone might still claim that the theory is valuable and argue that granting that the notion of rational preference presupposes the market and money, we can still explain a great deal with it. For this preference relation does express quantitatively the notion of use-value *in capitalist society* and thus can be used to determine the particular price-quantity structure of the market at a given time. In other words, transitivity of preferences is indeed rational only given certain institutions, and thus cannot be used to explain or justify these institutions; still, these are the institutions we have, and thus we can count on people to use the appropriate concept of rationality and therefore behave approximately as the theory says they should.

Such a move would concede a great deal, for it would entail giving up much of the attempt to justify capitalist institutions via principles underlying the demand curve. Nevertheless, some bourgeois economists find this line of defense attractive: leave the justification of the institutions presupposed by the use-value notion to other arguments, but point out that once these institutions are accepted the structure of the society at any particular time can be accounted for on the basis of the wishes, hopes, and desires of the members of that society.

It is our contention that the preference relation at the base of utility theory does not adequately capture the structure of use-value even in capitalist society. If our arguments are correct, then one cannot even expect people in capitalist society to have transitive preferences most of the time, much less all of the time.

In our opinion, utility theory does not adequately deal with the fact that preference is a *judgment* and all that this implies. Thus when a person prefers x over y, what we have is a *cognitive act*, for at the very least we demand that the person have some knowledge of the objects—enough at least to distinguish them and perhaps to identify them. Picking one item blindfolded and randomly from a box containing other items would not in any event be an act of preference. Consequently, a person's beliefs are essentially involved in any adequate theory of preferential judgment. But given this fact we are forced to ask, what are the objects of the theory? The bodies and events of the world, or these objects under the description provided for them by the agent making the judgment? We have here the *intentional* aspect of preference, which presents very serious difficulties for utility theory; for if

$$x \text{ is not preferred to } y \text{ by agent A}$$
$$\text{and } x = z, \text{ it does not necessarily follow that}$$
$$z \text{ is not preferred to } y \text{ by agent A.}$$

Thus under some descriptions the object x might be preferred to the object y, and under other descriptions it might not. Given this situation serious doubt is cast on the claim that the preference relation has *any* fixed properties, whether they be reflexivity, completeness, or transitivity.

There are certain other obvious consequences of seeing preference as a matter of deliberation or judgment. As one's immediate ends change, so do one's preference decisions. For example, if one wanted to build a table, hammers would be preferred to money wrenches, but if one wanted to install water pipes, then a monkey wrench would probably be preferred. Such a reversal is not due to changing tastes but a matter of differing immediate ends affecting one's choices. We can now see how restrictive it is to require that there be no changes in the agent's preference judgments. Such a requirement is tantamount to assuming that the consumer is *single-purposed*.

Utility theorists might object that the restriction is not so drastic as we have made it appear, that the agent's immediate ends are ultimate in not being subordinated to some higher end. For the theory to be applicable the agent must indeed be single-purposed, but only in the sense of having an overriding end to which he subordinates all other purposes. If the agent's immediate ends are themselves subordinated to such an ultimate goal, then his preference ranking can remain stable through changes in immediate ends.

In response to this objection we must ask what this single ultimate end is. It *cannot* be said that this purpose is the maximization of utility, because the existence of utility as a quantity to be maximized itself depends on the existence of this purpose. That is to say, before we can speak of utility as a quantity, and thus before we can speak of the maximization of utility as an ultimate goal to which all other ends are subordinated, we must first be assured that a person's preferences are structured in accordance with conditions (1)–(3). And this is precisely what is at issue here, i.e., whether (1)-(3) can be expected to be satisfied across changes in immediate ends, because of some more ultimate end. To appeal to the maximization of utility as such an ultimate goal would once again be to fall into circularity. Of course, one might try to avoid this problem by claiming that utility (or satisfaction, or pleasure) has a prior, introspectively verifiable existence as a quantitative entity the maximization of which can serve as an ultimate purpose. But this is precisely the sort of dubious psychological basis which utility theorists sought to avoid in appealing merely to the structure of a person's preference judgments.

Nor can it be said that the ultimate purpose is the accumulation of value. For this is the ultimate purpose only of capitalists and even of them only *qua* capitalists. As consumers they have other goals in contradiction to the accumulation of value, as the fund which they deduct from surplus value for their own consumption demonstrates.[15] Here it should be noted that an expressed purpose of some utility theorists is to find an analog in consumption theory to the motive of profit maximization in the theory of production, so as to strengthen the view that everyone in capitalist society, workers included, acts as a capitalist in making economic decisions. Thus we find S asserting:

> ... a rise in the price of movies relative to stage plays may cause the consumer to seek less of his amusement in the dearer direction. The consumer is doing here only what every businessman does when rises in the price of one productive factor cause him to adjust his production methods so as to substitute cheap inputs for the dear inputs. By this process of substitution, he is able to produce the same output at least total cost. Similarly do consumers buy satisfaction at least cost. [435]

The impossibility of finding an ultimate goal satisfying the requirements of utility theory highlights the ideological nature of this view.

But even if we confine our attention to cases where the agent is somehow single-purposed, the second aspect of deliberation mentioned above creates insuperable difficulties for utility theory. The fact that deliberation involves considering the known properties of alternatives with regard to their effectiveness in accomplishing one's purpose destroys any remaining plausibility the transitivity assumption might have had. For there is no necessity that the many different property-dimensions which are relevant to how well objects satisfy a given purpose arrange themselves transitively. This might most easily be seen by way of a hypothetical example. Consider John, a single-purposed individual who wants only to read good fiction. There are three properties which John looks for in a work of fiction: brevity, content or "message," and suspense. These are the good-making properties of fiction, as far as he is concerned, and he views them all as equally important. Suppose first that he is given a choice between books a and b, about which he knows only the following:

(i)

a has a better message than b.
b is shorter than a.
a is more suspenseful than b.

Which book would he choose? It seems reasonable to conclude that he would choose a over b, since a excels in two of the three good-making qualities, which he regards as equally important. There do not seem to be any grounds for calling this an irrational choice.

Now assume instead that he is presented with book b from above and another book, c, and asked which he would prefer, given the following information:

(ii)

b has a better message than c.
b is shorter than c.
c is more suspenseful than b.

It seems reasonable, on the same grounds as above, that he would prefer b to c, and that this is rational.

Finally, suppose that he is presented with the following information, which is consistent with that given in (i) and (ii) above, and asked to choose between a and c:

(iii)

a has a better message than c.
c is shorter than a.
c is more suspenseful than a.

Again on the same grounds we conclude that he would prefer c to a, and that this choice is rational.

But according to our conclusions it is clear that John's choices would violate the transitivity condition, since he would prefer a to b and b to c, but c to a, rather than a to c as transitivity would require.

The importance of our stipulation that John attached equal importance to the three qualities should be noted. Suppose instead that he ranked the qualities according to the following decision procedure:

> Message is the most important property; the book with the best message is to be chosen, regardless of how it compares to the alternatives in suspense and brevity. Suspense is next in importance; if the books have equally good messages, then the one with the greatest suspense is to be chosen, regardless of length. Only if the books rank equally in both message and suspense does brevity become a relevant factor. Then the shortest book should be chosen.

Using this valuation of the three qualities, John would choose a over b, b over c, and a over c, thus satisfying transitivity. Other valuations of the qualities are possible, some violating transitivity and some not. But it seems arbitrary, apart from a theory of fiction, to require any one of the valuations over the others. And there is no guarantee that an objectively valid theory of fiction, if one is possible, would require a valuation satisfying transitivity.

The minimum condition which any set of properties relevant to the achievement of a given purpose would have to satisfy in order for choices to arrange themselves transitively in each possible choice-situation is that it be possible to place all the various property-combinations on a single ordinal scale in accordance with degree of effectiveness in achieving the given purpose. The various factors relevant to the achievement of a purpose P must be reducible to a single quantitatively expressible factor, which we might call "P-effectiveness." There is no reason to believe, however, that such a reduction of many properties to a single property is possible for all or even most purposes P. The above example is a hypothetical case in which such a reduction is not possible (given John's valuation of the three properties). An actual case appears to exist in the field of nutrition. There are many different factors which are relevant to the nutritional qualities of food, and these factors are not reducible to a single factor which would allow us to give an ordinal ranking of plates of food in accordance with their nutritional value. Such examples[16] render it implausible that preferences are structured transitively most of the time.

We note in conclusion that commodity production reduces the most diverse objects (use-values) to a single quantitative value-dimension. The positions of various commodities along this dimension are expressed by their prices, and comparison of prices makes it possible to assess the effectiveness of various methods of production for the accumulation of surplus value (assuming labor-power has also become a commodity). Though this circumstance fails to render utility theory viable as a basis for the theory of consumer behavior, it does indicate the extent to which the utility concept is an ideological reflection of bourgeois production relations. Thus we reach the same conclusion in our analysis as did Marx and Engels in 1845-46 concerning very early formulations of utility theory:

> The apparent stupidity of merging all the manifold relationships of people in the *one* relation of usefulness, this apparently metaphysical abstraction arises from the fact that, in modern bourgeois society, all relations are subordinated in practice to the one abstract monetary-commercial relation. . . . For (the bourgeois) only *one* relation is valid on its own account—the relation of exploitation; all other relations have validity for him only insofar as he can include them under this one relation, and even where he encounters relations which cannot be directly subordinated to the relation of exploitation, he does at least subordinate them to it in his imagination. The material expression of this use is money, the representative of the value of all things, people and social relations.[17]

Chapter 16: Price Theory (S's Chapters 23-24)

THE U-CURVE

Perhaps the most important point of attack here is the ultimate refutation of diminishing returns, that ubiquitous tool of bourgeois economics. A close reading of the cost theory indicates that it stands and falls with this "law."

In explaining why marginal costs rise, S himself refers the reader to the discussion of the production-possibility curve, which, though not immediately related, is connected with other topics soon to be discussed (such as opportunity costs). Here the model presupposes fixed amounts of everything—the point is to allocate them. "The economy must really decide" WHAT, HOW, etc. (20). For "dramatic purposes" we are given a military situation in which "society" has to choose between different amounts of guns and butter. This is of course not a "dramatic" but distorted example, inasmuch as it concentrates on a case in which the aggregate capitalist (the state) does in fact make a conscious choice "for" society. This has application to a later alleged reason for increasing costs: namely that long-run equilibrium price will rise after satisfying an increased demand level, "because when a large industry (which has already achieved the economies of large-scale production) expands, it must coax men, ships, nets, and other productive factors away from other industries by bidding up their prices and thus its costs" (386).

S unfortunately confuses two unrelated processes. Although such reconversion problems do exist, they have nothing to do with increasing costs. The changed proportions of commodities take place by building new factories, etc., and not by converting cornfields into rubber plantations if the demand for automobile tires increases. And if there are such conversions, the resultant increasing costs last only for the length of the period of adaptation.

But S avoids the problem by admitting that when excess capacity is present "our economic laws may then be quite different" (21). "Different" from what? In the entire "peacetime" history of our mixed Keynesian economy the U.S. economy has never reached the frontier.

When S gets around to explaining and "proving" diminishing returns he always manages to come up with an example from agriculture (25 f., 539 ff.). In a further attempt to weasel his way out, S asserts that "increasing returns to scale" is not a "direct refutation" of the "law" because the latter presupposes that at least one "factor" remain constant, while the former deals with increasing all "factors" at the same time and in the same degree (28).

Here we encounter a controversy among bourgeois economists. S, following in the tradition of J. M. Clark and Joan Robinson, apparently sees diminishing returns as a part of the logical make-up of the universe, which later enables him to formulate other universal laws regarding rational choice. More precisely, Joan Robinson claims that the law of diminishing returns is a tautology which results from the definition of a factor of production: increasing doses of one factor added to a fixed factor must eventually bring about diminishing marginal and average productivity of the variable factor. "The Law of Increasing Returns differs from the Law of Diminishing Returns in that it cannot be reduced to a tautology. . . . The Law of Increasing Returns is a matter of empirical fact."[1]

That S shares this view is revealed by the fact that he relegates the latter "law" to the status of a digression (he does not even elevate it to the rank of law, a real insult considering his wonted largesse, but merely speaks of the "phenomenon" [28]).

For Clark, the law of diminishing returns "holds good,

not as a purely technical principle, but as a principle of human choice."[2]

Schumpeter on the other hand sharply criticizes this view: "The law of diminishing returns is of course an empirical statement—a generalization from observed facts that only further observation can either verify or refute. It is interesting to report that theorists have almost unanimously displayed an aversion to admitting this."[3] Schumpeter is partially correct: There is no theoretical underpinning to the law. There is however a theory to back up increasing productivity. And as we shall see shortly, empirical studies have not dealt kindly with the universal "law."

Since returns diminish, we are told, costs (both average and marginal) must increase. Historically, diminishing returns was a Ricardian theory of agriculture (refuted by Marx in theory and by statistics in every advanced capitalist society), which was then transported into industry. Bourgeois dissatisfaction with neoclassical price theory was given sophisticated expression by Piero Sraffa. In a now-famous article he suggested that it would be best to return to the classical emphasis on constant returns and/or costs. Sraffa gave this description of the quasi-conspiratorial situation of the time:

> In the tranquil view which the modern theory of value presents us there is one dark spot which disturbs the harmony of the whole. This is represented by the supply curve, based upon the laws of increasing and diminishing returns. That its foundations are less solid than those of other portions of the structure is generally recognised. That they are actually so weak as to be unable to support the weight imposed upon them is a doubt which slumbers beneath the conscious of many, but which most succeed in silently suppressing. From time to time someone is unable any longer to suppress the pressure of his doubts and expresses them openly; then in order to prevent the scandal spreading, he is promptly silenced, frequently with some concessions and partial admission to his objections, which, naturally, the theory had implicitly taken into account. And so, with the lapse of time, the qualifications, the restrictions and the exceptions have piled up, and have eaten up, if not all, certainly the greater part of the theory.[4]

From S's text and from others it would seem that this silencing has not yet ceased. How do we account for this? On a somewhat vulgar level we might discover the following circumstances which would make the increasing cost theory attractive to the capitalist class; for it justifies (1) a policy of high prices; (2) the capitalists' aversion to paying higher wages ("our costs are eating up our profits"); and (3) the capitalists' resistance to higher taxes (for the same reason).

In a revealing study by two economists, several hundred manufacturing capitalists (with factories "employing" from 500 to 5,000 workers) were sent graphs of eight cost curves and asked which one represented their firm's. Of a total of 334 replies, 18 indicated one of the three graphs corresponding to the marginalist U-curve; 316 indicated diminishing costs. Even more interesting were the written responses by some of the more articulate industrialists: "The amazing thing," wrote one, "is that any sane economist could consider No. 3, No. 4 and No. 5 curves [the U-curves] as representing business thinking. It looks as if some economists, assuming as a premise that business is not progressive, are trying to prove the premise by suggesting curves like Nos. 3, 4 and 5." And another said: "Even with the low efficiency and premium pay of overtime work, our unit costs would still decline with increased production since the absorption of the fixed expenses would more than offset the added direct expenses incurred."[5]

The point of these chapters, presumably, is to tell us that a "perfect competitor picks the quantity he will supply by referring to his marginal cost curve, so that P=MC" (453). Here profit will be maximized.

But this statement of course depends on the marginal-cost curve: it presupposes the U-curve. In this sense the entire price theory rests on the theory of costs. Or more precisely, it "depends heavily on three sorts of basic assumptions: concerning the psychology of buyers, the technological relationships of factors used in production, and the motivation of enterprisers who produce and sell goods."[6] Let us review these three pillars of price theory.

As for the psychology of buyers (by which is meant consumers of Department II commodities since capitalistic buyers when transforming the money form of their capital into its productive form are subject to a different sort of "psychology"), the notion of consumer sovereignty seems to be on its last legs. Thus Alvin Hansen expresses disbelief that any economist could still take this stuff seriously: "The process of consumer brain-washing has become a branch of psychoanalysis. Consumer wants are no longer a matter of individual choice. They are 'mass produced.' "[7]

Of course, not all bourgeois economists have seen the light. Aside from S and his King Consumer, there are other ideological throwbacks, like Chicago's Stigler, who are sticklers for obsolete notions and will stick to the "assumption" that consumers maximize utility with "mathematical consistency" "until a better theory comes along."[8]

As for the second pillar, technology, we have already dealt with this. At least we now know enough to state that where diminishing returns and the U-curve fall by the wayside, so must P=MC too. Since MC is usually a straight line ("L-curve"), MC≠P, but the difference between MC and P remains constant with different volumes of production, since P is by definition constant. On the other hand, the difference between price and average cost increases with production, and thus too the profit per unit of commodity. Every factory tries to maximize profit, but since the MC curve is L-shaped, the maximum profit is reached not by equalizing MC and P, but rather is obtained by the greatest production at the lowest costs of production.

Given this situation, one might wonder why S continues to feed us this model. He does not really provide an answer, but he is likely to concur with his oligopolistic competitor Bach, who adduces these answers: "the purely competitive model" could serve as a "norm," and "ideal," an "ought" for private enterprise; secondly, "We have to begin somewhere, and the pure-competition case is in many respects the simplest and easiest to understand."[9]

Pricing then in "pure competition" leads to "an organization of society's scarce resources that looks amazingly as if it had been guided by some invisible hand for the welfare of society as a whole."[10] In other words, it is the "optimality property" of MC (460) that makes the study of pure competition important. In his magnum opus S puts it this way:

> Marginal cost is not part of cost which must be met, and the equality of price and marginal cost has nothing to do with a recovery of full costs, determination of fair return on investments, correct imputation of factor shares, etc. Its purpose is to secure correct factor allocation, and avoid anomalous product allocation.[11]

Thus although the textbook purports to be an introductory *analysis*, we seem to be inundated with value judgments on how "society" ought to be organized.

The third pillar of price theory is the motivation of entrepreneurs—another psychological element. Now although in Chapter 23 S asserts that capitalists do in fact "refer" to their marginal-cost curves in making their production decisions, in Chapter 26 he says that "even if the firm is not itself tackling the problem with conscious awareness of the particular marginal tools of the theoretical economists, *to the extent that it is truly making a fair guess as to where its highest profits are realized*, it will be succeeding in making marginal revenue and marginal cost approximately equal" (507). This is analogous to the view in Chapter 22 on consumer behavior: although individual (consumer or entrepreneurial) behavior is the foundation, and although marginal-utility theory explains this behavior, even if behavior diverges it really does not matter (or better yet: it really does not diverge) since in fact it must be so because good vibes or profits are being maximized. But, unfortunately, this time bourgeois logic has outwitted S; here is the argument of the two authors whose survey of businessmen was quoted above:

> The reasoning of marginal price theory is valid if businessmen *believe* curves to be shaped as theorists assume, even though the curves are actually shaped as opponents contend; con-

versely, orthodox price theory is not valid if businessmen *believe* curves to be shaped so that their least cost points are at or near capacity, even though the curves really have the shape which conventional theorists maintain. Hence, marginal price theory stands or falls depending upon what businessmen think, because their short-run decisions to expand or to contract are based upon what they believe rather than what is actually true.[12]

In other words, if one wants to construct a subjectively oriented theory, then one must either explain motives or renounce subjectivism. And with that, all three pillars of price theory—psychology, technology, and motivation—are seen to crumble.

COSTS

We will now proceed to a closer examination of S's cost notions. Before doing this, however, we must first establish that S has failed to develop any general concept of cost on the basis of which the various cost components can be discussed systematically. To be sure, he states in a footnote that average cost "corresponds to the man in the street's rough notion of costs" (7th ed., p. 442 n. 5), yet we are not provided with any precise understanding of the concept of cost. (Two other footnotes (452 n. 3 and 470 n. 5) concede that in the "long run" price will equal average price and/or that marginal cost will be constant. This amounts to a renunciation of marginalism and the U-curve based on diminishing returns.) In point of fact, S has elaborated a notion of cost—albeit one that "the man in the street" probably is not acquainted with—namely "opportunity cost"; here cost is defined in terms of other commodities which we would have to sacrifice in order to obtain the one(s) we want (29).

Excursus on Opportunity Costs and the Backward-Bending Supply Curve for Labor The plausibility of the notion of opportunity cost allegedly derives from the fact that the economist "realizes that some of the most important costs attributable to doing one thing rather than another stem from the *forgone opportunities* that have to be sacrificed in doing this one thing" (473). As usual, of course, this is supposed to be another universal, with no relation to capitalism, money, etc. This principle describes what we might call a society of spilt-milk-weepers and/or sour-grapesters; for in fact everyone would appear to be preoccupied with whether or not he had attained more or less vibration or profit from a given decision.

The secret of the opportunity (as well as the implicit) costs is that it describes the reactions of capitalists to the equalization of the rate of profit. It is what Marx called the compensations grounds of the capitalist. In the third volume of *Capital*, he explains that once capitalism has reached a certain stage of development the equalization between the various profit rates in different industries and a general rate of profit for society does not take place solely on the basis of the movements of capital reacting to changing market prices; at this point the individual capitalists become conscious of the various differences that are being equalized so that they include them in their mutual calculations from the start. This means that every factor that makes a capital investment more or less profitable than another is calculated as a valid ground for compensation, without competition having to furnish repeated justification. However, the capitalist, able to see the world only from the upside-down vantage point of competition, does not understand that all these grounds for compensation relate to the fact that every capital of equal magnitude has an equal claim to the total surplus value produced. It *seems* to the capitalist (because in general the amount of profit he receives is different from the amount of surplus value "his" workers in fact produce) that his grounds for compensation *create* the profit, whereas all they do is equalize the share in the total surplus value.[13]

Actually, such a critique does too much honor to S, since this notion of opportunity cost is much more vulgar than the ones Marx was confronted with. To see just how vulgar, let us consider one example S mentions. He states that the cost of working "can be thought of as the . . . sacrificed amount of forgone-leisure" (473). This is integrally connected to Jevons' determination of wages by the "final equivalence of labour and utility." Since S does not use this as the main determinant but merely as one, we might as well deal with it here.

Jevons' scheme was as follows: "the larger the wages earned, the less is the pleasure derived from a further increment"; thus the marginal utility curve slopes down to the right. As for the labor or disutility curve, it first rises ("At the moment of commencing labour it is usually more irksome") or rather there is pain at first which is then relieved by a period of pleasure, and then toward the end of the day by some more pain. When the utility of the wages equals the disutility of working, the worker will quit for the day.

First we must point out that Jevons is dealing with the case of a small commodity producer (or natural economy producer), not a wage worker, for he presupposes that the worker receives the total produce. But even if we "correct" this item by substituting capitalist wages, the "model" is still nonsensical. The two curves are independent of each other—at least subjectively in the mind of the worker. That is, *regardless* of the pain involved, he must work as long as is necessary in order to get enough money to keep him and his family alive. He has no alternative; he is not free to choose whether to enter into this exchange or not (nor for that matter is the capitalist in the long run, as long as the total production of capitalist society is to be secured).

Jevons' examples all refer to precapitalist or incipient colonial-capitalist situations, in which an "undisciplined work force" will really only work part of the week to make enough to maintain its traditional-historical standard of living. Unable to grasp the differences between socioeconomic formations, Jevons seeks refuge in racism: "A man of lower race, a Negro for instance, enjoys possession less, and loathes labour more; his exertions, therefore, stop sooner."[14]

Objectively, Jevons' scheme does reflect, albeit in a very distorted and tenuous way, something real: namely that the wage must be high enough to reproduce the labor power of the worker ("pain"). But this refers to the total utility of the means of subsistence and not to any "final equivalence of labor and utility." Also, given the historically formed subsistence level of workers, it appears that Jevons is wrong on his own grounds: the utility curve of wages would—under real conditions of capitalism—never taper off; "absolute" (i.e., non-price-related) needs are so little satisfied that workers' wages would never be high enough to satisfy these needs under capitalism.

Plausibility could be obtained in theory only by letting the worker slave twenty hours a day (though even here he could still not make enough to satisfy needs)—a physical impossibility in the long run and with no relation to marginal utility.

As far as wage theory is concerned, Jevons' formula serves the very useful purpose of justifying abysmally low wages; for the lower the wage, the higher the marginal utility of the commodities purchased with it and, therefore, the greater the readiness of the worker to endure a greater disutility of labor.[15]

In and of themselves the categories "fixed and variable costs" can be useful when analyzing structural tendencies in the costs of individual firms as long as one is careful to relate them to the underlying causal tendencies of the total economy. Unfortunately S does not do this, so these two rubrics degenerate into sterile arithmetical relationships.

Although fixed and variable costs stand in no immediate relationship to either of Marx's pairs—variable and constant capital, circulating and fixed capital—they do reflect *some* of the phenomena of Marx's concepts. On the one hand, the attention devoted to fixed and variable costs within the individual firm—as opposed to certain marginalist notions—is rooted in the increasing organic composition of capital which finds expression in the increasing weight of the fixed costs vis-à-vis the variable costs. On the other hand, the increasing organic composition of capital cannot be directly reflected in the relative rise of fixed costs, because the former is a category of production, whereas the latter represents a peculiar mixture of elements of production and circulation. In the latter sense it shares some of the characteristics of Marx's "fixed capital." Thus, since variable costs include wages and raw materials, a relative increase in fixed costs may be said to reflect an increasing organic composition of capital by expressing the above-average growth of the plant and machinery component of constant capital.

From the point of view of the individual firm making the investment, increased fixed costs are incurred with a view toward raising productivity and thus lowering costs; if a firm is in the forefront of such an investment wave, it will be able to realize the goal of receiving (temporary) extra profits because its individual costs will be lower than those of the branch in general; this will in turn set off a chain-reaction among the other firms, which will be forced to follow suit if they wish to retain a significant capital-accumulation ability.

Once the forces of production as mediated by the specific developments in any particular branch have attained such a level that the fixed costs begin to dominate the cost structure, the goal of extra profits via diminished costs can be realized only if the increased fixed costs are distributed over a sufficiently large number of units of output; in other words, the number of commodities produced with the new machinery and plant must be so large that the depreciation costs charged to each commodity produced become small enough to justify the investment compared to the previous smaller-scale, more labor-intensive production methods.

This compulsion to attain a relatively high-capacity utilization rate is tantamount to a rise of the "break-even point" (455, 470) for the individual firm, which may even result in further expansions of capacity in the hopes of increasing productivity and lowering costs sufficiently to compensate for cyclically diminished demand. On the total social level, the result is a loss of "flexibility" in crises, since cutting back on the variable costs becomes increasingly ineffective.

COST, AVERAGE RATE OF PROFIT, AND COMPETITION

In this section we will examine the ramifications of S's inclusion in " 'full competitive minimum costs' a normal return to management services, as determined competitively in all industries; and a normal return to capital, as determined competitively by industries of equal riskiness" (472). In order to evaluate this definition with respect to its factual content, we must first summarize briefly some of the major elements of Marx's theory of price.

Cost-price, according to Marx, is what the commodity costs the capitalist—constant plus variable capital. But cost-price is not a real category of value production insofar as it contains two heterogeneous elements: the constant capital value is merely transferred from the means of production to the new commodities, whereas the variable capital does not enter into the value of the new commodity at all; for labor as creator of value takes the place of the value of labor power in the functioning productive capital. Now the cost-price and the value of the commodity are obviously different, namely the latter contains the value of the constant capital plus the entire value created by the living labor (value of labor power plus surplus value). In other words, what the commodity costs the capitalist and its production cost are not identical. In this sense one might say that Marx was the discoverer of the concept of social costs. And capitalist competition involves the possibility of selling a commodity at a profit below value precisely because of the difference between value and cost-price.

In other words, the existence of surplus value gives the capitalist a certain radius of action within which he can lower his selling prices in order to drive out his competitors without taking a "loss" himself. If the capitalist received back in the selling price (realized) less than the cost-price, he would then be forced to cut back production (unless he had additional capital or took out a loan) by not replacing obsolete machinery or by firing workers.

S's "break-even point" is totally different, since "breaking even" in this sense means obtaining the average rate of profit. Moreover, S's average rate of profit is determined by fiat without any objective explanation. To say that companies are breaking even when in fact they are making an average profit means to restrict competition to the garnering of (temporary) extra profit; although of supreme importance, this is definitely not the only type of capitalist competition. Extra profit is appropriated in a competitive struggle among capitalists in the same branch—and it is doubtless for this reason that bourgeois economists deal primarily with competition within a branch; the main exception to this is competition between substitutes (e.g., steel and aluminum). This is also important, but it is restricted to use-value.

But this is not so. There is also a competition between or among branches (not in use-values) for the splitting-up of the total surplus value produced each year. Various industries have different organic compositions of capital—that is to say, some have much greater expenditures for machinery and raw materials than for labor power, while others may have other combinations (e.g., fifty-fifty). This organic composition will in the last analysis be determined by the current technological structure of production in that particular industrial branch. It is clear that with an equal rate of surplus value in all branches, those branches with lower organic compositions, i.e., with relatively more variable capital, will produce more surplus value—alias profit—in relation to total capital invested and will therefore have a higher rate of profit. These differing rates of profits are equalized through competition among branches; this is done through a redistribution of the total surplus value, so that each branch receives a share proportionate to its total capital regardless of how much surplus value was actually produced within it. To effect this transfer, or rather as the consequence of this redistribution, the "original" commodity values are transformed into prices of production which comprehend the cost price plus a share of the surplus value proportionate to its share of the total social capital.

Without this equalization capitalism would collapse because (1) the resultant enormous disruptive disproportions between or among branches would make the use-value foundation of capitalism incapable of reproduction; (2) on the subjective side the psychological impetus essential to the whole operation (both on an individual and class-wide basis) could not be generated. This second point is clearly the rational kernel of "full competitive minimum costs."

Because it fails to understand this mechanism, bourgeois economics has nothing to say about the competition between branches which sets the average rate of profit.

What about competition within a branch? Here a market value is established which is the average value of the commodities produced in this branch. This will of course depend on the specific weight of the various producers: if the most efficient producers can supply most of the total demand, then the market value will gravitate toward the value of the commodities produced under those conditions. All producers will have to sell at this "price." But as long as there are less efficient producers, there will always be a gap between the individual value of the producers who are most productive and the average or market value (simply because the supply furnished by the less productive producers will raise the average); this means that there will always be an extra profit for those producers who increase their productivity before the others do. This extra profit is only temporary—it lasts as long as the other producers remain behind in "rationalizing" their productive organizations. This also means that within a branch there is no equalization of the rates of profit, for the capitalists belonging to the most productive group will always "beat out" the smaller, less productive capitals.

Here we also see the interaction between inter- and intrabranch competition. The question arises by how much the temporarily leading capitalist should cut his price. This means that the individual value of his commodities is now lower than the previous average (and lower than the previous low), and that he would "like" to continue selling his commodities at that old average, since this would bring about the largest profit per commodity unit. Of course he will have to lower the price at least a bit so that he can attract more buyers; how much will depend on how much of the total demand he can satisfy and on whether the total demand will increase as a result of the drop in price. The latter of course depends on total solvent demand and in particular, if we are dealing with a mass-production consumer-commodity industry, on wages. Now this limitation of solvent demand expresses itself in the limitation of demand for different commodities of various branches. To our individual capitalist this appears as the competition with other branches. Thus this interbranch competition affects the intrabranch competition by forcing the capitalists of that branch to adapt themselves to the new, most productive arrangement.

This latter mechanism has a specific cyclical appearance. During the upswing, demand always appears unlimited (or, as S describes the surface appearance: "an air of optimism begins to pervade the business community"—[260]), so that the more productive capitalists are not forced—in this short run—to lower their prices to the average social value. But once Department I has overproduced in terms of capital's ability to self-expand, a severe shake-up takes place via bankruptcies, mergers, acquisitions (in short, centralization of capital), which forces the industry to adapt itself to the most productive conditions. Those capitals that try to buck the trend will be forced out by the more productive capitals. In the end a new round will begin with even larger capitals which can produce even more productively.

Now the process of increasing productivity cannot be overlooked by bourgeois economists. Thus when S gets around to mentioning the situation we have just outlined, he admits that $P = MC$ has lost its validity and that we will have to deal with the imperfect competition in some other way.

Nevertheless, S's presentation of the historical insight of bourgeois science leaves something to be desired as far as truth is concerned. S notes that "economic textbooks of years ago" used to adduce the case of long-run industry-wide decreasing costs. This is followed by the word "actually," indicating that this approach is incompatible with perfect competition. Later he states that with external economies, all firms could expand together without rupturing perfect competition, but that this does not refute the destruction of such competition by "internally" decreasing costs (473).

Whose books is he talking about? How did the truth finally prevail among value-free scientists? As usual, S prefers to represent the neoclassical synthesis as timeless.

P. Sraffa provides some interesting material on this subject. He points out that originally Marshall derived the law of increasing productivity directly from the division of labor within a factory which in turn depended on the size of the factory. This Marshall propounded in *Economics of Industry*, first published in 1879. But when he noticed that all this was incompatible with free competition, Marshall abandoned this tack in his *Principles* in favor of external economies. This radical change passed almost unobserved, while the theory of value based on the "fundamental symmetry" of the forces of supply and demand remained unchanged; thus the foundation was substituted without causing any shock in the superstructure. Sraffa opines that Marshall's cleverness consisted in concealing this transformation. Marshall tried to deemphasize the novelty; in fact, he tried to pass it off as something commonplace, and he succeeded in having it accepted as a compromise between the necessity of a theory of competition, with which decreasing individual costs are incompatible, and the necessity of not departing too far from reality which was hardly a model of perfect competition. That external economies peculiar to an industry, which rendered possible the desired conciliation between scientific abstraction and reality, were a purely hypothetical and unreal construction was neglected.[15a]

Bourgeois explanations of competition-monopoly suffer from their insistence on the primacy of the market: they do not see that the sphere of circulation is merely the mediator of compelling forces which have their origin in the sphere of production. Competition is not an explanation but merely a reflection, a surface expression, of these forces.

But Marx, unlike bourgeois economists, whether contemporary or classical, developed a societal explanation for the transition to monopoly.

EXTERNAL ECONOMIES AND DISECONOMIES

An external economy of diseconomy is defined as an "effect on one or more persons that emanates from the action of a different person or firm" (474). Although this is not entirely clear, it appears that external effects are understood as a universal phenomenon. Whether they exist in socialism also is not clear, but probably they do, inasmuch as S avers that centralized planning must be transformed via decentralization experiments (634).

External effects obviously presuppose the existence of an inside and an outside. Inside and outside of what? Well, that we are really never told, since bourgeois economics cannot understand the dialectic of a commodity-producing society. Actually this question is not as simple-minded as it may seem, for bourgeois economics insists on centering the "what" on the firm, whereby the workers of the firm become part of the firm. Thus external effects are seen mainly as capitalists hurting or harming one another or as "consumers," or as "social overhead capital" rechanneled through the state. However, progress in capitalism very often takes place on the backs of the working class. What about the "harm" caused by productive activities *within* a firm? Is this an external "diseconomy" or is it "within the family"?

This is a very significant phenomenon known as social costs. But S, "coldly objective scientist" that he is, brushes this matter off as one which "can shift firm cost curves" and thereby "alter supply curves" (476), but which after all is one of those "evils" which "can be ameliorated by appropriate policies, within the framework of the mixed economy" (7th ed., p. 618).

Let us return to the workers who have suffered from external (or is it internal?) diseconomies as a result of activities within a firm. Now we know that as far as the constant capital is concerned, the capitalist recoups its gradual deterioration in the form of depreciation charges. Say that chemical vapors in a plant corroded some machines, an everyday occurrence in such factories; or that within a certain cycle machines will be used more intensively than is recommended. Given such conditions, these factors will be reflected in the depreciation figures.

But what about the worker? If he corrodes or is overworked, will he also have a compensatory depreciation fund? In Marx's theoretical "model" the answer is "yes." This may surprise those who think of Marx as a mindless supporter of the proletariat; however, Marx operates on the assumption that a worker's wage is equal to the value of his labor power. This means that if the production process in intensified, the worker would receive a higher wage because he would need more food, more relaxation, etc., to restore his labor power.

In practice, of course, things just don't work that way. In fact, depressing the price of labor power (the wage) below its value constitutes a source of enormous additional surplus value. And although this source of supplementary exploitation is not needed by Marx to "prove his case against capitalism," it is his concern with such phenomena that sets Marx against "pure" economists like S.

"Optimality Property" of P = MC

Let us now look at the "optimality" property of P = MC. One of the startling aspects of this discussion in S (460) is its naked apologetic intention: Isn't capitalism wonderful! But even when we deviate from P = MC, we have institutional stabilizers. Such an optimistic outlook was not always shared by bourgeois economists. Thus J. M. Clark expressed the fear that "unless private business can transcend its purely private character and absorb sufficient social accounting to keep these wastes within bounds, the result will be the discrediting of the system of private enterprise and a transition to some other system."[16]

Not so S. He is convinced that under perfect competition

where P = MC we have a Pareto optimum, that is a situation in which " 'you can't make any one man better off without hurting some other man' " (632). In other words, it is a situation in which "a planner could not come along with a slide rule and find a solution, different from the laissez faire one, which could improve the welfare of everyone" (ibid.). But as Dobb points out, the Pareto optimum does not provide any criterion of choice within the area in which it is possible for one person to gain more than another loses: "It merely expresses how the utility of any one individual can be improved on the assumption that the utilities of all other individuals in the community are held constant at some arbitrary levels."[17]

Something along these lines is admitted by S himself when he states that the existing distribution of income and property are the result of "past history" having no optimal property without a value system (640): "Only if abilities and *dollar-wealth votes were originally distributed in 'an ethically optimal' manner*—and kept so distributed by nondistorting, nonmarket interventions—could even perfectly competitive pricing be counted on (a) to produce an efficient configuration of production out on society's production-possibility frontier (and not inside it) . . ." (632). Now S, as one of the "defenders of the capitalist system," believes that deviations from optimum income, etc., distribution can be corrected by the state (640). Yet it is clear that no capitalist state has ever significantly interfered with the distribution of the means of production, for as S points out, this would lead to "our capitalist system's having to incur some costs (like ceasing to be capitalist). Since the distribution of "dollar votes" depends on the distribution of the means of production, maintaining the "original" distribution of the former would entail constant "nondistorting, nonmarket interventions" excluding the accumulation and centralization of capital—in other words, excluding the very system we all know and love so well.

Since, as S so generously admits, "laissez-faire perfect competition *could* lead to starving cripples; to malnourished children who grow up to produce malnourished children . . . for generations or forever" (632), he has not proved

> that the common welfare is in some sense necessarily served in the working of a competitive capitalism. . . . Of course, if persons received by way of income exactly the value, whatever that might mean, of services rendered, all would (Bastiat-like) indeed be harmony. Mathematical elaboration serves merely to disguise the irrelevance of the argumentation once this critical assumption has been made.[18]

The production-possibility frontier and its alleged optimality under perfect competition provides a fine example of the inability of bourgeois economics to understand the socio-historical nature of what they are describing. As Schumpeter noted, such theories involve "the creation of an entirely imaginary golden age of perfect competition that somehow metamorphosed itself into the monopolistic age."[19] Or as Joan Robinson put it, since there is such great income inequality under free competition, "Our world of monopolists therefore has not after all such a very high standard with which to compete."[20]

Bourgeois economists concede that the alleged optimality properties of competition are being chipped away, yet since they do not present the rise of monopoly capitalism as any sort of historically necessary process, but merely as the result of a conglomeration of technological and psychological factors, they can still offer the baffled reader "hope for limiting monopoly" (520).

Thus on the one hand bourgeois economists do not understand that monopoly is an expression of the constantly growing socialization of production, socialization of labor. In this sense monopoly is by no means something "external" to so-called competitive capitalism. On the contrary, it is an example of dialectical sublation: capitalism is negated, preserved, and raised to a higher level. Monopoly takes its roots in the most advanced sectors of capitalist industry. At the same time it further develops the (of course capitalistically antagonistic) socialization of production by uniting larger and larger capitals, producing different commodities on an ever-increasing scale with the exploitation of ever-larger concentrations of workers. On the other hand, to the extent that bourgeois economists do see the increasing socialization of production, they identify it wholly with the capitalist *form* of that socialization. In a socialist society there can be a complete monopoly over production without the problem of how to share the increased fruits of productivity improvements.

Blindness to changes in social-historical forms of relations of production permeates S: "If entry is really free, not only has perfect competition the nice property of ensuring that *each firm* ends up on an efficient curve and at the minimum point on it, but in addition the Invisible Hand ensures that the industry gets its Q from the proper number of firms as some are squeezed out or attracted in" (472). But as S himself admits in the footnote to this assertion, if there are diminishing costs, then, as Bain notes: "any industry can be highly concentrated consistent with efficiency."[21]

But we did not need S's curves to know where capitalism was leading. And if such mathematical "precision" adds nothing new to Marx's theory of capital accumulation and concentration, it does have optimal obfuscatory property: namely, it looks upon monopolization as a process that can be rolled back in order to synthesize the best of it and competition. This obfuscation has two aspects: first, it is theoretically false, inasmuch as it looks only at the "untoward" class consequences of the capitalist form of socialization of production, whereby it suprahistorically attributes "nonoptimality" properties to the content of that socialization per se; secondly, on a practical policy level it is demagogic, because it makes the reader believe that "our neutral state" can halt the process. Yet insofar as this process is immanent to capitalism, a bourgeois state would no more try to stop it than abdicate.

Chapter 17: Monopoly Theory (S's Chapters 25 and 26)

INTRODUCTION

Although "orthodox" monopoly theory in the past half-century has come to realize that the concepts of monopoly and competition cannot be treated as mutually exclusive opposites,[1] market or circulation-sphere approach still prevents it from taking account of the processes of socialization of production that underlie modern monopoly. We may exemplify this by using Chamberlin's notion of "product differentiation," to which S attaches central significance (485 ff.). To the extent this phenomenon touches on the question of monopoly at all, it hardly sees it as a cause but rather as a product of competition. Generally speaking, monopolistic structures are created by the processes of capital accumulation and centralization as mediated by the sphere of competition.

S's own hodgepodge classification (489) is but a further application of the circulation-sphere approach whose only virtue is the pedantically accurate, but socially meaningless restriction of the word "monopoly" to 100 percent market control. For even in the everyday language of business journals and newspapers, "monopolies" have come to assume the meaning accorded them in traditional Marxist literature—namely, the relatively few large capitals whose magnitude of accumulation and centralization have enabled them to gain preeminence in practically all branches of production on the basis of their above-average productivities, high organic capital compositions, integrated production facilities, control over sources of raw materials, etc. It is therefore hardly surprising that in these chapters S devotes no attention to the aggregate "concentration" of capital in present-day capitalist countries. In this sense, monopoly theory remains limited to the study of the individual firm or commodity in isolation from the economic processes as a whole.

MARGINAL REVENUE, THE RATE OF PROFIT, AND MONOPOLY PROFITS

We have cited evidence to the effect that entrepreneurial decision-making fails to utilize marginalist principles. The same holds true for marginal revenue. Thus J. Bain for example states that sellers "do not expressly balance the marginal increments of cost against the marginal increments of sales revenue for each possible extension of output . . . in order to determine precisely that price-output combination . . . which will yield the largest profit.[2] Another study indicated that many firms operate on the basis of a percentage profit mark-up to their costs. At U.S. Steel, for instance, standard cost is an average weighted by the volumes at respective mills.[3]

S concedes that this is so: "This theory therefore seems realistic. But it is not very informative. It stops tantalizingly short of telling us *why* the average markup is 40 per cent in one industry and 5 per cent in another . . ." (508). Nevertheless, such an account is compatible with the marginal analysis "so long as the percentage markup is subject to the pressures implicit in *MC* and *MR* analysis" (508). The first edition, instead of this eclectic optimism, had this rather modest follow-up: "There seems to be nothing to do about this unsatisfactory situation but try to specify a number of different competitive and monopolistic patterns . . ." (p. 511).

Let us see whether Marx's theory also "stops tantalizingly short" of the truth. In it, production prices are determined as follows: The first component is the cost of production. This includes only the wear and tear of the fixed capital plus the circulating capital times the number of turnovers per year (in bourgeois terms: total yearly sales turnover minus profit). The second component is the total advanced capital times the average rate of profit for the whole social capital. The advanced capital includes all the fixed capital (not just the amount worn and torn), but only the circulating capital advanced (not the total turnover thereof). It is therefore no mystery why the rates of profit as calculated on the costs of production ("mark-ups") are not equal.

Using his total capital advanced and the average rate of profit as a point of departure, the capitalist will calculate the "expected" mass of average profit. The next step in entrepreneurial reckoning will be the determination of the relation between this mass of average profit and the yearly costs of production—i.e., the rate of profit on the costs of production. The third stage is the determination of the price of production for each of the commodities produced by the company. This means that to the costs of production of each commodity is added the "expected" mass of profit in accordance with the general rate of profit on the company's costs of production.

What is particularly important here is that the method of calculating the profit in terms of percentage of the costs of production (or ex post facto in terms of the sum of sales) is a secondary form derivative of the calculation of the profit rate in terms of the advanced capital.

The fact that the rate of profit falls tendentially with the enlarging of the mass of profit has led to two false theories. On the one hand it is said that only the greatest mass of profit is the regulator of production; on the other, that diminishing returns is a universal law of production. Both these theories absolutize certain tendencies operating within narrow limits.

Now certain modifications take place once concentration has reached a given level ("monopoly capitalism"). In the previous chapter mention was made of extra profits obtained for temporary periods within a branch of production;

these were the result of a temporary achievement of higher productivity by certain capitalists which allowed them to sell above the individual value of their commodities but below their social value. With the formation of a few very large capitals within a branch this process takes on a slightly different form. For now certain capitals will assume a monopoly over the most modern forms of technology, the cheapest and most efficient raw materials, and the supply of qualified workers. (This development generates important consequences for the relationship between labor and capital inasmuch as the high and increasing organic composition of capital demands high capacity-utilization rates to make the use of this capital stock profitable. The "fixed costs" must be distributed over as many units of output as possible for unit costs to decline and thus the leeway for extra profits—the rationale for the investment in the first place—increases.) This means that these firms strive to avoid strikes and other potential threats to the continuity of production—at least during upswing and boom phases of the cycle. Because of their huge mass of profits they are in a position to pay above-average wages, which in part are to buy the "loyalty" of the workers. In this connection great pressure is often exerted on labor unions to take care of "discipline" by preventing "wildcat strikes," counter absenteeism, support "productivity" programs.

Several factors counteract this tendency toward consolidation of temporary intrabranch extra profits. First of all, competition among the largest capitals of each branch remains and intensifies. And the other type of extra profit—interbranch—acts as a second constraint on such monopolization, for this depends on raising the rate of profit of the entire branch over the average for the total social capital. If this is arranged on the basis of artificially created shortages in order to raise the price, it would conflict with the methods for raising intrabranch profits. Also, the extent to which such branch monopolies can be made quasi permanent depends on the possibilities for the flow of capital into them. On the one hand the increasing minimum capital necessary to start, the increasing specific weight of the fixed capital, and the active opposition of the entrenched monopolies all tend to preserve the positions of the "ins." On the other hand, the enormous amounts of accumulated profits which can be channeled through the credit system would tend to aid the flow of capital.

As Marx pointed out, monopoly profits are produced on the basis of the redistribution of total surplus value from other capitalists. This means that the capitalists on the deficit end of the redistribution will be making less than the average rate of profit. This can lead to mass bankruptcies and/or to a sort of client status of some smaller producers vis-à-vis the monopolists. These smaller producers then become subcontractors if they are not sucked up entirely.

Empirically this process finds expression in the ubiquitous phenomenon of the declining share of "proprietors" and the rising share of wage and salary workers in the total labor force. One of the prime functions of antitrust legislation is to modify this tendency so that the process of proletarization is not too abrupt and massive, for this could give rise to undesirable political movements.

In the light of the above analysis S's reasoning appears primitive: "Why do new firms enter the industry in the face of the fact that most existing firms are incurring losses? Apparently, partly out of ignorance and partly out of misplaced hope" (517).

Let us try to summarize the results of the above discussion concerning the relation between monopoly and competition in a different form. Our remarks on the relative consolidation of temporary extra profits do not imply that the essence of capitalism has changed; for extra profits were also present in earlier periods, but they merely shifted more frequently among a larger number of competing top capitals. Even under monopoly conditions individual capitals are now and then toppled; and this holds true also for extra profits derived from intra- and interbranch competition. This is how one author summarized the results of a study of the hundred largest industrial corporations in the U.S. from 1909 to 1960:

> Continued economic dominance is not accomplished through any size-generated immunity to market pressure, but rather by ability to respond to that pressure, to develop with developing

industries and products, to cross product lines where advantageous, and to drop activities where continued investment would fail to provide the basis for sound corporate growth. . . . Perhaps more than any factor, the disparity of economic growth among different industrial sectors has introduced instability among the ranks of the 100 largest.[4]

We must tread carefully here, for S will use such findings for his usual apologetics: "And just as a hotel may be always full—but with different people—so do we find the list of biggest corporations to be a changing one, but at a very slow rate" (112). What S would like to prove of course is that there is no tight-knit clique running the country. Also it would probably aid his thesis that the real "evil" of monopoly is that P is greater than MC, and not that profits are abnormally high, for it would seem to prove that such profits are not concentrated in one hand.

The simplest answer would be that all this is irrelevant—we are interested in the exploitative power of a class, which grows in the aggregate regardless of any shifts within that class. Also we might respond that although the names of the corporations and their commodities may change through the years, the same cliques remain in charge. Furthermore, we could challenge the thesis that "the most efficient engineering knowledge and economic combination of land, labor and capital are brought about by ruthless Darwinian competition" (7th ed., p. 91). The "flows" of labor and capital in the capitalist countries, oriented as they are toward profit, are highly disruptive; since they are not planned, they are indeed "ruthless"—particularly toward the working and unemployed population. The existence of Appalachias throughout the advanced capitalist world makes it appear somewhat doubtful whether "the profit motive is a good motive."

To document the shifts in capital structure we reproduce the following chart:

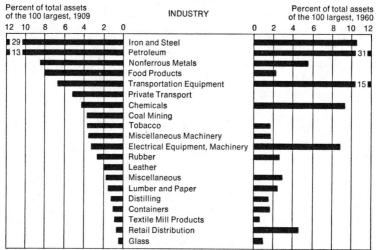

Assets of the 100 Largest Industrial Firms, by Industry, 1909 and 1960[a]

Source: Tables 7-2 through 7-7.
[a]Total assets, 1909, $8.7 billion; total assets, 1960, $125.5 billion.

Thus, for example, in 1909 the percentage of total assets among the largest hundred corporations broke down as follows per industry:
Iron and steel—29 percent; petroleum—13 percent; nonferrous metals—8.5 percent; food products—8 percent; transportation equipment—6.5 percent. Thus these five industries accounted for 65 percent of total assets among the hundred largest corporations. In 1960 we find this structure: petroleum—31 percent; transportation equipment—15 percent; iron and steel—10 percent; chemicals—9 percent; electrical equipment, machinery—8.5 percent, a total of 73.5 percent. We see that some branches have strengthened their positions, others have dropped out, etc.

THE "EVILS" OF MONOPOLY AND ANTITRUST LEGISLATION

The marginalist approach must also be seen in connection with S's assertion that price not profit is the real "evil" of monopoly. In order that the students "see this," S takes the example of the state's taxing the monopoly profit away: since the price remains the same, "the state has now become the villainous recipient of monopoly profit and has failed to correct the misallocation of resources" (517). Now there really is something to this. We can understand this perhaps in analogy to absolute ground rent, which would accrue to the state in case of nationalization of the land. The point is of course what the state does with the rent. It is not to be denied that the misallocation of resources under monopoly is perhaps somewhat different from the misallocation under competitive capitalism in the sense that the gap between actual and potential production is widened. The problem is that S sees this as a technological problem not connected with the capitalist mode of production.

In any event, a capitalist state cannot do anything to alleviate the problem, because to the extent to which it succeeded in easing entry into industries, etc. (520 f.), it would only once again set into motion the same forces of concentration and centralization that brought about monopolies in the first place.

And when S is not confusing technology with capitalism, then he blames the "ills" of capitalism on the psychology of consumers. Thus "if consumers were willing to sacrifice the differentiation of product," we could have fewer firms and lower prices. (Why this is so is not clear; the case at hand is the waste deriving from free entry with many differentiated sellers; if this were then supplanted by concentration of capital within a branch with a so-called standardized commodity, then we would have the "evils" associated with "oligopoly.") "But laissez faire has no way of deciding how much extra people ought to pay in return for the extra variety of products they enjoy" (516). Not only can laissez faire not tell us what "the net balance of advantage over disadvantage" is with respect to advertising, packaging, etc., "a priori reasoning cannot tell us; even study of the facts cannot lead to a conclusive answer independently of ethical value judgments" (515).

The consumer is after all king; and in the last analysis the value-free scientist must take his cue from him. In this sense it is only consistent for S to aver that "consumers should be made to pay for the smoke damage that their purchases make inevitable" (475). Yet one wonders then what the purpose of this book is, since its author emphasizes (7th ed., p. vii) that the "highest praise" of all would be for the student to keep it in his or her pocket when entering the polling booth. If science breaks down every time it comes to making a political decision, how on earth is this book going to help the "citizen"?

Section B of Chapter 26, "Modern Antitrust Problems," is so clearly apologetic, so devoid of any theoretical foundation, that all one can do is point out some of the grosser distortions.

While admitting the "evil" of excess capacity ("the desire of corporations to earn a fair return on their past investments can at times be at variance with the well-being of the consumer" [519]), S directs the blame at a nonexistent "society": "Having made the mistake of building the plants, society ought not to add the further error of failing to use them to best advantage" (ibid.). First of all, this is a deceptive and devious use of the word "mistake"; commonly understood it implies corrigibility. Yet this is precisely the reverse of what is happening in capitalism: the overproduction of commodities in the sense of supplying them in value terms exceeding the purchasing power of the consumers, and the cyclical overproduction of capital is immanent in capitalism. It is not a matter of hiring more and better-trained economists in order to avoid the disasters caused by trial-and-error methods of uneducated entrepreneurs.

Secondly, no conscious or self-conscious agent "society" built these plants. They were built under the control of individual capitals. The only thing that "society" may do, in the guise of the capitalist state, is to help these capitalists shift the losses "classically" inherent in overproduction crises back on to the workers—whether as sellers of the commodity labor power or as producers of the commodity labor power (i.e., as consumers) is irrelevant from this viewpoint.

As far as "dynamic research and monopoly" are concerned (520), this allegedly goes to prove that "all is not evil in any field." This is a perfect example of the bourgeois inability to understand the contradictory nature of "progress" in class societies. Bourgeois economists, instead of searching for the real historical process, explain the specifically capitalist form of increasing productivity as some sort of technological "evil." After debating the pros and cons of the matter, such as that research is used for improving the market rather than the technology, and that despite the enormous funds a large share of new inventions do not emanate from the monopolies, S delivers himself of the following warning: "A sensible student realizes this is indeed no black-and-white matter" (520).

In order to convince the reader "what government can do about monopoly" (521), S presents "in detail" a one-page fictitious study of public-utility regulation showing mainly that "the state steps in to protect the consumer by setting maximum rates."

The real purpose of "regulation" is to keep down the costs of production entering into the individual capitals. Since all large capitals use enormous amounts of certain basic "inputs" such as electricity, coal, transportation, communications, these industries are often "nationalized." They are then run on a nonprofit or deficit basis, charging lower prices than private capitalists would, with the working class as taxpayer in large part picking up the tab.

S's description of the development of antitrust legislation suffers from the ahistoricism rooted in the inability to see the societal basis and expressions of monopoly. In this view monopoly becomes an inevitable evil which men of good will can try to alleviate. In this respect S's historical review is reduced to a tradition of voluntarism, and the essential political aspects are neglected entirely.

Historically the function of the *relatively* strict antitrust laws in the U.S. has been to slow down the process of economic centralization which since the end of the nineteenth century has here proceeded further than in any other capitalist country. This course is motivated by the wish to preserve a class of small capitalists and to absorb potentially anticapitalist movements within this class and among farmers and workers.

This function is readily apparent in the antitrust regulations promulgated under Thurmond Arnold during the New Deal. As one rather realistic account of the period recognizes, "the bulk of Arnold's support came . . . from smaller businessmen or dissatisfied business groups unable to compete successfully with their larger rivals. . . ."[6] At a time, however, when increased productivity was the order of the day, consistent antitrust policy was sheer phantasy.

Yet for political purposes antitrust could be put on show in a demagogic manner: "In a time when Americans distrusted business leadership and blamed big business for the prevailing economic misery, it was only natural that an antitrust approach should have wide political appeal. Concessions had to be made to it. . . ."[7] But behind this façade lurked another reality:

> Action could be taken only in special or exceptional areas, against unusually privileged groups that were particularly hated and particularly vulnerable, in fields where one business group was fighting another, in cases where no one would get hurt, or against practices that violated common standards of decency and fairness. . . . The result of such activities, however, could hardly be more than marginal. . . . The Arnold approach . 9 . could and did break up a number of loose combinations; it could and did disrupt monopolistic arrangements that were no necessary part of modern industrialism. . . . But it made no real effort to rearrange the underlying industrial structure itself. . . ."[8]

In his discussion of U.S. antitrust policy in occupied Germany and Japan, S reveals himself to be the spokesman of the interests of U.S. capital. He presents the U.S. attempts to break up trusts in these countries as a type of good-Samaritan act which the U.S., a "pioneer" in antitrust action had long had in mind—while other countries took "a very lax view of the legality of monopolistic arrangements" (528)—but could only carry out in the wake of World War II. The following contemporary account sheds some light on the real intentions behind U.S. antitrust policy in occupied Japan:

> Admittedly, retention of the combines would enable Japan to restore her industrial potential more quickly, and thus make her a stronger potential ally in the event of another war. The question is, however, whether this fact would be equally true for the longer run and, indeed, whether there are not other reasons of immediate application such as our need to establish our right to world leadership of democratic thought [!!], which outweigh the temporary expediency of Japanese production.[9]

Chapter 18: Marginal Productivity Theory (S's Chapter 27)

> In advanced industrial countries it is more meaningful to think of the machine as the main determinant of output, with the worker attached to it, rather than the other way round. . . .
>
> —E. Domar, "Full Capacity vs. Full Employment Growth: Comment," *Quarterly Journal of Economics*, LXVII, No. 4 (November, 1953), 559

INTRODUCTION

Part 4 of S's textbook is largely devoted to demonstrating that Marx's overly simple labor theory of value, while providing "persuasive terminology for declaiming against the 'exploitation of labor,' . . . constituted bad scientific economics" (7th ed., p. 29). Our earlier, brief encounter with the theory of marginal productivity made us aware of its close relationship to the "vulgar-economic" nineteenth-century theories whose object of interest Marx dubbed the Holy Trinity (Land, Labor, and Capital). We are, therefore, hardly surprised when S states that the key to how the factors of production "get priced in the market place" will be the "economic theory of production" (534). For we have also become acquainted with this approach: the quantity theory of money which claims that commodities enter the market place without prices, and money without value. Adherence to this tenet makes a theory vulnerable to an arbitrary view of price determination as a process analogous to an auction. It will also come as no surprise that S's economic theory of production reveals itself to be a technologically based theory.

"DERIVED DEMAND" AND MARGINAL UTILITY

S starts his discussion with a few words about "derived demand." Now in Chapter 22 he skilfully avoided the matter of utility with respect to means of production; now he must face the music, or rather cacophony. We are told that capitalists buy machines and raw materials not for the good vibes they directly receive but for the "production and revenue" they hope to gain indirectly (557). The "and" here is gratuitous. If the capitalists could gain revenue without producing anything (which is done millions of times daily by bank capitalists, stock market speculators, et al.), they gladly would.

Then we are told that consumer "satisfactions . . . help to determine" how much the final product can be sold for and thus *"ultimately* determine the firm's demand for inputs" (ibid.). As we never grow tired of repeating, satisfactions, utilities, and the like can never determine prices quantitatively; insofar as demand can affect the deviations of market prices from value (or price of production), only solvent demand is relevant here. S takes this into consideration by inserting the phrase "are willing to pay for" between satisfactions and desires.

But then we are merely told that consumer demand can influence only capitalist *demand* for factors of production; the *pricing* of the factors is then in a sort of backhanded way "determined" by their supply and demand.

Obviously bourgeois economics is in a bind. Factor price is determined by nonprice factors; the only possibility for the fitting of such a rule within the "orthodox" theory is marginal utility. This it is supposed to do by explaining the commensurability of marginal products on the demand side and supply on the commodity markets. But because marginal utility itself depends on prices, it cannot serve to explain homogeneity and commensurability in commodity prices. On the micro level, factor incomes are not only physical but also value products; on the macro level, prices appear as the element of commensurability. Supply and demand cannot be the explanation of these prices, for they can explain only changes of prices and costs of production but not the genesis of commensurability in prices.

Since we have just mentioned how marginal utility disqualifies itself as price explainer because it itself rests upon price factors, we should develop this point further (incidentally, the objection is valid for marginal utility in its totality).

Within the labor theory of value labor plays the role of creating value although it itself has no value (that is in Marx's conception of the theory, which purges the classical theory of its "logical" inconsistency of referring to labor as the commodity the worker sells). In a purely subjectivistic theory, utility or vibes or whatever would play this role. But the subjectivists are not consistent; at some point the unmediated jump is made from moneyless, priceless utilitarians to commodity production, thus rendering utility invalid in its role as constant determiner, insofar as it becomes dependent on that which it is supposed to determine—prices.

To return to the question of factor-pricing. Here S in his wonted ahistorical fashion spares the student the tortuous tale of the development of the subjectivistic approach toward the price of the means of production. Let us look at the brilliant solution proffered by Carl Menger, the founder of the Austrian school. He maintains that the value of the means of production is equal to the prospective value of the final products plus a "margin for the value of the capital use and the entrepreneurial activity."[1]

This "solution" solves nothing. It merely confirms the existence of the phenomena of interest and profit in the capitalist mode of production. Moreover, it merely repeats the century-old mistake of Malthus criticized by Marx: namely, Menger like Malthus absorbs profit into the definition of value, so that the value of the commodity and the self-expansion of value of capital become confused and identified. What we then get is the value of a commodity equaling its value plus an excess over its value. This happily puts to rest the notion of the exploitation of labor in the exchange between capital and the commodity labor power and leads us to the familiar profit-upon-alienation theory (i.e., profit becomes a mark-up).

The factor-demand theory corresponds to a very undeveloped stage of capitalism, which in any case lost its validity (if it ever had any) at least two hundred years ago. As Menger puts it, only when our need for a final product cannot be met does a mediate need arise for means of production to produce this good.[2]

But as we have had occasion to point out before, that although in developed capitalism the commodities in Department II must ultimately be sold to the consumers, production in Department I maintains an independent existence in the phases of the cycle leading to crisis. With the ever-increasing organic composition of capital, the notion of Department I as being merely a derived demand for Department II becomes ever more unrealistic.

In general, then, we can say that marginal utility as applied to the means of production becomes self-contradictory. The "utility" of a production factor lies solely in its contribution to surplus value; marginal utility theory derives this utility "at the margin" of the finished commodities, although these can be of no utility to the capitalist producing them. At best one can say that if the marginal utility of the finished product is a price that includes costs, interest, and profit, then the utility imputation implies that the productive marginal utility depends on the contribution to the realizable value inclusive of surplus value.[3]

One last point before we leave this topic. S informs us that "effort involved in making coats . . . is of no interest to society for its own sake; we pay men . . . to sew because of the satisfaction to be gained from the finished product" (558). This may well be true of capitalist society: Production itself is not oriented at the self-expression of the immediate producers. But we must keep in mind that S claims to be dealing with the problems of "every economic society," with "technological facts." So without getting involved in moralizing, we might just note the hidden assumptions S builds into his "technological" models, a standard approach for bourgeois economists.

Far from being a precise statement about any economic system, S's remarks do not even apply to capitalism insofar as "society" as such has no interests. In fact, the only social formations for which the assertion would hold would be a slave or feudal society in which production is directed at satisfying the needs of the masters while the immediate producers do not work for the fun of it.

THE "TECHNOLOGY" OF PRODUCTIVE FACTORS

The next section introduces us to the technology of factor demand. Here we are told that since it is technologically difficult to dig building foundation without a shovel, an "obvious consequence is this: The amount of labor demanded will depend on its wage rate, but the labor demanded will depend also upon the price of machines" (534). How the transition from hands and shovels to wages and prices is to be effected remains S's secret. But once we are there, he cannot refrain from adding this gem: "By raising miners' wages, John L. Lewis created good business for power tools" (*ibid.*). The implication of course is that *technology* places wage workers in this dilemma: Either be happy with your lousy wages or we'll replace you with a nonunionized machine!

Now we get to the tricky matter of how to separate the physical products of the various factors given their interdependence. This is done allegedly "by the processes of supply and demand, operating in perfectly or imperfectly competitive markets and modified by government laws" (535). As we shall see, supply and demand play only a subordinate role in the general formulation of the solution, while in chapters 28-30—devoted to particular solutions of land, labor, and capital—marginal productivity, which in the general formulation is supposed to play the determining role, disappears, to be replaced by a meaningless supply-and-demand theory.

Although we will go into this greater detail in Chapter

21, let us stop here to discuss the notion of capital productivity. S does not bother to define it at this point, although this does not stop him from measuring it. In Chapter 30 he states that the productivity of capital goods is a "technological fact" (609). What is this productivity?—"that annual percentage yield which you could earn by tying up your money in it. What is the same time . . . net productivity is that market rate of interest at which it would just pay to undertake" the investment (599). Thus, what does S mean when he says that the "average rate of improvement" of capital productivity is one or two percent a year? That the interest rate rises annually by this amount? Hardly. (We will return to this in Chapter 27, but we merely want to point out here that S is mystifying his readers by withholding the definitions themselves from them.

Before he picks up the microscope again S explains why the "return per unit of capital" (Is this physical revenue? Rate of profit? Interest rate?—we are not told) has not diminished as a result of the reduced labor it has to work with. The answer: technology, the "offsetting" factor. In fact, "Technical improvements by themselves would probably have raised profits on capital had not the diminishing returns to increasing capital per laborer been taking place as an offset" (537).

This is truly a textbook example of S's lack of understanding of the dialectic of the falling rate of profit. The "would have . . . if had not" shows that S does not see that technical improvements and the more rapid growth of constant over variable capital are inseparable: they are two sides of the same process. It is ironic that although S claims technology as the field par excellence of bourgeois economics, it is invariably inserted as a theoretically unmediated deus ex machina.

In other words, it is precisely the accumulated surplus value previously produced by workers which enables them to produce the next round of capital even more productively; and the more productive they are in this sense, the more surplus value can be accumulated and employed by the capitalists *against* (and not "in cooperation" with) them in order to extract even more surplus value the next time round.

> The connection here to the falling rate of profit is close: . . . That the procedures for the production of relative surplus value by and large amount to: on the one hand transforming as much as possible of a given mass of labor into surplus value, on the other hand to employ in relation to the capital advanced as little labor as possible; so that the same reasons which permit raising the degree of exploitation of labor, forbid exploiting with the same aggregate capital as much labor as before.[4]

In other words, the mass of capital is not increasing more quickly than the mass of labor "because of thrift on the part of society" (537)—whatever that is supposed to mean—but because increasing productivity in capitalism is expressed by the ability of a given mass of labor to put in motion ever larger masses of capital.

Now we arrive at the crucial link in the marginal productivity story: marginal products of the factors. This is turned into an adaptation of the diminishing returns of Chapter 2 and dubbed "the law of diminishing marginal-physical-product." Thus we get: "the extra product or output added by one extra unit of that factor, while other factors are being held constant" (537 f.).

It seems appropriate to elaborate on our earlier critique of diminishing returns. First of all, as Lenin emphasized, added increments of labor and capital presuppose changes in the level of technology; in order to increase significantly the amount of capital invested in the land, for example, it is necessary to invent new machines, new systems of farming, etc. In comparatively small measures, added increments can come about without changing techniques; and in this sense the so-called law of diminishing returns would be valid—namely, that unchanged technical conditions allow for very narrow limits (relatively) to increments.[5]

For as we pointed out in Chapter 2, and as S verified for us, this so-called law abstracts from technological change.

This, as we shall soon see, is integral to J. B. Clark's argument.

Even within its own framework the so-called law doesn't do much in the way of explaining. Thus one of its major postulates holds that the increments taper off—that is, not that absolutely less is produced, but rather more is produced but the size of the additions diminishes. Let us look at the conditions under which this is supposed to take place. How are we to arrive at, say, an increased number of workers with the same amount of capital? We could of course assume that two workers rather than one will use the same saw; since only one is necessary, the productivity of each would decline. This is of course an extreme case; but in general, if we, as S & Co. do, attribute maximization drives to the capitalists, it is not clear why any machine would have fewer workers on it than is optimal. Any increase then in the number of workers should lead to a decline in each individual worker's productivity. If the number of workers previously hadn't been optimal, then we must assume that the capitalist wasn't behaving rationally.

J. B. Clark avoids this problem by assuming that the value of the capital goods remains unchanged, but that it changes its shape: "Capital . . . lives, as it were, by transmigration, taking itself out of one set of bodies and putting itself into another, again and again."[6] More specifically, Clark assumes that the given value of the capital goods remains unchanged but that the means of production are replaced by more, cheaper, and less efficient ones, so that the increased number of workers have enough machines, but that they are less efficient.

Under these circumstances it is not at all clear that what we will get would be a series of diminishing increments; in fact, it is very likely that we would get an *absolute* decline in the production of use values. That is, the increasing number of workers is not enough to compensate for the diminishing productivity. In any case, this is a quantitative problem which in the abstract is indeterminate and in no way represents a technological law.

Historically, an increased number of workers without a

concomitant increase of capital is a rarity. This is valid both for the situation of an unchanging organic composition of capital, and even more so for the case of an increasing organic composition, in which the number of workers declines relative to the constant capital, so that an increasing number of workers would be possible only where the physical volume of means of production increased even more rapidly.

In fact, the "law" of diminishing productivity is refuted by all possible variants of the relations between labor and capital: (1) with unchanged technique both factors can increase only simultaneously—labor productivity does not decrease; (2) with a rising level of technology the number of workers decreases relatively—labor productivity rises; (3) "only under the pathological 'variant' of lowering the level of technique can the number of workers grow with an unchanged capital, but even in this case the productivity of labor is not lowered as a result of the growth of the number of workers, but, just the reverse, the number of workers increases . . . as a result of the lowering of the productivity of labor."[7]

Having established the essentially shaky basis of the law of diminishing productivity, we can procede to J. B. Clark's theory, which, according to S, can show "how to allocate two (or more) cooperating factors among the total product they *jointly* produce" (589).

Clark wrote his major works during a critical juncture in the development of U.S. capitalism. His magnum opus appeared in 1899. The years 1898-1902 represent the high point in the monopolization process that began after the Civil War. And it was also the time of the Spanish-American War, the more or less official entry of the U.S. into the imperialist camp.

But let us listen to Clark himself:

> The welfare of the laboring classes depends on whether they get much or little; but their attitude toward other classes—and therefore the stability of the social state—depends chiefly on the question, whether the amount that they get, be it large or small, is what they produce. If they create a small amount of wealth and get the whole of it, they may not seek to re-

volutionize society; but if it were to appear that they produce an ample amount and get only a part of it, many of them would become revolutionists, and all would have the right to do so. . . . If this charge were proved [exploitation—ML], every right-minded man should become a socialist; and his zeal in transforming the industrial system would then express and measure his sense of justice.[8]

Although Clark emphasizes the need to "enter the realm of production," his conception of production in capitalist society is something less than realistic: "Think of society as an isolated being, turning its collective energy to the making of one thing till it has enough of it and then making another . . . we find it doing what a solitary man would do under the influence of the law of diminishing utility."[9] And he expresses his essentially antiproduction standpoint clearly: "The man as a consumer is the owner of the man as a producer."[10]

So despite a veneer of production, Clark gives us the usual Crusoe-type harmonistic interpretations of capitalism.

Excursus on a Left-Wing Bourgeois View of the Factors of Production These remarks should not under any circumstances lead us to conclude that the main difference between capitalism and socialism or communism consists in income distribution.

The bourgeois economist Erich Preiser[10a] writes that the major defect of marginal productivity is its view of income distribution as determined primarily by natural and technical factors and its neglect of the social conditions which first explain the relative magnitude of the incomes flowing to the various social classes.[11]

In Chapter 51 of the third volume of *Capital* Marx speaks of a more critical bourgeois consciousness which admits the historical viability of the forms of distribution but clings firmly to the historically unchanging nature of production. He had in mind John Stuart Mill. Today we might compare Preiser to Clark; for the latter specifically claims to have discovered a "natural law" controlling the distribution of income "of society."[12]

But although Preiser critically offers the notion of private property in the means of production without which the personal agents would receive no income, what he is really saying is that given this private property, the production-factor theory is basically correct. In a socialist society the same factors would be at work, but, since there is no private ownership of the means of production, income would be centrally redistributed. In other words, these distributional free spirits as Marx points out, ban history from production, whereby behind our backs bourgeois relations are assumed as eternal laws of nature of society in abstracto.

The point is that neither in capitalism nor in socialism can one ignore that production determines distribution, and that since production relations change historically, distribution relations do as well. If there were no difference in the production relations between capitalism and socialism, it would be difficult to understand why the distribution relations should be different.

The change in property relations from capitalism to socialism mentioned by Preiser is not enough. Here we get an analogy of sorts with piracy or plunder: capital(ism) continues to reproduce itself, but some bad guys come and take the produce as a tribute (whereby they may act like Robin Hoods).

Regardless: land, labor, and capital continue to produce a specifically identifiable and imputable *value*; the manner of its distribution is another (nonnatural) matter.

Thus reads this theory in its enlightened version. But we know that in capitalism only labor creates value. Here we have the confusion of the simple labor process with a specific societal production process as well as the confusion of the *sources* of production and distribution.

Once labor has been confused with wage labor, the product of labor with wages, and the value created by labor with the value component represented by wages, "the other value components, profit and rent, appear over against wages just as autonomously and must result from sources specifically different from and independent of labor."[13]

Marx admits that the ownership of labor power, capital, and land *causes* the various value components to fall to the share of the owners of these factors and transforms them into revenues for these owners. Is Marx merely saying what Preiser said? No—because Marx calls the existence of revenue as being value-creating a *semblance*. The point of the entire seventh section of the third volume of *Capital* (as well as of the chapters on wages in the first volume) is the mediation of this semblance with the essential production relations of the capitalist mode of production.

Thus Preiser cannot fulfill his promise to supply the social conditions which explain why "an economic subject receives income altogether," because he himself, like Clark, conceives of the autonomization of the means of production over against the worker as a property inherent in the former as objects, as a characteristic immanent in the means of production as such.

In other words, the rational kernel of Preiser's approach is that the class monopolization of the means of production enables the capitalist class to appropriate (to get distributed to itself) the product of the surplus labor. The quantitative extent of surplus labor is increased under the capitalist mode of production; by this we mean that part of exploitation consists not only in the fact that nonworkers function as representatives of general social needs, but also in the fact that the quantitative determination of necessary labor is depressed below what it would be in a socialist society. For example, in a post capitalist society the direct producers would individually consume a larger portion of what they produce—they would eat better, would have better clothes, dwellings, etc.

What Preiser & Co. do not understand is that when Marx says that it is private ownership of the Trinity that causes the various value components to fall to their owners, this is in a sense a tautology, inasmuch as these value components represent production relations which presuppose or imply private ownership. Marx is *not* saying that the value components are there, and that it is merely the private ownership that causes them to fall to different classes. The two are merely two sides of the same expression of the relations of production.

THE MATERIALISTIC BASIS OF CLARK'S THEORY

Let us now turn to a more detailed analysis of how Clark goes about "unscrambling the separate contributions."

We have noted some of the more important developments which took place during Clark's creative years. We must add one more: the new wave of intensification and "rationalization" of the capitalist labor process that began about that time. In the 1880s meat factories introduced assembly-line production; in 1884, the first business-management school opened at Wharton. And also at that time Frederick Winslow Taylor started his experiments to increase labor productivity "scientifically."

Since Clark experienced only the beginnings of this process, his theory is flawed by an essential ambiguity, or rather by two self-contradictory views: the first, or primitive, view, from the standpoint of the calculating entrepreneur whose factory apparatus consists nonuniformly of modern and overaged machines; and the second, or progressive view, which reflects the development of assembly-line production. Since Clark did not foresee the enormous technological development, he arrived at the law of diminishing marginal productivity.

CLARK'S FIRST, OR PRIMITIVE, THEORY

Under the conditions outlined above, Clark's theory of additional workers being hired to tend the same amount of capital in different but less efficient form becomes understandable. Having established the background against which Clark's theory must be seen, let us procede to his search for a case "in advanced society" in which labor gets its entire product. For, "If there are marginal laborers, in the sense in which there are marginal quantities of wheat, cotton, iron, etc., then these final or marginal men are likewise in a strategic position; for their products set the standard of every one's wage."[14] Clark conjectures that there is no point in searching for a "rude state" where men have "not capital enough to complicate the problem of wages."[15] The fact that he has no qualms about speaking of wages in a society in which there is no capital would indicate that he has some difficulty in grasping the essence of capitalism. And in fact the entire marginal-productivity theory is characterized by a confusion of simple commodity producers who after completing production own the result and capitalist wage labor.

Clark believes he has found men who have masters but need share nothing with them:

> There are mills and furnaces so antiquated . . . that their owners get nothing from them; and yet they run, so long as superintendents can earn their salaries and ordinary workers their natural wages. There are machines that have outlived their usefulness to their owners, but still do their work and give the entire product that they help create to the men who operate them. . . . Everywhere, in indefinite variety and extent, are no-rent instruments; and if labor uses them, it gets the entire product of the operation. . . . So long as an *entrepreneur* can keep such an instrument in his service, and gain anything whatever by so doing, he will keep it. When he loses something by its presence, he will abandon it.[16]

Thus in order to find a wage worker who gets the entire product he produces, Clark selects one who works with machines that are already completely amortized. This being so, Clark reasons, no interest need be reckoned for this machine and deducted from the value of the remaining commodities produced with its aid.

Here we must interject that Clark assumes a static situation—that is, one in which there is only interest and no profit. But Clark's concepts of interest and profit are more akin to those of profit and extra profit respectively, the latter being a temporary gain. His confusion on this matter (which is now more or less accepted by all bourgeois economists including S) was probably conditioned by the enormous growth of trusts and fictitious capital in his time.

To return to Clark's worn-out machines: even within the bourgeois framework it ought to be clear that despite the (probably fictitious) lack of fixed capital, the capitalist still has to make expenditures on circulating capital. The bourgeois concept of "working" capital does not include Marx's variable capital (i.e., wages), but it does include raw materials (also finished goods and warehoused goods). Thus "interest" would still have to be made on the circulating capital, for as Paul Douglas states, "working capital of course normally 'produces' value for its owner"[16]—unless Clark wishes to make the absurd assumption that this production process takes place without raw materials.

To summarize Clark's primitive view: he has constructed a superficial parallel to the theory of rent; on the "macro" level additional workers can be employed only on worn-out machines (in the rent theory this would be equivalent to the worst land) or on already fully utilized machinery. This construct leads to the notion of diminishing marginal productivity.

CLARK'S SECOND, OR MORE PROGRESSIVE, THEORY

Later in his book Clark admits that the margin of employment offered by an existing particular stock capital goods is but a fraction of what could be offered by the same amount of capital in a different physical form.[17] As mentioned above, Clark assumes that the new capital will be cheaper and less efficient. On this basis he erects his second, or more progressive, view.

Here he pictures an "isolated community" with a 100 million of capital and a thousand workers. Now he adds a second group of one thousand workers. In order to accommodate them, the capital structure (with the value remaining constant) must be altered; thus each worker now operates with only $50,000 of capital instead of the earlier $100,000. Thus the productivity of *all* the workers diminishes.

Then Clark proceeds to calculate:

> The product that can be attributed to this second increment of labor is, of course, not all that it creates by *the aid of the capital that the earlier division of workers has surrendered to it*; it is only

> what its presence adds to the product previously created. With a thousand workers using the whole capital, the product was four units of value; with two thousand, it is four plus; and the plus quantity, whatever it is, measures the product that is attributable to the second increment of labor only. There is a minus quantity to be taken into account in calculating the product that is attributable to the final unit of labor. If we take, first, all that it creates by the aid of the capital that is surrendered to it, and then deduct what is taken from the product of the earlier workers and their capital by reason of the share of capital that they surrender to the new workers, we shall have the net addition that the new workers make to the product of industry. . . . Two facts are now clear . . . (1) The difference between what the first division of workers created by the use of the whole capital and what they now create is an amount that is solely attributable to the extra capital which they formerly had. (2) The difference between what one increment of labor produced, when it used the whole of the capital, and what two increments are now producing, by the aid of that same amount of capital, is attributable solely to the second increment of labor.[18]

Extremely important changes have obviously taken place in this second view. First, all workers are equally productive because the apparatus has been adapted to the increased labor supply. Secondly, as a result the notion of the marginal product itself disappears: the value of the marginal labor is no longer equal to the marginal product created by it, for the marginal product is equivalent to the product of any unit. The value of the marginal labor equals the difference between the present and the previous product.

In any event, Clark is faced with this dilemma: if the productivity of all workers is not equal, then "interest" must obviously result from exploitation of the nonmarginal workers who receive the wage resulting from the lowest productivity of the marginal workers; if on the other hand the productivity of all workers is equal, then it becomes impossible for Clark to explain the existence of "interest" as a residue.

Although the second view destroys the primitive notion of the indifference zone and the stability of the capital structure, it is self-contradictory; for although it recognizes the technological adaptability of the capital structure, it denies technological progress by insisting upon replacing good equipment with worse. The "law" of diminishing marginal productivity does not flow from this conception, but rather is imposed upon it.

The absurdity of this version can be seen on the "micro" level: if, during the transition to mass production along assembly-line methods (which is the process the second version reflects) the capitalists were to replace their machinery with inferior models, they would be destroyed by their competitors.

THE CONNECTION BETWEEN CLARK AND MODERN PRESENTATIONS

As will be noted S (537-40) sticks to the primitive version Clark developed. This is only natural since Clark's diagrams also applied this version. S admits that rent (or interest) is a residue resulting from the fact that the non-marginal workers do not receive the products they produce. In other words, S here avoids developing a theory of capital productivity. On the other hand, he finds it necessary to exonerate the landowner (or entrepreneur) from the charge of "profiteering" in the usual sense of the word" (whatever that is): "Whether fair or unfair, all men are alike; all landlords are free competitors who can demand or not demand as they like; so it is inevitable that all the workers get paid the MP of the last worker" (540). This boils down to the following: (1) capitalists can "demand" the difference between the products of the least efficient worker and those of all other workers because they have a monopoly on the means of production; (2) if there is a consumer's surplus equivalent to the difference between the price one is willing to pay and that which one actually pays, there is a producer's surplus equal to the difference between what one is willing to pay a worker and what one is willing to force the worker to be willing to produce.

S claims that marginal-productivity determination of

wages flows from the rules of free competition, but as Crosser points out, this notion appears to belong to the feudal era. And contrary to S's assertion that Ricardo would have acknowledged Clark's advance beyond him and seen Clark's scheme as agreeing with his own theory of rent (541), it must be pointed out that classical rent theory took as its point of departure given wages and profits and determined rent as the remainder, whereas marginal productivity can only lead to optimal-factor maximization when factor prices are assumed as given, even though Clark's theory is supposed to explain these prices.

Significantly, in the first edition of his textbook S admitted this latter point; he emphasized that marginal productivity "is not a theory that explains wages, rents, or interest; on the contrary, it simply explains how factors of production are hired by the firm, once their prices are known" (526). Beyond this he asserts that "the problem of distributing social product by identification of factor shares" is a "false" one (528).

One element in Clark's theory of distribution is that of imputation. This theory is supposed to tell us how large the contribution of each factor is. Notice: this is not at all what the first element was supposed to do. Nevertheless Clark is under the delusion that the theory of marginal productivity and that of specific productivity (or imputation) coincide or answer the same question. But this is patently false; for the maximum "demand price" is a determinate magnitude, whereas factor contributions to value production are not. By determining specific productivity as the product of marginal productivity times the number of units of the factor, Clark arrives at the coincidence of the demand price of a given quantity of labor (power) and its absolute productivity. There is no exploitation.

As we see, the Clarkian theory of distribution rests upon two contradictory principles: the theory of marginal productivity implies that labor productivity depends on the relation between labor and capital, and that, therefore, it depends on the quantity of capital it works with; the theory of specific productivity on the other hand assumes that labor productivity is solely dependent on the character (quality) of labor, and is, therefore, the same for different units of labor.

It is not clear why the obviously more apologetic second version has been largely dropped by contemporary bourgeois economists, especially in light of the fact that they are at least as interested in defending capitalism as was Clark.

Chapter 19: The Theory of Ground Rent (S's Chapter 28)

In Chapter 28, S undertakes to "show in detail" how the aggregated demand curve together with the supply curve "determines the distribution of income to owners of the different factors of production" (7th ed., p. 530); the example used to illustrate "these general principles" is land rent. As usual, the underlying methodology is that of one graph being worth a thousand theories.

THE ALLEGED CONSTANT SUPPLY OF LAND

Let us see why the supply and demand curves at their point of intersection determine the equilibrium price. S's reasoning consists in the assertion that if the price rose above this level, demand would decline, since some landowners could not rent their land, they would bid down the price. This derives from the fixed nature of the supply so that "this factor would be willing to work for less if it had to" (568); "under competition there is nothing" the landowners can do since they cannot alter the supply (563).[1]

As Marx observed, it is insipid to assert that the landowner cannot withdraw his land from the market in the same way that a capitalist can withdraw his capital from a particular branch of production; ownership of land gives him the power to do so until the economic situation will allow him a higher rent. Nor can the capitalistic farmers who are the lessees stop them from withdrawing it. For a withdrawal of capital from agriculture would—unless demand dropped—have the effect of pushing the market price of the agricultural commodities above their value, thus permitting rent, while a flow of new capital into agriculture could not have this same effect because it is precisely this competition of the capitalist farmers that allows the landowner to extract an extra profit from the former, forcing them to be satisfied with the average rate of profit.[2]

Historically, this withdrawing of land from use by the immediate producers has served the function of forcing the latter into the wage-labor force (including the ranks of reserve army of the unemployed); having been deprived of the main means of production—the land—these former peasants become free laborers during the decisive phase of "primitive accumulation of capital."[2a]

RENT AS EXTRA PROFIT

At this point S inserts a literary-historical reference to Ricardo, who, it is reported, stated that the price of corn is high not because the price of corn land is high but rather, the price of corn land is high because the price of corn is high (560). In order to evaluate this statement we must first provide an abbreviated explanation of Marx's theory of rent.[2b]

As we have pointed out, agriculture is no different from industry as far as capital is concerned—both are fields for profit-making. The laws of the creation of value and surplus-value are no different. The only difference lies in the historical accident that in agriculture there is a noncapitalist class which intervenes and on the basis of its monopoly over the means of production land can appropriate part of the surplus value.

In agriculture as in industry there is a struggle for extra profits; also, as in industry, there are extra profits stemming from inter- and intrabranch competition. In the case of industrial interbranch competition the surplus value is redistributed not in accordance with how much was produced in each branch but rather according to how much capital was employed in each. This means that from branches in which the organic composition of capital was low—that is, where relatively more variable capital was employed—and where relatively more surplus value was produced, some surplus value was redistributed to those branches in which the organic composition of capital is higher (where relatively more constant capital is used). The mechanism that effects this redistribution is competition in the form of the free flow of capital from one branch to another. This mechanism, the equalization of the rates of profit for the total social capital, presupposes the unhindered flow of capital to those branches where the rate of profit is momentarily higher from those where it is lower.

In the case of monopoly over the ownership of the land this free flow is hindered. Furthermore, as a result of historical development, during most of the capitalist era the organic composition of capital in agriculture has been below average—that is, below that in industry. This means that relatively more surplus value is produced here. But, in the absence of the free flow of capital, instead of this extra profit's being redistributed, it is retained within the sphere of agriculture; however, it is not retained by the capitalist farmer, but rather by the landowner in the form of rent. This rent Marx calls absolute rent. It is a permanent extra profit rooted in the differing organic composition of capital (specifically lower) employed in agriculture; the monopoly over the land allows this extra profit to become permanent.

Although Marx calls this type of rent the one most adequate to landed property[2c] it was not known in Ricardo. Ricardo could not have discovered such a rent because it would have contradicted his understanding of the labor theory of value. He would have contradicted his theory of value had he stated that the same quantity of labor in agriculture created more value than in industry. The point is that value and price of production are not identical, so that after redistribution of the surplus value the two diverge. In any case, Marx showed why absolute rent existed.

So far we have looked at the case of interbranch competition and the permanent extra profit resulting from it in agriculture—absolute rent. Now let us look at intrabranch competition. As we know, in industry the capital which gains a temporary productivity advantage can sell its commodites above the individual value of its commodities but at or below the market (or average) value of the entire supply; it thereby gains the difference as a temporary profit. In order to effect an analogous transition to agricultural conditions, we could imagine an industry in which water power was used instead of some other source; the user of this free source, which has no value because no labor went into its creation, would enjoy an advantage over his competitors; his individual value would be below average and he would therefore make an extra profit; if he had exclusive control over the water, he would have a permanent extra profit; if he did now own it but rented from someone else, he would have to pay the surplus or extra profit to that owner and settle for the average profit for himself.

The same would be true in agriculture. Land which is more fertile or closer to the markets would give a greater advantage to its users; to the extent that the land is owned not by the farmers who use it, they would have to pay this extra profit to the owners. This extra profit then also becomes permanent—instead of being garnered successively by various capitalists, it is siphoned off in the form of differential rent. This was the only type of rent Ricardo recognized.

Now we can understand the Ricardian thesis which S relates. In his *Principles*, Ricardo states: "Corn is not high because a rent is paid, but a rent is paid because corn is high; and it has been justly observed that no reduction would take place in the price of corn although landlords should forego the whole of their rent."[3] As we explained above, Ricardo recognized only differential rent. Denying absolute rent, he asserted that the least fertile or worst land paid no rent; and since the value of the products of agriculture "is regulated by the productiveness of the portion of capital last employed on the land and paying no rent . . . therefore rent is not a component part of the price of commodities."[4]

But this position is valid only for differential rent: whether the landlord pockets it or whether the farmer gets to keep it is irrelevant precisely because differential rent is a form of intrabranch competition: the extra profit is merely divided up differently among various producers and idlers (landowners) in that branch.

But this is not true of absolute rent, which is a form of interbranch competition. The rise of the organic composition of capital or the abolition of the monopolization of the land (nationalization by the bourgeois state), leading to the elimination of absolute rent, would lower the price of production of agricultural commodities and raise the price of production of industrial commodities until the point had been reached at which the redistribution of surplus value had brought about an equalization of the rates of profit. In this sense absolute rent is a cause of the "high price of corn."

In passing it may be remarked that S's use of the term "value of land" is irrational. As has been pointed out, the price of land (which can have no value since it embodies no labor) is in reality the capitalization of the rent; in this sense the price of corn land can rise independently of the value of the commodities produced on it as well as of the rent since the capitalization also depends on the rate of interest; if the latter should fall even with a constant rent, the price of the land—the price of the permanent rent income—would rise. For example, a rent of $100 with the interest rate at 5 percent would mean a land price of $2,000; if the interest rate fell to 4 percent, the price would rise to $2,500—in other words the rent is more expensive to buy.

In a distorted way, S's discussion of implicit costs itself indicates the influence of rent on commodity prices. Marx has outlined this influence as follows:

> Rent—as the price of land—may not directly determine the price of the product, but it determines the mode of production, whether much capital is concentrated on little land or little capital is dispensed on much land, whether this or that type of product, cattle or corn, is produced, the market price of which best meets the price of the rent, for the rent must be paid before the term is over which it contracts for. So that rent may form no deduction from industrial profit, pasture is turned into farm land, farm land into pasture, etc. Therewith the rent determines the market price of the individual product not di-

rectly, but indirectly inasmuch as it so distributes the proportions of the species of products, as supply and demand best bring forth the price for each one, that the market price can pay the rent.[5]

As Smith, and Marx after him, showed, subjective theories of opportunity cost are not needed to understand that the rent on the land for the main subsistence crops directly determines the market price of the other commodities. Thus for instance, if corn is the staple, then rent determines price indirectly; however, the rent on grazing land is not determined by the market price of meat; just the reverse: the market price of meat is determined by the rent paid on corn land. This raises (or can raise) the price of meat above its own price of production and even value, because it must also pay for the rent which the land would bring if it were being used to grow corn.

RENT AS A "SURPLUS"

In light of the discussion on costs and surplus it seems paradoxical that S should state that rent is a surplus (562). Does this mean that bourgeois economics has become more "honest" since Marx's time, that it now recognizes that rent is a part of surplus value?

First of all, S makes his statement in the context of a discussion of Henry George. The introduction to him is rather weird. We are told that as more and more immigrants came to the U.S., "Each acre of land had more and more people to work with" (562). But, as S himself points out, since there was still a frontier, this was not an inevitable result of immigration: all that would necessarily happen is that more acres of land would be farmed. In fact, it was not until after World War I that U.S. agriculture became intensive. S does not care about facts or consistency; thus some pages later, he turns around and says that in America "we find extensive agriculture" because land is plentiful and labor scarce (565). As we know, the amount of land can be made "scarce" by withdrawing some of it from the market, but since S sees landowners as helpless pawns he disregards this; on the other side, it is not clear how labor can be scarce when millions are out of work. This is yet another example of S's refusal to look at the social situation—namely capital as the pivotal social relation and determination of what is "scarce" and what is "abundant"—and his restriction of economics to alleged technobiological relations between man and land.

But to return to Henry George. Next we are told that as a result of the increased number of workers per acre, "in a sense . . . the land became more productive" (562). Which "sense"? Marginal productivity sense, of course, because the factor land has more labor to "work with." But then this would have to be true of machines too; but we know that machines don't improve with use—in fact they wear out. "The earth, on the other hand, treated correctly, improves continually."[6]

Following this we read: "In any case its [the land's] competitive rental value certainly tended to rise" (562). Rent—and, a fortiori, the price of land—has nothing to do with absolute levels of productivity. In fact, it very often is the case that where productivity is lowest—where farm prices are thus highest—rent is lowest, or perhaps even nonexistent; for we must remember that differential rent can be paid only where there is a difference between individual and market value; where the producers with the highest costs—lowest productivity—predominate, they cannot pay such a rent.

In any case, what S is probably trying to say is that when certain people gobbled up all the land, those who still wanted to farm had to pay monopoly prices—probably purely speculative prices bearing no relation to value, that is, theoretically no longer determinable. This finds its expression in the statement that "those who were lucky or farsighted enough to get in on the ground floor and buy land early" made "handsome profits" (562). We will not go into a historical discussion of this, since even cowboy pictures show the violence connected with the primitive accumulation of land in the U.S.; also, we know about the enormous graft involved in the acquisition of the huge tracts of public land by the railroads.

The upshot of all this is that "many people began to wonder why lucky landowners should be permitted to receive these so-called 'unearned land increments' " (562). Henry George fits in here in that he "crystallized" sentiments. We are told that "it is not likely that anyone running on the single-tax ticket will again come so close to being elected mayor of New York City as George did in 1886" (562).

As might be expected, this account does not accord with historical fact. Regardless of George's subjective motives, he played a somewhat reactionary role in the development of the American labor movement. During the 1880s that movement, although containing definite socialist elements, was as backward as U.S. capitalism was undeveloped. Class relations between capital and labor had not yet been consolidated. Theoretically the labor movement was still quite confused when George appeared on the scene with a definite, well-formulated homespun theory. Contrary to S, George's "central tenet" was not that land rent is a surplus, but that with the nationalization of the land, or rather the transfer of all land rent to the state, the problems of capitalism would disappear. It is this latter sentiment—the elimination of the "problems" associated with capitalism—and not merely wondering about lucky landowners' unearned incomes that George "crystallized." And that is why the Central Labor Union supported his mayoral candidacy in 1886. George's function was to divert the attention of the working masses from the real contradictions inherent in capitalism.

Now comes the main point. S says that he agrees with George that pure land rent is a surplus "which can be taxed heavily without distorting production incentives or efficiency" (562). He explains this on the basis of the strictly limited supply of land and the inability of the landowners to do anything to counteract this. Of course, we might say that rent is a surplus in the sense that it is only the ownership of the entire globe by a few people which enables them to appropriate as a tribute part of the surplus labor produced under capitalist conditions, whereby this process is concealed by the fact that the capitalized rent appears as the price of the land—a mere commodity which can be bought and sold for an equivalent like any other "honestly" traded commodity.

But S is not really radical when he says this (especially in light of the nonsocial explanation he provides), since bourgeois economists were calling for nationalization of the land almost 200 years ago. S cannot explain any of this because he does not concern himself with ancient history—namely anything that happened before about 1930. But it is crucial for the understanding of the position of land rent within capitalism to see how land ownership was really a social relation that preceded capitalism, a relation which capitalism inherited and remolded in its own image. The only rationale from the capitalist point of view in retaining land ownership by the aristocracy during the struggle with feudalism was that it was absolutely necessary that the workers—or future proletarians—not be able to remain on the land, possible refuge from the developing capitalist mode of production. Once this process took place, the ownership of the land by a class other than the capitalist became a barrier to capitalist development. One example of this "attitude" on the part of the capitalist class toward land ownership was its alliance with the working class in England to abolish the corn laws so that food would be cheaper (the capitalists' goal of course was to lower the value of labor power). It is thus clear that whereas the capitalist is a necessary agent of the capitalist mode of production, the landowner is superfluous.

It must be remembered that S is not suggesting that rent be abolished; all he says is that it can be taxed away without interfering with efficiency. At the same time he emphasizes that this is not true of profits and interest, which are allegedly not "unnecessary" surpluses; taxing away these incomes would interfere with maximum efficiency. In other words, the income rent in the sense of a revenue accruing to certain people may be done away with (after the fact, through taxation), but it is still needed for pricing efficiency.

Let us examine this proposition. The first part of it, namely that the class of landowners may be abolished, is analogous to nineteenth-century demands along these lines. As far as pricing is concerned, the matter is not quite so clear. The fiction of an absolute rent which is then funneled in toto to the state makes no sense (we must keep in mind that bourgeois economics does not deal with this type of rent). Differential rent would of course remain as long as there are differences in productivity of labor resulting from differences in fertility and as long as the capitalist market value existed.

There would seem to be nothing inconsistent with taking S's reasoning further and saying that the income accruing to entrepreneurs and capitalists could be given to the state while marginal-productivity pricing would remain in effect; this would be state capitalism of a sort, impossible in practice but possible in theory (except that capital is not in fixed supply as is land).

The discussion is significant because it reveals the radical ahistoricity of bourgeois economics. S cannot get himself to say that the "surplus" nature of rent is an expression of land ownership as belonging to a mode of production that antedates capitalism. That one mode of production can become historically superfluous and be replaced by another would set a precedent for capitalism's eventual demise which S categorically rejects.

Chapter 20: Wages (S's Chapter 29)

I. REAL WAGES IN THE UNITED STATES IN THE POSTWAR PERIOD

S is not interested merely in money wages, but also *"in real wages*—in what the wage will buy" (571). As an example, he states that "money wage rates doubled from 1960 to 1973; however, since prices increased about 50 per cent in that period, real wages increased by only one-third" (ibid.). S relies on these figures to refute the Malthus-Marx "iron law of wages"; for he claims this "survey of rising living standards . . . showed how unrealistic for the West is this notion of a bare-minimum, long-run supply curve of labor" (574).

Let us examine these data carefully. Since S has provided no sources, we can only guess that by "money wage rates" he means hourly wages. In point of fact, however, we discover that between 1960 and 1972 (since the book appeared in March of 1973 he could not have used 1973 data) the "average hourly earnings of productio or nonsupervisory workers on private nonagricultural payrolls" rose by 74.6 percent from $2.09 to $3.65.[1] Since the Consumer Price Index rose during this period rose by 41.6 percent, real wages rose by 23.2 percent.[2] And if we look at real weekly wages—in this case measured in so-called constant 1967 dollars—we note that they rose by 19.1 percent from $90.95 to $108.36.[3]

A more precise measurement of real wages must also deduct income taxes and social-security contributions from the "deflated" wages. Using this magnitude ("real spendable earnings"), we calculate that from 1960 to 1972 weekly wages rose by 17.5 percent, from $82.25 to $96.40.[4] From 1947 until the end of 1973, these wages had risen from: $66.73 to $95.08, or a mere 42.5 percent during the period of greatest prosperity in the history of capitalism.[5] And if we look at the period which ushered in "full employment"—namely large-scale intervention in Vietnam—we see that from 1965 through April, 1975, the spendable average weekly earnings of private nonagricultural workers actually declined from $91.32 to $86.70.[6]

SHARE OF WAGES IN NATIONAL INCOME

In light of the great length S goes to in his eagerness to persuade reader that wages constitute a large and growing share of national income, it is necessary to explain that this phenomenon should not be seen as contradicting Marx's notion of secularly increasing exploitation. We will merely enumerate some of the factors that would have to be taken into account if one were to undertake an empirical verification of an increasing rate of surplus value. (1) Not all "wage and salary earners" create surplus value; in fact, such "productive" workers are becoming a dwindling proportion of the total labor force, a fact which is reflected in various theories of the "service economy." Thus, if the share of wages in national income should remain constant while the share of surplus-value-producing workers in the total number of wage workers declines—a common phenomenon—a rise in the rate of surplus value may be presumed. (2) Claims concerning the rise of the share of wages in national income must always be set in relation to the development of the share of wage and salary workers in the entire labor force; for if the number of those persons receiving capital income declines in relation to those receiving wage income, then it is evident that a constant (or even rising) share of wages in national income assumes a different meaning because a larger number of people must share in it. If one takes account of this aspect, then the share of wages in national income actually declined during the 1950s and 1960s in Japan, West Germany, France, and Italy. (3) A part of the salaries of executives, managers, et al., must be deducted from the wage share of national income, since it in fact represents a part of corporate profits. (4) Capital's share is lowered by the continual shifting of profits into depreciation funds.

POPULATION AND WAGES

S's explanation of the (rapidly diminishing) gap in wage levels between the U.S. and Western Europe has a familiar ring to it: "Supply and demand are such in America, compared with Europe, as to lead to a higher real wage here" (572). What is correct in the ensuing discussion is commonplace and has remarkably little to do with marginal productivity. Basically it can be reduced to the fact that productivity and intensity of labor have been higher in the U.S., and that at least partially as a result of the historical situation of a shortage of workers in the U.S. during part of the nineteenth century, the U.S. working class has been able to fight for and retain that historical element in the value of their labor power. This relationship may not be interpreted to mean that a one-to-one correspondence exists between productivity (or intensity) and wages, so that the higher the productivity the higher the wage level. In fact, the relative wage—that is, wages as a share of value added—declines with increasing productivity; in other words, the rate of surplus value increases.

With respect to S's account of labor's support of anti-immigration legislation in the post-World War I period (584), the principal function of mass immigration, according to John R. Commons, was its creation of "America's reserve army of the unemployed."[7] Thus in only six of the twenty-five years prior to World War I did unemployment in manufacturing and transportation fall below 4 percent; however, for eight years it stayed above 10 percent.[8]

Labor's opposition to mass immigration was further due to the fact that foreign workers were often "contracted out" as strikebreakers.[9]

The postwar depression brought the rate of unemployment to 21.2 percent. It is to be questioned whether the capitalist class was not similarly interested in cutting off the flow of potential unemployed once this "socially and politically" dangerous level was reached. Also, immigration police permitted the continued flow of more highly skilled types of workers for which developed capitalism had a need. Once the period of extensive growth had come to a close, the continued flow of industrial serfs from Eastern and Southern Europe had become unnecessary.

This forms the basis of S's "suggestion" of a "theory" of population which would let population grow exactly to the point at which "increasing returns end and decreasing returns begin" (573). The only thing wrong with this "theoretical suggestion" is that it is precisely what every capitalist state has been doing. When a particular national capital is in need of an immediate increase of its work force and cannot provide it by itself it imports workers, and when the need subsides it stems the flow or even deports them.

II. THE WAGE-FORM

S's fundamental theoretical position is revealed in the opening sentences of the chapter: "A man is much more than a commodity. Yet it is true that men do rent out their services for a price. This price is the wage rate . . ." (572). In this connection we may also note that the Clayton Act (1914) decreed that labor is not a commodity. At that time, Samuel Gompers, the head of the AFL, delivered himself of this pronouncement: "Labor power is not a product—it is the ability to produce. The products of labor may be bought and sold without affecting the freedom of the one who produces or owns them—but the labor power of an individual cannot be separated from his living body."[10] This is precisely the sort of unreason that Marx sought to refute. The facts that products may be bought and sold (i.e., are commodities) and the existence of wage laborers (capitalism) are the two fundamental relations that shape all others in bourgeois society. It is impossible for producers to remain "unaffected" by a situation in which, to use S's terminology, what, how and for whom are determined by others. The absence of such "self-determination" at a time when it is materially possible constitutes a negation of freedom.

We have also previously commented on the irrationality of wages as the price of labor. Labor has no price and no value—it creates value. If the commodity-value is determined by the amount of social labor expended in its production, then it is clear that the value of labor would involve us in a tautology.

III. SUPPLY AND DEMAND ON THE LABOR MARKET

We shall here attempt to demonstrate that the superficial phenomena dealt with by supply-and-demand theory are rooted in the underlying processes of capital accumulation. Since Marx is specifically singled out as the chief adversary, we must first analyze S's absurd critique of the function of the reserve army of the unemployed.

MARX, S, AND THE RESERVE ARMY

S's attempt to impute to Marx an iron law of wages can only be explained by his ignorance and the wish to make Marx look ridiculous in the eyes of those who know nothing of the subject. Marx took great pains to refute this theory, and it directly contradicts his own conception of the role and limits of trade unions. In light of this, it is understandable that S has drastically changed the text over the years. Thus in the 7th edition he explained Marx's conception of the reserve army of the unemployed as follows: "In effect, employers were supposed to lead their workers to the factory windows and point to the unemployed workers out at the factory gates, eager to work for less. This, Marx thought, would depress wages to the subsistence level" (7th ed., p. 546). In the 8th edition, he inserted the following parenthetical phrase after "Marx thought": "or is interpreted as having thought." It is of course S who had been thus "interpreting" Marx. But in the 9th edition he outdoes himself in scientific dishonesty by changing the text to read: "or is scientific by naive Marxists to have thought" (574)!!

Even more significant as a recognition of the reserve army is a footnote in which S concedes: "The labor force sometimes tends to grow in recessions: when a husband is thrown out of work, his wife and children may seek jobs. Tending to cancel this [!?] is the fact that women and other workers are, under prosperous conditions, attracted into jobs by plentiful employment conditions. . . . When full employment finally reappeared, new entrants were finally coaxed back only to withdraw again in the 1969-1970 Nixon slowdown. When employment opportunities expanded after 1965 and again after the 1969–1970 stagnation, new entrants were drawn into the labor force in vast numbers" (577 n. 2).[10a]

Marx never stated that the reserve army brings about subsistence-level wages. S is here ascribing to Marx his own views on wage formation which Marx himself made fun of. As with any commodity, the value of labor power is determined by the socially necessary labor-time for its production and reproduction. This includes not only the means to keep the commodity in good repair (or rather the average for its kind), but also those to keep his replacements (wife and children; the same is true for women obviously) in a similar state; it must also include the educational costs of preparing this particular labor power. On the other hand, as Marx emphasizes,

> The scope of the so-called necessary needs, as well as the manner of their satisfaction, is itself a historical product and depends therefore largely on the level of civilization of a country, among other things it also essentially depends on this: under what conditions and therefore with what customs and demands on life the class of free laborers has been formed. In contradistinction to the other commodities therefore the value determination of labor power contains a historical and moral element.[11]

It is important to see this clearly: Marx applies his objective theory of value also to the commodity labor power; this value is independent of supply and demand. As with any commodity, supply and demand can only determine deviations of the price from this value. Capitalism has a built-in mechanism which allows it to expand operations without calling forth a demand for labor commensurate with the absolute increase in capital. S attempts to criticize Marx on the basis of a strawman he has erected. He sets up a graph to see whether a sharp rise in wages will lead to unemployment, which in turn will lead to subsistence wages. As far as the first part is concerned he agrees: "At this high wage, there would indeed be unemployment, as alleged" (574). By whom?! Marx never said that wages determine unemployment; just the reverse. What he said was: "By and large the general movements of the wage are exclusively determined by the expansion and contraction of the industrial reserve army, which corresponds to the periodic change of the industrial cycle."[12] S has done a little projecting here, for it is his side in this game that sees the wage as causal.

SUPPLY AND DEMAND FACTORS

Similar misunderstandings of the nature of wages crop up in S's discussion of the lump-of-labor fallacy. While according this thesis "its due," S objects to its contention that "there is only so much useful remunerative work to be done in any economic system" (576).

S would respond to "technological" unemployment with retraining—it is nothing less than the "optimal" solution, and much superior to restricting production the way those wrong-headed workers suggest.

So-called technological unemployment is not new. It is inherent in a system which revolutionizes methods of production anarchically, in which the organic composition of capital is raised, and above all, in which all workers are crippled by the division of labor. The views of bourgeois economists on this topic have not changed since Marx's time. Marx scorned sycophants who were unable to see any but the capitalist utilization of machinery, for whom the exploitation of the laborer by the machine is identical with the exploitation of the machine by the laborer, and who reproached all those who protested the capitalistic use of machines with holding up progress.

In this connection S's discussion of a shorter work week deserves attention. He finds it especially galling that workers are not willing to take a commensurate wage reduction: "What worker could be against a free present of more leisure" (576)? He finds it even more irksome that such aspects of class struggle do not fit into the neat individualized trade-off schemes he favors (396 n. 12); for such strictly harmonistic views are useless when dealing with an antagonistic society in which one class enjoys less of each (and/or a relatively smaller increase).

S's pro-employer bias is made obvious by his claim that "there is no doubt that drastic shortening of hours would imply lower real wages than a full-employment economy is capable of providing" (576).

There are several ways of refuting this. First, one could take the empirically least likely yet "theoretically possible" case that profits are merely cut. Secondly, one could take the empirically confirmed case of shorter hours being followed by an increase in productivity and/or intensity of labor. This is in fact the classic case of capitalism, in which the shorter day was a necessity if the workers were to survive the next round of speed-ups. S's denial of the possibility of an increased standard of living with a shortened work-day is the sheerest apology. Why is it that as a result of the eight-hour agitation in the 1880s and 1890s wages went up as the number of hours decreased?[13] This line of reasoning is dictated by the "modern" technique of granting money wage increases while taking it back in inflated commodity prices. S concurs with this when he states: "The general average of money wages can rise at the 3 to 3½ per cent annual national average of real productivity increase without leading to rising price indexes or the expropriation of profits" (7th ed., p. 564). This is a clear admission that the rate of surplus value must remain at least unchanged, that it may not be lowered; if the workers try, the capitalists and their compliant state will merely preserve profits through inflation, while compliant economists will devise theories to put the blame for inflation on greedy BIG LABOR.

It is instructive in this regard to look at the treatment accorded this theme in the first edition, at a time when labor apparently was regarded as the underdog, and thus S felt compelled to dwell on the seamier side of capitalism:

> Modern capitalist society seems so imbued with a feeling of guilt over the existing inequality of income that almost everyone believes in the desirability not only of higher wages, but of much higher wages. Consequently, the demands of workers are literally insatiable. An employer cannot buy them off at any price. All he can buy is a little time; but in a few months the workers will be back for more.
> The above remarks are stated as facts without any expression of approval or viewing with alarm. It should be said, however, that there is nothing sacred about the traditional fraction of two-thirds of the national income going to wages and salaries [p. 531].

This passage is complex compared with its parallels in the more recent editions. On the one hand we get a more critical attitude toward the class division of income: it is admitted that a shifting of income from capital to labor (that is, wages rising faster than productivity increases) need not result in inflation (theoretically). The absurd talk of profit expropriations is not there yet; in fact, even the mention of squeezing profits is placed in quotation marks. On the other hand, the old S still shines through in attributing greed to the oppressed.

It is also significant that the talk about the incompatibility of "full employment" and noninflation is directly related to the alleged disappearance of the reserve army. Whether this army has in fact disappeared is irrelevant: what is significant is the *theoretical* concession on the part of the bourgeois economists that its disappearance makes it difficult to keep down wages and/or keep inflation under control.

S's mention of highly paid athletes is as relevant to a discussion of wage theory as the example of rare postage stamps for the discussion of value theory. Such a discussion, of course, helps confuse the reader by asserting that wages are paid to a mixed bag of people, including the rich and the poor. That this is the general course of reasoning can be seen from S's similar theoretical statement denying the foundation of all of capitalism: abstract labor: "There is no single factor of production called labor; there are thousands of quite different kinds of labor" (580). The enormous mobility of U.S. workers, which represents the shunting back and forth of various quantities of human labor among different branches of production, is an especially poignant expression of this "single factor."

We did not need S to tell us what is correct in the discussion about "equalizing differences" in wages. Smith presented that quite clearly two hundred years ago,[14] and Marx considered the differences so obvious (which was not to demean Smith's earlier accomplishment) that he merely mentions them as empirical facts that can be read up on in Smith.

As for the "nonequalizing differentials," called "differences in labor quality," Marx analyzed these under the viewpoint of the difference between qualified and unqualified labor power. This is not just a terminological change; for as we noted above, S has a Malthusian (biological) approach to population insofar as it affects the supply of labor. Thus he speaks of "the irreducible differences in biological and social inheritance" as causing wage differentials to persist "even in the long run" (583).

"Natural attributes of workers have little to do with wage differentials. Most tasks performed by workers require relatively little training; also, experience shows that one person can learn a variety of such skills; and thirdly, the learning and unlearning of such skills is determined—by and large—not by nature or whim but by the direction and scope of capital accumulation. It is the structure of the place of production that determines whether the labor power of an individual worker has any exchange value; for just as with any commodity, if there is no use value for others—in this case, if no capitalists have any "use" for this specific labor power—then the socially necessary labor time which entered into the creation of that labor power, and thus its exchange value, is reduced to zero.

IV. LABOR MARKET "IMPERFECTIONS": LABOR UNIONS AND CAPITALIST COUNTERMEASURES

Instead of being given a description of the struggle between two classes, we are told that: "As far as the economist is concerned, the final outcome is in principle indeterminate—as indeterminate as the haggling between two millionaires over a fine painting" (587). This negates the fact that in a wage system the capitalist remains and must remain the master. That system is so constructed that it can never endanger capitalism.

Marx explains this. If wages continue to mount, they can do so under two conditions: (1) that this rise does not disturb the accumulation of capital; (2) that this rise does disturb accumulation by cutting profits so greatly that the capitalists temporarily throw in the towel. When capital ceases to appropriate the "normal" amount of surplus labor, investment is cut back, thereby exerting increased downward pressure on wages.

But Marx is also careful to insist on the causality: in the first of the two conditions just mentioned it is not the absolute or relative decrease of labor which makes capital superfluous, but rather the increase of capital which makes the exploitable labor power insufficient; and in the second it is not the increase of labor that makes capital insufficient, but the decrease of capital that makes the exploitable labor power (that is, the going price) superfluous.

Marx shows that it is incorrect to view the size of capital and the size of the labor force as independent of each other; he sees the relation between capital, accumulation, and wage rate as the relation between the paid and the unpaid labor of the same working people.

On the basis of this analysis Marx arrived at the conclusion that basically unions can serve a defensive role in resisting the most brutal encroachments of capital on the well-being of the workers. S's discussion of whether unions have raised wages does not make sense unless one understands this underlying situation.

As for antiunion (in the sense of antilabor as antagonist of capital) legislation, the struggle around Taft-Hartley is portrayed in this way: "the electorate became fed up with strikes and rising prices. Labor was no longer considered the underdog; and people felt that the Wagner Act had been one-sided, favoring labor and putting all the penalties on the employer" (143). In fact, however, the Taft-Harley Bill, which was bound up with the anticommunist legislation of the postwar era, was drafted by corporate lobbyists of large corporations.

S's position on this legislative activity is interesting. On the one hand, he knows that it is a "difficult research task" to measure the inequality that unorganized workers talk of when they speak of the need for labor unions (583). On the other hand, he hints that New Deal legislation perhaps went too far, creating reverse excesses (586 n. 4).

Beyond "collective bargaining" S seems to be unaware of all forms of class struggle. Thus he never mentions the movement for shorter hours. Nor does he mention the existence of everyday local plant resistance carried on against speed-ups, etc. What he does deem fit to mention, however, are "more subtle restrictions on the labor supply: explicit union limits on work loads (artificial limits put on number of bricks per day, width of paintbrush, standby orchestras, number of looms attended, and similar 'featherbedding' labor practices) and implicit understandings forcing a slowdown of the working pace" (585).

The key word in this passage is "artificial." This means that every order the bosses pass down concerning activities within the factory is in some sense natural, official, for real—in any case not artificial. S has formulated a Marxist insight here: the capitalist is absolute despot within the factory. Insofar as the workers have rented out their services for the day, they have nothing to say about the productivity attained with the commodity they lent. As long as the commodity is returned in good shape (the "rent" includes depreciation), the owner has no right to interfere.

To the extent that workers have no control over the process of production, it is "natural" (S admits this in the first edition, p. 89) for them to seek "artificial" limits or devices that will destroy their health and their jobs (that is, nullify the use value of their labor power). If it were true that (as in socialist countries) structural changes in production and corresponding changes in the education and training of the workers could be planned and thus the uncertainty, frustration, and outright economic disaster accompanying the capitalist form of such changes for workers could be eliminated, then of course "lump-of-labor" would be a fallacy because in such a society there would be no limit to the amount of useful and "remunerative" work. But as long as workers act on the basis of their experience with promises about "offsetting retraining policies that create adequate job opportunities and new skills" (7th ed. p. 547) they are likely to continue to be suspicious of those who praise capitalism without understanding it.

WAGES AND UNEMPLOYMENT

A crucial part of this chapter is devoted to explaining unemployment—mainly in terms of high wages. The discussion opens with this assertion: "The ability to strike succeeds in exacting wages increases higher than the increases in physical productivity" (7th ed., p. 563). If a "sometimes" were inserted between "strike" and "succeeds" it would not be wrong; but as it stands, it implies that every strike does this, thereby establishing a fallacious connection between strikes and inflation (at least as far as causality is concerned).

Connected with this is the assertion that wages never drop: wage stickiness is an alleged expression of the "imperfect" labor market: "When there is a considerable increase in unemployment—as in sluggish 1970—do wage rates drop as they would in a competitive market? History answers, No" (582). Yet even in the postwar period wages dropped between 1945 and 1947, 1950 and 1951 (in absolute terms the 1945 average was not reattained until 1952), 1956 and 1958, 1965 and 1967, and 1968 and 1969.[15]

S holds no brief for those who deny the miraculous properties of our mixed economy. First he shows us a graph indicating that unemployment was dropping in the 1960s, despite the present length and depth of unemployment. Undaunted, S assures us that if it were not for the unpleasant side effects of inflation, we could use fiscal-monetary tricks to get us back to "full employment." Alas, not even this wish has come true. S would rather revile the critics of the status quo by labeling and libeling their attribution of rising unemployment to intensified structural unemployment as "facile"; we are told that "careful" studies would show that geographic differentials in unemployment are narrowing.

Having polished off all the "facile" objections he can conceive of, S very generously admits in a footnote that "only the intractable situation of high Negro unemployment remains as a puzzle and problem, as also does the problem of getting unemployment down well below 4 per cent . . ." (7th ed., p. 564 n. 11). By early 1975 the problem was to keep the rate for blacks between the ages of sixteen and nineteen below 40 percent.[16]

If everything else fails, S can still offer us an incomes policy. Its main function is to centralize still more the automatic efforts of capitalists to prevent workers from "expropriating profits." Although S distorts the matter by claiming that there is class impartiality here (or at least reports that both sides claim to be disadvantaged without himself offering an opinion), this is hardly the way incomes policies work.

Between 1966 and 1969 net real income of a British median wage worker with three dependents rose from 732 to 748 constant 1959 pounds. The approximately 1 percent annual increase in wages during the incomes policy period

(1965-69) "contrasts with an annual gain in industrial productivity of over 3 per cent." In light of the fact that income tax payments of the average worker rose from 1966 to 1969 by 147 percent, it is no wonder that one study concluded: "Public policy on wage taxation may itself be the most potent of current inflationary forces. It also explains our coincidence of accelerated inflation with spreading recession."[17]

In January, 1972, unemployment in Britain reached one million for the first time since the onset of World War II.[18] Yet S claims that Britain is one of the countries that have sought a policy to hold down wage increases to a rate "compatible with productivity advance and stable price" (7th ed., p. 565). He admits that no "definitive solution" has been devised, but one wonders whether the solution is not to keep wage increases *below* productivity increases (that is, to shift income from labor to capital); this is in fact what happened in West Germany, where the incomes policy provided for linking wage increases and productivity only during "business-cycle peaks," while periods of recession and upswing saw the "scissors" opening very much to the disadvantage of the working class. Thus, Ernest Mandel reports that during the recession of 1967 *nominal* wages (i.e., money wages minus taxes, but not deducting cost of living increases) dropped 3.6 percent while productivity rose from 5 to 11 percent (according to different estimates).

In light of the crumbling house of cards S will doubtless continue to extol the wonders of "manpower training, improved worker mobility, and better placement services" (7th ed., p. 564); these are necessary, former Secretary of Labor Hodgson implored, in a letter to the *Wall Street Journal* of November 26, 1971, in order to "correct imperfections" like "the inefficiency in letting nature take its course in bringing the job hunter and the job together."

Chapter 21: Interest

This chapter will be relatively short since much of the material dealing with interest—particularly the division of profit into entrepreneurial profit and interest—has been analyzed elsewhere. Moreover, S himself admits that he is merely summarizing in "an uncritical way" traditional theories of capital/interest (596).

PROFIT AND INTEREST

If the (nonclassical) bourgeois notion of profit is somehow connected with that which Marx calls extra profit, then interest in some way resembles profit (this is confused because it also refers to the market interest rate of banks). Already in Marx's time it was possible to see from the orientation of vulgar political economy that the main ideological "benefit" of "correlating" capital with interest lay in the eradication of the connection to the *production process*: all we now have is a sum which begets a larger sum. Whether the agent of self-expansion appears as money or as the "thing" (that is, physical object) capital is irrelevant: both ignore social reality and both are adequate automatic fetishes.

We already know the marginal productivity of labor and capital theory in its major theoretical outlines. In that connection it was pointed out that Clark had a weird notion of capitalism inasmuch as he assumed a total break between "capitalists" and "entrepreneurs." But since the entrepreneur is not assumed to own any capital, he must exert a demand for all the capital he employs. But this is obviously incorrect inasmuch as total demand for capital is much smaller than the existing capital. There is then in general a confusion between capital and loan capital.

But it is impossible to explain the demand for capital if one denies that this capital bears profit for the demander. Either the entrepreneur demands means of production as capital, in which case it is impossible to limit "capital productivity" to interest (for then the entrepreneurial profit would disappear and with it the raison d'être of the demand); or he demands means of production as commodities, in which case both the entrepreneurial profit as well as the interest on the capital disappear (for the means of production merely have their value transferred to the new commodities).[1]

FACTORS OF PRODUCTIONS AND REVENUES

The first piece of business in this chapter is "a rather arbitrary division" of the so-called factors. Land and labor are given; capital is produced by the "economic system itself" (596). But then we are told that "capital goods . . . can be rented out in the competitive market just the way acres of land or hours of labor can be rented out" (597). Without belaboring the point, we must point out that labor is an activity which does not belong to the worker but can exist only when combined with objects and instruments of labor; and even if S meant labor power this is also misleading, since a worker does not have the choice between renting out his ability or using it for himself—what should he do with the ability to operate a crane while sitting home. (S cannot possibly answer this by asking what the capitalist should do with the crane at home, because the whole purpose of this discussion presumably is an attempt to pass off the capitalist as someone who has all this "stuff" which he could employ himself but which he for some reason prefers to "rent out."

Then we come to the section on the capitalization of assets, one containing very misleading notions. As Marx explained, the form of interest-bearing capital brings about a situation in which every money revenue of a regular or periodic nature is transformed into interest; if the interest rate is given, one can then "calculate" the capital which *would* bear that sum. Capitalization is necessary to understand the forms and movements of fictitious capital (stocks, bonds, government securities, etc.); Marx also uses it to determine the "price" of land, which is really the price of the ground rent determined on the basis of the interest rate. Although Marx does use the "device" of capitalization, he is careful to emphasize the theoretical foundation and causality. But with S all we get is a formula: plug in! And if you don't believe it, "check our formula"—do the arithmetic. This is what Marx meant by interest as "automatic fetish" totally removed from the real process of self-expansion of value.

Is it then true that "to see how assets get capitalized" we should look at the "simplest case of a piece of land"? This will allegedly clarify how "capital goods get priced in the market at their "capitalized value" (597). But as we have seen, capitalization is the formation of fictitious capital (bonds, etc.) or of a *fictitious* price (land): it is senseless to reverse this process and use it for real capital: one does not find the value of capital by empirically determining its periodic money revenue and then plugging it into the interest rate! The value of capital is determined independently (by the value of the commodities making up the constant and variable capital); similarly, the expanded value of the capital—the surplus value it "creates"—is determined by how much surplus labor is appropriated. This method of determining the value of capital represents an advanced stage of bourgeois disintegration: so deeply has the origin of profit been weeded out of its concept that the method for determining fictitious capital values is now transformed into the model for the real capital values.

EXCURSUS ON "HUMAN CAPITAL"

While implicitly conceding that wages do not lend themselves to capitalization treatment, S does extend it to slave wages and to educational investment in human capital.

What we just said about the superficialization of the category of interest—every periodic money income is transformed into, or to use S's phrase, "may appear as," interest (597, n. 2)—is repeated now for the category of capital. Since bourgeois economics would not be bourgeois economics if it had a sociohistorical concept of capital, it is not surprising that capital becomes—"may appear as"—any "thing" that spins off money income. As for slavery, it was involuntarily entered into; S would doubtless say that the "revenue" received from the slave's work would be the interest on the capital "invested" in him by the slaveowner; this, of course, makes a mockery of any attempt to distinguish between socio-historical epochs.

"PRODUCTIVITY" OF CAPITAL

Having set the stage with one total irrelevancy, S puts the reader in the mood to accept further superficialities by posing a "now we ask ourselves this question" which has nothing to do with what preceded or what follows: "Why do people ever bother to transform the primary factors of labor and land into intermediate capital goods or into capital? The traditional answer is: It is a technological fact of life that you can get *more future consumption product by using indirect or roundabout methods*" (598).

First, "people"; and then "bother." Which people in which society? In our wonderful mixed-economy society only one class of "people" make any decisions about capital formation, and for them it is really no "bother." Now these "people" do not make their decisions on the basis of whether future consumption will increase as a result; in fact, as monopoly shows, future production and consumption may even be cut back—the point is what is happening on the profit side.

"From this basic technological fact" S now makes a super-duper leap to "an important economic conclusion": "capital has a net productivity (or real interest yield)" (598). We must watch carefully at this point because S has cleverly strung out a series of definitions of net productivity of capital which begins from a technological fact of increasing productivity of human labor and winds up with vulgarization.

What do we know about the first stage? All S has done is to apply the appearances in their uncomprehended form of capitalism to noncapitalist societies. The productivity of capital consists first of all in the formal subsumption of labor to it: this is the compulsion which it exerts on the workers to work beyond the fulfillment of their immediate needs—not in the sense of fulfilling these other needs, but rather in making them work a longer period of time than is necessary for the production of the use-values they customarily need. The extra labor goes to the production of two elements: use-values for the nonworking, capital-owning class; and means of production for expanded reproduction (accumulation). Capitalism shares the first of these elements with other class societies (slavery, feudalism, etc.); the form of this exploitation is, to be sure, essentially different, but the aspect of class exploitation is the same. This is not why Marx viewed capitalism as progressive. Its real productivity consisted in accumulating in a production-oriented manner the objective results of previous exploitation of labor: the products of labor now are marshalled in a massive manner over against the laborer as the basis for more and increased exploitation.

But this is only a relatively primitive stage of the rule of capital. The really mysterious relation between labor and its objectified products arises (this is partly associated with the thrust toward the development of relative surplus value) when not only the product, but also

> the forms of societally developed labor, cooperation, manufacture (as form of the division of labor), factory (as form of societal labor organized with machinery as its material basis) present themselves as *developmental forms of capital* and therefore the productive powers of labor developed from these forms of societal labor, therefore also science and natural forces present themselves as *productive powers of capital*.[2]

This is the first stage of S's saga of capital productivity as "that annual percentage yield which you could earn by tying up your money" in any particular "project" (599). By this time we can begin to see how productivity and profitability diverge. It finally dawns on us when S states that a synonymous definition would be "that market rate of interest at which it would just pay to undertake" the investment.

S is quite clever. He sandwiches capitalism in-between two nonclass societies, imputing to the latter the relations of capitalism and to capitalism their relations. Thus like these societies, capitalism becomes a society in which there is collective, conscious planning on what to produce to satisfy needs; and these societies in turn use the anarchic "device" of an interest rate they have no need of because they can plan directly.

No discussion is of course complete without dragging in our old friend the law of diminishing returns. It tells us that "as more and more capital goods . . . become available to work with the limited supply of natural resources and land and with the more slowly growing number of workers . . . society and the private investors will run out of new projects with as high net productivities as the previous ones" (599). As a result interest rates and investment yields will fall.

Since bourgeois interest is related to the notion of profit in our terms, this would seem to be an expression of the falling rate of profit. And in fact it resembles Adam Smith's explanation of the falling rate of profit from accumulation and competition. It also shares with Ricardo's conception the feature of declining productivity. Marx rejected both insofar as he showed how the rate of profit drops even though, or rather precisely because labor, in its capitalist form, has become more and more productive (it can set more and more objectified labor in motion but relatively less surplus labor time).

EXCURSUS ON INFRASTRUCTURE

Let us look at S's example of a bridge with a net productivity of 10 percent, while the market rate of interest is 11 percent. He states that until the rate drops to 10 percent, it will not be "worth" building the bridge. For whom? For "a community," for society, or for private investors?

Let us look at this more closely. First of all, his chosen example is bound to obfuscate matters; he has hit upon a type of operation which involves so much capital, and so much constant capital in relation to variable capital, that it has traditionally been undertaken only by nonprofit state organs; or more recently also by large joint-stock corporations which must be satisfied with interest (dividends) instead of the full profit. Such operations (railroads, highways, bridges, ports, etc.), today called infrastructure, can be undertaken by private capital only when it can be done with a "profit" (i.e., when it throws off at least as much as bonds, etc.); furthermore, capital must be sufficiently concentrated to attain the size needed by enormous projects which take a long time to complete (slow turnover of capital); such transportation/communication projects must correspond to a certain level of the productive forces of those industrial capitals which will consume them: in other words, they must be "worth" their exchange value.

However, even when such a project is not "attractive to private investors" because they can find more "productive" investment opportunities elsewhere, it may nevertheless be undertaken because it is an essential use value for the society which needs it "at any price." In that case the operation is undertaken by the state: it is "financed" not by capital but by revenue in the form of taxes. This can be done only if the society has the labor-time available for it without withdrawing any from that needed to reproduce the aggregate labor power of the society.

Here we can see the productivity of capital in action. Let us say that it would take one hundred workers one year to build the bridge; the value of labor power is such that it would take six months of labor to create that value. The productivity of capital consists in forcing the worker to work twelve months while paying him for six. Nevertheless, the capitalists do not make the workers work twice as much just for the fun of it: the extra labor is needed both to do the job and to make it profitable. If the subsumption of labor under capital were still incomplete, that is, if the workers were still in a position to refuse to work the surplus labor-time, then the state of course could not work magic: it cannot build the bridge with one hundred times six months of labor. The other half of the labor would have to be provided by another contingent of workers who would receive their wages from taxpayers; these would either have to work a little bit extra in order to pay their taxes without causing their labor power to go unreproduced in full, or because of taxation they would be indirectly working surplus time by having part of their necessary time siphoned off to the state.

"WAITING" AND "ABSTINENCE"

Since Chapter 12 has dealt with the Keynesian conceptions of the interest rate and its determinants, there is no need to go into details here. Clearly the alleged supply determinant is a bunch of apologetic nonsense: those who "do" the capital formations are in reality demanding that other people "abstain and wait"; of course this sort of waiting is self-reproducing.

S cunningly avoids this issue—when he mentions the two magic words he sets them in quotation marks (604). Otherwise he speaks of patience and impatience (605). But as we already know from the discussion of consumption and saving, S likes to "aggregate" and thus make the class relation one affecting society as an undifferentiated whole. Thus in the text, "the community" is the subject that is sacrificing, saving, consuming, etc. Only in the fine print of the appendix does S indicate that interest is as much caused by capital productivity as by "the fact that savers must be paid for the unpleasant task of 'abstinence' or 'waiting' " (611).

It would have been nice if S had bothered to tell the reader something of the history of these terms, but alas he is a "modern" economist for whom time begins with the mixed economy. So let's fill in a bit. The venerable Nassau Senior (1790-1864) made the term abstinence fashionable for obvious apologetic reasons. Marshall, not quite so ignorant of political-social issues, thought the term was misunderstood and believed "with advantage" to be able to replace it with waiting. It was misunderstood, he wrote, because the "greatest accumulators of wealth are very rich persons, some of whom live in luxury," and can thus not be thought to live abstinently. "What economists meant was," he continued, "that, when a person abstained from consuming anything which he had the power of consuming, with the purpose of increasing his resources in the future, his abstinence from that particular act of consumption increased the accumulation of wealth."[3] In other words, Marshall set waiting against "impulsive grasping at immediate satisfactions." What nonsense! Can Rockefeller really be said to have abstained from guzzling billions of barrels of oil so as to increase his wealth? And even if we translate the natural form of their means of production into money, is it really possible for someone to spend billions of dollars? "Waiting" is equally absurd—they are not waiting for future enjoyment because they will never consume it.

PRECAPITALIST INTEREST

In a section entitled "ancient misconceptions about interest" S throws together a good deal of ahistorical material which makes him look very critical as compared to his predecessors. Aristotle was rather silly because he didn't realize when he "said it was unfair to charge positive interest for loans," that since capital is scarce and hence productive, "if I did not pay you interest, I should really be cheating you out of the return that you could get by putting your own money directly into such productive investment projects!" (602 f.).

As for "cheating," that is true—but suprahistorically it is not correct. As Marx noted in reply to a nineteenth-century English author who also viewed interest as a principle of natural justice:

> The justness of transactions which take place among agents of production rests upon the fact that these transactions derive from the relations of production as a natural consequence. The

legal forms in which these economic transactions appear as acts of will of the participants . . . can as mere forms not determine this content itself. This content is just as soon as it corresponds to the mode of production, is adequate to it. It is unjust as soon as it contradicts it. Slavery on the basis of the capitalist mode of production is unjust; similarly cheating with respect to the quality of the commodity.[4]

As for consumptions loans, it is not enough to say that because they are "less important" than production loans the latter determine the rate of interest. In a self-reproducing capitalist system it must be obvious that interest can be paid only if there is a mechanism through which the capitalists pay back their loans without causing a diminution of their capital stock—otherwise capital could not accumulate and there would be no capitalism. That this was not the case in precapitalist societies, that usury under certain historical circumstances became a lever of dissolution of previous economic formations, etc.,—all this finds no mention in S. Moreover, S inverts the real meaning of "Biblical utterances against interest and usury" when he characterizes them as "loans made for consumption rather than investment purposes" (603); for the ruling classes lent slaves and poor peasants money to be able to exploit their labor directly when they could no longer pay back their debts. What is true is that the loans of the *ruling class* during the Middle Ages were primarily for consumption, and this in fact is still the case today in many Asian countries.

INTEREST RATE "MANIPULATION" AND "CRISIS MANAGEMENT"

Clark confused the demand for loan capital with the demand for capital. S reproduces this error to the extent that he talks of "the existing stock of capital" as being "auctioned off" by the rate of interest (600). This is no quirk on S's part, since one of the presuppositions of Keynesian theory is that control over the interest rate is an essential point. To the extent that the investment decisions of many corporations are not made on the basis of this rate, much of the Keynesian bag of tricks is neutralized.

Tucked away in a discussion of zero interest rates is a "qualification" indicating that perhaps our mixed economy isn't so wonderful after all. Thus not only in 1932, but "Even today, if the profit rate (pure interest rate plus premiums to cover risk) got forced down to 8 or 10 per cent before taxes, business as a whole might be unwilling to undertake an investment level equal to desired full-employment saving" (604 n. 8). We are told that once the Fed had shot its bolt and gotten the interest rate down to zero, its power to "coax out" more investment would have dissipated:

> Therefore it is conceivable that an impasse, a kind of Day of Judgment for our mixed system . . . might arrive when conventional measures to stimulate investment could not restore full employment and let our optimistic managed money" work itself out smoothly and fully. . . . And if that unhappy day should ever approach, more extensive remedial programs (such as insurance of risk loans or new institutions to provide venture capital) would have to be imaginatively explored [613].

This is the first and only time in the whole book that S hints that perhaps a repeat performance of the 1930s may be a possibility.

Of course, S is not saying that the case is hopeless; he does present some new "policy tools." But the admission is significant because in general he denies the possibility of crisis.

The point of course is keeping capitalism alive politically—by political means. S never explains these Keynesian policies in class terms. They are always good for everyone. Keynes at least possessed the optimism of a bourgeois—he spoke openly in class terms, as exemplified by his description of the measures taken to finance World War I:

> The war inevitably involved in all countries an immense diversion of resources to forms of production which, since they did

> not add to the volume of liquid consumption goods purchasable and consumable by income earners, had just the same effect as an increased investment in fixed capital would have in ordinary times. The investment thus required was . . . on such a scale that it exceeded the maximum possible amount of voluntary saving which one could expect. . . . Thus forced transferences of purchasing power were a necessary condition. . . . The means of effecting this transference with the minimum of social friction and disturbance was the question for solution.[5]

He goes on to reject the proposal of "the financial purists" which would have raised the entire sum by taxation on the grounds that it would have

> to be aimed directly at the relatively poor, since it was above all their consumption, in view of its aggregate magnitude, which had somehow or other to be reduced. It would have meant, that is to say, a tax of (say) 5s. in the £ on all wages, perhaps more. No government engaged in war could be expected to add to its other difficulties the political problems of such a tax.[6]

Then Keynes opts for rising prices rather than lowering money wages because this would provoke less working-class opposition while the effect—"the resources released would not accrue in the first instance to the Government . . . but to the entrepreneurs in the shape of exceptional profits . . . because the margin between the money-proceeds of production and its money-costs would be widened"[7]—would be the same.

It is interesting that in admitting that this whole process is similar to capital formation in peacetime, Keynes is also admitting what we have wrung from him before—namely that consumption is not the goal of capitalism inasmuch as "the psychology of the community is such that" the marginal propensity to consume would cause losses to capitalists if the capitalists used all of increased employment to satisfy the "increased demand for immediate consumption."[8]

We might say that S's refusal to speak in open terms is another example of how the cash value of a doctrine lies in its vulgarization.

S has been so impressed by the crises of recent years that he has—together with the term "neoclassical synthesis"—also deleted his previous "confident reply" from later editions, according to which this synthesis "can successfully fight off the plague of mass unemployment and the plague of inflation" (7th ed., p. 581). But this development cannot surprise S, for he appreciates the tremendous significance for capital theory of the fact that "each night we go to bed realizing that the next morning will have some surprises for us" (606).

Chapter 22: Theories of Profit
(S's Chapter 31)

In the end, business profits can be regarded as a fee. A fee for financing, maintaining and managing the U.S. economy.

—McGraw-Hill Advertisement, "The $400-Billion Misunderstanding," in *Business Week*, July 22, 1972, pp. 70-71.

Since profit is allegedly a residual magnitude whose "components" we have dealt with, we will restrict ourselves here to the various "views" which S describes. (The fact that S has abbreviated this chapter in the ninth edition is of ideological interest, for this doubtless marks an attempt to pacify those whose "hostility toward profit" (8th ed., pp. 599 f.) has so disturbed S. This is clear from the fact that he has now added a new little section: "Sixth View: Profit as Marxian Surplus Value"; however, proof that this is a half-hearted addition is delivered in form of a footnote telling the teacher that this part may be skipped [622 n. 3].)

IDEOLOGICAL MISSION

Whereas the classical bourgeois economists still understood profit in class terms, S sees it as a "complex" matter; for the most part this complexity consists in so gross a distortion of the category of profit as to sever it from its social base. In the end, not only capitalists but workers too make profits. This idea is not of course original; it has been around at least as long as the Holy Trinity—the notion that wages, interest, and rent are actually created by corresponding "factors"; since profit could no longer be identified with capital (this honor fell to interest), new "sources" had to be invented. This chapter merely goes through some of them.

The key sentences in this chapter, and in a sense in the whole book as far as its social "mission" is concerned, follow S's description of three "views" of profit as implicit factor returns, returns to innovation, and for risk-bearing:

> If you point out the above to a person who feels vaguely critical toward profit, you may confuse him and make him uncertain as to what it is that he is against. His hazy notion of a capitalist as a fat man with a penchant for arithmetic, who somehow exploits the rest of the community, calls attention to a fourth possible meaning of profit, *namely profit as the earnings* of monopoly [8th ed., p. 597].

It is no exaggeration to claim that this is in fact a function—if not the conscious purpose—of this whole book and of all bourgeois education: to confuse those who are "vaguely critical" of the profit system. This "source" of profit is thrown in as a sop, but we must remember that the chapters on monopoly have already asserted that the profits associated with monopoly are not the evil.

THE VARIOUS "VIEWS"

The chapter opens with a discussion of the "statistician's" view, which breaks down into several kinds. Let us see what they are: Implicit factor returns have already been discussed in connection with opportunity costs and the hybrid nature of the income of small commodity producers (or service producers). Since S himself admits that "much of what is ordinarily called profit is really nothing but interest, rents, and wages under a different name" (619), we can exclude this category from the discussion of profit as a discrete category. In any event, this first "view" does wonders in dispelling the "hostility" toward profit by letting wage "earners" share it.

We have also met, and criticized, the second rubric, profit as "reward to enterprise and innovation," in connection with temporary extra profit. This profit exists, we are told, because perfect competition does not now exist, never did, never will, and never could. The "heroically abstract assumptions" (630) involved in perfect competition are not transparent in their function. On the one hand, they seem designed to give the reader the impression that he is being confronted with a pair of categories (perfect—imperfect) analogous to the Leninist pair—premonopoly and monopoly capitalism. Yet this is obviously not right, since premonopoly capitalism did exist. Maybe one could change the analogy to the distinction Marx made between commodity production and capitalism, or between surplus value and profit. This would gain some plausibility from the statement that the "model . . . is not a picture of the real world as we know it when we step outside the library" (630). Yet this is similarly invalid, for Marx's distinction is based on the Hegelian understanding of the relation between essence and appearance: surplus value is "there," whether you see it on the surface or not. Perfect competition is not.

In any event, from the admission that perfect competition is a dreamworld S makes a quantum jump to: "In real life somebody must act as boss and decide how a business shall be run" (620). The justification for the eternal nature of the capitalist authority structure of production is of course lacking. But then in an equally unmediated way we are brought back to capitalist innovators "in the world as we know it" (620). This then leads into the discussion of the distinction between wages of management and innovational returns. S reports that Schumpeter ruled out the former as a part of profit. S seems to agree with this because he adds: "Although these executives run the business they are paid wages much like anybody else. Management of this type is a skill not different in kind from other skills . . . .People who possess this skill are bid for in the market place . . ." (620).

Now this managerial wage has had an interesting career.

Called wages of superintendence in the nineteenth century, it was an attempt to justify profit as an income deriving from labor. This had become necessary once the Holy Trinity had established itself as an integral part of vulgar economics. Since interest was now connected with capital, it was essential to find out where profit came from. On the other hand, interest now became attached to capital as possession—it had nothing to do with capital in production. The managers could point to their own "wages" as uniting them against those anonymous forces of capital. But this is not dangerous, because interest-capital, although it assumes the role of the social existence of capital, no longer has anything to do with labor, no longer represents exploitation of labor. The ownership of capital appears as a relation between two capitalists.

S states that, as a result of huge corporations and managers, it is easier to understand Schumpeter's distinction today than it was fifty years earlier. Yet one hundred years before that the utopians had developed this insight. We quote Marx's paraphrase of these authors because it is almost precisely what S says:

> The labor of superintendence can now be bought on the market like every other labor power and is relatively just as cheap to produce and therefore to buy. Capitalist production itself has brought it about that the labor of direction, completely separated from capital property, whether one's own or others', runs about on the street. It has become totally useless for the capitalist to execute this labor of direction.[1]

If S did in fact subscribe to this view, he would be forced to explain the extremely high salaries of corporate executives as a result of "the tremendous qualitative differentials among people" (580). But it is not only Marxists, as S hints (625), who understand these salaries as a part of total profit (or surplus value):

> The high incomes of top executives can in fact be understood only if we bear in mind that they are in a position in which they can fix their own remuneration. Supply and demand do

not take us far here, nor does the concept of "productive contribution," dear to the hearts of economists. Here "power" is a more enlightening term than the forces of the market.[2]

As far as the innovative aspect is concerned, its rational kernel is already familiar to us within the framework of the concept of extra profit. The personalization of this phenomenon in the "innovator" is misleading in that most inventions belong to the corporations in which the researchers are salaried employes—or they stem from independent inventors who sell their patents to corporations.

The next "type" of profit—"monopoly profit"—has already been dealt with on a general level, so here we will concern ourselves only with the new aspects S inserts into the discussion.

This section provokes a significant admission, which like all other such statements is relegated to a footnote: "If there is great inequality in the distribution of ownership of factors of production, then even under the most perfect competition (where pure profit is zero) there can still result a very rich, possibly idle, minority of plutocrats surrounded by masses of lower-income people" (623 n. 4). The "if" is a generous concession. This in a nutshell actually constitutes a self-refutation. The whole theory of perfect competition was held up as a model of efficiency against which any society could be judged, and now it is conceded that because one class owns all of the means of production in their objectified form there must be a class-income dichotomy.

The purpose of this section was to show those doubting Thomases that what they objected to was monopoly profits. For this reason S once again finds it necessary to haul in the unique factor of production story so that workers can be the large monopolists just like the capitalists. But after reducing monopoly profits to rent, wages, and interest, he claims that *"much of the hostility toward profit is really hostility toward the extremes of inequality in the distribution of money income that comes from unequal factor ownership"* (8th ed. p. 600), a source which must be kept apart from monopoly.

In the first place this merely strengthens the case of our

"vague critics"; for they should not restrict their "hazy notions" of fat-cats to monopoly, but extend it to the whole system since there is *in fact* enormous "inequality of factor ownership." What S does not seem to grasp is that it is the ownership of the "factors"—the fact that some people own capital and others labor power—that brings about the inequality in ownership, and through that the inequality in income. This S himself more or less admits in the chapters on monopoly when he indicates that concentration and centralization of capital are a continuously self-reproducing process into which it is necessary to intervene again and again so that matters do not get out of hand. Thus the hostility toward profit is really the hostility toward the whole profit system.

S is thus being consistent when he claims that "it is misleading to talk about 'a profit system.' Ours is a profit-and-loss system" (8th ed. p. 599). Pity the poor capitalist who gets "a kick in the pants from unions or from fate in general" (586). If S means the workers get what the capitalists lose, then this would indicate that there is a real struggle going on for the division of the pie—a fact which is denied throughout this entire book; but if he merely means that one capitalist loses what another gains, then this is totally irrelevant as far as a theoretical analysis of the profit system is concerned—because this refers to a whole class.

S's last line of resistance is that everyone wants a piece of the action; this means that the "pursuit of profit" is merely "trying to get as much as he [the businessman] can for the resources at his disposal. (This is not different from what a worker is doing when he changes occupations or joins a union.)" (8th ed. pp. 599-600).

At this point S treats us to a hitherto secret definition of profit: unnecessary surplus earned by factors. But S can hardly blame "people" for this understanding since it was bourgeois economics itself which created the notion of profit upon alienation: namely that profit was a mark-up created in the sphere of circulation by selling at a higher price than one buys at. In this sense "unnecessary" is wrong; it is also wrong in the sense that the capitalist system could do without these "surpluses"—this is the correct part of S's dislike of profits taxes. But it must be emphasized that the surplus over and beyond what the worker gets is "unnecessary" today—there is a class that pockets the difference and this is unnecessary today, as is their sole power to decide what to do with the part of the surplus that is reinvested.

THE SOCIETAL SIGNIFICANCE OF THE PRAISES OF PROFIT

The "sermon on profit" must rank as one of S's supreme displays of stupidity and infamy. One might still accept the assertion that "profit seeking is simply seeking of self-advantage" (8th ed., p. 601), for these two characteristics of the bourgeois epoch are not unrelated. But S is not promising any utopia: "shirkers get low incomes. And earnest people, born stupid and with weak muscles, also get low incomes for all their earnestness. Smart go-getters get high incomes. . . . So it goes" (ibid.). If this is the best of all possible worlds under nonexistent perfect competition, the real world is even worse. S does not seem too disturbed about what the shirkers, the inherently stupid and weak would do if they ever heard him talk about them in this way. Nevertheless, to the extent that capitalism keeps producing "shirkers" and the genetically "stupid," dealing with them becomes a political problem. The tax system is the answer: "democracy" can redistribute income. If in fact the tax system does not redistribute income to the poorer people, we are forced to conclude that we either do not have a democracy or that the poor—the majority—are altruists intent on increasing the incomes of the rich. There is a rational aspect to S's claims: if a radical left-wing government were to reduce the income of the capitalist class, it is very likely that this class would experience a "distortion of incentives" which would lead to open civil war. But what S wants to prove is that profit is an eternal aspect of human nature, and that to block that pursuit is bound to interfere with efficiency whatever the economic system.

The description of profit as a "coordinating device" is not

quite correct in the sense that it guides *all* of us; for it gives the impression that capitalism is one gigantic "profit-sharing" system. Although it is true that wages may be higher in branches where profits are greater, the "rationality" in seeking a higher paying job so that one may keep one's family above water is hardly to be equated with the transformation of one's capital from one form into another in order to accumulate more. And when S asserts that both workers and capitalists get "penalized" when they "overdo" the satisfaction of consumer wants, one must really ask whether the Ford family suffered the same penalties when the Edsel folded as did the workers who found themselves out on the street.

Imperialism and the World Market
Introduction to Chapters 23-27

> The decadent international but individualistic capitalism, in the hands of which we found ourselves after the war, is not a success. It is not intelligent, it is not beautiful, it is not just, it is not virtuous—and it doesn't deliver the goods. In short, we dislike it, and we are beginning to despise it. But when we wonder what to put in its place, we are extremely perplexed.
>
> —J. M. Keynes, "National Self-Sufficiency," *Yale Review*, XXII, No. 4 (Summer 1933), 760 f.

The overriding purpose of the four chapters that make up Part 5 of S's book (plus the chapter on "underdevelopment") is to persuade the reader that, just as within the U.S. the messy problems of pre-Keynesian capitalism have been banished, so too on the international scene a just and harmonious world order—at least in the FREE WORLD—reigns supreme. This treatment is reflected in the structure of the book; thus, as just mentioned, what must strike every reader as a flaw in this tranquil setting, namely the enormous poverty of the countries which those who fancy themselves the First World call the Third World gets shunted off into Part 6, Current Economic Problems, which is filled up with other anomalies like poverty, racism, unemployment, socialism, etc. These topics represent accretions of the afterthought variety: in other words, every new edition or so includes a new topical subject to indicate that S is not ignorant of the real problems of the real world. Unfortunately, these "problems" stand in no relation to the text—written basically a quarter-century ago, at a time when such problems presumably had not yet arisen—although S claims that the latter provides the solution to the former.

Much of what we have learned up to now, for instance, our previous discussions of money, gold, profit, etc., will prove to be useful in understanding these chapters. Before we enter into our systematic critique we would like to elaborate on the all-pervading harmony of these chapters.

As we already know, its self-consciously non- or even anti-class standpoint is a fundamental feature of bourgeois economics. Both on the empirical and theoretical levels, we have emphasized that these theories in part derive the essentially nonantagonistic nature of capitalism's "flaws" from the alleged nonexistence of social classes.

Now it would seem, on the basis of the obvious disparities in the levels of material existence between the capitalist countries of North America and Western Europe and the rest of the capitalist world, that the reader might be led to become skeptical toward earlier assertions of harmony. Yet on the surface there is an important countervailing factor at work here; for it is precisely the nonclass nature of each national capitalism that transforms all international "problems" into "frictions" and "tensions" among internally unified and uniform nations.

When S does speak of these "frictions," it is always in the context of a transitional phase of adjustment to higher planes of welfare. This for example plays an enormous role in the theory of comparative advantages, which decrees that in the long run it is better for a nation to sacrifice an entire industry in order to put its scarce resources to more efficient use.

We have noted that S's approach is not shared by all his colleagues; thus, since our book is a critique of S only insofar as he is representative of contemporary bourgeois economics, it will be necessary to comment on divergent views. Nonetheless we will show the fundamental unity of these superficially radically differing theories.

This other wing, which for want of a more precise term

we will call left-wing liberal, is not consolidated or institutionalized (we abstract here from the coherent blocs of economists from the "developing" countries); and although they are not outcasts cut off from access to the standard journals, etc., they are commonly treated as well-intentioned individuals of peripheral and/or gadfly significance.

In a sense this cavalier attitude on the part of orthodoxy is justified inasmuch as the liberal critique is not really very "high-powered": in the main it restricts itself to confronting the established theory with empirical findings suggesting the inadequacies of the explanatory power of the theory. Such an approach does not faze orthodoxy, which marches to the tune of a different drummer. Often one or two responses ensues: either the partial validity of the findings is admitted, which leads to a further "refining" of the assumptions (usually tantamount to a renunciation of contact with reality), or the annoying critic is condescendingly informed as to what theory is all about. This is not to say that we hold the empirical refutation to be worthless: on the contrary. The point, as we shall soon see, lies rather in the inability of the left-liberals to present an immanent theoretical critique and to develop their own coherent theories.

The cause of this inability must be sought in the circumstance that these critics share the fundamental propositions common to all bourgeois economics; they merely object to certain corollaries which appear to them out of tune with reality. Since they accept the base upon which the offending theories rest, they can only refute them by an appeal to "facts."

We would now like to demonstrate this by an example which at the same time allows us to concretize our earlier remarks on the notion of harmony.

Our example is the Swedish Social Democrat Gunnar Myrdal, the most prominent proponent of the view we have termed left-liberal. Myrdal believes fully as much as S that the Keynesian welfare state has overcome the traditional problems of capitalism pointed out by Karl Marx. On the other hand he stresses the great inequalities between the "West" and the Third World, which he sees as widening and accentuated by selfish policies on the part of the former. Here is how he explains the causal mechanism at work:

> *The welfare state is nationalistic.* . . . Thus, tremendous forces of vested interests, often spread out among broad layers of the citizens, are so created that they can be mobilized against abstaining from policies that hurt underdeveloped countries. In this case it is wrong to put the blame on the "capitalists," as is often done by some ignorant radicals. *On this point the people are the reactionaries.* . . . Governments and officials should not be blamed. . . . They respond to their peoples who are prejudiced.[1]

What is common to Myrdal and S is the view of "the" nation or the people. All bourgeois economists operate with this class-undifferentiated conception of capitalist society. And even those economists who recognize the interests of certain groups—Myrdal does as does S, who usually picks out various industrial workers as the offending group responsible for forfeiting the comparative advantage of the U.S.—do so only by opposing these interests to an alleged general interest which is being violated.

In other words, all bourgeois economists fail to see that the political and economic antagonisms and contradictions of the bourgeois state internally must somehow find their expression in the external activities of this state—i.e., in the interrelations among bourgeois states.

For the left-liberals this means that (many of) the evils of imperialism are admitted and described without suggesting, and/or by explicitly denying any causal connection to the various national capitalisms. This distorted approach has its historical roots in the liberal tradition. Thus Max Horkheimer, then head of the Institute for Social Research, chastised the German exiles in England in the 1930s who continued to attack fascism without mentioning capitalism: "He who does not want to talk about capitalism should keep quiet about fascism."[2] Applied to our liberals the saying might read: He who does not want to talk about capitalism should keep quiet about imperialism.

As to S, he, of course, is not guilty of this inconsistency since he talks of neither capitalism nor imperialism. But as we shall see, certain inherent contradictions are involved in S's view of the state. At this point we might point to a certain irony in this connection: S was so busy propagating the mixed economy (i.e., state) as the solution to capitalism's internal problems that when he comes to speak of the state in its external operations he cannot perceive its particular functions and limitations.

DISCUSSION OF S'S GENERAL OPENING REMARKS

In introducing the four chapters of this Part, S makes three points, all of them methodological in nature, although they are not presented as such.

The first point relates to the systematic significance of foreign trade within this book and within the capitalist or mixed economic system: "In the earlier chapters of this book we took international trade more or less for granted. Here . . . we wish to analyze explicitly the interesting economic problems arising as soon as an economy engages in foreign trade" (643).

Now in and of itself there is nothing wrong with such a procedure; Marx too abstracted from foreign trade in order to grasp the laws of value and surplus value production in their "pure" form. The point here is how trade is introduced.

By this we do not mean whether the author has succeeded in executing a smooth stylistic transition from one section of his book to the next. What we do mean is this: foreign trade, like all capitalist phenomena, has a certain historical genesis and fulfills certain functions within the world capitalist system. Although there is no one-to-one correspondence between these two aspects, there is a significant relation inasmuch as capitalism is a self-reproducing system; that is to say, if foreign trade has undergone significant functional changes, then these must have been brought about by other changes within capitalism. In any event, neither one can be understood without the other. Concretely, one cannot understand the early history of capitalist trade without pursuing the later development of capital leading to the approximation of its own concept. On the other hand, merely confronting contemporary reality without understanding its origin and its direction is equally one-sided and distorted.

The basis of S's introduction of foreign trade leads us to his third point: he derives the importance of international trade more or less exclusively from the alleged fact that it "offers a 'consumption-possibility frontier' that can give us more of all goods than can our own domestic production-possibility frontier! . . . *Each of us ends up consuming more than he could produce alone*. The world is out on—and not inside—its true production-possibility frontier" (643).

In order to discuss this in a comprehensible manner, we will have to anticipate the later discussion of comparative advantages. It will be clear to the reader by now that S has introduced foreign trade on the basis of the new and/or additional use-values which it allows "us" to consume. In one sense this is indeed consistent since S sees consumption not only as the subjective goal of the mixed economy, but also as its objective end.

Without going any further now, we might merely point out that S's claims for consumption would have to meet with some skepticism on our part: How can he assert that the capitalist international division of labor permits us to consume more than we could produce alone when: (1) U.S. workers now do not even consume all they produce; (2) U.S. workers do not even produce all they could produce (unemployment, unutilized capacity, "waste," etc.)?

Returning to the second (methodological) point made by S in his brief introduction: this deals with the structural arrangement of the chapters. Thus, Chapter 33 deals with monetary mechanisms whereas the following two are devoted to "the basic real factors which underlie international trade and which are often obscured by the monetary veil that covers all international transactions" (643).

Although everyone knows that you can't eat gold or paper money, to portray the physical products of the labor process as "real" within an economic system whose very existence is distinguished by the production of "veils," whether they be commodities, money, value, profit, wages, rent, etc., is both demagoguery and what we may call metaphysical materialism. By this we mean an approach which sticks to "the facts," the objects of immediate perception, without understanding that to say something economically significant about a table in ancient Greece and one in today's U.S. one must do more than point to the differences of their production functions (i.e., that they embody different proportions of living and dead labor); for a table built purely as a use-value is not the same as one built only "partly" as a use-value and "partly" as a profit-maker. One of the things that makes Marxism superior to bourgeois science is that it takes the "veils" very seriously and tries to explain their origin and inevitable existence in certain societies; but merely to characterize them as "obscuring," without explaining why the "real" which they obscure cannot otherwise exist in capitalism and why the "real" is not in fact "really real"—this sort of metaphysical materialism means the renunciation of all science precisely because it fails to explain what is specific about capitalism.

On the basis of this brief discussion we can now outline how the Marxist approach to foreign trade and the world market will differ. What is "real" in capitalism is neither the physical product nor the veil, but the contradictory unity of both in the commodity (this at least on the basic level; we would then have to look at more complicated phenomena like capital, etc.). This is why Marx begins *Capital* with the commodity which is the contradictory unity of use-value ("the real") and value ("veil"), whereby he explains how another "veil" inevitably arises from this contradictory unity—namely money.

Similarly, on the world market one does not, as S does, start with a physical product like Vermont maple sugar or with dollars. Now one might ask, why the word "similarly," why can't we proceed *exactly* as Marx did within a country? A good question, and we will deal with it below.

At this point we merely warn the reader that Marx's theory of international value, of world money, etc., like his theory of money itself, is perhaps the most difficult part of his entire theory. Furthermore, Marx himself never completed this international aspect of his theory, and so we must try to develop a theory from his fragmentary remarks and from the works of later Marxist writers; the subject is still generating great controversy among Marxists and no complete theory exists yet. As far as possible we will try to keep an immanent critique of S, but at intervals we will have to break off the "narrative" to develop the Marxist theory so that our critique will remain comprehensible in its orientation.

Chapter 23: The World Market and World Money: Theoretical and Historical Outline (S's Chapter 33)

Some U.S. producers and processors maintain the Japanese are buying shrimp for purely monetary reasons. They would simply rather have shrimp than dollars, it seems. "They're overloaded with American dollars and they're almost spreading them around the world like funny money...."

—"For Some Reason Japan is Buying Lots of Shrimp," *Wall Street Journal*, December 1, 1971, p. 36

I. THE WORLD MARKET

S opens his discussion by asking how trade takes place (644); this presumes that his reference to an alleged enlarged consumption-possibility frontier on the preceding page has already adequately answered the question of *why* foreign trade takes place.

We know that use values are not the dominant aspect of capitalist reality and therefore cannot have the dominant explanatory power within the theory S ascribes to them.

The why of foreign trade must take into account historical changes in the function of that trade. Because capitalism is a self-reproducing system, some relation must exist between the changing functions. This calls for some revision insofar as foreign trade helped give birth to capitalism (that is, it predates capitalism).

Marx saw the rise of commodity production in the trade of surplus products between non-commodity-producing communities; this was the beginnings of production not for use but for barter. This in turn caused some members of the community to engage solely in production for others outside the community.

Something analogous took place in the transitional period between the dissolution of feudal societies and the rise of capitalism. Traders mediated among the producers of various goods in various countries. At this stage, the desire for new and probably locally unobtainable products—most likely luxury items—sparked this process. Regardless of the motives of the consumers, this at first accidental trade of surplus led to a production for exchange. In this way trade increased the volume and variety of value production, and by helping to dissolve the feudal societies also helped give birth to capitalism. But once the capitalist world market exists, it will be capitalist production, now dependent on that market, which will give the impetus to further trade.

In the beginning S appears to have been right: expanding consumption was the motive behind trade (though not the motive of the plundering traders themselves). But let's see what happens from here.

Once capitalism has created its own basis, the necessity of a world market becomes clear:

> If the surplus labour or value were represented merely in the national surplus produce, then the increase of value for the sake of value and hence the extraction of surplus labour would find a limit in the narrow-mindedness, the narrow circle of use-values, in which the value of the national labor is represented. But it is only external trade that develops its true nature as value by developing the labor contained in the value as social labor, which is represented in an unlimited series of various use-values and indeed gives abstract wealth its meaning.[1]

Marx obviously was not ignorant of use-values, but he interprets them as phenomena capable of embodying different social relations at different times. We also see that for Marx the development of foreign trade was bound up with the development of human labor. Marx—and here he was certainly not alone—saw the incorporation of more and more societies and more and more types of concrete labor in the world market as a civilizing force. Although he believed that the crises of capitalism would also be intensified by this process, he was aware of the extraordinary expansion of human productivity arising from capitalist industrialization and the world market accompanying it.

S appears to be so engrossed in his ideological mission of proving that world capitalism is a harmonious whole that he fails in the elementary task of impressing upon the reader the extent and significance of the tendency toward objective unification brought about by capitalism (while on the other hand he exaggerates the aspect of *subjective* unification by totally neglecting the divisive powers of the national capitalist states).

S's use of British racing cars as an example of foreign trade may be calculated to what the reader's interest, but it hardly deals with two of the major functions of foreign trade—to cheapen the elements of constant capital (machines, raw materials, fuels) and to cheapen the means of subsistence of the working class (the variable capital); the former helps to raise the rate of profit by lowering costs, and the latter, by raising the rate of surplus value. This will obviously have a positive effect on the accumulation of capital. Importers will buy abroad if the lower prices enable them to make a greater profit; these individual capitalists clearly need not be guided by societal ends in making the decisions which influence capital accumulation.

II. WORLD MONEY

The upshot of S's discussion is that "ultimately" a U.S. purchaser of the British car must pay the producer in his, namely British, money: trade "between nations with different units of money introduces a new economic factor: *the foreign exchange rate*, giving the price of the foreigner's unit of money in terms of our own" (644). This passage indicates that paper dollars, pounds, etc., are fiat money—as S has repeatedly insisted—i.e., which are money only within the nation's sovereign territory. Yet, as we already know, money in this view is merely a technical means to facilitate barter; it, according to bourgeois economists, serves here only as a means of circulation and/or payment. Thus on the international level as well, barter and money are mechanically united, thus permitting them to be just as easily separated. This will enable S to apply his supply-and-demand analysis to determine exchange rates, thus abstracting from the fact that exchange is exchange of commodities—having value—and not barter, and that money itself has value.

Following this section S seeks to determine the principles underlying the formation of exchange rates, whereby he distinguishes several cases (645). This "case-study" approach makes it impossible to grasp the historical and logical factors at work in the structural modification of the international monetary system—or more accurately, this barter-means of circulation approach ignores the essence of the system, and leads S to adopt an approach which looks at superficial changes.

Thus it is neither on account of its historical importance nor as a result of the fact that it is "one of the easiest cases" to master that we begin with the gold standard, but rather because it expresses most clearly the essential relations of the world market.

A. THEORETICAL ASPECTS

Marx attempted to show that the development of commodities and commodity production was accompanied by or expressed itself in a parallel development of money:

> With its exit from the internal sphere of circulation money sheds the local forms of standard of price, coin, fractional currency and token of value which sprout there and reverts to the original ingot form of the precious metals. In world trade commodities unfold their value universally. For this reason their autonomous value form also appears over against them here as world money. It is first on the world market that money functions in its full scope as the commodity whose natural form is at the same time directly the social form of realiza-

tion of human labor in abstracto. Its mode of existence becomes adequate to its concept.[2]

In other words, capitalism will not reach its full flowering until it has taken hold of the whole world; but this does not happen with each capitalist nation developing to maturity in isolation or even with nation after nation successively completing this development; rather the full development of capitalism within each nation is dependent on its interaction with other countries. It is only on the basis of this incorporation on a world level of all human labor and the latter's reduction to abstract labor that capitalism becomes capitalism.

The extensive development of abstract labor, and therefore of commodity production, must find its adequate expression in world money. This money serves the functions of: (1) universal means of payment; (2) universal wealth (i.e., transfer of wealth from one country to another where the transfer in commodity form is not possible, such as loans). Since in international trade commodity exchange is the realization of the commodity form of capital, and such transactions are usually undertaken as credit operations, it is the first function—the means of payment—that will predominate on the world market. This of course means that just as within a country not all exchanges are mediated by real money, thus too on the world market gold is needed only to pay the balances remaining after all reciprocal debt demands have been compensated.

When S begins to deal with this system of gold money, he states that "by definition, there would be no foreign exchange rate problem" (645) if gold bars were used or if each national currency were defined in terms of a fixed weight of gold, since then each currency could be set into relation to each other easily arithmetically.

By whose definition? What S and all bourgeois economists would like to do is to counterpose fixed and flexible exchange rates in this way: with the former the whole price structure and income structure of a country must accommodate itself to changes in trade, whereas in a flexible or free exchange-rate system the rates of exchange themselves do the accommodating. However, S insists that it is only with the exchange rate that "a new economic factor" is "introduced" (644), whereas a gold standard leaves foreign trade "essentially" like domestic trade (645).

This approach misses the essential peculiarities of the modifications brought about by international trade. By making the exchange rate the central issue, S is able to present the sphere of circulation as the fundamental problem, thereby creating the illusion that international "disequilibria" can be cured by certain institutional changes in the monetary mechanism.

S's description of Hume's gold-flow equilibrating mechanism again attests to S's ahistorical approach. He would like to make us believe that Hume deserves much credit for destroying silly mercantilist notions of yesteryear, which he so caricatures that the reader must assume the mercantilists were nitwits. Other than the fact that the mercantilists preceded Hume and Smith, we are told nothing about them—not who they were, when they lived, etc. These authors wrote at a time—the sixteenth and seventeenth centuries—when the greatest part of production still took place under feudal conditions; this means that commodity production had not yet become dominant. The mercantilists were "farsighted" in the sense that they recognized the monetary form of wealth as the universal form, in contrast to all other commodities. In other words, they were anticipating the basis of value production by regarding the labor producing the commodities for foreign trade—which would be exchanged for gold and silver—as the source of true wealth.

S apparently approves of Hume's mercantilist critique. Its first part, as related by S, refers to the absurdity of maintaining a large gold stock. But all S says is that "If" this merely means that an increased gold stock leads to a proportional inflation, then there is no benefit from this (647). This is obviously true, but the point is whether inflation is the inevitable result. We know that Hume's theory of money was based on the quantity theory of money; S characterizes that theory as "crude" (ibid.) and refers to the whole classical mechanism as "oversimplified" (7th ed., p. 625), so that we do not know his real position. Yet the reader is left with the impression that large gold stocks are ridiculous, an opinion shared by S and most—but not all—bourgeois economists.

Although S has told us that with the exchange rate a new economic factor is introduced, he fails to grasp what is specific about international trade. We have advised caution in talking of nations as class-undifferentiated wholes, yet: "In the exchange rate—no matter how the private interests of every nation divide the latter into as many nations as it possesses fullgrown individuals and the interests of the importers and exporters of the same nation stand over against each other—national trade receives a semblance of existence. . . ."[3] By this Marx means that despite the different and opposing interests that may be affected by changes in the exchange rate, that is despite the fact that the effects will not be uniform, the exchange rate itself will affect the various national interests in a way which will *not necessarily* be valid for other nations.

Let us now look at S's explanation of exchange rates. S's theory rests upon this basis: "Although money prices are quoted in international trade, in the longest run there must really be an international *barter* of goods and services" (8th ed., p. 630). And if we have not guessed it before, S now informs us that "the forces of supply and demand will determine" the exchange rate (647). It is obvious that nothing is going to be explained: if supply and demand cannot determine the equilibrium price on commodity markets, it also cannot explain exchange rates. By viewing exchange-rate changes as mere monetary expressions of bartering, S reduces money to its fluid form of means of circulation and payment; money as a necessary form of value itself is lost sight of.

S does not explain why "Americans want to buy so many English goods at the existing $2.40 level and Europeans want so few American goods" (647); he is content merely to state this, and to see what happens once a new level is reached. In other words, the influence of the exchange rate itself on supply and demand is central, whereas the determinant of supply and demand is shunted off.

According to S, the U.S. demand curve for pounds "comes from our desire" to import British goods, make trips, finance troops in Britain, finance foreign aid, finance U.S. investment there, pay British owners of U.S. stocks and bonds and productive capital (648). Let us for the time being separate trade from all the other categories. It is clear that this sudden "desire" for things British must somehow find an explanation. Since for the most part Britain does not export commodities to the U.S. not obtainable elsewhere or here, we must assume that these imports have become cheaper than imports from other countries or domestic production. It is of course the "cheaper" that needs explanation, for in international trade two circulation acts must be completed: one must sell one's own commodity in order to realize dollars, and then one must sell the dollars for pounds in order to buy the British commodities. Thus a change in the exchange rate can arise on either side of the Atlantic: from a change in the value either of U.S. or of British commodities. In other words, in order to "get behind" the supply and demand curves we must investigate the conditions of value production in each country and the peculiar manner in which these changes are reflected in exchange rates.

Before doing so, however, we must mention the other factors S sees as determining supply and demand curves. True, they do influence the exchange rate, but it is also true that equating them with imports and exports blurs important distinctions. Thus, for example, S himself admits that capital exports will be accelerated from a country with an overvalued currency to one with an undervalued currency. This would appear to be a case where capital exports are determined by the inability of the first country to compete with the second on its home ground; this would normally be reflected in a negative or declining trade balance of the country with the overvalued currency. In other words, here the factors determining supply and demand manifest themselves most clearly in imports and exports, whereas capital exports would be—at least in part—a derivative phenomenon. Moreover, other, not directly related factors, such as financing the U.S. imperialist beachhead in Europe, would have to be brought in to deal with capital exports. And these are obviously even further removed from the sort of abstract theoretical analysis called for here.

B. A MARXIST THEORY OF EXCHANGE RATES

At this point we must interrupt the narrative to present a Marxist explanation of exchange rates. A Marxist theory of the international monetary system must take as its point of departure the peculiarities of this sphere vis-à-vis value production within a nation. Within a nation the value of a commodity represents the expenditure of human labor of every ordinary human being; and although this average labor is given for any country at any time, it varies from country to country and from time to time.

This national average labor is the essential foundation of Marx's theory of value; without it there could be no regularity in the economic processes; no scientific laws concerning economics could be formulated; in fact, no sense could be made of capitalism altogether: it would appear chaotic.

However this foundation was not an arbitrary "assumption" necessitated by Marx's model, for forces at work within capitalism bring about this average labor. On the one hand on the production end all capitalists feel compelled to keep up with and overtake their competitors. But since the average labor is not a condition established by the subjective desires of the workers but by the capitalist enterprises they work in, this same competitive compulsion tends to bring about an average labor throughout the country. Thus the value of a commodity is not determined by any amount of labor spent on its production, but rather by the *socially necessary labor* as determined by the socially normal conditions of production and the socially average degree of labor skill and intensity.

There is a compulsion within a branch of production for average conditions to prevail and for these average conditions to become increasingly more productive; on the other hand there is also a compulsion for society's total of labor power and capital to be distributed among the various branches of production in accordance with the needs of capital accumulation in those branches. Marx calls the expression of these immanent forces within capitalism the law of value. The question is to what extent these conditions prevail among nations so that the law of value may also operate on the world market. Two prerequisites of this functioning of the law of value are the unimpeded mobility of labor and capital. It is precisely the function of the bourgeois state to set limits to this mobility of labor and capital; in fact, contrary to the alleged laws of international laissez-faire as propagated by S, the formation of the various national capitals and their interaction has been characterized by the intervention of the various national states in order to create conditions under which their national capitals can compete with the others. There is a dialectic involved here: the national states have the power to hinder the free mobility of capital, labor, commodities etc., that is, they have the ability to crush competition of other national capitals, but it is done with the intention of creating long-run conditions under which its national capital can compete more effectively. To put it more abstractly; the state has the power to interfere with the workings of the law of value in the short run, but this law will asset itself in the long run, and every state must bow to it.

There is a good deal of migration of laborers and there is an enormous amount of trade and capital import and export, but there is only a blocked-tendency world-average rate of profit and there is no world state. And yet commodities are exchanged on the world market. In what modified form does the law of value assert itself on the world market?

> In every country there prevails a certain average intensity of labor below which the labor producing a commodity consumes more than the socially necessary time and therefore does not

count as labor of normal quality. Only a degree of intensity rising above the national average alters, in a given country, the measure of value by the mere duration of labor time.[4]

The measure of value is the duration of average labor-time. The value produced by one hour's average labor is constant: it was the same in 1900 as today, although the concrete use-values produced in that time have increased enormously. If given branches of production or firms are able to increase the intensity of "their" laborers, this means that these laborers produce more value per hour.[5]

At some point the other producers will be forced to match this pace, and when they do a new average intensity will have formed. This does *not* mean that now all producers produce twice as much value per hour; rather it means that a new average labor producing the *same* amount of value per hour has been established; the extra surplus value disappears, but the measure of value remains unchanged.

> Otherwise on the world market whose integral parts are the individual countries. The average intensity of labor varies from country to country; it is greater here, less there. Thus these national averages form a scale whose unit of measure is the average unit of universal labor. Compared with the less intensive, therefore, the more intensive national labor produces more value in the same time, which expresses itself in more money.
>
> The law of value is modified still more in its international application by the fact that on the world market the more productive national labor also counts as the more intensive whenever the more productive nation is not forced by competition to lower the sale price of its commodity to its value.[6]

There the world market apparently harbors a mechanism similar to the one bringing about extra surplus value within a country. The more productive labor counts as the more intensive in the sense that the commodity value will not be lowered to the individual value—that is, increased intensity does not lower the value of the commodity in the short run—more commodities are produced but the value per commodity unit remains unchanged (until this new higher intensity becomes the new average); similarly, this exceptionally productive labor will reap extra profit for the capitalist insofar as in the short run competition does not force the innovating capitalist to lower his price to the new, lower social value (resulting from the generalization of the higher productivity).

To go on with Marx's presentation:

> According as in a country capitalist production is developed, the national intensity and productivity of labor also rise there above the international level. The different quantities of commodities of the same kind which are produced in different countries in the same labor time therefore have unequal international values which are expressed in different prices, i.e., in different money sums according to the international values. The relative value of money will therefore be smaller in a nation with the more developed capitalist mode of production than in the one with the less developed capitalist mode of production.[7]

In commenting on this last part of the passage, let us assume that U.S. workers produce 100 cars per day, British workers 75, and West German workers 50, with British conditions of production coinciding with the average conditions. If 100 grams of gold are equal to the value of the average work day, then the national values of the cars will be 1, 1.33, and 2 grams respectively, whereby 1.33 equals the world market price. Thus the U.S. will gain a surplus profit, whereas West Germany will be selling below its national value. If the relative value of money is smaller in the U.S. then the U.S. needs less time to buy one gram of gold but with this gold can buy more hours of labor embodied in the commodities of the less productive nations. Although there is equal exchange on the world market in terms of value—i.e., of international value—less national labor time is being exchanged for more.

It will be clear from the previous discussion that the exchange rate will express the relation between the national money form of value and world money or, what is the same, the relation between national value production and what Marx called universal labor.

But universal labor, as opposed to the average labor within a country, is an abstraction of exchange on the world market; unlike the average labor on a national scale, it is not an immanent condition of production, although the increasing export of capital in the past two decades has created a situation in which production conditions in the major capitalist nations begins to approximate one another. How does this exchange abstraction become concretized?

The example cited above was misleading insofar as it gives the impression that every national labor on the world market gets weighted in the scale of universal labor according to the rank which its country occupies in that scale.

In fact, differences of intensity and productivity can only work themselves out through competition of specific branches of production. Let us illustrate this with the following example of three countries producing three commodities: U.S., U.K., and West Germany; cars, whisky, rubber. We set the dollar, pound, and mark in a 1=1=1=1 relation, whereby one unit of national currency represents one national labor day. Under these assumptions we get the following as a point of departure:

	U.S.	W.G.	U.K.
Cars	$50	DM 150	£180
Whisky	$25	DM 40	£ 66
Rubber	$ 5	DM 20	£ 12

Obviously under these conditions, that is with absolute productivity and intensity "advantages" of the U.S., the latter would develop a very large trade surplus, whereas W.G. and U.K. would develop large trade deficits. Under these circumstances the demand for U.S. commodities on the part of U.K. and W.G. will increase; this appears as an increased demand for dollars, but it is merely a reflection of the demand for the cheaper U.S. commodities. The fact that more pounds and marks must be paid to buy dollars means that more commodities can be bought with dollars than with the other two currencies. Under these conditions the dollar will appreciate relative to the other two currencies, whereby the pound and mark will depreciate relative to the dollar. This in turn means that the national labor of the U.S. will be expressed in higher values on the world market, and that of the U.K. and W.G. in lower values. In this way the national labor of each country becomes part of the scale of universal labor. On this basis one U.S. labor day is set equal to one universal labor day, that of W.G. to $1/2$ universal labor day, and that of the U.K. to $1/3$; thus $1 = DM2 = £3$. With respect to the above branches of production we get:

	U.S.	W.G.	U.K.
Cars	$50	$75	$60
Whisky	$25	$20	$22
Rubber	$ 5	$10	$ 4

From this table we see that the U.S. has lost its leading position in the production of whisky and rubber and has retained it only in cars, even though the U.S. continues to produce the former two commodities in the same amount of labor time—that is, in less time than the U.K. and W.G. expend on these commodities.

The reason that the smaller amount of national labor time embodied in U.S. commodities is represented in more value than the greater amounts of U.K. and W.G. national labor time is that through the modification of the law of value on the world market

> every branch-specific labor of a country must be weighted according to the rank which the national labor on the average occupies on the scale of productivities and intensities. This mechanism can have as a result that a branch of a nation, although it in international comparison produces most productively, nevertheless in price competition falls behind the branch of that nation which produces most unproductively. This can take place because the relative productivity advantage of this branch vis-à-vis international competition is less than the average productivity and intensity advantage of the nation in ques-

tion vis-à-vis the other nations, which latter advantage determines its rank in the international scale and therewith its exchange rate.[8]

The reader should keep in mind the double process of international value formation: (1) on the aggregate social level—through the rank of the national labor on the scale of universal labor; and (2) through the individual capital—through the competition of the national capitals within a sphere of production.

C. A SHORT HISTORICAL OVERVIEW OF THE GOLD AND "DOLLAR" STANDARDS

1. *Gold* S opens this section with the bold statement that there is "of course nothing sacred about gold" (650); he then proceeds to mention other objects which "would do" too. What they or even gold "would do" or do do is not clear. It is doubtful, however, that S was restricting himself to the use-value aspect of the matter. By his use of the word "sacred" and the inclusion of paper napkins as a possible substitute for gold S would like to give the impression that the value aspect of gold is also irrelevant. This is consistent with his belief that fiat paper money is the essence of money. This cavalier attitude toward gold has long been good form among bourgeois economists who fancy that this is all part and parcel of the "modern" economists' ability to overcome the irrationality of capitalism.

S's account of the problems of the gold standard is pedagogically very confusing; for in discussing the influence of the gold supply on the monetary system at a time when there was internal gold circulation, he tells the reader that this is "very relevant for our own day" (7th ed., op. cit. p. 627). It is clear that economizing on the use of gold in circulation through the use of paper money/credit will in large part deal with the problem of gold supply under a gold circulation standard as far as the internal price structure is concerned; however, the problem of current interest which this material is supposed to be "relevant" to is so-called international liquidity. As S sees it, the opening up of more gold mines toward the end of the nineteenth century and the increased use of the credit pyramid "enabled the world to keep on the gold standard and stave off deflation up until the 1929 crash. But this did involve a strain on international liquidity, and some experts actually attribute that slump to an increasing shortage of world liquidity" (652).

The point here is that the gold is not some sort of external physical production factor controlling the fate of capitalism: if only we could find more gold mines, crises would be forever banished. (Though this is not S's view, he at least implicitly imputes it to unnamed supporters of the gold standard.) S argues that as a result of lagging gold supply there was a sagging price level in the last third of the nineteenth century:

> This gave rise to much social unrest. In an ideal world of perfect price flexibility, where the Quantity Theory worked smoothly both down and up, falling prices should not have mattered much. But as Hume himself insisted, prices and wages tend to be sticky downward; and falling price levels tend to lead to labor unrest, strikes, unemployment, and radical movements generally. Precisely that happened in the US and other countries during the 1875-1895 era of populism [650 f.].

We must admit we find this baffling both on a theoretical and a factual level. Why falling price levels should lead to "unrest" is not clear. Everyday experience in the past few years would lead one to believe that rising prices do not exactly lead to calm. If both rising and falling prices lead to "unrest," it would appear that capitalism will have very few rest periods.

But is S correct? First of all, it is clear that if wages rise, remain the same, or drop less than prices do, real wages will not have declined. Let us look at the period under question. Using 1900 as our base year (i.e., all the magnitudes are set equal to 100 in 1900), we see that from 1875 to 1895 nominal wages sank from 95 to 94, the cost of living from 104 to 92, resulting in a rise in real wages from 91 to 102.[9] It is of course true that this period did nevertheless witness fairly intensive class struggle in the U.S. How do we explain this? The reason lay in the accelerated development of capitalist accumulation following the Civil War: the working class was rebelling against the exploitation of their labor power in capitalist factories, an exploitation not restricted to the amount of bread on their table.

Germany also experienced a vast strengthening of a socialist labor movement during this period in which real wages also rose.

In England, on the other hand, this period produced a "business trade unionism"—in other words, a departure from dealing with the broader political issues of class struggle and a concentration on consolidating union power with respect to improving the living standards of the union members.

In view of this information we cannot accept S's presentation as accurate. In addition, the fall in price levels during this period was in any case not wholly caused on the gold side, for it was also a time of greatly increasing productivity in manufacturing industry, which would have caused prices in that premonopoly period to drop, abstracting from the factor gold.

Before turning to the "dollar standard" we wish to comment briefly on S's treatment of the gold standard and its historical evolution. First we are told that it was on account of Britain's "prestige" that other major capitalist countries adopted the gold standard. We assume this to be a euphemism for the economic and military power which made Britain the dominant capitalist power of that period. On the other hand, Britain's prestige apparently was not great enough to force these other countries to join it in the great harmonious experiment of free trade. Why was Britain's prestige great enough to bring about the one but not the other? Presumably because the national sovereignty of the competitors was not severely impinged upon by the gold standard, whereas it most definitely was by free trade. Britain's internal gold standard was merely a reflection of the fact that it, as the first developed capitalist nation, developed the monetary system most adequate to that economic structure. The evolution of this gold standard on a world scale meant that capitalism itself was creating an international capitalist system also with its most adequate monetary system.

A critique of the rest of S's narrative on this subject is made difficult by its vague and folksy tone, an approach devoid of historical content; in fact, there is no chronological indication of when "small" countries like the Philippines began to hold the currencies of "big" countries like the U.S. which were on the gold standard (that is, whose currencies were still convertible into gold), a development commonly called the gold-exchange standard. This modification of the gold standard was programmatically put forward at the Genoa Conference in 1922, which was to formulate monetary reforms to deal with the disruption of the old system caused by the war-induced inflation. Since gold could no longer cover the inflated paper currencies, it was suggested that the foreign currencies of countries still on the gold standard be held in reserves to function like gold as a cover for paper in circulation.

S goes on to state that as long as the "small" country can remain on this gold-exchange standard "the effect would be much like the pure gold standard, but with great economizing on gold" (651). For whom would it be the same? Or what would be the same? One gets the impression S means things would be the same for the "small" country. Perhaps; however, now the various currencies were linked not only through the "neutral numeraire" gold, but new explicit credit relations were being constructed. In fact, one of the main reasons that Benjamin Strong, then Governor of the New York Federal Reserve Bank, turned against this gold-exchange standard was the fear that it "facilitated a pyramiding of credit on small gold holdings in center countries; that the conversion of foreign exchange balances into gold might force the center countries sharply to increase their discount rates and so to bring about the very deflation that the advocates of the League [of Nations] study feared."[10]

2. *The So-called Dollar Standard* We salute S for his courage in mentioning this phenomenon at all (even if a portion has disappeared again in the 9th ed).

The origins of the dollar standard are related in admirably bold outline: "During the Great Depression of the 1930s, political unrest and fear of Hitler's aggression caused an avalanche of gold to flow into the U.S. After World War II *the world was in fact on a dollar standard*" (652). The next few lines deal with the assertion that the dollar had replaced the pound as the key currency. That there must be some difference between the position of the pound and the dollar can be seen in S's own "example," according to which the Bretton Woods Conference defined currencies either in terms of gold or the dollar. But this is something new, something that the pound had never been involved in during its "heyday."

At this point S concedes that the position of the dollar gave the U.S. "in effect, something of the same privilege of creating money out of thin air that the commercial banks enjoy domestically. . . . To a degree, this key position gave America the right to get a certain amount of goods at no real cost. But it also put a special responsibility on America to keep its balance of payments in order" (8th ed., p. 630).

As to the "privilege" the U.S. gained from the mechanism, the analogy to a commercial bank does not appear accurate to us. It would appear more accurate to state that the U.S. gained a role in the capitalist world similar to that of the Federal Reserve–Treasury within the U.S.— namely its ability to print paper money.

When the state prints up paper money, the result is inflation and presumably a redistribution of income within the country. This would appear to be analogous to the present situation on the international level. It arose at Bretton Woods because the West European countries confronted their periods of economic reconstruction unable to complete the tasks alone; without gold to buy U.S. capital "goods" and consumer "goods"; without the present economic potential to produce exports with which to import U.S. commodities. If the U.S. had continued merely to export to these countries, then sooner or later the whole process would have come to a halt. It is in this context that the Marshall "aid" must be seen; for without credits or grants there would have been no exchange whatsoever.

To return to the paper dollar: S states that "America" acquired the "right to get a certain amount of goods at no real cost." But who is America? And from whom did it get these "goods at no real cost?" For the most part these dollars were used to buy capital—whether in productive or money form—abroad. This is not America, but the capitalist class, and more specifically the international monopolies with foreign plants. Now remember our analogy to paper money emission within a country: an inflation-induced redistribution of income follows. Something like that must occur internationally: parts of the value produced in other capitalist countries are being redistributed to U.S. capitalists.

Bourgeois economists are wont to view the matter of loss and gain one-sidedly with respect to the dollar standard; either the U.S. gets nothing from it or it suffers from having less leeway in its domestic economic policy and international balance of payments. But precisely this aspect would appear to constitute the difference between the key currency system in the 1920s and the dollar standard; for in the former case the U.S. was subject to certain constrictions which in the end caused the system to break down on account of the unwillingness of the U.S. to subordinate national capital accumulation needs to the requirements of international world money requirements.

At the present time it would appear that the power of the U.S. to issue paper money internationally eliminates at least a large part of the constriction usually associated with a key-currency nation; it is prevented from dealing with it effectively on account of its international monetary responsibilities—in fact after World War II it was the European countries, in particular Britain, that wanted some mechanism to protect it from the expected depression, recession, or slump in the U.S.

Moreover, regardless of the institutional set-up in the 1920s, the U.S. would not have been in the best possible situation to throw its weight about on the international level because the British banks were still preeminent there. Ever since before World War I the U.S. capitalist class sought to displace Britain as the leading finance capitalist on the world market. Such a position is a powerful lever for fostering commodity exports, capital export in the form of direct investment and portfolio investment, floating international loans to foreign corporations and governments, etc.

That the U.S. role of world banker depended in large part on its industrial capital preeminence does not refute the fact that there was a very definite strategy afoot. After all, it was not for nothing that the U.S. Treasury Secretary at the time of Bretton Woods, Henry Morgenthau, Jr., declared it to be his main objective to "move the financial center of the world from London and Wall Street to the United States Treasury. . . ."[11]

III. HISTORICAL ASPECTS OF THE WORLD MARKET AS A DETERMINING FACTOR OF NATIONAL AND INTERNATIONAL CAPITAL ACCUMULATION

The stated purpose of the second part of Chapter 33 is to "go behind the demand and supply curves of international trade to examine each item involving foreign exchange payments and see how they all combine" (8th ed., p. 631). Instead we are given five pages devoted to a breakdown of the various elements of the balance of payments into formal classifications and three pages of extremely suspect historical material and current aspects of capital movements. The first five pages are of course necessary and useful as a guide to balance of payments tables, but they can hardly be viewed as going beyond supply and demand, for no concrete analysis is involved, merely a description of the categories.

S presents "the four stages typical of the growth of a young agricultural nation into a well-developed industrialized one" (659). By reviewing how the U.S. historically passed through these stages he hopes to "consolidate understanding." Aside from the inaccuracies in the account itself, the most pernicious aspect of this approach is its implicit advice to the "poor" countries: if you too want to grow up and be industrialized like us, then you'll have to do it the way we did it.

The phenomenon S outlines here with respect to the U.S. represents the reenactment of a similar process which took place in England in the eighteenth century; this is but one aspect of the uneven development of capitalism over time and among countries at a given time. There has been a long succession of dominant capitalist powers who indirectly helped the rise of the national capital about to supplant them. This process is connected with the overaccumulation of capital on the national level; the falling rate of profit makes it imperative to withdraw a portion of the national capital from the home country and to invest in countries where, because of the lower organic composition of capital, the rate of profit will be higher and/or in countries where the extraordinary conditions of labor exploitability make enormous profits easily accessible.

In the case of Holland, at a time when capitalism was in the early part of its development and the mode of relative surplus-value production was in a state of underdevelopment as a result of the state of technology, the overaccumulation of capital set in rather early. When we speak of the decline of a great power, we do not mean that the capitalist class of that nation has become totally impoverished. In fact, in the case of Holland, that country's bourgeoisie has retained its international rentier status until the present day; for example, Holland is the only major Western European country which maintains more direct investment in the U.S. than the U.S. does in Holland.

Yet in spite of this relatively lucrative outlet for Dutch monopoly capital, the Netherlands today is a second-rate capitalist power; France and England, which in the nineteenth century also began to suffer the same fate that had befallen Holland in the eighteenth, are also minor powers today. It is this aspect of international capitalist power that S loses sight of not only in this section but throughout the section on the international economy. Instead we are presented with a movement on the part of all countries through time to ever higher states of welfare.

S gives no inkling that anything of the sort described above could have been happening in the development of the U.S. Instead we are told that England and Europe lent to the U.S. "in order to build up our capital structure" (660). "In order to" is S's own version of intentions; they actually invested in order to make profit, regardless of what happened to "our capital structure." The fact that the U.S. happened to become a major capitalist power, which is not true for any other major areas of European investment in the nineteenth century, is only peripherally related to the foreign investment, considering the relatively small amount involved. The U.S. would doubtless have become a great power on its own.

Rather the point of this section is to support the thesis that today's capitalist investment in "underdeveloped" countries will build up their capital structures as well, and that furthermore this is the only historically tried and proven way.

Next we learn that from 1873 until World War I, U.S. capital movements were "nearly in balance, our new lending just about canceling our borrowing" (660). This is a good example of S's formal approach via the double-entry bookkeeping method without telling us what the underlying contents of these sums mean. First of all, the period itself is too comprehensive to be meaningful, for it covers two different eras in U.S. development. Thus during the first period, from 1873 to 1896, the U.S. imported almost four times as much capital as it exported, whereas during the second period the proportions were almost reversed.

Behind the formal balances there is also the hidden factor of the qualitative changes taking place in the industrial structure of the older and newer capitalist countries. As Rudolf Hilferding pointed out, the two rising powers of the period, the U.S. and Germany, both "export above all industrial capital and thus extend their own industry the working capital of which they in part receive in the form of loan capital from countries with slower industrial development but with greater accumulated capital wealth."[12] By this Hilderding means that direct investment abroad in a sense represents an extension of the national capital insofar as the capitalists making the investment retain control over the operations of the plant and may reinvest—including "repatriation" of their profits—as they choose, thus extracting the maximal advantage; the providers of loan capital on the other hand, England, France, Netherlands, were relegated to a much more passive position as mere creditors.

We now watch the U.S. enter the stage of "new creditor nation," which was ushered in by World War I. There is a certain irony here in S's use of qualitative and quantitative changes. On the one hand, S's quantitative discovery of balance hid a qualitative change in the relation of the U.S. to Europe and Latin America; now on the other hand, given an obvious qualitative change, S tries his best to make light of the matter: "When the warring countries suddenly became avid customers for our exports, we sent them goods in return for barren gold and fancy gilt-edged certificates" (706).

That all this wasn't quite such a surprise gift which happened to fall into the laps of the American "people" is described by William A. Brown, Jr., in his standard work on the gold standard:

> For at least a decade before the passage of the Federal Reserve Act ways and means of promoting American export trade in manufacturing goods had been actively discussed in the US. . . . There had been an increasing desire to provide American exporters with facilities in foreign countries comparable to those built up during the nineteenth century by British banks and during the latter part of the nineteenth century and the first part of the twentieth century by Italian and other foreign banks. . . . Though the facilities of this system provided American commerce with cheap and efficient financing, the increasingly competitive nature of American exports of manufactures rendered dependence on these foreign facilities distasteful to those engaged in an aggressive expansion of American trade. There was a strong feeling that the use of sterling accep-

tance was a handicap to American trade because it strengthened the preference for British goods already built up by long standing connections and by British controlled enterprise throughout the world. . . . From the day on which the war broke out Americans began to lay the foundation for an extension of American banking abroad and therefore, for the provision at the points of origin of foreign business, of a supply of bills drawn under American credits. The war did not lay the foundation for this movement, but it swept away the obstacles that had impeded its development.[13]

World War I brought about the disintegration of the world market in its traditional form; trade treaties lapsed and currencies collapsed, thus becoming inconvertible. After the war the major capitalist nations sought to pursue a policy of economic autarchy in order to prepare themselves for the imperialist war. Moreover, the years 1920-22 brought on a new depression (in 1921 the rate of unemployment in the U.S. reached 11.9 percent). Under these conditions there developed "a trend toward economic self-sufficiency and high tariffs . . . in both Europe and the Western Hemisphere."[14]

1922 marks the year of the Fordney-McCumber tariff in the U.S. which served to secure the domestic market for the agricultural and industrial producers who were suffering from extreme overproduction.

Therein lies the predicament that U.S.—and to some extent British—capital had gotten into. Large reparations payments were forthcoming, but the debtors (above all Germany) were in a period of disaccumulation (that is to say, the existing stock of capital in its physical form was not even being renewed), while the creditors were suffering from overproduction and overaccumulation crises. Payments by the debtor nations in the form of commodities would only exacerbate the problem of overproduction.

Some groups of capitalists (for example the New York National City Bank) favored the cancellation of the debts. The industrial capitalists were afraid that a cancellation and thus reduction of tax burden for the German industrial capitalists would increase their competitive position on the world market. U.S. and U.K. capitalists were interested in a deindustrialized Germany which would serve as a colonial area (as indeed all of middle and eastern Europe were supposed to) in the sense of producing raw materials and selling out its industrial potential to the U.S. and U.K. for colonial-type wages.

Thus we find objective differences between the victorious states and the debtor states, among the victorious states, and among factions of the capitalist class within the victorious as well as the debtor states. Since S is either unwilling or unable to pursue these issues and to discuss them, he is left with no other explanation than "our psychological state of mind."

We cannot go into the causes of the Great Depression here, but apportioning "blame" to various countries (660) it clearly does not constitute a scientific explanation. S implies that foolish "Main Street investors" who kept throwing their money away were partially responsible for the crisis. First of all, let us not forget that although the Allied Powers defaulted on approximately $9.5 billion of war debt to the U.S. government, it is not the capitalists who supplied the commodities that were purchased with this loan who lost out on the deal; nor the U.S. capitalists who bought the bonds which financed the loan, for they too were paid their interest; rather it was the U.S. taxpayers who kept paying taxes to support the debt payments on the U.S. national debt who had to take the loss.

Secondly, the fact that much U.S. loan capital was being sent out of the country did not depend on the psychological propensities of U.S. investors to pick lemons: the point is that toward the end of the 1920s the U.S. was suffering a severe crisis of capital overaccumulation, i.e., the same vast scale of productive reinvestment of surplus value could not be maintained. This was responsible for the shift of loan capital to domestic speculation (stock market) and capital export. Although the debts in the wake of World War I doubtless exacerbated the situation, this was a classical overproduction crisis of capitalism which existed independently of poor investment choices (in fact, caused those choices to turn out to be "poor").

We now turn to the fourth and final stage—that of mature creditor nation, a blissful state apparently attained only by Great Britain, which in turn brings us to the next part of S's argument—namely that we need not "feel sorry" for Britain on account of her passive trade balance: "Her *citizens* were living better because they were able to import much cheap food and in return did not have to part with much in the way of valuable export goods. *The* English were paying for their import surplus by the interest and dividend receipts they were receiving from past foreign lending" (660—our emphasis). This statement can be broken down as follows: (1) the whole population of England as an undifferentiated mass was affected uniformly by the phenomenon under study; (2) this mass of people was living better; (3) this resulted from imports of cheap food; (4) domestic production could be consumed at home instead of being exported as payment for the imports; (5) payment followed in the form of U.K. foreign-investment income.

Although S in two places here refers to all of the English people, he specifically refers to the benefits accruing to the working class alone and only in their function as consumers. We deduce this from the reference to cheap food, which cannot be a prime concern of the capitalists as consumers, and the landowners were opposed to all food imports since they posed a threat. First let us look at the narrow argument that the working class gained as consumer. What sort of goods did England import from its colonies? Sugar, tea, tobacco, etc. The matter is hardly as straightforward as S would have us believe; in fact, the statistical calculation of consumption items alone is still a matter of dispute. Although certain better-paid workers undoubtedly gained from this "arrangement," S has in fact provided neither proof nor sources.

So who did benefit from the situation? U.K. investment abroad meant a higher rate of profit for the capital involved because the organic composition of capital as well as wages were lower in the colonies, and in many cases monopoly positions allowed monopoly profits. This in turn has a positive effect on the rate of profit at home. Thus when S says that nineteenth-century foreign investment was "twice blessed: it blessed him who gave and him who received" (660), the first part is correct; for it "blessed" the British capitalists in the form of a higher profit rate abroad and a higher rate of surplus value at home.

This hints at the salubrious effect of British imperialism on the workers. With a large portion of British surplus value being exported abroad in the form of capital, both potential output and jobs were being destroyed. Between 1850 and 1900 the unemployment rate remained above 4 percent during twenty-four of these years, or approximately half the time; during seventeen years the rate reached 6 percent or more; and for three years it exceeded 10 percent.[15] The unemployment picture would therefore be one indication that *the* English were not uniformly "twice blessed" by imperialism. As we know, capitalists invest abroad mainly because the "commercial return" there is higher, or alternatively, that continued investment at "home" would press profitability downward. Thus it must be emphasized that capitalists are responding to "market pressures" by going abroad; to support continued investment at home under these circumstances would be class-suicidal philanthropy.

Now we come to the last part of S's statement, his assertion that the foreign investment income "paid" for the import surplus. This is a very tricky point insofar as it appears to transform the mathematics of the formal balance of payments into a causal foundation. In one very important sense, S is right: England was in a position to get more than it gave; it was able to import more commodities than it had to export. This meant a tribute was being paid to England; it also meant that other countries were exporting more commodities than they were receiving, a definite loss to them. This much then is true.

S is not asserting that somehow English workers were getting tea for nothing. Philanthropic capitalists did not offer to give workers five pounds of tea for the price of four because they, the capitalists, had "paid the difference" in their foreign investment income. No, workers continued to pay the whole price as it were. To simplify the matter let us assume that British capitalists export capital to Ceylon for a tea plantation. Part of this tea can be now exported to England where other workers will pay for it; perhaps other countries will "pay" by in turn exporting other goods to Britain, which will, of course, also be paid for. The point is that if we only look at the sphere of circulation where exchange of equivalents presumably takes place, we will never discover the origin of getting something in return for nothing. This "trick" takes place at the source of production, where surplus value is produced. Applied to our case, this means that the surplus value produced by the plantation workers in Ceylon will be realized somewhere along the line of the trade channels we have just mentioned. Whether the case is domestic production or imports and exports, surplus value will always be realized by equivalent exchange. In the instance of foreign trade the origin is obscured even more by the intricacies of international payments. The tribute is to be seen in the surplus value produced abroad and in its various forms of realization.

Thus the exploitation is to be sought in the colonies themselves. Their loss consists in their exporting more of their annual product than they import; S's contention that the difference is made up by foreign investments in the colonies simply is not true.

A look at the structure of British investments and trade might be useful, since S does not deem this essential to his disquisition on the blessings of the system. He does not differentiate between the relatively unpopulated colonies like the U.S., Canada, Australia, New Zealand, which soon were populated by European emigrants, and the older civilizations like India, Africa, Latin America, whose already populous areas were subject to foreign domination. Of British foreign investment at the outset of World War I, which totaled about $18 billion, almost 40 percent went to the advanced capitalist countries to be.[16]

Without going into the matter any more deeply, the trade and investment structure was extremely complicated; generalizations about trade, etc., without going into the specifics of the countries involved can be very dangerous. S insists upon speaking of Britain and "the rest of the world" in answer to the question whether the latter's export surplus did not worsen its situation; S replies "not necessarily" because "normally" British investment permitted "the rest of the world" to produce more than enough to pay off British investment-income claims (660). The sense of the "not necessarily" and the "normally" does not reveal itself until one reads on and finds that "of course" things did not always "operate quite so smoothly," but apparently only because not all investments were "wise" and those annoying "political" problems of colonies and "nationalism" "complicated" matters.

Now S's assertion is true for the U.S., Canada, Australia, etc.; these countries were able to pay back the profits the British capitalists "earned" without being crippled. But it must be remembered that even in the nineteenth century the U.S. was a power to be reckoned with. The U.S., an enormous nation with vast resources, could have become an industrial power with or without British investment. What is perhaps equally important is the absence of a sovereign government in a colony like India. The conquest and maintenance of control over such colonies demanded large government expenditures; there was also a need for building the "infrastructure." This produced a large government debt there. Instead of inefficiently having each individual British capitalist in India exploit his workers even more to pay this debt, the Indian government took out loans from British capitalists and paid them interest. It was then left to the Indian government to withdraw these funds more efficiently in turn from the Indian population in the form of taxes.

It is hard to see how government expenditures on nonproductive activities such as building up a military to keep the people in check for the benefit of the British can be regarded as "paying its way." Furthermore, a significant portion of British investment in the colonies flowed into mining which was basically direct investment kept under British control and management.[17] The same would be true of many plantations such as tea, etc. Inasmuch as almost all of this production was geared to the needs of Britain, it was, as it were, a foreign body in the colonies. In this sense it is not correct on S's part to refer to it as "domestic" production.

Thus we are basically left with the railroad investments. These too would appear to have played different roles in the U.S. and in the colonies. In the U.S. they seem to have been purely investment activities—that is, portfolio investments for the purpose of income; the railroads themselves (and canals, too) were to be used as the infrastructure of the U.S. economy determined by the needs of U.S. capitalism.

In India on the other hand the railways were built to facilitate British exploitation of raw materials and markets for the purposes of self-expansion of British value.

That S can propagate such erroneous views at a time when their refutation has seeped into the general consciousness of students does not appear to be idiosyncratic; of the major economics textbooks we could find only one with anything even remotely resembling a realistic description of the situation:

> Imperialism . . . exerted a peculiarly deforming impulse to the underdeveloped—indeed, then, totally undeveloped—economies of the East and South. . . . Malaya became a vast tin mine; Indonesia a huge tea and rubber plantation; Arabia an oil field. In other words, the direction of economic development was steadily pushed in the direction that most benefited the imperial owner, not the colonial peoples themselves.[18]

The result today is that the economy of the underdeveloped nation is badly lopsided, unable to supply itself with a wide variety of goods. This statement too is incorrect, for "the East and South" were not "indeed . . . totally undeveloped"; Deane among others points out that British manufactured exports found restricted entry into China because "local manufactures were often at least as good and always a great deal cheaper" (*The First Industrial Revolution*, op. cit., p. 53).

Excursus: Import Surpluses and Stagnation—Some Hypotheses Before we leave this rather extended commentary on this section we must try to tie up the discussion of trade and "stages" in the balance of payments. S warns us not to "feel sorry" for Britain's passive trade balance, because after all *"it is imports and not exports that add to a nation's well-being"* (8th ed., p. 639). And these import surpluses do represent exploitation although its fruits are distributed far from uniformly. Yet in a deeper sense, we ought to "feel sorry" for Britain, or, more precisely, Britain's ruling class ought to start feeling sorry for itself—and, contrary to S's pious wishes, does. We mean that the import surplus is an expression of the developing or developed rentier status of a now or soon-to-be has-been power.

Imports are not the measure of "well-being" of a capitalist country because consumption does not drive that society; the world market represents an extremely important mechanism for strengthening the forces that ward off the development of crises within a capitalist country (although the world market will also foster the crisis since all escape routes turn into dead ends in the capitalist industrial cycle). A passive trade balance signalizes declining competitiveness of the national capital on the world market; this in turn stems from a relative lagging behind of this national capital in the development of its productive forces with respect to other national capitals.

Thus on the one hand an import surplus is a sign of the relative decline of national capital, and on the other it indicates that this national capital will soon be involved in various structural crises insofar as its exports no longer enjoy ready access to the world market.

But we also must look at the problem historically. In the middle of the nineteenth century when England entered its free trade phase it was by far the most advanced capitalist nation in the world; yet it experienced a passive trade balance. It would appear as though the reasoning just outlined does not apply to the "case" of England. Or perhaps the "case approach" altogether should not be applied.

In any event we would like to present a hypothesis concerning Britain in the nineteenth century. We have posited certain competitive pressures favoring export surpluses; or, alternatively, we have stated that such surpluses, at least among the advanced capitalist countries, were associated with the most productive national capitals, whereas trade deficits indicated relative stagnation. We might look for the roots of England's peculiar position in the historical situation of the time. The very fact that England had a head-start in its capitalist industrialization exerted an adverse influence on its trade balance; that is to say, the other countries were not yet sufficiently industrialized to fulfill the role of good markets for English exports. But there is another reason as well. The competitive forces we spoke of in large degree refer to countries competing in the export of the same commodity or type of commodity (machine tools, aircraft, chemicals, generators, etc.); in the middle of the last century British foreign trade basically consisted of importing commodities it could not produce.

Regardless of this historical situation, we reject S's view that one should not "feel sorry" for a "mature creditor" country with an import surplus. In typical fashion he appears to favor "progress" at all times regardless of the short-run harm this may cause individual producers or countries.

S is referring to the international economic scene where, as we pointed out above, the individual capitalist states are in a position to limit the pressures of competition. The point with S is that he is not merely wishing that the world were run harmoniously, but he is also contending that the theory he presents helps to understand the world as it is and that the reader can become an informed citizen by mastering this theory. It is precisely this "idealistic" approach which militates against an understanding of national policies. The sort of "philanthropic" approach to international trade S seems to advocate has never been and never will be the basis of the economic policy of any capitalist country. And today the situation is no different than it was yesterday. The bawling of U.S. capitalists and their government agents over the "first trade deficit since 1893" is not a sham; the U.S. is becoming less and less competitive on the world market. One of the main troubles with S's discussion is his failure to explain real—as opposed to the arithmetical—relations among the various items in the balance of payments. All we are told is that a plus must offset a minus "for it is a tautology that, *What you get you must either pay for or owe for*" (658). This statement is in itself very enlightening, for as we already know it can only refer to the sphere of circulation and can otherwise only obscure the real sources of gain and loss on the world market. But going beyond this we must try to establish some relations. That S is unable to do this is borne out by his treatment of capital movements as mere "loans private citizens make" and his pedagogic admonition to treat them "like any other exports and imports" (ibid.). During the 1960s U.S. export surpluses were diminishing while capital exports were increasing. Direct investment abroad was in part an attempt to overcome the diminishing competitiveness of U.S. commodities. In the short run this can enhance the productivity of the European competitors by introducing more advanced methods of production there; in the long run, however, it is likely to foster equalization of productive conditions among the major capitalist nations.

Appendix: The Phenomenal Form of the Varying National Conditions of Accumulation in the Bretton Woods System—Over- and Undervalued Currencies In our discussion of the appendix we will focus on the account of over- and undervalued currencies given by S. This appendix first appeared in the 6th edition (1964).

The 8th and 9th editions depart from the previous two insofar as West Germany has now replaced England as Europe's representative. Aside from this problematical approach of lumping all West European countries together, thus blotting out important differences, S also is unclear on the time spans involved. On the one hand there might be some merit in speaking of Europe as a whole inasmuch as in the postwar period those countries, unlike the U.S., sported certain common features. This may well have been true of West Germany and Italy and perhaps of France too; however, England in large measure suffered the same stagnation which prevailed in the U.S. More importantly, the period was not uniform even in Western Europe; one must distinguish between different stages of postwar development if one is to make sense of the monetary situation.

Perhaps the most disturbing aspect of the whole presentation is the absence of any statistical information. This makes matters very difficult if not impossible for the student, especially the beginning student who is probably not familiar with the necessary sources and who would expect a beginning text to furnish at least some direction.

The first section of the overvaluation discussion is devoted to a description of its origin. S begins his account by "let[ting] productivity in Europe grow faster than in America" (7th ed., p. 642). There then follows a very brief description, culminating in the statement that overvaluation "results from the more rapid technical change abroad, which partially closed the gap between their technology and ours and lowered their relative costs" (665). Since productivity is defined technologically S has assumed what has to be explained; in other words, he "lets" productivity increase faster in Europe; from this he draws a straight line to overvaluation of currencies; and then he explains the latter in terms of technological change which is merely a repetition of the "let" clause.

Although productivity is a concept which relates to use-value production, use-value production takes place within a certain social system whose specific characteristics determine how technology develops. To look at the technological results without seeing what creates, fosters, or limits them is to miss the causal aspects of the process.

With reference to postwar Western Europe we must of course take war-caused destruction into consideration. Western Europe, forced to rebuild much of its productive facilities, was at a distinct advantage, for this enabled it to start with the most modern and efficient plants. Thus both total output and productivity increased more rapidly in

West Germany than in the U.S.: the annual rate of growth of total output from 1950 to 1960 equaled 7.6 percent in the former and 3.2 percent in the latter; whereas the per capita rate equaled 6.5 percent and 1.6 percent respectively.[19]

Aside from this and from the additional circumstance that the production facilities were modernized more rapidly in an ongoing manner in Western Europe, there is the further growth factor of channeling labor into the most productive spheres on the Continent by withdrawing workers from previously small firms (also farms), the construction of mass production facilities, etc.: in short, the capitalization of previously non- or small capitalistic producers.

Equally important in the process of accelerated capital accumulation in Western Europe was the extreme exploitation of the working class. In large part this exploitation was made possible by an enormous reserve army of the unemployed. In West Germany, for example, the source of this labor supply consisted of the three million who left the G.D.R. and former German areas, foreign workers from Italy, Turkey, Greece, etc., starting in the late 1950s, ex-farmers, small commodity producers and entrepreneurs, and women. As Charles Kindleberger points out, West Germany's "miracle's" "sine qua non was the elastic labor supply which held down wages and maintained profits and investment."[20]

This mechanism of keeping wages low can be seen in the trend in the share of labor in national income. By comparing net wages (i.e., minus taxes) with (net) national income, one economist has determined that in West Germany labor's share did not regain the 1950 level until 1961.[21] And when one further considers that wage and salary earners as a percentage of all "gainfully employed" rose during this period, then that share of national income must be spread over a larger share of the population.

This is the social meaning of S's gracious "realistic" assumption that wages did not increase as quickly as productivity (665). The significance of the reserve army can be, as it were, independently controlled with the examples of Britain and Japan. The former country had a relatively low rate of unemployment in the 1950s which enabled the labor unions to exert much greater resistance to "rationalizations" of the production process, a resistance force in part responsible for the British lag in growth. As for Japan, we merely refer to an official government publication which itself points to enforced savings through inflation and low wages based on an "excess labor force" as part of the key to Japanese capital accumulation.[22]

The increased productivity of Western Europe finds no expression in the currency relations. Yet S's conclusion that as a result U.S. exports "dwindle physically and (probably) in value" (665) is unclear since U.S. exports in fact doubled in the 1950s.[23] And although it is true that U.S. capitalists will under these conditions begin to transfer production abroad (capital export), it does not automatically follow that current account balance of payments will be harmed by this, since repatriated profits exceed U.S. capital invested abroad.

But this is not enough: other countries became more competitive on the world market because the exporters were able to underprice their U.S. competitors not only on the basis of lower national values, or prices of production, but also because their costs of production gave them an objectively greater leeway.

In connection with the overvalued dollar country (U.S.), S is mainly concerned with the lower aggregate employment and income resulting from the drop in exports (although the drop is not in any case in absolute terms); for the undervalued currency countries S focuses on the inflation (if there had been full employment previously) and on the fact that with the terms of trade turned against the latter they are, "so to speak, throwing away goods" to the U.S. which is getting them for "barren gold or mere dollar IOUs" (666).

What remains to be explained is the specific position of the dollar in an international monetary system of fixed parities. In the immediate postwar period the U.S. productivity advantage guaranteed it large trade surpluses; at the same time this absolute hegemony made the dollar acceptable as a world currency. The fact that the U.S. trade balance becomes negative at the same time that the surplus countries no longer are willing to hold on to their dollars is merely an expression of the one basic process of tendential equalization of production conditions in all advanced capitalist nations.

Up until now S has stressed the advantages accruing to the U.S. and the disadvantages accruing to the undervalued-currency countries; we have also seen that the underlying unity of productivity differentials is not emphasized. Very little attention is devoted to the reasons that West Germany or Japan was willing to put up with this situation for so long.

Bourgeois economists admit the existence of "special interests" which attempt to thwart "progress." What social forces are at work behind the special and the general interest?

In our discussion of the exchange-rate system we spoke of the modification of the law of value that takes place on the world market; on the one hand, there exists an institutionalized tendency toward unequal exchange insofar as the countries with above-average productivity and intensity can exploit their labor on the world market as producing more value (one must keep in mind that this refers to absolute terms of productivity and intensity); thus this would work to the favor of the U.S. in the postwar period against Germany or Japan. (This is not inherently connected with the paper dollar as world currency; it would also be true of any two countries with different positions on the scale of universal labor. The advantages accruing to U.S. capital specifically from the dollar's position are additional.) On the other hand, this tendency does not exist in isolation; for there is a compensating mechanism in the form of exchange-rate changes on the part of the countries with lower absolute productivities. Such national capitals can expand their market shares through devaluations and competitive price advantages on the world market.

When S discusses the possibilities for correcting overvaluation he suddenly becomes much more realistic; he briefly mentions inflation in Europe, deflation in the U.S., a "miracle" of greater productivity in the U.S., devaluation of the dollar and up-valuation of European currencies, continued gold shipments and dollar accumulations, U.S. troop withdrawals from abroad, tariffs, exchange controls, etc. These are in fact some of the factors that must be taken into account when a national capital is faced with the decision concerning exchange rates. Now it is clear from our discussion that the workings of the law of value on the world market would necessitate a realignment of currencies; if none took place, the monetary crisis would finally become an international trade crisis. But even though in the long run the mere existence of international capitalism requires these changes, there is no reason to believe, as S would have us do, that individual national capitals are going to forgo temporary advantages in their competitive struggles without a struggle; and this struggle takes place both among factions of the national capital and among national capitals.

The realism of this section appears to reach its climax in the section entitled "The Achilles' Heel of Classicism," where, if we understand it correctly, it is hinted that little if nothing can be done to discredit the "discredited notions of the mercantilists" under conditions of over- and undervaluation. Immediately following this S advises the reader to look at Chapters 34 and 35 on comparative advantages and tariffs which "would be unanswerable" "if" prices and wages were everywhere flexible and/or exchange rates were flexible and thus no over- and undervaluation occurred (667). Yes "if," but the whole point of the Bretton Woods system was to free the various nations from having to relinquish control over their national economic policies as required by the gold standard.

We do not have time to develop this theme at length, but we would like to try to show some of the factors involved in upward valuation in Germany and Japan. Prior to the 1969 revaluation of the mark a struggle raged in Germany concerning this "decision." Among the arguments against revaluation were these: (1) since the West German economy is relatively heavily oriented toward exports, the adverse market situation resulting from revaluation would hurt the entire economy; (2) the subsequent cheaper imports would weaken the domestic markets for certain already weak branches such as coal and steel, textiles, agriculture; (3) revaluation would diminish entrepreneurial propensities. On the other hand, there were certain consequences to be expected from not revaluing: (1) a continued export boom would relatively diminish domestic supply while the continued inflow of U.S. dollars would increase the domestic money supply (via the gold-exchange standard in which Germany is a non-key currency country) thus accelerating inflation; (2) the economy becomes increasingly dependent on exports and thus on the trade and tariff policies of other countries which sooner or later must take restrictive measures against West German imports; (3) capital concentration will be fostered (this results from the fact that the exporters can avail themselves of large cost economies on the basis of their producing for a market much larger than that served by the purely domestic producers); (4) since Department I commodities ("capital goods") preponderate among West German exports, a further growth of exports would serve to accentuate the differential growth of the two departments, which would have negative effects on the industrial cycle; (5) the inflation-induced tendency toward a drop in real wages will be compensated for by increased wage demands which can be met with the higher profits but which will affect different branches differently according to their competitive positions and will thus further accentuate discrepancies in this respect.[24]

There was no single correct answer. Each side was correct because each side represented certain interests. If the West German economy was to remain a stable capital accumulating economy, then every measure would have to be flanked by others. Given the importance of the export industries, one could not revalue to an extent which would harm them; on the other hand, one would have to revalue enough to give the other national capitals more leeway in their competitive struggle. Those who favored the upvaluation had in mind more the long-term possibilities of an expanding West German economy within an expanding world market than the economy in general, since the relatively small devaluation would have to be a "foul compromise" anyway.

Another example of revaluation as a political-economic problem and struggle of interests can be seen in Japan. Despite a 17 percent upward revaluation in December, 1971, Japan is still widening its export surplus. But one must also take into account the peculiar foreign trade structure in Japan: approximately two-thirds of Japan's imports consist of raw materials, a very high proportion for a major industrial nation. Given the comparatively severe import restrictions and tariffs of Japanese trade policy, it is to be doubted whether the enhanced position of Japan on the scale of universal labor attendant upon a revaluation of the yen will really redound to the benefit of the "broad and scattered consumer interests" as so many bourgeois theoreticians fancy; given this protection from foreign competition it is more likely that domestic profits will rise as a result: "Japan as a whole depends on the outside world for about three-fourths of the raw materials it uses. Increasing the yen's value automatically lowers the cost of these materials here and thus cuts the cost of manufacturing."[25] At the same time of course it is pointed out that the "shake-up" in Japanese industry resulting from its higher prices on the world market will really be beneficial to Japan since it will eliminate "inefficient marginal producers" and "free millions of workers" and "speed capital" into "more sophisticated fields." All this may well be true, but the branches concerned are not going down without a fight, nor is the capitalist state about to engage in wholesale euthanasia. Just as in the case of West Germany, the capitalist state in Japan is developing flanking measures in case of revaluation. Recent measures concerning the export of capital are not merely a "neutral" mechanism to disaccumulate large dollar reserves. These capital exports are meant to strengthen Japan's external position.

Chapter 24: World-Trade Theories (S's Chapter 34)

One tells us, for example, that free trade would bring into being an international division of labor and therewith assign to every country a production harmonizing with its natural advantages.

You believe perhaps, gentlemen, that the production of coffee and sugar is the natural attribute of the West Indies.

Two hundred years ago nature, which pays no heed to free trade, planted neither coffee trees nor sugar cane there.

And it will perhaps not take a half-century before you will no longer find either coffee or sugar there, for already the East Indies through cheaper production have successfully taken up the cudgel against this allegedly natural attribute of the West Indies. . . .

One more circumstance must thereby never be lost sight of: namely that, just as everything has become a monopoly, there are today also a few branches of industry which dominate all others and assure the peoples primarily producing them dominance on the world market. . . . It is truly ridiculous how the free traders point to the few specialties in every industrial branch in order to throw them onto the scales against the products of everyday use which can be produced most cheaply in those countries where industry is most developed.

If the free traders cannot comprehend how one country can enrich itself at the expense of another, we should not be surprised, since the same gentlemen want to comprehend even less how within a country one class can enrich itself at the expense of another.—*Rede über den Freihandel* (Speech on Free Trade), January 9, 1848, in Marx-Engels *Werke*, IV, 456 f.

SPECIALIZATION: AN UNINTENTIONAL BOURGEOIS ANALOGY BETWEEN THE OPPRESSION OF THE "THIRD" WORLD AND THE OPPRESSION OF WOMEN

S begins his discussion with this assertion: "Again and again we have seen how specialization increases productivity and standards of living." This chapter will allegedly extend this established fact to the international sphere (668). We cannot agree that S has really provided the reader with any proof other than the dubious "mathematical proofs." He has previously stated that specialization rests on "interpersonal differences in ability"; these he takes to be "natural," whereas the "differences" specialization "accentuates and creates" apparently are "acquired" (52 f.). In this chapter, it is the former that absorb practically all of his theoretical and policy-making attention; the latter recede into the background.

Since S himself explicitly extends the advantages of specialization to "regions" (52), we must follow up the negative side.

S might maintain that the banana producers can barter their bananas on the world market for other goods and second, it does not really matter whether the emphasis is on coffee beans or steel. However, as we shall see, this might be true in a world of "harmony." Secondly, it "just so happens" that the countries concentrating on a few agricultural export products belong to the poorer nations. Thirdly, one must pay attention to the use-values under consideration: no major power is going to suffer irreparable harm if its supply of bananas and coffee is cut off; and although substitutes for unobtainable raw materials can be found, there are certain limits beyond which the power aspirations of any nation would be severely restricted.

The peculiar manner in which use-values are lost sight

of, and individual and collective processes mixed, can be seen in S's exemplification of the principle of comparative advantage. He resorts to the "traditional example" of the best lawyer who is also the best typist in town. Although he is better than his typist, rather than "give up precious time from the legal field" he magnanimously lets her type.

Before we make the leap to nations, let us analyze the subtle logic at work here. First of all, S has both stacked the deck and destroyed his own emphasis of the difference between comparative and absolute advantage by "endowing" his characters with a certain "package" of "resources"; for in the vast majority of cases the secretary has no hope whatsoever of becoming a lawyer—her productivity in that area is zero. One important point here is that certain social power attaches to certain positions; no one, not even S, would deny that capitalists have greater social power than their secretaries. And, to quote S, "So with countries" (669).

But to continue with the secretary: this division of labor is not optimal with respect to world production; for, as many bourgeois economists readily admit, "The principle of comparative advantage does not call for having each task done by the man who can do it most efficiently. That would mean having Jones divide his time between fishing and coconut picking, while Smith does nothing."[1]

The only reason S comes to the conclusion he does is that, contrary to his stated method of sticking to barter and production functions, money wages have been sneaked in. Presumably the reason lawyers do not do their own typing is that secretaries "come so cheap."

The "traditional" example points up the logic of oppression inherent in bourgeois economics; just as women may continue pecking away at the keys while the men folk take care of business, so too the developing countries of the "Third" World may resign themselves to producing coffee and bananas relaxed in the thought that the ruling class of the steel-, chemical-, etc., producing countries will run the world for their benefit.

Thus the basic tenor of the theory of comparative advantage is that nations, like "people," are better "suited," "fit," etc., to produce certain commodities than others. How they got to be that way is not germane to S's reasoning: similarly, the fact of one-sided development itself is taken for granted rather than explained (specialization will obviously not suffice inasmuch as certain countries seem to be able to specialize in more items and with less deleterious results than others); and finally, the power relations inherent in the production of certain use-values is altogether neglected and, in fact, implicitly denied in this world of harmony.

"NATURE" AND COMPARATIVE COSTS

Let us now look at how S explains why certain countries are (not how they got to be) better suited for some activities than for others. "The first link" in comparative-advantages thinking, according to S, is the *"diversity in conditions of production between different countries"* (668); by this he means that each country is "endowed with certain quantities of natural resources, capital goods, kinds of labor, and technical knowledge or know-how" (ibid.).

The first thing that strikes us here is the use of the term "endowed"; on a fairly superficial level this is a static approach. But let us look at the enumerated factors more closely. With respect to the natural resources one might be inclined to agree that here we are indeed dealing with endowments. Thus, certain mineral deposits, bodies of water, etc., do indeed predate human activity. But even their being "endowed with certain quantities of natural resources" in itself says little; if a society's development is such that it does not know what to do with these resources, then they are irrelevant; on the other hand, an "advanced technology" may compensate for the absence of certain raw materials by manufacturing synthetics; and finally, the colonial or imperialist control of a raw-material source in a formally sovereign state may also go a long way toward overcoming such "faulty" endowments.

As for the other factors S mentions (labor, capital, and

"know-how"), these reveal even more clearly the static nature of comparative-advantages theory. Obviously they are not "endowments" in the sense of "original" natural resources; they have been developed in the course of a specific social and historical process; the mere fact that on the basis of a certain development one country at a given time may, according to the tenets of comparative advantage, be better suited to produce a certain commodity than another in no way implies that the processes leading up to this condition were not a misdevelopment; in other words, the fact that some countries produce rubber and others use it does not in itself mean that somebody must be doing something right.

An interesting situation arises: so convinced are bourgeois authors of their theory as a guide to practice that actual trade patterns are taken to be expressions of the "law" of comparative advantage, which per se means that a world optimum is being attained. Thus Bela Balassa admits that there is not sufficient information to explain reallocation of resources as dependent on comparative costs; instead he uses as an "alternative solution" " 'revealed' comparative advantage": "Since the commodity pattern of trade reflects relative costs as well as the influence of nonprice factors, such as goodwill, quality, and the availability of servicing and repair facilities, the 'revealed' comparative advantage of the industrial countries may be indicated by their trade performance with respect to individual industries."[2]

Having set down "the first link," S goes on to say that this is why different countries have different "production possibilities"; from this he deduces that although every country could try to produce everything, not all could succeed and/or only "at a terrific cost" (668 f.). However, except for certain items which a nation may be unable to produce at all, it would take an extremely complicated analysis to determine which "costs"—producing or not producing—are greater in the long run. We use the word analysis here not in the post factum sense of determining why a country specializes in some commodities, but rather in the spirit of the bourgeois myth that such "national cost" calculations are actually made prior to "deciding" in favor of one of the alternatives.

That capitalism does not "plan itself" and that comparative advantage is a theoretical expression of this phenomenon insofar as it avoids dealing with the origins of a given "product mix" can be seen in the following statement by Kindleberger:

> Differences in comparative costs come about not only because of differences in factor endowments but also through specialization in different commodities. To a degree the choice of whether the US or Britain specializes in one kind of an [sic] automobile or another ... may be determined by *historical accident*. The *fact is that, with each specialized*, a basis for trade exists, since each can produce one good cheaper than the other.[3]

Kindleberger's choice of such a relatively innocuous example as different cars is a curious one; it would appear much more important to investigate why one country produces sugar "best" and another steel. We have italicized "historical accident" in the cited passage to emphasize the nonplanned aspect; we can accept "accident," whether historical or otherwise, only in a limited sense. A science of the international division of labor would have to study the conditions under which the currently dominant structure originated; this would mean for example showing that the noncapitalist world did not make a "policy decision" in favor of sugar, cotton, etc., on the basis of its favorable production factor "mix," but rather that economic and in some cases direct military coercion on the part of European capitalist powers were instrumental in making the "decision" for these countries.

In a different context S himself has conceded that the usual textbook approach leaves something to be desired:

> No one will deny the importance of iron, coal, power, rainfall and fertile plains as localizing factors. But there is little that the proportions-of-the-factor analysis can add to our understanding of the matter. We should be giving the show away if we were

to descend to such fatuities as: the tropics grow tropical fruits because of the relative abundance there of tropical conditions.[4]

As long as comparative advantages and its "modern" variant, factor proportions, remain on the surface of society and history they will indeed remain bogged down in "fatuities," unable to explain either the use-value or value aspect of foreign trade. Although it is true that in a "rational" world not every area would produce everything, S has definitely not proved that, other than for the very shortest run and within the narrowest of calculations, "it pays" for all countries to specialize in what they happen to be specializing in.

RICARDO'S THEORY AND ITS MODERN BOURGEOIS DISTORTION

This is one of the rare passages where Ricardo receives mention, let alone praise. We will forgo any discussion of S's introduction of Ricardo and instead provide our own by citing a passage from Ricardo indicative of the uncommonly harmonistic tone of the principle:

> Under a system of perfectly free commerce, each country naturally devotes its capital and labour to such employments as are most beneficial to each. This pursuit of individual advantage is admirably connected with the universal good of the whole. By stimulating industry, by rewarding ingenuity, and by using most efficaciously the peculiar powers bestowed by nature, it distributes labour most effectively and most economically; while by increasing the general mass of productions, it diffuses general benefit, and binds together, by one common tie of interest and intercourse, the universal society of nations throughout the civilized world. It is this principle which determines that wine shall be made in France and Portugal, that corn shall be grown in America and Poland, and that hardware and other goods shall be manufactured in England.[5]

And finally, as Ricardo notes, "it would undoubtedly be advantageous to the capitalists of England, and to the consumers in both countries" that wine and cloth be made in

Portugal by transferring English capital and labor thither; alas, "the fancied or real insecurity of capital" will thwart such an absolute optimum.[6]

Now let us look at S's explication of Ricardo's theory. First we are told that just as Ricardo worked with two countries and two "goods" "for simplicity," he also "chose to measure all costs in terms of hours and labor" "for simplicity" (670); and lest we become apprehensive about using a theory Ricardo himself recognized to be "unrealistic" (8th ed., p. 27), S reminds us that the Appendix will show us how modern advanced treatises avoid this pitfall.

First of all, it is not accurate to say that Ricardo "chose to measure all costs" in terms of labor time. The term "cost" itself is misleading. Cost within the tradition of bourgeois international economic theory has meant either subjective cost in the sense of the pain of labor or abstinence attendant upon saving or, in the "modern" version, opportunity cost (this notion underlies S's production possibility frontiers). Ricardo was not an adherent of this notion of cost; and his notion of cost of production also referred to the labor embodied in the means of production.

In any case, it is false to assert, as does Gottfried Haberler, that the labor theory of value "assumes that the factor 'labor' is the sole means of production."[7] If by "means of production" is meant "factor of production," then this is palpably false, since it refers to the production of use-values, in which land, labor, and means of production all participate; and if by this is meant, as S charges, that "labor would get all the income" (7th ed., p. 29), it is equally false. However, in Ricardo's treatment of foreign trade, profit is in fact left out of consideration, not because he imputes all income to labor, but because he reasons in terms of fictitious nations instead of the concrete processes of capitalist commodity production.

S in his presentation talks exclusively in terms of wages and/or countries, although completely gratuitously he speaks of international trade as being mutually "profitable" (669); doubtless the word is used in its nonscientific sense here to mean some sort of gain, yet nowhere do we find any discussion of the role of profit in international trade. The gains he speaks of are higher wages and lower prices, whereby the latter must again be reduced to higher real wages, since "America" is constantly being identified with its workers as consumers. Does it appear likely that any "law" of capitalism, such as that of comparative advantages, would forcefully bring about higher wages? Some light may be shed on this topic by looking at the intentions of those who were associated with the origins of this theory. As Jacob Viner observes in his standard study of the history of international trade theory:

> The classical theory of international trade was formulated primarily with a view to its providing guidance on questions of national policy. . . . This was . . . more conspicuously true in the field which is sometimes called "the theory of international value," where the problems were expressly treated with reference to their bearing on "gain" or "loss" to England, or on the distribution of gain as between England and the rest of the world.[8]

And bringing the issue more up to date, Viner adds that comparative advantage "has continued to command attention mainly because of its use as the basic 'scientific' argument of free-trade economists in their attacks on protective tariffs."[9]

Marxist theory not only criticizes "modern" comparative advantages theory, but also sees the roots of contemporary apologetics in this sphere in the original structure of the theory in Ricardo. To begin with, Ricardo emphasized the use-value aspect of foreign trade to the exclusion of any investigation of the value aspect. It is of course true that to the extent that a "nation" can receive use-values which it otherwise could not have produced itself, or can consume a greater quantity of use-values without increasing the number of labor hours it must expend, it has "gained." In other words, foreign trade based on comparative advantages *can*, under certain circumstances, be *one* way to economize effectively on the expenditure of living and dead labor on a national scale. Whether this happens under capitalism is another matter. That it is not so intended by the economic agents themselves would be admitted by all bourgeois economists from Smith to S, but this would not bother them as long as there are forces at work in capitalism that bring this about regardless of the subjective motives of these agents. Where in fact such economization of national labor time does take place, we may say that the rational kernel of comparative advantages has manifested itself; to the extent that it does not take place, or is overcome by other "perverse" factors connected with the current international division of labor, we may say that the theory is apologetic inasmuch as it claims overall gains for everybody and the whole world.

We agree with Ricardo's discovery that, from the point of view or use-values, comparative advantages *can be* a useful guideline to national foreign-trade policy. S states that "trade is *indirect* production. It is efficient production. Efficient production is always better than inefficient production" (691). The first two assertions may be true; the last, characterized by claim of universality, is not. This may seem ridiculous given the general meanings of efficient and inefficient, but we shall see otherwise.

There are certain ironies involved in the bourgeois theory. Although Ricardo explicitly refers to the exchange of one hundred hours of labor for eighty, he does not investigate the possible consequences of such an exchange on a continuing basis; and S, although he explicitly refers to foreign trade as indirect production, persists in treating foreign trade problems as essentially belonging to the sphere of circulation. But at the same time that certain countries are "gaining" on the basis of comparative advantages, a process of absolute advantages and disadvantages is also taking place; this stems from the fact that the relative advantages are not necessarily distributed evenly between the exchanging countries. To the extent that such absolute advantages and disadvantages accumulate at different poles, something very different from the harmony imagined by bourgeois theory ensues. In the long run such transfers of national labor from one country to another can represent a significant source of accumulation for the one set of countries and of drain on accumulation in the other.

One of the major weaknesses of Ricardo's theory was its unreflective use of national labor time. This may strike the reader as a strange objection coming from a Marxist. The reason for this objection is this: although labor is the foundation of capitalism as well as every other economic formation, labor does not *appear* as the creator of value in capitalism and therefore the economizing of labor is not the major goal, but the enhancement of profit. We know that there are competitive forces at work within a national capitalist economy causing each individual capitalist to increase the productivity of "his" workers precisely in order to increase his profit. But we also know that what is true for the individual capitalist need not be true for the aggregate national capital. Thus it is precisely this process of increasing profits for the individual capitalist that leads to the falling rate of profit on the aggregate capital. Not in an analogous manner, but nevertheless based on the same totality of relations between the aggregate and the individual capital, increasing productivity for the individual capital does not necessarily lead to increasing aggregate productivity. What is particularly important here is the absence of an economic agent concerned with increasing "national" productivity.

It is true, of course, that a higher position on the scale of universal labor will enable a national capital to operate more profitably on the world market (in the sense that each individual component of the national capital involved in exporting will "enjoy" extra profits). It is possible for the national capitalist state to work in the direction of improving the competitiveness of its national capital, yet most often this takes the form of improving or maintaining the position of certain branches regardless of international productivity comparisons. This does not stem from a "perverse" refusal to bow to the "law" of comparative advantages, but rather from the fact that capitalist productivity does not coincide with the economizing of national labor.

This does not mean that a capitalist economy that transfers its labor time without equivalent receipt of foreign national labor time is not undermining its source of capital accumulation; nor does it mean that the "country" receiving the "extra" labor time has not come into possession of an additional source of such accumulation. It merely means that such transfers can take place concretely only through specific branches, and within them through specific capitals; and to the extent that this is so, we are then dealing with the productivity peculiar to capital which is essentially uninterested in the global reduction of national labor time in the sense of allowing the workers to consume more without having to work more.

Thus in order to grasp the specific processes of comparative advantages, we would have to go beyond national labor time saved. By looking at labor expenditure alone Ricardo fails to see national values and prices which include both costs and profits. However, when we look at matters on this more concrete level we see that individual capitals can sell their commodities on the world market profitably without appropriating the whole of the surplus labor embodied in the surplus value; in other words, part of the national surplus labor may be transferred to capitalists of other countries. This might result in lower consumer prices, although if it does so too successfully the national capitalist state may intervene with tariffs, quotas, or subsidies. In the case of raw materials not in competition with domestic production, lower costs and higher profits for the domestic capitalists consuming these raw materials productively result. If the market expanding strategy fails to boost capital accumulation in the exporting country, then a stop may have to be put to the global transfers of national surplus labor.

A relevant concretization appears to be absent in S, but others have felt compelled to present the theory in a more realistic form; thus Charles Staley employs the following pedagogical approach:

> The Ricardian approach is very abstract and stark, which bothers students. Traders make decisions on the basis of com-

paring money costs and prices, not ratios of amounts of resources used. Money costs are influenced by wage rates and by exchange rates when one purchases abroad. By ignoring these, might we not have left out something important? How do we know that we come out with the correct answers if we consider only comparative costs? To answer these questions, it is necessary to *recast* Ricardo's data into monetary form.[10]

Staley then proceeds to do the "recasting" so that the theory retains its validity through the influence of supply and demand on exchange rate.

Another author, Peter B. Kenen, exemplifies the theory by using changes in wages, prices, etc. Let us see how this mechanism works. Kenen sets up a situation in which the U.S. has an absolute advantage in coal vis-à-vis the U.K., whereas both have equal productivity in potatoes; this causes U.K. capitalists to buy U.S. coal, bringing on unemployment (of coal miners) in the U.K. and excess labor demand in the U.S. (since during this transitional stage potato farming continues); this will cause wages to drop in the U.K. and to rise in the U.S.; hence, U.K. potatoes become cheaper and production is shifted to them from the U.S., resulting in a new equilibrium. In summary Kenen states: "The wage-rate changes will have offset America's higher productivity, allowing Britain's comparative advantage in potato-growing to *show through* as a lower price."[11]

For our purposes it is irrelevant that Staley and Kenen (as well as S) continue to regard wages as the only costs in this "simplified" model; we might just as well substitute national values for wages. As we have pointed out, it is not sufficient for any given branch of industry of the nation exhibiting the highest productivity and intensity of labor (i.e., to be at the top of the scale of universal labor) merely to appear on the world market as it were and to expect to be competitive on the basis of the good name of its national capital; in other words, mere participation in the national capital does not guarantee success on the world market for all individual capital components.

Rather account must also be taken of its specific productivity vis-à-vis this branch in other countries. If for example the relative productivity advantage of America's clothing industry (to use S's example) vis-à-vis Europe's is less than the average productivity and intensity advantage of the U.S. national capital vis-à-vis Europe's (i.e., their relation to each other on the scale of universal labor), then despite America's absolute advantage (that is to say, despite the fact that it can produce the clothing in less national labor time), its clothing commodities will appear on the world market with higher international values and will thus be in a weak competitive position.

This then is the rational kernel of the theory of comparative advantages. But there are a number of phenomena that we have to consider here. First, a basic tenet of this theory consists in the allegation that it "makes it possible for everyone to be better off" (673); that as a result of it "the sum total of human happiness is increased" (675). This is not necessarily so either within a nation or among nations. Within a nation this modification of the law of value on the world market tends to sharpen the uneven development of the various capitals, because in the upper-half of the scale of universal labor only those capitals can prosper on the world market which produce with a productivity and intensity at least corresponding to that of the national capital as a whole; those that do not will be crushed in international competition. These branches will not, of course, disappear as rapidly as the "simplified model" suggests; in fact, despite comparative advantages they will probably not disappear at all. As merely one example among thousands, consider the U.S. textile industry; rather than being a dying industry, textile production has increased, though not so rapidly as U.S. manufacturing in general. It is not among the most productive U.S. industries; it has the lowest "assets per employee" figures of all industries and its international productivity position is deteriorating. Consequently, the U.S. has been a net importer of consumer textiles since 1955, and of industrial textiles since 1963.[12] None of this has prevented the industry from "earning" about $250 million dollars in profits in 1971, although its 6.2 percent "return on net worth" was only about two-thirds that of some

5,000 "leading corporations."[13] A major ingredient in the survival of this industry is the relatively low wage level made possible by mass migration of production facilities to the largely unorganized South. Thus in 1972 gross average hourly wages in textile mills amounted to $2.73, or approximately 72 percent of the $3.81 for all manufacturing workers.[14]

This points up a real problem with bourgeois comparative advantage theory: it identifies low production costs with high efficiency or productivity; yet these low costs may in large part stem from low wages—not necessarily lower than that of competitor nations, as the U.S. example shows, but lower than the average wage level in that country. In the "Third" World nations these wages are of course also absolutely lower, but here we must also take into consideration that a part of their competitiveness on the world market derives from the monopsony low prices they receive.

S's answer to all this is: that may be so, but the point is that the U.S. would be better off by scuttling its textile industry and getting into some expanding, dynamic new industry. Here again we confront the problem of the fictitious national interest. On one level we can answer that the economic and political problems inherent in such a "phasing out" of such an enormous investment (net worth of $4 billion; more than 2 million workers) might well be the straw that breaks the camel's back in a country with more than 5 million unemployed. But more fundamentally on another level we would have to answer that in order for comparative advantages to have significance beyond the moral appeals to greater efficiency for the "whole" nation, it must prove that there are processes at work which also act on the individual agents of production so that the objective "law" may find expression in the actions of these subjects. For capitalism this means of course that the individual capitalists are forced by the "market" to abandon the production of clothing and go into food production; to prove this S would have to show that the rate of profit would be higher if this step were taken. Does such an equalization in fact take place? It is possible and in fact inevitable that surplus value (and in the "national sense," surplus labor) will be redistributed through the world market, so that the more developed capitals will appropriate part of the surplus created by the workers in the less developed countries. If S has admitted that it is possible for a country to price itself out of the world market by "sky-high" wages or profits (667), then in another context he has also admitted that "it is simply not true to say that the theory of comparative costs proves that one country cannot continue to 'undersell' another in every commodity"[15] (and let us add—by "bargain basement" low wages or profits). If the national rate of profit is lower than that of the competitor countries, then it is possible to accept that rate from foreign trade, thus surrendering part of the surplus value in order to retain or expand market shares; it is also possible that a branch will accept less than the national rate of profit simply because there is no alternative. Furthermore, it is also possible for a firm to make more than the average rate of profit on foreign trade; in other words, on the basis of foreign trade according to the principles of comparative advantage:

> The advantaged country receives more labor in return in exchange for less, although this difference, this more, as in general with the exchange between labor and capital, is pocketed by a certain class.[15a]

By failing to take into account any of these "finer details" S is able to state so emphatically that all gain from free trade takes place according to the "law."

"OTHER CAUSES OF INTERNATIONAL TRADE"

Although the "law" of comparative advantages should presumably be sufficient to decree trade, S does find it necessary to introduce more realistic "other causes"; yet here too we find the inability to present causality properly. In this context S adduces "decreasing costs," since specialization with mass production "is most fruitful when there is a widely expanded market"; such a consideration "would strengthen the case for international exchange of goods" (674).

There is obviously something to this description, but with S it appears as if this complicated political-economic process were a matter of humanitarian choice designed to bestow upon the world a cornucopia of goods, a suspicion confirmed by S's lighthearted remark that even with no differences in comparative costs between two countries "it might pay for them to toss a coin to decide who was to produce each of two goods," subject to decreasing costs (674). There is no understanding here of the circumstance that the proliferating growth of the domestic market is not the harmonious picture which derives from looking only at use-values. In the first place, this process does not only result from the technological considerations of mass production; the fact that much of the national product must be sold abroad also reflects the limited internal purchasing power.

Perhaps even more significant than the absolute limitation of the domestic market is the uneven development of the various branches of a national economy which forces some of these to seek markets abroad. As long as the world market as a whole is expanding, or at least as long as the industrial cycle of the major capitalist countries has not become synchronized, there will be no crisis; but when the market is shrinking, the struggle for who loses least intensifies. It is hardly a case of "nations," let alone individual capitals, flipping a coin to determine who will be allowed to specialize.

S's attempt to move this proposition with the formation of the Common Market only testifies to the weakness of his position. The EEC was created at a time of cyclical upswing; the development of the basic electrical and chemical industries in particular pointed up the need for a larger market; the quest for markets was felt even more sharply by these countries once they had recovered from the war destruction at a time of a shrinking world capitalist market, the result of the creation of socialist states (especially Eastern Europe). S's assertion that "freer international trade is often an efficient way of breaking up monopoly positions" (674) must be looked at in this context. S hedges with the "often," and then adds this footnote: "Still, one must concede that violently decreasing-cost situations might under free trade lead to bigger monopolies . . ." (674 n. 3). The "still" of course contradicts the text; and it is interesting that S places the refutation of tariffs in the text and leaves the "advanced" student the choice of hunting out the cons in footnotes.

In any event, this is quite relevant to the Common Market; for one of the main effects, if not goals, of the Common Market was to guarantee the markets of the six countries "their" own monopolies and to create further concentration and centralization of capital so that these monopolies would be in a position to compete more favorably with U.S. capital.

Unlike S, we do not posit an absolute antithesis between monopoly and competition; in fact, monopoly is an expression of increased competition. Thus on the international level increased trade may lead to increased concentration and centralization of capital, which at the same time means greater competition within the national capital and among national capitals.

COMPARATIVE ADVANTAGES AND TARIFFS

The remainder of the chapter is devoted to a discussion of tariffs. We will do well to approach this section by way of a sentence which was dropped from the 8th and 9th editions, i.e., that comparative advantage is an "oversimplified" theory "as far as our rushing out to make immediate applications to real life is concerned" (7th ed., p. 657). Yet the whole book is allegedly oriented at precisely such "applications," and the chapters on trade indicate very strongly that policy recommendations as well as analysis of reality are implicit in the theory. In fact, however, reality and policy largely run counter to the text.

The discussion of tariffs moves only within the realm of

short-term consumption optima; that any serious long-run structural "problems" may arise from constantly adapting to the "law" of comparative advantage is simply not considered. Although S agrees that the theory was unrealistic in the 1930s, in view of the chronic unemployment, he carries on the discussion on the assumption that such a situation will never arise again: "To the extent that we can in the future . . . count on the successful macroeconomic management . . . to banish chronic slumps and inflations—to that extent will the old classical theory of comparative advantage retain its vital social significance" (680; apparently, what has been "banished" is the neoclassical synthesis itself, which from the 7th to the 8th editions has been replaced by various circumlocutions).

We do not claim that the protectionists are "right" and the free traders "wrong"; on the contrary, they are both "right" to the extent that they call attention to different real aspects of the contradictory situation of a national capital. S is "right" in saying that protection among developed capitalist countries is a sign of inefficiency; and doubtless in the long run no major *capitalist* country could withstand the international pressures. On the other hand, S is wrong in his blanket assessment to the effect that protection will hinder "potential growth" (680); as a succession of countries including the U.S., Germany, and Japan has shown, protection may be a necessary element of growth at certain historical points.

What we are concerned with here is the fact that S's analysis provides the reader with no standards by which to judge actual trade policy. The manifold forces that might be at work in tariff policy are ignored.

Appendix: The Factor-Proportions Theory of Trade S's presentation is eclectic insofar as he fails to distinguish between comparative advantages and factor proportions. The essence of this theory is to be found in Point Number 1 of the appendix summary (690): namely that a country will specialize in the production of labor intensive commodities if it is "labor-rich."

We may mention here three types of critique: empirical, immanent bourgeois, and Marxist. To begin with the empirical: The factor proportion theory sailed along quite nicely from the 1920s until the 1950s, when it was put to empirical test. The first and most famous of such studies was done by W. Leontief, who determined that

> an average million dollars' worth of our exports embodies considerably less capital and somewhat more labor than would be required to replace from domestic production an equivalent amount of our competitive imports. America's participation in the international division of labor is based on its specialization on labor intensive, rather than capital intensive, lines of production. In other words, this country resorts to foreign trade in order to economize its capital and dispose of its surplus labor, rather than vice versa.[16]

This came as quite a shock, since everyone agreed that the U.S. was capital-intensive, rather than labor-intensive. Leontief tried to save the factor-proportion theory by conjecturing that one man-year of U.S. labor was equivalent to three man-years of foreign labor, and thus the U.S. was labor-intensive. Ever since, an enormous literature has begun to accumulate concerning the Leontief "Paradox." We need not enter into a description of the further course of this debate, especially since it is still in full swing.[17] Our sole purpose was to show that on an empirical level serious objections have been brought forth against the orthodox theory and that it is incumbent upon S at least to mention the existence of such an imposing body of literature.

Situated as it were half-way between theoretical and immanent bourgeois critique is another type of approach we will illustrate with two authors. The first is the Swedish economist Staffan Linder, who has pointed out that industrial countries import an increasing amount of manufactures from one another rather than producing them domestically and that such trade bulked larger than similar trade between industrial and "developing" countries. He was of the opinion that, given these circumstances, the factor-proportion theory was no longer of relevance.[18] S implicitly recognizes this objection but without making it clear to the reader. Again the admission comes in a footnote in the subsequent chapter. First he asserts that comparative advantages teaches us that "we benefit most by trading with countries of the Far East or the tropics which have economies very different from ours" rather than with similarly industrialized nations (696). Then the footnote follows: "This argument must be qualified and amplified. Backward countries, so poor that they have little real purchasing power with which to import, at best can export little to us. Most trade today is between industrialized countries" (696 n. 3).

S seems to have a very dialectical conception of "qualified and amplified" since a contradition always results from these footnotes. All it means is that the theory does not explain trade movements. And if these countries have "little real purchasing power" to buy our imports today, then they must have had little in the past as well, and thus the theory never had any validity; or, one could salvage the theory historically by admitting that these countries have grown relatively poorer—but S of course cannot do this, since he in fact asserts that factor prices tend toward equality internationally.

Like Linder, a German author has noted the trend toward specialization in manufactures among industrially advanced capitalist countries; in other words, these countries are increasingly exporting and importing the same commodities.[19] It would appear that the aim is a type of monopolistic competition, with certain firms producing a very specialized type of commodity making import necessary. But we should keep in mind that the competitive aspect is still strong. Thus it was recently reported that at a time when German machine-tool exports were booming and about to replace the U.S. primacy on the world market, imports were gaining an ever-growing share of the West German domestic market; in fact what had happened was that West German producers concentrated on "highly profitable sophisticated machine tools, such as numerical control models," leaving the home market "open for the less expensive standard tools."[20]

There is no need to go into a separate Marxist critique of

the factor-proportion theory inasmuch as it is only an application of marginal-productivity theory already criticized in Chapters 18-22. (Since the immanent bourgeois critique has become very technical we will not go into it. We will merely summarize that the major objections relate to the assumption that production functions are everywhere the same—that factor reversals are empirically insignificant. [See B. S. Minhas, "The Homohypallagic Production Function, Factor-Intensity Reversals and the Meckscher-Ohlin Theorem," *Journal of Political Economy*, LXX (1962), 138–56; Romney Robinson, "Factor Proportions and Comparative Advantage: Part I," *Quarterly Journal of Economics*, LXX (May, 1956), 169–92. Staley, *International Economics*, op. cit., Chap. 5, offers a good summary of this literature.]) We will confine ourselves to pointing out that Marx emphasizes that such a theory is caught up in the confusion of distribution and production, that it cannot distinguish between value production and income distribution to the "factors of production," and thus does not see how production lies at the base. To refer to "factor prices" as the determinants of international competition fails to consider that it is the development of the productive force of labor as reflected in the production of surplus value and that the accumulation of capital determines international competitiveness regardless of the subjective motivation of the agents of production according to local factor costs; here Marx shows how the latter merely confirms the already existing bourgeois notion that value is determined by factor costs also on the international level.[21]

FACTOR-PRICE EQUALIZATION

This section (690) presents Ohlin's argument that even free commodity trade without factor movements will tend to equalize factor prices. It is curious that S's modesty prevents him from mentioning his own contribution to this subject—a "proof" that complete equalization must result.[22]

But whether one adheres to the "strong" or "weak" case for factor-price equalization, it is clear that this theory has no relation to reality, and that when, as in Chapter 38, it is implicit in policy recommendations to the "developing" countries by the imperialist powers, its apologetic content becomes manifest.

On the basis of the discussion in this chapter we are now ready to look at S's analysis of trade in his next chapter and in Chapter 38. As a preliminary to this, especially in light of the fact that S gives the reader the distinct impression that international trade is actually guided by the "laws" laid out here, we offer the following research results by Jan Tinbergen, who determined that on the basis of capital resources, capital-labor proportions and manpower availability:

> The Soviet Union would be the world's producer of computers, which means that IBM would have other things to think about. And it may provoke a wistfully pacific thought or two (even a wry smile) to learn that it would seem efficient, given the availability of capital and labor, for weapons to be built in the US and ammunition . . . in Eastern Europe. Professor Tinbergen is not irrational enough to think this rational finding will be adopted. . . .[23]

Chapter 25: The Development of Imperialist Trade Policy (S's Chapter 35)

The monopolization of the noncapitalist areas of expansion in the old capitalist states as well as outside in the overseas countries became the slogan of capital, while free trade, the policy of the "open door," has become the specific form of defenselessness of the noncapitalist countries vis-à-vis international capital and of the equilibrium of this competing capital—a prestage of their partial or total occupation as colonies or spheres of interest. If until now alone England has remained true to free trade, then primarily because it as the oldest colonial empire found in its enormous possession of noncapitalist areas from the very beginning a basis of operations which until most recent times offered almost limitless prospects for the accumulation of capital and which in fact placed it beyond the competition of other capitalist countries. Hence the general rush of the capitalist countries to isolate themselves from one another through protective tariffs, although they are at the same time commodity buyers of each other in ever greater measure, are more and more dependent on one another for the replacement of their material conditions of reproduction, and although protective tariffs today, from the standpoint of the technical development of the forces of production, have become completely dispensable, indeed, they frequently lead on the contrary to the artificial conservation of obsolete modes of production.

—Rosa Luxemburg, *The Accumulation of Capital*, Ch. 31; German ed., *Gesammelte Werke*, VI (Berlin, 1923), 366

HISTORICAL FUNCTIONS OF TARIFFS

Here again the most prominent feature of this chapter is a radically ahistorical point of view which finds expression in the failure to offer even a skimpy review of the development of capitalist trade policy. It is not merely for the record that we insist upon the need for at least some historical analysis; for although trade policy has doubtless undergone considerable change, there is a very definite historical continuum essential to an understanding of contemporary policies and views.

However, this chapter does contain a modicum of realism insofar as it deals with the explicitly political topic of "group interests" pressuring the state; and even though he cannot ignore them, S—and here he is joined by practically all other textbook writers—does his best to minimize the problem. Thus with respect to the reason for generally harmful tariffs, S posits the traditional concentration of producer interests against scattered consumer interests (695). The point about these explicitly political discussions is that they are meant to depoliticize the issue by shifting attention to individual motives without focusing on the specific social causation and its broad historical and national base.

Thus it is only in the context of areas where the connection between economics and politics can no longer be ignored that S can afford to make such a statement: "Most arguments for tariffs are simply rationalizations for special benefits to particular pressure groups and do not stand up under analysis" (704). We would say that all bourgeois theory is one large "rationalization" of "special interests" for the capitalist class; but even with respect to free trade we find that "rationalization" abounds, both within one country and among various countries. S himself admits that there is but one argument for free trade—namely that it is beneficial for everyone. Yet as S has also admitted in one of his scholarly contributions: "Free trade will *not* necessarily maximize the real income or consumption and utility possibilities of *any one country*. . . ."[1]

To return to the historical aspect, we would like to review briefly the development of the relationship between free trade and protectionism to see what changing underlying political-economic factors are at work. The following lengthy quotation we believe offers great insight into certain historical changes that find reflection in the ideological sphere:

> When the nineteenth-century liberal spoke of the greatest good of the greatest number, he tacitly assumed that the good of the minority might have to be sacrificed to it. This principle applied equally to international economic relations. . . . The modern utopian internationalist enjoys none of the advantages, and has none of the toughness, of the nineteenth-century liberal. The material success of the weak Powers in building up protected industries, as well as the new spirit of internationalism, preclude him from arguing that the harmony of interests depends on the sacrifice of economically unfit nations. Yet the abandonment of this premise destroys the whole basis of the doctrine which he has inherited; and he is driven to the belief that the common good can be achieved without any sacrifice of the good of any individual member of the community. . . . It is for this reason that we find in the modern period an extraordinary divergence between the theories of economic experts and the practice of those responsible for the economic policies of their respective countries. Analysis will show that this divergence springs from a simple fact. The economic expert, dominated in the main by laissez-faire doctrine, considers the hypothetical economic interest of the world as a whole, and is content to assume that this is identical with the interest of each individual country. The politician pursues the concrete interest of his country, and assumes (if he makes any assumption at all) that the interest of the world as a whole is identical with it.[2]

In fairness to Carr's own views it must be noted that he wrote this during a period of world capitalist depression—that is to say, at a time when the national capital's inherent drive to "look after itself" manifests itself most strongly as a result of the shrinking world market; when it is no longer a matter of the competitive division of the profits but rather of the losses; when "competition is transformed into the struggle of the hostile brothers."[3]

But in an objective sense it is not "unfair" to focus on the attitudes prevailing during this period since they marked an important developmental stage in the history of international capitalism. The periodic crises of the nineteenth century were in large part reflections of the internal crises of British capitalism; to the extent that Britain occupied a historically unique monopoly position on the world industrial market, its crises became those of the world market. During the last quarter of the nineteenth century this hegemony came under strong attack, especially from the U.S. and Germany; this meant of course that the world market would begin to assume more of an autonomous cyclical shape precisely because it was now for the first time becoming a *world* market.

This fourth quarter of the nineteenth century is (at least in Marxist literature) associated with the transformation of competitive into monopoly capital. But we have to be more precise in delineating this change. First of all, the world market was characterized by the breaking of the British monopoly position; with the development of several powerful national capitals, competition was first now becoming possible.

But what about the national level? This was of course a period of great capital concentration and centralization; and one must of course also take into consideration that with the then less developed state of the forces of production, certain production processes could be monopolized for a longer period of time than is possible today. It was the time of the formation of the oil, steel, tobacco, meat, and aluminum trusts in the U.S. At the same time, however, there is no absolute long-run monopoly under capitalism and thus this period was also marked, for instance in the U.S., by the fiercest competition.

Now let us see how tariffs fit into this development. In the earlier part of the nineteenth century tariffs had in the main fulfilled the function of "protecting young industries" from the all-powerful industrial hegemony of Britain. These tariffs fulfilled their function and world market competitive industries did arise. (We attribute no absolute significance to these tariffs; that is, as S rightly points out, protection beyond a certain level may impede advancing productivity, whereas free trade might force domestic procedures to adjust themselves to the most advanced state of productivity. This was apparently the case with Denmark; until the middle of the nineteenth century this was one of the least productive agricultural nations, but it was also one of the few without agricultural tariffs; this forced the Danish farmers to become more mechanized while the formerly advanced nations fell back.)

In other words, enormous dumping was taking place: monopolists, freed of foreign competition, could raise domestic prices to enable them to undersell their foreign competitors abroad. Given this general trend stemming from structural changes in capitalism, it is not very enlightening to portray the desire for tariffs on the part of these large industrial exporters as merely "irrational" as S does. Engels, for instance, agreed that it was "stupid" for German exporters to ask for tariffs at a time when they were already very competitive; this was tantamount to giving away the surplus value to foreigners and compensating oneself by lowering real domestic wages through monopoly high prices. But Engels was not surprised at the "stupidity" of these exporters; for availing oneself of short-run profits at the "expense of national rationality" is the rational mode of capitalist behavior.

We do not intend to pursue this description of the history of trade policy. Suffice it to say that protectionism of varying degrees characterized the period up to World War I and then again the period between the two World Wars, in particular the Great Depression.

TARIFFS AMONG ADVANCED CAPITALIST COUNTRIES

S admits that "certain noneconomic arguments . . . may make it desirable national policy to sacrifice national welfare in order to subsidize certain activities admittedly not economically efficient" (692). But there is more here than meets the eye. First of all, there is the definition of "economic": reduced to its simplest terms this means determining whether "the benefit to consumers" later "would be enough to more than make up for the higher prices during the period of protection" (701 f.). The key here is "benefit to consumers," for S apparently there is nothing "economic" in the process of production itself—at least not for the workers involved. Thus S would probably consider it a noneconomic decision, that is a decision based on noneconomic criteria, if in a postcapitalist society the workers were to decide to consume less and work less, or if to discontinue the use of certain machinery from the capitalist era despite its greater efficiency because working on such machinery was so debilitating that the extra consumption would not justify it.

There is of course a certain rationale for S's approach—namely that in capitalism the workers have no such choice; first, because their power to limit the work week is limited; and secondly, because their standard of living is so low compared to what they *know* it could and must be under the given development of the forces of production that they cannot afford to reduce consumption.

As for S's distinction between tariffs and subsidies, this is largely irrelevant since such subsidies are usually regarded as no less of an interference with free trade than tariffs. That S recommends subsidies on the basis of their being more transparent to the "public" and thus allow it to "decide whether the game is worth the candle" (693) can only be regarded as tongue-in-cheek demagoguery. First of all, a sudden price raise would make it very clear to consumers that they were paying more for domestic development, whereas a subsidy, given the general taxation and appropriations approach of "modern" taxation, would in fact hide the extra expense from everyone except those who pored through pages of individual entries in the government's revenue and expenditure sides of the budget. Thus S's recommending the proposal which would conceal the "real cost." Secondly, if S were really so interested in making the "public" aware of its contribution to the "national defense" his opportunity to speak came in Chapter 9, where he briefly mentions direct and indirect taxes; but he made no such plea on behalf of direct taxes on the basis of their being more transparent.

We shall skip over most of the material on the "grossly fallacious arguments" partly because we have dealt with this above. But just to give an idea of the "special" interests lobbying tariffs, we produce the following figures showing exports as a percentage of GNP for leading capitalist countries in the year 1971:[4]

Belgium	44.1%	Sweden	21.0%	Italy	15.0%
Holland	38.0%	Finland	20.8%	Australia	14.1%
Ireland	29.7%	Canada	19.7%	France	12.8%
Switzerland	23.9%	FRGermany	18.0%	Japan	10.6%
Denmark	21.7%	U.K.	16.5%	U.S.	4.2%

These figures are not to be understood in any absolute sense; that is to say, we are not asserting that there is any one-to-one correspondence between the degree of export orientation of any economy and its tariff policy. This should be obvious from the data for Japan and the U.S., which are often cited as the most protective nations. Our purpose in presenting these figures was merely to give the reader some impression as to the relative trade dependency of various national economies on the world market.

One reason for this lack of one-to-one correspondence between export orientation and trade policy lies in the concrete structure of production; as we have had occasion to note before, one must also investigate which branches are heavily committed on the world market, which firms among those branches, how heavily concentrated the domestic market is, whether these branches are key for the industrial cycle, etc.

Beyond this one must consider that a nation which exports a large share of its national product is also likely to be importing a similarly large share. (Certain oil-exporting nations are an exception). This would lead one to expect that such countries would also be interested in raising their tariffs so as to keep import prices down. It would seem plausible, for example, that they would want to keep down the prices of raw materials since this would keep industrial costs down. But here too one must look at the specific conditions instead of judging globally.

In this context it would be instructive to look at the chart S provides (703) along with its astoundingly meager commentary. But at least the chart does provide some historical comparison for at least one country (though the source is not given). All we are told is how U.S. tariffs evolved in the aggregate; and it is asserted that "if comparable figures were compiled for other countries" we would see that the U.S. is no longer a laggard in free trade (8th ed., p. 679). Of course such statistics do exist although they are difficult to compile and one finds various measures (in part determined by varying methods of calculation in various countries).

Beyond this comparison it is also necessary to look at the specific commodity structure of the tariffs, which S neglects to do. It is common policy for the U.S. and other advanced capitalist nations to establish a hierarchy of tariff rates; in other words, the average tariff rates for nations conceal varying rates for different types of commodities. In general, industrial raw materials are burdened with the lowest tariffs since these enter into the costs of production of industrial firms and higher tariffs here would impair the competitive position of exporters on the world market. There is, however, also a complicating factor here: namely, where domestic producers of these raw materials or synthetic substitutes for them exist, there is pressure to raise tariffs. In the U.S., tariff policy has been created—on this issue—on the basis of a compromise between the interests of domestic users of raw materials and the U.S. multinational firms producing or marketing these materials on the one hand, and domestic producers on the other, whereby the tendency in recent years has been to make tariff policy more in line with the interests of the former while giving subsidies to the latter.

With respect to foodstuffs, similar contrary interests exist. On the one hand the capitalist class as a whole is interested in cheap food imports which help to keep the cost of living and thus variable capital as low as possible (whereby here again one would have to differentiate: those branches with above-average organic compositions of capital—i.e., "capital intensive"—would be less interested than those with lower organic compositions); on the other hand, the capitalist class also has an interest, especially in Europe where this tendency manifests itself clearly in Common Market agricultural policy, in preventing mass destruction of the small farmers for reasons of political stability.

TARIFFS AND THE "THIRD" WORLD

The advanced capitalist countries also tend to raise tariffs according to the degree of fabrication or processing a product has undergone; this has a particularly unfavorable effect on exports from "developing" nations with respect to raw-materials processing and manufactures. This subject has been engaging the attention of those capitalist forces concerned about not killing the gold goose that laid the golden egg.

Even within the discussion now underway on how to integrate the "developing" countries into the world market without causing undue harm to the established imperialist interests, it is obvious whose interests will be paramount. Thus commenting on the "costs" involved in implementing a plan to grant "Third" World nations temporary tariff preference, one author has noted "that the developing nations will be induced to produce those manufactures which the governments of the rich countries feel their countries can import with least injury to their own producers rather than those goods in which the developing countries might be most efficient."[5]

But here as elsewhere in a society built on antagonistic interests, one should not be surprised if certain surface phenomena seem to contradict what some Marxists have often portrayed as the monolithic "interests of capital." Thus respect to the proposed measures to grant "developing" nations temporary tariff relief, it seems that other nations may also be pushing this proposal for their own reasons.

Since we now have some notion of how comparative advantage is "violated" by the imperialist powers when it is to their advantage, let us see how S treats this. Although he spends little time on the matter, he does enter into the discussion when he specifies some conditions under which interference with free trade may "begin to score some weighty points" (699). The first such argument S labels "diversification to reduce terms-of-trade risk"; under this scheme countries will cut back on the production of the agricultural commodity they are heavily committed to on the world market in order to develop production of some other commodity for export. Even S's language is revealing: "To avoid the perils of 'monoculture,' Latin American economists advise the use of tariffs" (700). First, the use of quotation marks around monoculture presumably expresses S's dissociation from the term—possibly because it is used by opponents of comparative advantage theory, even though it well describes many economies. Secondly, despite the fact that S acknowledges that the argument "certainly deserves careful attention," one wonders why only "Latin American" economists are pushing it. Could it be that economic theory's "technical concepts . . . are no more than codified common sense,"[6] or perhaps, more likely, that economic theory, especially on the international level, is greatly affected by whose national interests are at stake?

Thirdly, S's own interpretation of this strategy as being similar to that pursued by an investor who does not want to put all his eggs in one basket would seem to miss the point. It is not so much the risk reduction that must be emphasized here but the content: namely, industrialization as a method of raising living standards which is not open to many agricultural notions.

The remainder of S's discussion appears to miss the point entirely. First of all, it is entirely unclear why he insists that the whole argument is based on the assumption that government knows better; could there not be a case where capitalists desirous of starting up new production induce the government to introduce tariffs on this commodity? The argument becomes more incomprehensible as S goes on. Next he states that "if the future risks are genuine and are foreseen by private investors, those investors will not be misled by temporarily high profits into investing in these few industries." So convinced is he of the "law" of comparative advantage that he asserts that since these industries have no "genuine long-run comparative advantage . . . there will be no effective tendency to specialize in them" (701). Let us go through this strange reasoning slowly. The first sentence would seem to be a tautology: if an investor foresees a loss, he just won't invest. So why is it that "investors" are "misled" into these ventures? These terms themselves prejudice the argument, for while they may be adequate to the task of describing how a trust fund allocates its wealth, it has absolutely nothing to do with the concrete situation in "underdeveloped" countries. First, who are the "investors"? If we are speaking of the typical agricultural producers for the world market, then these may in large part be very poor peasants who produce small quantities and sell them to local dealers. These are not investors; they are in large part subsistence farmers who are not getting high profits, whether temporary or not.

So why do they remain in "business" instead of "diversifying"? Why do they insist on engaging in industries with no "genuine long-run comparative advantage"? Answers to questions such as these are not S's forte. Instead, there is the implied answer that the phenomenon does not even exist. Our answer is that these producers have basically no alternative, for there are few cases in which a Thai rice farmer is going to make it big by opening a steel plant.

S might say, then let him become a worker in that steel plant. Fine, but who will open the plant? The whole point is that imperialist trade structure makes it extremely difficult for "Third" World nations to enter the world market in manufactures. This is precisely why the state must intervene to provide the industry with the most favorable initial conditions possible. S's argumentation here is disjointed: on the one hand he urges extreme caution concerning state intervention since its "comparative-advantage forecasts," if wrong, may hinder development (701). Although S finds it necessary to issue this warning concerning government intervention, he implies that the "market" is never wrong about future comparative advantage; he devotes no attention whatsoever to the developmental blocks thrown up by concentrating on one or two agricultural exports. The problem here is bound up with the strategy of agricultural exports as a means of gaining foreign exchange needed to buy industrial products. If these prices are not stable, or if they show a downward trend, then development programs based on them will be in trouble. Here then are two connected issues: the long-term decline in the terms of trade for agricultural products on the world market, and the short-run fluctuations. Both afflict "developing" countries who are stuck with the commodities imperialism under the guise of the natural law of comparative advantage foisted upon them.

Now to proceed to the other side of S's disjointed argument against state intervention: this is offered in the context of a discussion of tariffs for infant industries. While admitting in theory the advantages of such a tariff, S sees as the major drawback the practical problem of the industry's failure to gain the government support needed to overcome the entrenched power of the already dominant producers (702). If this were really the problem, then why did S feel compelled to issue all the caveats about state intervention? In fact, the most likely case is that of a national bourgeoisie's taking over state power precisely in order to push forward some sort of national industrialization program.

The rest of S's discussion is ambiguous. Although he admits that the infant industries argument had more validity for the U.S. in the past century than today, and more for "underdeveloped" nations today than "developed" ones, he does not make the crucial comparison: its validity for the U.S. in the last century versus "underdeveloped" nations today. On the surface it would seem that if it worked so splendidly for the U.S. then why not for Brazil today? With respect to "infant economies" S cautiously agrees that "a strong case can be made for using moderate protection" (702); yet we find this standpoint wishy-washy at best. In the first place, this runs counter to S's facetious attitude toward "Third" World industrialization programs in Chapter 38. Secondly, this avoids the whole issue as to whether such industrialization attempts can be regarded as analogous to those of the nineteenth century. We do not doubt that a certain amount of industrialization will be pushed through by these "developing" nations and that for a variety of reasons and points of interest the imperialist nations will not oppose certain directions. What we are saying is that along capitalist lines it is impossible for the "Third" World countries to break through the hegemony of these imperialist powers similar to the way in which the U.S., Germany, and Japan broke through Britain's domination in the nineteenth century. That is to say, the industrialization will in large part be effected in terms which will cause the least disruption to imperialist interests. The autonomous interests of capital in the "Third" World nations—let alone the interests of the people—will not be able to assert themselves as did those of the U.S., etc., in the nineteenth century.

TARIFFS AND THE WORKING CLASS

With respect to tariffs designed to raise labor's share of national income S is constrained to concede that according to the Ohlin proposition the relative share in national income falling to the scarce factor will be lowered by the introduction of free trade.[7] After mentioning this as a possibility for the sake of "objectivity," S proceeds to pooh-pooh the notion since with American labor "such an important and flexible factor of production, it seems likely that other laborers would gain from expanded trade more than those hurt would lose" (697).

S supplies the justification for this several pages later when reviewing the case for tariffs to prevent unemployment. The answer: "rational macroeconomic management" (alias the neoclassical synthesis) makes it unnecessary to "tolerate a gap between actual and potentially producible product" and thus provides jobs in other industries (700).

We may first point out that S himself adopted a rather different position on tariffs a quarter-century ago:

> It is perhaps not so obvious, but it is none the less true that free trade has had the same harmful effects upon the vested interests of the whole laboring class in America (and landowning class in Europe) as would the removal of all immigration barriers. What maximizes world or national output will in this case lower the absolute real returns to even so "important" and "versatile" a factor as (American) labor. . . . Advocates of freer trade—and I consider myself in this class—must not overstate their case. Protection can help special groups; it can even help special large groups.[8]

Well, S might reply, no one ever denied that certain groups might be hurt by free trade, but I wrote that at a time when the neoclassical synthesis had not yet proved itself. It would then seem that the answer lies in the efficacy of "rational macroeconomic management."

But it is precisely this "tool" that has been called into question lately. This is not the place to offer a detailed account of the success or failure of the neoclassical synthesis as a practical tool in maintaining full employment. But we should at least be made aware of the theoretical approach underlying S's concern with unemployment. He does not deny that free trade will cause some unemployment; this is fine as long as new jobs are created. (Actually this is a generous interpretation: more precisely, S implies that the unemployed textile worker may not find another job, but that his "hurt" will be outweighed by other workers' gains.) This approach is summarized more generally in a book not uncritical of U.S. capitalism:

> Concern with diagnosing the causes of original unemployment leads to a theoretical dead end. The diagnosis must be based on reasons for lack of re-employment after disemployment occurs or after new labor force entrants are not newly employed. The reasons for the original disemployment are of no concern if re-employment is assured.[9]

By refusing to investigate the causes of "original disemployment" one is neglecting a very important feature of capitalism; for although even in postcapitalist society production of certain products will be eliminated or reduced and that of others introduced or increased, such changes being planned will be foreseen, and thus the "structural manpower" problems associated with "creative destruction" and "external diseconomies" will not prevail. And such problems will not prevail for another important reason as well: the very narrow education and training characteristic of capitalist wage workers can be eliminated.

The point, however, is precisely whether capital accumulation rates are high enough to overcome (temporarily) the increasing organic composition of capital attendant upon increasing productivity so that new surplus-value creating labor can be employed. The current "Buy American" legislation sponsored by U.S. trade unions appears to be based on the thesis that U.S. capital has more or less reached the end of the line as a great capital-accumulating society, for it contends that U.S. productivity can no longer compensate for the higher wages in the U.S. and that capital accumulation can no longer create enough new jobs in new branches for those thrown out of work by foreign competition.

On the one hand the labor unions are realistic enough to see through "business" arguments to the effect that U.S. trade deficits and consequent lost employment are necessary in order that foreign countries be in a position to acquire dollars to pay profits to U.S. multinational corporations abroad. On the other hand, the acceptance of the capitalist mode of production by the unions involves them in a contradictory strategy.

Their answer is to reduce the impetus to produce abroad by taxing such profits more heavily. In the end, however, this increased domestic profitability will come only at the expense of the American working class.

Thus, by accepting the framework of capitalism, and by understanding "labor" merely as a coequal "factor of production," trade unions may easily wind up fighting particular interest struggles and even abandoning the interests of the working class within capitalism, although, given their assumption of a declining competitiveness of U.S. capital, there is something to their protectionist strategy.

Chapter 26: Aspects of the World Market and International Currency Crises (S's Chapter 36)

Revolutionary change which shakes confidence in the fair treatment of private property is incompatible with rapid economic expansion.
—David Rockefeller, "What Private Enterprise Means to Latin America," *Foreign Affairs*, XLIV, No. 3 (April, 1966),

Whatever one may think of the "domino" theory, it is beyond question that without the American commitment in Vietnam, Asia would be a far different place today.

The U.S. presence has provided tangible and highly visible proof that communism is not necessarily the wave of Asia's future. This was a vital factor in the turnaround in Indonesia, where a tendency toward fatalism is a national characteristic. It provided a shield behind which the anti-communist forces found the courage and the capacity to stage their countercoup and, at the final moment, to rescue their country from the Chinese orbit. And, with its 100 million people, and its 3,000 mile arc of islands containing the region's richest hoard of natural resources, Indonesia constitutes by far the greatest prize in the Southeast Asian area.
—Richard M. Nixon, "Asia after Viet Nam," in *Foreign Affairs*, XLVI, No. 1 (October, 1967), 111

Introduction

This is one of the chapters referred to above as an accretion of the after-thought variety: although it purports to "put to work" "all the principles" of Chapters 33-35 "to help understand the contemporary international scene" (643), it must be seen as an implicit acknowledgment of the somewhat less than smooth functioning of the international capitalist system and of the failure of orthodox economics to develop an analysis of predictive value. In reading this chapter one does not get the impression that one has been adequately prepared for the existence of such "problems" as are touched on here; for the "principles" espoused in the preceding chapters led one to believe that capitalism was not afflicted with what Marxists are wont to call internal contradictions. Not that S goes quite so far, yet some of the issues mentioned here might lead one to suspect that there are perhaps problems our mixed economy cannot successfully resolve.

Our primary objective in this chapter is to place the empirical material S presents in a theoretically and historically mediated context. First, we will examine the political-economic origins of the post-World War II development in the international capitalist economy; then we will analyze the origins and functions of the most important supranational "institutions"; and finally, we will discuss some fundamental aspects of the recent and/or current international economic crises.

I. PREHISTORY OF THE CURRENT STRUCTURE OF THE INTERNATIONAL ECONOMY

A. THE CRISIS OF THE 1930s AND WORLD WAR II

S's attitude toward the 1930s is ambiguous: on the one hand he appears to be hinting that if only the Keynesian policies had been instituted, the Depression could have been avoided. Thus, he says that "contractionary monetary and fiscal policies" merely accentuated the GNP gap, whereas the deficit spending attendant upon World War II finally brought on full employment (8th ed., p. 682). On the other hand, he sees, rather realistically, that a single nation cannot make the transition to Keynesianism in an otherwise un-Keynesian world without suffering severe losses on the world market—unless it is willing to sever connections with the world markets.

These then are the two, not very conclusive, views that S seems to hold on the 1930s, and on that note he leads into an extremely abbreviated account of the round of devaluations with "as it happened." Let us try to piece together briefly what happened. These devaluations were due to onerous internal and foreign debts, the result of steep price drops. In the agrarian countries the devaluation was the immediate result of the passive balance of payments caused by the drop in world-market commodity prices; export surpluses could no longer meet the interest and amortization of the foreign debt. In England a temporary passivity of the balance of payments, strong gold outflow, and the sudden withdrawal of large parts of the short-term capital on deposit in London brought about the departure from the gold standard. In the U.S., on the other hand, the devaluation was not caused by an outflow of gold (in fact, there was an active balance of payments) but was consciously initiated to lighten the debt burden in order to redistribute profits between industrial and loan capital in favor of the former. But the U.S. departure from the gold standard did not suffice to devalue the dollar (the trade and payments balances were too favorable), so Roosevelt, wary of using the openly inflationary method of the printing press, chose a unique method: the purchase of gold at a higher price than would correspond to the exchange rate of the dollar for gold francs—in other words, the artificial lowering of the dollar exchange rate.[1] That this situation of "unbearable debts" is not such a "never-never land" as S intimates can be seen from the current situation in the U.S.

> Obviously, there is a considerable truth to the contention that much of the post-World War II prosperity in the U.S. was based on the accumulation of a mountain of debt.
> There are some who contend that, with the debt so large and rising steadily, the interest burden is becoming more than the economy can bear and that, eventually, a substantial part of the debt will have to be liquidated the hard way, through a rise in failures accompanied by considerable deflation.[2]

The devaluations thus had the double function of restoring profitability within the national capitals and making them more competitive on the world market. Aside from the self-defeating aspects inherent in the competitive devaluations emphasized by S, one must not forget that they also represent transfers of national value from one national capital to another. Moreover, the two goals are to some degree contradictory since the first requires the rise of domestic prices and the second the fall or constancy of export prices.

Without getting involved in a lengthy discussion of the various tactics used by the various national capitals to shift the greater part of the loss onto one another, we want to indicate that the matter is somewhat more complicated than S leads us to believe. He gives us the impression that the departure from the gold standard was the key to success for England and Sweden, for example. But the fact that these two countries "were already recovering nicely from the Depression" while the U.S., Germany, and France were still wallowing in it does not prove much. First of all, England really never participated in the boom of the 1920s to begin with, so that it did not have that far to fall. The depression did not develop to the same degree in England even before it left the gold standard in 1931.

S provides absolutely no material concerning the changes brought about by the Depression and World War II with respect to international investment. During the Depression, the many private and public bankruptcies reduced outstanding investment and future investment "propensities." More concretely, whereas British total foreign investment remained more or less constant, the U.S. investment position deteriorated. The following is a tabular comparison of the long-term U.S. investment position in 1929 and 1939:

U.S. PRIVATE INVESTMENT ABROAD

	1929	1939
Long-term (total)	$15.4 billion	$11.4 billion
direct	7.6	7.3
portfolio	7.8	4.1

U.S. FOREIGN LIABILITIES

	1929	1939
Long-term (total)	$5.9 billion	$8.7 billion
direct	1.4	2.9
portfolio	4.5	5.8
Net position	9.5	2.7

Source: Cleona Lewis, *The United States and Foreign Investment Problems* (Washington, 1948), p. 26

The long-term U.S. investment position may have deteriorated sharply during the Depression, but this was not uniformly so; the U.S. became a debtor toward Europe but remained a creditor toward the countries of the Western Hemisphere where it maintained over 70 percent of its investments.[3] However, the U.S. maintained its direct investment whereas it suffered losses with respect to its holdings of foreign debt (government and private bonds, etc.).

During World War II, U.K. foreign assets were sharply reduced from approximately $18 billion to $4 billion; Germany, France, Netherlands, Italy, and Japan also witnessed either total or very large reductions of their foreign assets. The U.S. position improved during the war, so that by 1945 the British and American empires both amounted to approximately $14 billion in assets with a net creditor position of about $4 billion.[4]

B. THE AFTERMATH OF WORLD WAR II

Although the political context of S's description of international events following the war requires analysis, the information he does present is uncommonly informative. To begin with the period of the "dollar shortage": without U.S. "gifts," loans, and investments, the European capitalist nations would not have had the "liquidity" to purchase the means of production and consumption from the only nation in a position to sell them—the U.S.

But this "technical" mechanism for "creating liquidity" concealed other relations—the incorporation of these national capitals into a newly reconstructed imperialist world market which, despite the fact that it involved direct subordination of the weaker national capitals of Western Europe to U.S. capital, also was subject to autonomous laws of motion beyond the control of even the strongest national capital. This relationship between anarchy and planning on an international scale must be understood, for in general bourgeois economics is unable to explain both sides; one must see that it was possible at a certain concrete historical juncture for a uniquely powerful national capital to "create" an international monetary system geared to secure its short-term advantages without its simultaneously being in a position to "create" a system which could remain under its conscious control.

Since the international monetary system was not (only) a technical mechanism for restoring world trading links, its "success" was not uniquely tied to the planning wisdom of the founders of Bretton Woods; rather, the success of the "dollar standard" must be analyzed in connection not with the circulation of the dollar as technical means of facilitating barter, but with the fundamental conditions of the general world-wide postwar upswing of the capitalist world. The dollar was not merely a temporary replacement and/or supplement vis-à-vis gold as international money, but also represented—as do all currencies—money capital; in this way, dollar "flows" are also capital flows, proof that the many contradictory processes within the national capital will also find some expression on the international level.

It is important to bear in mind this complex when dealing with the various post-World War II plans and organizations, because the impression has been given that in some planned way all the old problems plaguing international economics are being eliminated. However, money is not just thrown into the sphere of circulation—it is done so in accordance with regularities stemming from the production and realization of value; to be sure, the state can interfere within certain limits, especially externally, on the world market on behalf of its national capital. Such "interventions," however, are always embedded in and delimited by the interests of the national capital and the expansion or contraction of the world market.

Having indicated in somewhat theoretical terms why the Bretton Woods system was not some sort of "neutral tool," let us approach the same subject from a more explicitly political point of view. First S makes absolutely no effort to place these events in any historical context. The sharp struggles which took place during and after World War II among the various capitalist allies and among various segments of their ruling class receded into obscurity during the era of cold-war prosperity; the contradictory forces at work in the plans of the U.S. for recreating postwar capitalism in its own image are given little attention. Students are not told that the formative phase of the glorious Anglo-American friendship involved jockeying as to how much of its empire Britain would have to sacrifice in order to obtain U.S. "aid"; thus for instance, during the finest hours of our English allies, when they were sacrificing their blood, sweat, and tears, we asked them to throw their colonies in too while they were at it. This took place at the time of lend-lease negotiations, when Churchill begged the U.S. not to connect this with the demand for the renunciation of Imperial Preference (this was the special tariff system within the British Empire which made the intrusion of outside powers more difficult and which the U.S. was most anxious to dispose of to strengthen its world market position), for this would "enable enemy propagandists to say that the United States was capitalizing on British adversity to seize control of the British Empire."[5]

Presumably the U.S. would have been strong enough to exist on its own without large trading with capitalist Europe and could have waited until these economies had pulled themselves up by their bootstraps.

But the 1920s and 1930s had already demonstrated the revolutionary dangers inherent in such a strategy, and with the rise of socialist Eastern Europe it became obvious that a repetition of that first postwar period could well spell the end of capitalism globally, and thus in the U.S. as well. Thus, the post-World War II plans on the part of the U.S. were in reality attempts to restore the viability of capitalism in the long run while securing U.S. capitalist hegemony at least for the short term. The gifts and grants and loans made by the U.S. can be regarded as insurance premiums, and, as we shall see, it was not the beneficiary who would end up footing the bill.

S states that chronologically the aid programs ran as follows: UNRRA, Marshall Plan, then "shift" toward NATO and other military alliances—e.g., Truman Doctrine and Greece (708). UNRRA had been set up during the war to ward off starvation situations; financed by the U.S. and administered by the United Nations, it was to be disbanded in 1947 before it had actually completed its task. Thus La Guardia, ex-Mayor of New York, the administrator, asked the UN General Assembly in 1946 that a Food Fund be established to continue the work; all nations except the U.K. and the U.S. favored this approach. They decided that individual nations should give help as they saw fit, the first step, or at least the first major manifestation, of U.S. policy to use its unique economic force in the postwar period to secure its leadership in the international capitalist power structure.

The rest of S's chronology is wrong—for the Marshall Plan did not precede "our" military involvements in time nor would it in any case be proper to speak of a "shift" from recovery to military programs. To set the record straight, the Truman speech now referred to as his doctrine was made in March, 1947, whereas Marshall's did not come until June of that year; and whereas the Marshall Plan did not go into effect until the next year, "aid" to Greece was more urgent.

Let us see exactly how the U.S. aided Greece when it was "threatened" by communism. In 1944 the Communist-led army was clearly dominant and enjoyed large popular support; in the ensuing civil war with the discredited monarchist forces, victory would have been theirs had not "aid" been forthcoming.

But in 1946 civil war erupted again in Greece. According to Hugh Seton-Watson, this was dictated not by Moscow but rather by the "repressive policy" of the ruling government.[6] This policy in turn was pushed by Britain, which was determined to "install in power the discredited monarchy and its blindly vengeful rightist supporters."[7]

The only problem Britain had at this time was that its economic weakness prevented it from carrying out its imperial tasks effectively; Britain also had to admit its inability to defeat the "threat" of communism in Greece. As usual, the U.S. was glad to oblige—and this was where the Truman Doctrine came in. The Truman Doctrine in general was an attempt to circumvent international bodies such as the U.N.: thus with respect to Greece, the U.S. decided to ignore a U.N. plan for reconstruction. Basically the U.S. needed Greece for its strategic Mediterranean position with respect to Mideast oil and the Soviet Union.

That there is something suspicious about S's description can be seen from his inclusion of Yugoslavia ("even") (708) among those getting "aid"; it must be remembered that the other countries were being aided because they were "threatened" by communism. But Yugoslavia had, as it were, already succumbed to the disease—so how could we treat a dead patient short of military force? The point here is that the U.S. was not interested in saving democracy or soldiers' lives—the goal was to save markets and possibilities for capital investment (that Yugoslavia is a relatively small country is as little a refutation as is size in the case of Vietnam).

Digression on U.S. Direct Investment Abroad and the "Multinational Corporation" Tucked away at the end of S's minidiscussion of the Point Four Program, we find this statement:

> Besides these government plans, we have been privately exporting our "know-how." Many of our largest companies are establishing branch factories abroad; often the capital is largely raised there, with Americans supplying the technical knowledge. Some people throw up their hands in horror at the thought of our helping foreign nations to become our industrial competitors. . . . In terms of selfish long-run economic interest there is some factual basis for this gloomy view—as the post-Marshall Plan economic revival of Europe and Japan well illus-

trates. However, in terms of both long-run political interests and altruism, helping others to develop is deemed definitely good policy for the United States . . .[709].

Two aspects of this statement are remarkable: first, it is the only mention in the whole book of large-scale U.S. direct investment abroad; and secondly, it has been handed down now in an unaltered fashion through edition after edition. We consider the first point important, since the chapter is after all entitled "Current International Economic Problems," and the phenomenon under discussion has attained such significance that it has penetrated popular consciousness. Given the enormous changes that have taken place since World War II in this area, only someone who spends only a minimum of time on each new edition to liven it up for the "modern" student could reprint this section unchanged.

No attempt is made to provide a detailed account of U.S. direct investment abroad or of similar tendencies in other major national capitals. Though the main force of our criticism of S is not directed at his failure to offer such an account, to the extent that he contends that his theory immediately flows into such practical, concrete applications, he must be held accountable in this respect; similarly, if he does make the effort to summarize the major "problems" in this area, it is incumbent upon us to determine whether he has made a representative selection.

In order to understand the processes covered by the catchword multinational corporations, we must understand the connection between the overaccumulation of capital and the falling rate of profit within a national capital and the workings of the world market.

In Chapter 23 we introduced the concept of overaccumulation of capital to explain the phenomenon of capital exports by more "mature" capitalist nations to developing capitalist nations. At that point we were mainly interested in the export of loan capital (investment in "paper") in the context of S's discussion of "stages of development." Here, however, we are no longer dealing with "old" and "new" capitals, but rather with the reciprocal export of capital by highly developed national capitals, as well as their capital export to nations which will probably never become developed capitalist nations. The contemporary situation is, furthermore, complicated by the circumstance that in large part the export of capital now means direct investment abroad instead of the traditional reliance on loan capital.

How are we to explain this new situation? We hinted at the answer when we pointed out that as early as the beginning of this century the then two most dynamic capitalist powers, Germany and the U.S., were simultaneously importing loan capital and exporting capital for direct investment purposes. There were probably two major causes of this phenomenon at that time. First, we may hypothesize that, whereas in England a general overaccumulation of capital had set in which fostered the withdrawal of segments of the total national capital and its transfer in the money form of capital to territories offering a higher rate of "return" in the U.S. and Germany opportunities for the short-term expansion of the domestic market still abounded. The situation in these two countries was such that the process of monopolization—creation of trusts, cartels, etc.—had progressed so far that these branches of industry—iron and steel for instance—had developed ahead of the rest of the economy; one very important way to overcome these disproportions was to expand the market by producing abroad.

At this point the question may be raised—then why not just export commodities, why export the production facilities themselves? There are several reasons, and we may collect them all under the second major cause of direct investment. Among these was the then burgeoning system of protectionism: in order to overcome the tariff barriers of other countries, the highly cartelized and protectionist countries such as the U.S. and Germany found it necessary to set up production abroad. (This is one similarity to the contemporary situation, in which the U.S. has been investing very heavily in the Common Market countries).

Another reason for this trend lay in the attempt on the

part of these newer capitalist powers to compensate for the enormous advantage Great Britain enjoyed as a result of the unique financial power of London as the world's banker, which enabled it to gain the upper hand in financing commodity exports by British capitalists.

The third reason, closely connected to the foregoing, relates to the need on the part of the would-be imperialist powers to overcome the very substantial economic and political advantages inherent in the structure of the British Empire. One form this attempt assumed culminated in the colonial struggles of a productive base in foreign countries.

This summary of the rise of direct investment among the nascent imperialist powers at the time of the turn of this century can serve as the starting point for an understanding of the enormous growth of such investments in the post-World War II period. The factors mentioned were the concrete causes of the general need to overcome the falling rate of profit. Certain of these specific causes are still valid today (such as need to overcome tariff barriers), but others are still to be determined.

But before we can pursue this matter further, we must look at the other aspect underlying this process—the influence of the world market. In fact, perhaps it cannot even be characterized as "another aspect," since the interrelation between the two must be considered in investigating the cause of these "capital movements." The drive toward the establishment of a world market, toward the capitalization of all nations, is inherent in capital. Periodically, during times of world depression, the national capitals qua national states try to stem this tide. Nevertheless, there is a secular trend in the sense that despite the periodic "setbacks," the interconnectedness of all national capitals is intensified; this process does not, however, exclude the intensification of the "reverse" motion: that is to say, the possibility of crises remains and this very interconnectedness can conceal the roots of deeper crises precisely because the national capitals will find it increasingly difficult to sever their ties to the world market. But this also means that attempts to protect the national capital will also be increased and intensified.

The so-called multinational corporation is the chief mechanism by which the world market relations have been deepened in the post-World War II period. Lenin recognized long ago that capital "flows" were the prime forces at work in this respect. But in his time it was the export of loan capital (buying of stocks and bonds in foreign corporations and states, bank lending, etc.) that predominated; today direct investments are the dominant form. Prior to World War I, 60 percent of foreign loans issued in the advanced capitalist countries were directed toward the perennially "underdeveloped" countries, but today such loans are much less significant because the risks involved are too great. Although direct investment in these countries has also dropped relative to direct investment among the major capitalist powers, still it has increased significantly. The reason for this difference is explained by the fact that whereas the recovery of loans depends on the development of the local economy, making a profit on direct investment is relatively independent of that economy and can be guided much more directly by the investors. By this we mean that the "underdeveloped" countries must be competitive enough to obtain enough foreign exchange in order to pay back the debts, but the world market and tariff systems limit this possibility of gaining enough foreign exchange. Thus the countries find themselves unable to pay back their debts and thus few loans are offered. Hence the "poor credit rating" of these nations.[8]

The other main reason for the shift from the export of loan capital is linked to the structure of finance capital; in the last sixty to seventy years a great capital concentration in the largest corporations has taken place, and they (together with their group banks) are now able to self-finance a large share of their expansion. This is in sharp contrast to the period about the turn of the century when large sums of capital, stemming from a relatively broad layer of rentiers, was centralized in banks for foreign loans.

Related to this circumstance are the structural changes in capitalism itself, largely influenced by the Keynesian mode of staving off the more blatant crises, which makes for the protracted idling of productive capital, preventing its transformation into the internationally mobile money form; in other words, permanent excess capacity binds previously mobile capital to the national sphere.[9]

The reasons for the vast increases in "international production" are not the same for all advanced capitalist nations, although the general precondition for all the nations involved has been the postwar upswing on the world market. Of particular interest in this context is U.S. direct investment, particularly in the West European countries.

In the immediate postwar period the U.S. was not a senile power buying securities in the new, young, vigorous economies of Europe. The U.S. enjoyed an enormous productive advantage over the European countries, and it was reflected in the gigantic total trade surplus it accumulated during these years; between 1945 and 1952, the excess of exports over imports reached $43.524 billion.[10]

On the other hand, the secular stagnation of the 1930s reappeared between World War II and the Korean War, which provided great incentive for U.S. capital to invest abroad. Given the low wages in Europe one would have expected U.S. corporations to make a rush for profits there. Yet U.S. direct investment in the Marshall Plan countries increased by less than 30 percent between 1945 and 1950 (from $1.768 to $2.272 million). For this there are probably two major reasons. First, the great instability in these countries threw doubt on the ability of capitalism to survive there. Secondly, the large corporations were making big profits from exports guaranteed by the U.S. government; between 1945 and 1951 the difference between "goods and services" exported and imported by the U.S. equaled $49 billion; this amount represents the "gifts" and loans made by the U.S. during this time.

But of course foreign investment was not caught nodding during this period: the weakness of the West European "partners" was used to strengthen the U.S. position in "contested" areas. Thus U.S. direct investment in the following areas increased as follows between 1946 and 1950: Canada—50 percent; Latin America—60 percent; West European colonies—95 percent; other "underdeveloped" areas—120 percent.[11]

But with the political and economic "stabilization" settled by the early 1950s, it became clear that this was a good time for U.S. corporations to gain control over European markets from the inside. This is how an Executive Vice President of Caterpillar describes the situation for one individual capital:

> Caterpillar had no foreign investment prior to 1950, but it had been exporting U.S.-manufactured goods all over the world for many years. A major impediment arose as World War II ended and the nations of Europe began to recover from the physical and economic devastations of that war. Several countries had hundreds and even thousands of Caterpillar-built tractors within their boundaries, but they had no US dollar exchange to purchase repair parts from the United States to keep them running. . . .
> Caterpillar's first major response to this situation was to create a British company to subcontract the manufacture of parts to British companies. It purchased the parts as they were manufactured . . . and shipped them to any part of the world where pound sterling was more readily available than US dollars for use in making payment. (Virgil Grant, "The Multinational Company," in Federal Reserve Bank of Chicago, *The International Monetary System in Transition* (Chicago, 1972), pp. 109f.)

From 1950 until 1957, the year of the founding of the Common Market, U.S. direct investments in Western Europe rose from $2.272 to $4.151 billion, or approximately 83 percent.[12] Yet this still does not represent above-average increases in investment, and during this period West European investments continued to average about 15 percent of total U.S. investment abroad.

With the formation of the Common Market, however, a decisive turning point was reached:

> The big challenge came when the European Community was created in 1957. The six countries making up the market agreed to have a uniform import tariff which, in the case of track-type tractors, was to be 16 percent. Prior to creation of the market, the rate on tractors shipped to Germany and Belgium, the two largest customers, had been only 6 percent. Since there were

two tractor manufacturers in Germany, two in France, and the big Fiat plant in Italy (which, incidentally, was built with Marshall Plan funds), we could not hope to compete in that market by exporting from the U.S. The 16 percent tariff would make our prices too high. It was clear that we had to have a factory in one of those six countries. A thorough study of the situation resulted in buying the assets of one of the tractor factories in France with 150 employees. That company now has 1,800 employees. We have since located a second company in the European Community in Belgium in response to a challenge to our rubber-tired loader line. It employs 2,300.[13]

And in fact we see a similar picture on the aggregate level; the following table shows the increase in U.S. direct investment from 1957 to 1970 and compares it to the general increase in U.S. direct investment in all countries:

	1957 ($000,000)	1970 ($000,000)	% increase
Total	25,394	78,090	208
Western Europe	4,151	24,471	494
Common Market	1,680	11,695	596

Sources: For 1957—F. Hartog, "Trade Arrangements Among Countries: Effects on the Common Market," op. cit., p. 109; for 1970—*Survey of Current Business*, October, 1971, p. 32

Thus by 1970, Western Europe accounted for 33.4 percent of total U.S. direct investment, compared to 16.4 percent in 1957; similarly, the Common Market more than doubled its share, from 6.6 percent to 15 percent. This increased share has been accompanied by an enlarged share of U.S. corporations in the industrial production of Western Europe.

Here we begin to see the very complicated nature of these huge U.S. investments in Western Europe. The U.S. presence doubtless had salutary effects on the growth of capitalism in these countries, although at the same time it was U.S. capital that was gaining control over ever-larger shares of the source of capital accumulation.

A further aspect of this complex process relates to the

very nature of the "multinational" corporation; for once U.S. capital has become deeply involved in, say, Western Europe, it is subject to the same vicissitudes of the industrial cycle as the local national capital. This means that in periods of "recession," the subsidiaries of the large U.S. corporations will cease to play the role of the chief mechanism for intensifying the interconnectedness of all national capitals through the world market; large capital investments in one country cannot be so easily transferred elsewhere, and thus "U.S." capital remains the profit- or loss-bringing property of U.S. owners, though economically it is subject to the laws of motion of the national capital it is embedded in.

The structure of the capital relations between the U.S. and Western Europe offers a good example of the sort of U.S. advantage which may soon be brought to a halt. Whereas the greater part of U.S. investment in Western Europe falls in the category of direct investment, the overwhelming proportion of European investment in the U.S. falls in the category of loan capital (private and state, short- and long-term). To the extent that these countries were "willing" to finance the various imperialist ventures of the U.S., some of which directly and indirectly also aided the European capitalist systems, European loan capital was being transformed into U.S. industrial capital in Western Europe, whereby the U.S. capitalists gained from the difference between the interest rates they had to pay and the rate of profit on their investments.

The complicated nature of the increase in U.S. direct investment finds further expression in its relation to the development of the competitiveness of U.S. capital. Although the original U.S. investment in Western Europe was not necessarily a sign of domestic stagnation, the continued investment in the 1960s was definitely related to an inability to compete via exports. U.S. capital export was in large part a response to the decline in its competitive position. It is important to understand the causality. Although U.S. capital export was in large measure dictated by the opportunities of higher profit rates, increasingly it came to be an admission "that there are advantages in producing in the foreign market, which would suggest that the foreign-produced goods could outcompete the comparable United States product."[14]

The U.S. multinational corporations have obviously contributed significantly to equalizing conditions of production among the developed capitalist nations, although "equality" has by no means been reached. Nor, given the absence of a world capitalist state, will it be attained; for in periods of declining rates of accumulation each national capital takes care of itself.

It would be a mistake, however, to believe that U.S. capital is inevitably headed for defeat. Let us consider whether the cumulative effect of the enormous profits made by U.S. firms abroad might not act as a surplus-value injection, to compensate for the insufficient profitability of U.S. domestic capital. The following table shows the capital "flows" associated with U.S. direct investment between 1961 and 1970 (minus figures mean outflow):

	($ billion)
U.S. direct investment abroad	−28.8
Borrowing abroad by U.S. direct investors	11.2
Interest payments on borrowing abroad	− 1.3
Income from direct inv. abroad	41.8
Receipt of royalties and fees	12.4
Total	35.3

Source: Susan Foster, "Impact of Direct Investment Abroad...," op. cit., p. 172.

Thus during this decade U.S. "multinationals" returned "home" about $35 billion more than they invested. It may be true that profits derived from exports cannot function as a stimulus toward an upswing—insofar as the profits realized abroad first had to be produced domestically—unless the conditions of exploitation at "home tendentially allow of high rates of accumulation anyway." (See Neüsuss, et al., *"Kapitalistischer Weltmarkt...,"* op. cit., p. 102.) This construction, however, is not valid for profits stemming from direct investment abroad precisely because they were produced under conditions of exploitation superior to those of domestic capital.

With respect to the possible effects of "autonomous" injections of surplus value, it is obvious that the advantages stemming from this foreign profit accrue to those capitals with foreign investments. This is also a definite impulse for concentration, which in turn leads us to the last aspect of direct investment: its significance to United States capital as a whole.

First of all, U.S. direct investment abroad is concentrated among the largest monopolies. Only a very small percentage of all U.S. firms have any such investments, and even within this group the concentration is great. With respect to individual corporations, a major study done several years ago investigated the foreign "involvement" of *Fortune* magazine's 500 largest industrials for that year. It determined that 386, or 77 percent maintained foreign operations. Using five criteria of sales, earnings, assets, employment, and production, it divided these 386 companies into groups according to their "relative involvement in foreign operations": 48 percent maintained less than 10 percent foreign operations; 32 percent between 10 and 24 percent; 18 percent between 25 and 50 percent; and 2 percent greater than 50 percent.[15] The "involvement" of these largest corporations is even greater today.[16]

II. WORLD MARKET AND INTERNATIONAL MONETARY "INSTITUTIONS"

A. THE "WORLD" BANK

For S, the origin of the International Bank for Reconstruction and Development is extraordinarily simple:

> Since the U.S. is more developed industrially than the rest of the world, there is no doubt that South America, the Orient, Europe, and Africa could profitably use our capital for their industrial development. Such capital could be expected to increase their production by more than enough to pay generous interest and repay the principal [709].

At this point S leads us into the founding of the IBRD and IMF with a "therefore." And this is where the "cunning of reason" enters the scene; for although the rhetoric surrounding the founding of the institutions centered on the aspects encompassed by the name of the Bank, S has unwittingly put his finger on the real function of these institutions: the creation of the general conditions for "safe" international investments.

Why did the more grandiose plans of the Bank recede in the early postwar years? At a certain point in the roll-back strategy the U.S. considered "multilateralism" an inefficient if not potentially dangerous instrument; hence it opted for more openly direct control of the operations. Although Treasury Secretary Morgenthau defended the view in 1945—against Senator Fulbright—that the Bretton Woods system be "wholly independent of the political connection" (this in the context of a discussion of a proposed $10 billion low interest loan to the Soviet Union),

> as relations with the Soviet Bloc deteriorated, the political significance of Fund and Bank operations naturally increased. Several of the Soviet satellites were members of the institutions. The United States was understandably reluctant to permit the granting of financial assistance to members of an increasingly hostile bloc of nations.
>
> Indeed, the growing hostility between East and West was forcing the American Government to seek ever greater control over the disposition of the resources it was making available to other nations. . . .
>
> In the case of the Bretton Woods institutions, of course, resources had already been put under international control. But it was not too late to ensure that the resources of the Fund and Bank were employed in conformity with American political interests. The powerful voice which the U.S. had in the operation of these institutions soon began to make itself felt.[17]

With the U.S. decision to take direct control over the "reconstruction" process in Western Europe through the Marshall Plan, the Bank had to orient itself toward other goals, to act "as a safe bridge over which private capital could move into the international field."[18]

The ways in which the Bank serves this function are manifold. The fact that the Bank can perform this function altogether derives from a homogeneity of interests of the imperialist nations to keep access to the "Third" World open to capitalist investment; and although the U.S. is still the first among equals in the Bank, it must be understood that the Bank itself represents a coordinated response on the part of "First" World to the "threats" of the national liberation struggles.

Shonfield has characterized the advantages of a supranational bank for the imperialist lenders:

> The association of the Bank with a country is also taken to provide some insurance of international good behavior. . . . It is generally believed that a country would hesitate . . . before . . . defaulting on a World Bank loan.
>
> At the same time it is able to act as a kind of shield to foreign companies which want to develop some mineral or other natural resource in a distant spot, but are anxious to be protected against the political risks that are run by a rich and isolated alien concern operating in the territory of a poor nation. Thus, for example, the American steel companies, who wanted to develop the manganese deposits of the Gabon on the west coast of Africa, were able to avoid a direct connection with the business, because the Bank took the initiative, once the American interest in the manganese had been firmly established, and made a loan—knowing that it would be able . . . to sell rather more than half of the loan obligations to American insurance companies, who were standing ready to buy. These combined operations of the financial house, the large industrial corporation, and the Bank are an interesting extension of modern investment practice. . . . In time this may, indeed, become the standard formula for large-scale company investment in the natural resources of an undeveloped country. . . .[19]

A division of labor has developed between international organizations such as the Bank and private "investors"; in large measure the former has assumed the task of investing in the "infrastructure" of the "underdeveloped" nations. The reason for this division of labor is clear: investments in infrastructure are not immediately profitable; thus such projects may "tie up" considerable amounts of capital for a long time. Traditionally investors in such projects have had to be satisfied with interest rather than the full profit, and, of course, given a choice, large capitalist corporations will take the latter.

Such investments in infrastructure can also stem from so-called bilateral public capital, and sometimes a consortium is formed by the Bank to coordinate the "aid" programs of many nations to a large "development plan" (as, for example, with respect to India and Pakistan). Despite the general preference for multinational programs for reasons of "safety in numbers," there is the opposing consideration that such participation as a rule excludes the possibility of "tying" funds to purchases from the "donor" country. Such "aid" will of course meet with opposition from those national capitals or branches whose export position is deteriorating anyway. But this latter aspect should not make us lose sight of the fact that under certain historical conditions "multilateralism" can function as a means of penetration for one of the participating national capitals. That this was the case in the postwar period was emphasized in an article in *Business Week* of May 6, 1972, which quoted a high American official at the IBRD as saying: "If we didn't have the World Bank and IDA we'd have to create them. They cut through the barbed wire of the old colonial preferences and give us equal access to the markets of South Asia and Africa."

While U.S. taxpayers financed approximately $1.8 billion in paid-in capital to the Bank and IDA, by the end of 1970 U.S. capitalists had obtained orders amounting to more than $3.5 billion; when one adds the net income accruing to U.S. banks, etc., on 37 percent of the IBRD's outstanding debt, one sees that "U.S. equity-type investments and donations have been repaid two times over at least."[20]

The "flow" of loans for infrastructure and related areas is not unconnected with the needs of private capital. It is essential to understand that given such a meshing of investment policies, the only result of IBRD lending can be the further integration of the "underdeveloped" countries into the world capitalist market as further objects of imperialist exploitation; since loans are often withheld if the development purposes to which they are to be put do not coincide with those "perceived" by the Bank as having priority, and since anticapitalist measures find little acclaim at the Bank, those countries that get caught up in development via "international" institutions also find the rules of development narrowly prescribed.

We will now examine the origins and operations of the International Development Agency by scrutinizing S's optimistic view of the ability of the "borrowing lands" to repay their loans with "generous" interest. The Pearson Commission report to the IBRD, however, estimates that by the end of the 1970s debt-servicing will swallow almost all new private and public lending.

S's statement contradicts the actuality. According to him (8th ed., p. 687), "an embarassing volume of profits" gave rise to the largesse known as the IDA and IFC. The rise of the IDA was in fact the Bank's response to the prospective defaulting on many of its outstanding loans; rather than alter its policy on "creditworthiness," the Bank chose to open a more flexible branch which would offer lower interest rates and longer terms of payment.

Thus in 1970, when the foreign-exchange debt of these countries had reached $55 billion and was rising twice as rapidly as export earnings, McNamara stated that he shared the concern of these countries. But just in case, it was announced that in October of that year the Bank would start work on proposals for international investment insurance to protect foreign business against "expropriation and other hazards."[21]

All S tells us is that increasing portions of the Bank's profits goes to support its "soft" loan policy. Let us look at this more closely. First of all, the fact that in every new edition S repeats the bit about the "embarassing" profits, advancing the year (1964, 1967, 1970) up to which they have accumulated, merely confirms Shonfield's opinion that "if the development problem were being treated with the urgency that is required in order to make an impression on world poverty during the decade of the 1960s, IDA would be the senior partner of the World Bank."[22]

In the second place, S gives an incomplete, and thus distorted, view of the financing of IDA. Through 1970 the IBRD has transferred $485 million to IDA, while IDA had lent $2,886,130,000.[23] In other words, less than 17 percent stemmed from the Bank. The chief source of funds for IDA are the richest members of the Bank—and precisely this has been the cause of disruption, since the U.S. on occasion has so delayed its contribution that IDA lending fell off.

S's description of the IFC is even more misleading, because this institution does not even make the "soft" loans IDA does; rather, it has emphasized its "merchant-banker function" to such an extent that "one or two countries have found its terms so stiff that they have refused to use this source of finance for development."[24] For a bank not pursuing profit "per se," IFC was doing a pretty good job of hot pursuit, as witnessed by its average annual return of 9.08 percent.[25]

B. INTERNATIONAL MONETARY FUND

With the exception of a brief reference to the "hopes" of the IMF founders, no attempt is made to place the IMF into any historical context; since the function and development of the IMF is not problematized in the analysis itself, it is no wonder that S cannot go beyond vague talk about "disappointment" and "strains" (8th ed., p. 688).

As S notes, the IMF grew out of the same conferences which gave rise to the IBRD: what he does not say is that it also became integrated into the postwar imperialist strategy.

The final plans establishing the IMF codified the outcome of yet another intense struggle or world hegemony between the U.S. and Britain. The plan proposed by Britain, worked out by Keynes, was geared to the expected debtor status of Britain in the postwar period; in essence it provided Britain with overdraft facilities, reducing the drain on gold, since the latter was being supplanted by credit ("bancor") allocated on a basis favorable to Britain in the first place. Since the U.S. would obviously be the major creditor nation, this plan did not sit well with it, especially in light of the fact that unused bancors would lapse after a certain period.

This, combined with the built-in voting bias granted to the British Empire, did not fit into the emerging U.S. strategy of removing control over the reconstruction period from multilateral organizations.

The IMF, as it developed from the White plan put forward by the U.S., enabled the U.S. to assume an unprecedented position of power in the international financial system. One should not to ascribe to the U.S. the unlimited powers which find their source in the whims of the U.S. ruling class. What we mean here is that U.S. capital's strategy for hegemony accompanied the objective possibility for this power, and more specifically related to the international monetary system, corresponded to certain conditions necessary for the dollar's ability to assume the role it did.

Given the great concentration of gold in the U.S. (that is, both the fact that other countries had little gold and that the U.S. gold stock exceeded the dollars outstanding), given the relatively enormous commodity production taking place in the U.S. (which means that commodities could be bought by all dollar holders), given the role of the U.S. in world trade and finance (which permitted other countries to use the dollar as a means of payment and circulation)— given all these conditions, it was possible for the dollar to become world paper money. That all this was realized depended on the political pressure the U.S. was able to exert on the other countries; however, since no other country was in the objective position to fulfill this role, the other capitalist nations were confronted with an accomplished fact. The system that evolved was also necessary for the whole capitalist world so that in the medium run the other countries could "live with" it.

One of the major failings of the section on the IMF is its inability to prepare the way for an understanding of the collapse of the system. At the very least S would have to point out that along with the power the U.S. obtained through the ability to issue world money came the inherent instability of a monetary system based on the national currency of one particular country.

This is the inherent constriction of every credit system: to the extent that international trade and capital transactions grow more quickly than the gold supply, the reserve currency must be increased. In this process there comes a point at which the needs of availability of "liquidity" are bought at the expense of convertibility into gold. Once this point has been reached, it is merely a matter of time until the concrete conditions develop in the reserve country which will react on the other nations through the international processes of circulation; at such a time an economic crisis in one country can be transmitted to others which did not suffer an endogenously caused crisis.

Yet S himself "almost" provides the clue to the collapse of the Bretton Woods system when he asks why the dollar-DM exchange rates should remain unchanged after twenty years when "German productivity might outstrip America in an unpredictable way" (720). The only problem with this sort of reasoning is its tendency to locate the cause of the "disequilibria" in the technical workings of the IMF. But as we have pointed out, the exchange rate changes reflect the changes taking place among the various national capitals in their ordering on the universal scale of labor; in the long run such changes may be "predictable" or "unpredictable" as far as their specifics are concerned, but the uneven development inherent in capitalism assures their occurrence.

If this system has suffered crisis after crisis, then this in part stems from the U.S. insistence on, the European acquiescence in, the role of the dollar; but this also depends on the circumstance that there were radical changes in the scale of universal labor which had to find expression in national capitals resisting the changes being brought about by the workings of the law of value on the world market in order to secure certain important short-run trade advantages.

An example of S's technically oriented approach in his treatment of the various actions taken to "save" the pound sterling (8th ed., p. 688). Yet the underlying cause of this string of crises was the attempt of British capital to retain its imperial power despite its failure to establish the requisite international monetary system. In order to preserve its colonies and its competitiveness vis-à-vis U.S. capital, Britain was compelled to export more capital than it received back in the form of profits from the colonies; for this purpose as well as for the maintenance of the London money market it became necessary for Britain to build up trade surpluses. And it also became necessary to build up currency reserves large enough to guarantee gold or dollar convertibility to the sterling holders.

The pound devaluation of 1949 signaled the defeat of this strategy, although this did not prevent British capital from persisting in it. (It should be noted that IMF rules provided for Fund approval of devaluations in excess of 10 percent; in a sense this protected the U.S. against large competitive devaluations and accompanying dumping.)

The increasing inability in the 1960s to achieve these two goals of export surpluses and currency reserves stemmed from the limits of productivity and competitiveness of the British economy: the next attempt to overcome these difficulties culminated in the attempt to "modernize" British industry through governmental tax, price, and income measures. The deflationary policy curbed imports but failed to bring about a long-term improvement of productivity, and thus of the balance of payments; similarly, inflationary policy led to an outflow of reserves and the bankruptcy of "stop and go" economic policy.

The measures taken by the IMF in conjunction with the pound crisis in November, 1967, described by S (8th ed., p. 688) represented a temporary compromise on the part of the imperialist nations to bring about a devaluation rate for Britain which would neither endanger their own trading policies nor force them into a further round of competitive devaluations.[26]

The last part of our discussion of the IMF deals with the intertwining of its activities and those of the IBRD with respect to "underdeveloped" nations. The reader might well ask what this discussion is supposed to refer to since S does not mention this subject at all. Precisely: when S speaks of devaluations recommended by the IMF to deal with indebtedness, he refers to "a country" without making any distinction between the effects such a policy will have on "First" and "Third" World countries.

That the international monetary system exerts different pressures on the imperialist and the imperialized is not peculiar to the Bretton Woods set-up: it was equally so during the nineteenth century, the "heyday" of the gold standard. As far as the "periphery" countries are concerned, "international cooperation" as embodied in the IMF has done nothing to alleviate the crises associated with the "automatic mechanism" of the gold standard. And this for good reason: the same features that characterized the nineteenth-century relationships still continue to characterize the "underdeveloped" nations and their dependency on the "core" countries.

In considering the essential differences between advanced and "backward" capitalist nations in this respect, we would have to emphasize (1) the difference in industrial structure which enables the advanced capitalist countries to substitute for imports when necessary and to increase exports by diverting from domestic production;[27] (2) difference in trade structure which makes "underdeveloped" economies more dependent on a limited number of commodities and limited markets, thus narrowing its maneuverability; (3) difference in financial structure, and thus power, which enables the advanced countries to receive a large share of their foreign exchange from investment abroad and other non-commodity-export-related items, whereas the "underdeveloped" nations must rely heavily on their volatile commodity exports.[28]

Thus, far fewer advanced nations were forced to devalue their currencies, and those that did were not subject to the same harsh developments experienced by the "underdeveloped" countries. When one of the latter countries comes to the IMF for a loan, it is usually in dire financial straits (including the danger of defaulting on its international debts, which would have far-reaching consequences for any nation intent upon remaining in the capitalist system); it is therefore not surprising that the IMF uses this opportunity to intensify the existing relations of dependence.

The political goals connected with IMF policy were clearly shown in the case of Cuba, which in 1959 turned to the IMF for help in restoring the foreign-currency reserves squandered under Batista. As the *New York Times* reported: "If Dr. Castro is to get large-scale aid for his budgetary and balance-of-payments problems, he will have to agree to a stabilization program proposed by the IMF. This would involve credit restraint and a balanced—or nearly balanced—budget."[29] But since such a policy would have effectively vetoed Cuba's agrarian-reform and employment programs, Cuba was compelled to pursue its developmental programs within another economic system.

A quarter of a century ago S was honest enough to admit the political content of the IMF and IBRD, and the possibility of just such developments:

> In the Fund and International Bank, we have pledged ourselves not to force our economic doctrines on the rest of the world. . . . If a socialist government abroad wishes to supplement its income tax structure with a policy of curbing imports of luxury goods in favor of necessities, then we may privately disapprove. But without risking the charge of supporting [!] imperialism and being a propagandist, we cannot raise objections. Yet that is what insisting upon free exchanges comes close to doing. On what insisting upon financial belt-tightening measures abroad often appears like to foreign eyes.[30]

In fact this has been the course pursued by the IMF over the years. IMF recommendations for the decontrol of exports and imports, for devaluation, for cutting government expenditures, balancing the budget, etc., all lead to a vicious circle strengthening the dependence of the "underdeveloped" countries on the "aid" of their exploiters.

C. GENERAL AGREEMENT ON TARIFFS AND TRADE

It is characteristic that S does not provide the reader with any information on the evolution of GATT. Had he done so, it would show the very opposite of the harmonious setting into which he puts the capitalist world. GATT arose amid the same general postwar conditions we have described before. It was the successor to the "still-born" International Trade Organization, which died as a result of insurmountable antagonism among the allies, chief among them the British refusal to abolish the Imperial Preference system which granted Britain special advantages in trade with its Empire. Another aspect of dispute centered on the European countries' "being required, through the forceful persuasion of the U.S., to give up trade controls which were necessary to defend their balances of payments and standards of living."[31] And finally, then as now, the U.S. insisted upon reciprocal tariff reductions, despite the fact that its tariffs were generally higher. In the end GATT was formed as a weak substitute, an organization which allowed all sorts of escape clauses and which the U.S. as well as others have disregarded when it was to their benefit.

During the 1950s the further push toward tariff reductions was thwarted by a recrudescence of U.S. protectionism based on the fear of the recreated Western European competition.[32] The Kennedy Round must be seen in conjunction with the creation of the EEC with its higher common tariff policy; although the U.S. had in part attempted to come to grips with this barrier through massive direct investments, this was only in part successful, and it was of little help as far as agricultural exports were concerned. The new-found interest in tariff reductions resulted in large from this need to overcome the tariff barriers. Although some "progress" was made toward lowering tariffs, the fundamental disputes concerning the EEC, the U.S., and Japan exist to this day. Almost every day brings new reports of U.S. or European attempts to "fend off" Japanese exports, while the U.S. and Europe continue to battle among themselves.

One of the major points of dispute concerns agricultural exports from the U.S. to the EEC. S characterizes French insistence upon high tariffs as a "wish" which leaves comparative-advantage geographers (!) and economists unimpressed (8th ed., p. 689). But this "wish" happens to be one of the cornerstones of the French support for the EEC, since France, as the strongest agricultural producer in that group, is intent upon securing an unencumbered outlet for its surplus farm products in the EEC. On the other hand, with the EEC as its largest export market for agricultural commodities, the U.S. is not likely to accede to French "wishes" very easily.

Another major dispute surrounds the relations to the "less-developed" capitalist nations. This encompasses two aspects. The first refers to the preferential-tariffs pacts between the EEC and numerous south European and African nations. "Bargaining" on this issue should also prove to be "difficult"; on the one hand, the EEC nations, especially West Germany, have created a favorable access route to the penetration of African and Arab markets which they have no intention of sharing with the U.S.; the U.S., on the other hand, has been struggling to improve its market share in Africa, where it has still not overcome the tight control established by the original European colonial powers.

In sum, then, beneath the veil of technical-sounding tariff reduction debates a significant competitive struggle is taking place among the major capitalist powers to capture new sources of capital accumulation.

D. EUROPEAN ECONOMIC COMMUNITY

"For the great mass of the people there has been no broad improvement in conditions generally."[33]

Aside from the goals of free trade and free "movement" of capital and labor, S does not provide us with any of the objective forces or subjective motivations which brought about "one of the most exciting international developments of the century" (712); in fact, from the meager description offered in these few paragraphs, it is not even demonstrated that anything "exciting" took place at all.

As we have already noted, several economic and political forces were at work in forming the Common Market. A partially correct interpretation of some of these factors was provided even prior to the formation of the EEC by Jacob Viner in his study of customs unions:

> For the U.S. however, the political and strategic interest in a stable and prosperous and strengthened Western Europe, and the economic interest in a Western Europe able to pay for the imports necessary to maintain its economic and political health, are clearly of much greater importance than the size of the market which Western Europe offers for American exports.[34]

In other words, in the early postwar period the U.S. was willing to accept an increasingly competitive Western Europe in exchange for an anticommunist bulwark. This interpretation, though providing us with some insight into the relationship between the U.S. and the EEC, does not reveal its whole complexity. Sidney Dell takes us a bit further:

> On the one hand integration was seen as a means of building up the strength of Western Europe in the conflict with the East. . . . Another motive for European unification, on the other hand, has been the desire to create a counterweight to the overwhelming predominance of the U.S. in the Western world.[35]

This interpretation introduces the further information that, going beyond U.S. willingness to put up with a new competitor in the form of a Western European economic union, the Europeans themselves had resolved to overcome the U.S. political-economic hegemony.

This, however, does not mean that Western Europe's "desire" to set up a counterforce to the U.S. merely sprang from some sort of Gaullist delusions of grandeur. To begin with, neither the U.S. nor the Europeans were concerned with imports and exports exclusively; the enormous build-up of U.S. direct investment in Western Europe provided the main stimulus to further efforts at economic integration, whereby of course the formation of the EEC itself spurred the very phenomenon that was at the root of the unification efforts: U.S. investment. With their newer technology and larger size the U.S. firms were gaining a firm place in the European economy.

In this connection it is useful to adopt Ernest Mandel's

distinction between the absolute and relative need for interpenetration of capital in the EEC. Under the former he understands the fact that: "Certain sectors of industry demand such intensive investment to attain profitable production that even all the companies in that sector in each individual Common Market country together cannot provide it."[36] He names three examples: supersonic aircraft, space exploration, and space telecommunications. Under relative dependency on the interpenetration of capital Mandel understands the following process:

> In theory, West Germany, France and Italy might be able to sink sufficient capital to set up large competitive computer industries in each of these three countries. But this hypothesis is unrealistic for two reasons. First, it goes against the principle of spreading risks—more capital would be sunk in one sector of industry than its expected profits would justify. Second, three similar firms would lead to massive overproduction. There are not enough buyers in the European or the world market for three such firms. There is, therefore, a *relative* necessity for the interpenetration of capital: given the size of the market, in an ever increasing number of branches of industry there are only a limited number of companies which can operate at a profit.[37]

Here we see that there were objective forces as well pushing toward West European integration; and from preliminary studies it would appear that the accompanying concentration movement in the EEC has helped close the gap between the European and the U.S. firms.

Missing from S's narrative is the special function of the preferential trade agreements established by the EEC with the "associated" African states. According to Dell, this system was equivalent to the advantages secured by Britain in its empire or by the U.S. from its relation to, say, the Philippines; this despite the fact that "it had been taken for granted that discrimination of this sort was on its way out with the colonial era."[38] As Dell also notes, this neocolonial arrangement was particularly attractive to West Germany which was totally excluded from colonial sources of profit after the two World Wars.

This need on the part of the EEC countries to establish new profitable relations with ex-colonies provides part of the explanation for the divergent interests of Britain and the EEC. As Dell puts it, for the continental nations of Western Europe, in contrast to Britain, "the problem was not how to hold on to existing influence but how to rebuild a glory and prestige lost during the years of war and occupation. There was a world to gain and nothing to lose from a pooling of sovereignties."[39]

Britain on the other hand was still essentially bound up with its Empire, an advantage which it would have to forgo in some form or another as the price of entry. This does not mean that monopoly capital in the U.K. was blind to the advantages of joining and to the dangers of not joining.

Of course British monopoly capital was interested in joining on its own terms; when these terms were rejected, Britain led the effort to form the EFTA. S explains this grouping on the basis of its being "anxious over the progress of the Common Market" (712); S does not quite understand this "anxiety" since such progress "ultimately" will "lead to net benefit" for others; but in any case this is a paltry explanation. In point of fact, as Dell notes, the EFTA was formed in order to put pressure on the EEC rather than as a serious effort at economic integration.[40] Britain hoped to convince the EEC to adopt its plan of a large free trading zone without common tariffs for outside trade, without regulation of relations to colonies and without inclusion of agricultural products. But the EFTA proved to be too weak to realize Britain's plans.

DeGaulle's opposition to a broadening of the Common Market was not entirely unfounded from the point of view of French capital, which from the beginning approached the EEC defensively: through customs and tariffs it wanted to protect itself from U.S., U.K., and Japanese competition. This stood in sharp contrast to the needs of West German capital, which approached the EEC aggressively; it saw in the Common Market a vehicle for overcoming the narrow confines of the German market and penetrating the rest of Europe as well as colonial areas. The conflict of interests between France and Germany, although it still exists today, given the unchanged underlying needs of the national capitals, was somewhat alleviated by the death of DeGaulle and the recognition on the part of U.K. monopoly capital that further delay in joining the EEC could be tantamount to permanently losing its place on the world market to superior U.S., EEC, and Japanese competition.

Excursus on the "Mobility" of Labor In the course of this discussion we have concentrated on capital export and import; in fact, this has been true of all the chapters on international economic relations. Yet labor mobility has become increasingly important in recent years, especially in Western Europe. Foreign workers have assumed the role of the reserve army in the sense of offering mobility from branch to branch as well as in the sense of moving into and out of the work force in times of high accumulation and depression.

Charles Kindleberger testifies to this internal aspect of mobility when he states that "unrestrained by ownership of property or burdened by possessions" the foreign workers "can readily effect geographic changes."[41] Further evidence of this role was supplied even more recently by West Germany's Minister of Labor and Social Affairs, Walter Arendt, who, while praising the "regional mobility" of these workers, warned that with lengthened stays and the eventual transfer of their families to West Germany this mobility would slacken and infrastructural investments would increase to the point at which the disadvantages would outweigh the advantages.[42]

In fact, it is well possible that in the coming years the surplus value created by these workers will be exported to their homelands and be used to exploit their compatriots; if profitability weakens in West Germany, then capital can be exported instead of labor power imported. This reciprocal relationship fits in well with West Germany's increasing capital exports geared to strengthening its position on the world market against other strong national capitals.

Striking proof of the other aspect of mobility—into and

out of the work force—was given during the West German recession of 1966-67 when the foreign labor force was reduced by about 300,000; this showed West Germany's ability to export unemployment to the countries from which their migrant laborers came.

This ability to shift the brunt of the unemployment onto foreign workers, who not only leave the labor force but also the country, may exert a very divisive influence on the working class in these countries; the foreign workers in essence fulfill the same role as blacks and Puerto Ricans and Chicanos in the U.S. in this respect. This similarity is also to be observed in the nature of their employment; for the foreigners are almost exclusively manual workers, allowing the natives to move into "white collar" positions of various sorts.

It is in this context that we must seek to understand the "free movement of labor" fostered by the Common Market. With the increasing need for workers during the late 1950 and 1960s, new policies intended to attract and integrate immigrant workers, but also to control them better, were introduced. One such measure was the free labor-movement policy of the EEC, designed to stimulate the flow of the rural proletariat of southern Europe to West European capital. But here, too, there were conflicts among the various national capitals, based on their need for such workers. West Germany, with no empire and thus without its own colonial source of workers, was perhaps most aggressive in its search; yet its refusal to concede priority to the recruitment of emigrants from Common Market countries, because of the more favorable conditions under which it could obtain workers from non-EEC countries, has led to only a partial realization of the free-labor movement policy.

That this movement of labor is called "free" corresponds to the ideology of capitalism: that is to say, it is a type of freedom peculiar and necessary to a certain mode of production, but which is celebrated as part of the human condition. This particular movement of labor is free in the sense that all wage labor is free—there are no slave or feudal relations that prevent the laborer from selling his labor power elsewhere. It is also free in the sense that the worker had the choice between work and starvation. Most of the foreign workers come to Europe because unemployment is high at home.

As far as Western Europe is concerned, high proportions of foreign capital and labor appear to have become a permanent feature of postwar development. In part one cause is common to both "factors of production": the high rates of accumulation characteristic of these economies during this period. But at this point the similarity ceases, and here we can begin to see the difference between free movement of capital and free movement of labor. Capital, by and large, came not because it was idle and starving, but because the rate of profit was higher in Europe (in part because there were so many foreigner laborers to exploit). But we must remember that there is a strong element of compulsion of the market variety here too: if foreign capital had not exploited these sources of accumulation, then competitors would have.

Foreign capital, in contrast to foreign labor, was not discriminated against, was not forced to "work" in the least profitable industries, was not recruited because it had nothing better to do, was not shipped home when a recession caused trouble for the domestic capitalists.

The mere arrival of additional capital did not lower the rate of profit in general, at least in the short run—in the long run all capital accumulation will, by increasing the organic composition of capital, tend to lower the profit rate—but rather increased it by introducing new methods of extracting relative surplus value.

Thus on the whole, the "factors of production" capital and labor experience entirely different situations when they happen to meet on neutral ground.

III. THE INTERNATIONAL MONETARY CRISIS

Although S points out many of the factors responsible for the dollar "shortage" and "glut," he is unable to see the two phenomena as necessary aspects of one and the same process. In the early years the positive trade balance for the U.S. derived from its large productivity lead over the Western European nations; the very fact of this advantage necessitated the U.S. balance of payments deficits in order to provide the world capitalist economy with "liquidity." The reason that the gold outflow from the U.S. at first "went unnoticed" (713) was that with the general upswing in the world capitalist economy in general and the commodity cornucopia in the U.S. in particular Europeans had "faith" in the dollar. In the 1960s the changing relations in productivity began to manifest themselves in the U.S. trade balance. The competitive position of the U.S. deteriorated steadily. In and of itself there is nothing spectacular about such a development: given uneven development among national capitals it is necessary for such gaps to be constantly closed and opened. What was significant here was that because the national currency of this national capital had been elevated to world paper money, the survival of the entire international credit system was at stake.

The transition from chronic to acute dollar crisis first took the form of rising gold prices, the result of the fact that at a certain point the European nations ceased to be interested in the overvaluation of the dollar because it threatened the value of their large foreign exchange (i.e., dollar) reserves; at the same time they began to fear adverse effects on their surplus trade and payments balance when the U.S. began to take measures to protect its balance. These European countries did not become "apprehensive" that the dollar "might" be devalued (716); the prices on the gold market indicated that it already had, and the declining trade position of the U.S. demonstrated that the dollar had depreciated vis-à-vis other currencies. This meant that the dollar's function as reserve currency and key currency had been seriously impaired, that the dollar was not "as good as gold," and that the exchange rates were no longer accurate reflections of the relations among the national capitals as value-producing units.

The introduction of flexible exchange rates might provide an illustration of what Marx called the sharpening of contradictions stemming from false legislation based on false theories of money. This theory of floating exchange rates is based on the bourgeois theory of the exchange rate as determined by supply and demand on the foreign exchange markets. This approach is incorrect in part because it fails to see the formation of exchange rates as an expression of the relations on the universal scale of labor; in this sense there is no equality among the various entries in the balance of payments, for the trade balance reveals more clearly than any other entry the changes taking place among the national capitals. Floating exchange rates, however, are based on all transactions taking place on the foreign-exchange markets (all private and state capital movements, etc.), thus blurring in practice what is also blurred in bourgeois theory.

By putting into practice a false theory, this "reform" would doubtless lead to exchange rates incompatible with the law of value, and unless corrected, would also lead to the same delayed and shifted type of crises that we have seen under Bretton Woods.

The same constraints present in all the other systems also impinge upon the flexible rate system. And finally, the dollar ceased to be the intervention currency because the other nations were no longer willing to support the exchange rate.

A. GOLD

We cannot here attempt an exhaustive treatment of the question of gold as world money. Instead, we will analyze S's treatment of two important aspects—the two-tier gold system and an increase in the "price" of gold.

S's description of the origin of the two-tier gold market follows a time-honored bourgeois tradition: Crisis ("time had run out on the precarious gold-and-dollar standard"); men of good will meet to solve their common problems ("the ten leading nations of the world met"); a new successful system arises ("Up until 1973 it has been working very well indeed") (722).

Yet this meeting of the Group of Ten and its decisions differ little in their orientation from other, similar conferences and the systems they generated.

When studying this or any other international monetary conference, two important aspects must be kept in mind: (1) since "technical" problems are not responsible for the contradictions which surface in the various crises, technical solutions will merely delay and shift the crisis; and (2) despite the fact that it is generally in the interest of all capitalist nations to have a functioning international monetary system, each system contains advantages and disadvantages for each national capital (parities, key currency, reserve currency, gold "price") which makes it imperative for each to assert its special plan.

S's description of the two-tier gold market is not consistent. On the one hand he states that "time had run out on the precarious gold-and-dollar standard"; on the other hand, he asserts that the new arrangements have worked "very well." But the purpose of the new arrangements, if we understand S correctly, was to block out the disruptive influences of the gold hoarders and speculators. Had this succeeded, one could say that S was correct. But the basic problem, as S himself points out, relates to the danger that Fort Knox would be "stripped" of all its gold. And that "danger" remained even after the speculators and hoarders were cut off from gaining access.

The point is that the splitting of the gold markets, far from securing the dollar, represented an admission that the dollar no longer played the role of reserve and key currency: for these two functions depended on the convertibility of the dollar into gold, and this convertibility in practice no longer existed even among central banks. Yet S announces triumphantly: "Outside the IMF Club, gold has finally been completely demonetized. Its price is freely set by supply and demand, just like the price of copper, wheat. . . . For the first time in 15 years the international financial structure has been able to be completely indifferent to the vagaries of hoarders and the ups and downs in free-market gold prices" (723).

A careful analysis of this reasoning will prove worthwhile inasmuch as it will show that the inability of bourgeois economics to understand gold as an expression of the fundamental contradiction of capitalist commodity production ultimately leads to its inability to see the phenomena now manifesting themselves as international crises and even to understand the plans which the bourgeois economists themselves have formulated and put into practice.

First of all, what does it mean that gold has been demonetized? It would seem that S means that only the fact that the U.S. had committed itself to paying $35 per ounce made gold money, and now that it had shed this obligation—except within a limited sphere—gold was no longer money. Unfortunately for S, this does not prove that gold has been demonetized; on the contrary, the *removal of gold convertibility has tendentially demonetized the dollar as world money*.

As far as the domestic sphere is concerned, this line of reasoning basically rests upon the false identification of money as measure of value with, on the one hand, money as standard of price, and on the other, money as means of circulation. This results in the belief that because paper can replace gold as means of circulation, the measure of value need not have any value, that its value is conventional, established by the state. Now we know that gold need not circulate in order to function as measure of value; and, in fact, for national purposes gold need not even be accessible to private citizens (convertibility is not necessary). This is the rational kernel of the "fiat" theory. This does not mean, however, that the state can create all the paper money it wants; for the laws of circulation will merely deflate it to the value of gold that would be in circulation (the standard of price has been changed). Thus it is not "gold backing" in the sense of convertibility that gives paper money a value domestically, but rather the representational relation of paper to gold as a measure of value.

In this sense, we see that removing gold from circulation in the U.S. has not demonetized gold. It is true, however, that the U.S., through its temporary power of maintaining the gold "price" at an artificial (in the sense of not corresponding to the law of value or, if you wish, the "law" of supply and demand) level, has been able to violate this representational relation within the U.S. This has provided the "institutional" framework within which the inflationary forces of the extended credit system could find full expression.

The point is not that a "law" of capitalism has been violated, but when and how that law will reassert itself; for this is but another illustration of the ability of the state to delay and shift crises.

According to S: *"Money, as money rather than a commodity, is wanted not for its own sake but for the things it will buy!* We do not wish to use money directly, but rather to use it by getting rid of it; even when we choose to use it by holding it, its value comes from the fact that we can spend it *later on"* (276). We contend that with this definition, S has refuted both his own claim that the value of paper money does not derive from gold and his assertion that gold has been demonetized through the inconvertibility of the dollar. First of all, the function of gold as "a heavily defended 'last ditch' reserve"[43] contradicts S's notion of money as a mere tool for facilitating barter. Secondly, if money is not wanted for its own sake but only for what it can buy, then the fact that dollar holders were no longer satisfied with what they could buy with dollars proves that the dollar was no longer world money. Indeed, dollar holders wanted to use it "by getting rid of it"—in exchange for gold. Once they could no longer get gold, which was the only commodity they wanted at this point, the dollar became a first-ditch reserve—it was the first to be ditched.

The open admission by the U.S. of its inability to convert dollars to gold was simultaneously a tacit admission of the artificial gold parity.

This leads us to S's second statement, that with the splitting of the gold markets the international monetary system had finally thrown off its cross of gold. Just the reverse. The existence of a free gold market has made public what previously only experts knew: that the dollar was overvalued. The rise of the gold price to a multiple of its official dollar parity now makes manifest the forces that have been disrupting Bretton Woods for years.

Neither the proponents of a higher gold "price" nor S in his critical remarks see that the existence of crises under the gold standard did not derive from the gold standard, but rather that their form was merely determined by the international monetary system then in existence. Thus when S states that mixed economies will not subject themselves to the deflationary possibilities of a gold standard, all he is saying is that the crises will continue to be delayed and shifted.

In any event, we have seen that on the contrary, modern mixed economies have been pulled into the international monetary crises against their "will"; the interconnectedness of the national capitals is an objective tendency of capitalism as a world system and any monetary system will have to express this tendency in some significant way. Certain systems may permit certain capitals to "go their own way" in the short run, but in the long run, as long as there is no crisis which specifically leads to a decomposition of the world market into trading and currency blocs, no country is immune to the elements of crises.

More specifically, with reference to raising the price of gold, if gold continues to play a role in the "next" international monetary system, then its "price" will doubtless be raised. S does not explain the factors involved in such a move, but rather is concerned with reinforcing the enlightened prejudice he has fostered against gold. Most of the arguments he offers are totally irrelevant from a scientific point of view. His only reference to the price rise per se is a derisive one: "But at the stroke of a pen, the shortage of international liquidity will have disappeared" [723]. How ironic! If anything, this should have been said about the creation of SDRs—but no, that was a "rational international system" (727). Here, where it is not a matter of "raising" any price but rather of eliminating political controls which had prevented gold from exchanging at its value, S finds it necessary to speak of pen strokes, giving the impression that something foolishly artificial is taking place. This stands in sharp contrast to his indictment of minimum wage laws, rent control, etc., as inefficient interference with the laws of supply and demand.)

As we have already indicated, if gold remains an important part of the international monetary system, then the gold "price" will rise toward its real value. This is a "rational" step because it will release the liquidity which had been suppressed by the U.S. ability to keep the price down. This is not "the solution" to the threatened breakdown, although by spurring on gold production it will doubtless provide increased liquidity later on as well. Nor does this mean a return to the gold standard: this is a strawman S uses, but the two are not related. There will be no return to the gold standard because it is incompatible with present-day Keynesian methods of dealing with crises. But this in no way rules out a fundamental role for gold in other systems. This in the end is also admitted by S, when he says IMF reforms will *"build around* gold and *supplement* it" (724), but again it stands in no relation to his arguments elsewhere in the text, except as a contradiction.

B. SPECIAL DRAWING RIGHTS

Finally, we turn to the latest attempt to solve the world monetary "muddle" by use of sophisticated hylo-alchemical techniques—"paper gold." In contrast to the seventh edition, which at least mentioned the existence of criticisms of this reform even if it did not elaborate on them, the eighth and ninth editions are the usual Samuelsonian celebration of that which is; the only reservation voiced is a brief appeal to the future—"success of the system is not yet assured" (727). But since none of the three editions offer any explanation of the prerequisites of such a system, it seems appropriate to begin with this aspect.

A hint in the right direction is provided by S himself—to be sure in connection with floating exchange rates—when he lets the protagonist say: "within a country like the United States there is one central government, one Federal Reserve and money system, and one labor market in the sense that workers can migrate to a low unemployment region. All these features are lacking internationally" (725). This is all true, but it belongs in the section on "paper gold," because it points up the barriers to the creation of "fiat" money internationally. Even more important is the lack of full capital mobility and its competitive expression in real tendency toward an average rate of profit; and most importantly, whereas the tendency toward an average rate of profit finds political expression on the national scale in the bourgeois state, there is no world state.

This essential aspect of any attempt to create paper gold has not been absent from discussions surrounding the reform plans, although it often appears in the more harmless guise of "national sovereignty." We may introduce a review of those discussions by picking up one of S's remarks to the effect that such a system runs into the same criticisms usually aimed at international languages like Esperanto—namely how to agree on it (7th edition, p. 698).

One interesting approach—though only implicitly analogous—is offered by an economist who comes to a correct view of gold as the only world money despite, or perhaps on account of, an incorrect understanding of the essence of money:

> All modern currencies that circulate within the territories of countries are essentially fiat monies, that is, money established by governmental decree. Sovereign governments also exercise control over the issuance of their national money supplies. However, their *legal* monetary sovereignty does not extend beyond their borders.
>
> A full-fledged international money would require the existence of a supra-national issuing authority. . . . In this world of sovereign nation-states, a universally accepted international money does not exist. . . . In the absence of world government, there is no other type of financial asset that receives international monetary acceptance fully equal to that of gold. . . . In a world of nation-states, there is nothing that could fully replace gold as international money.[44]

Eugene Birnbaum, quoted above, is so fixated on the essence of money as fiat money, as an artificial creation of man, that he rejects the possibility of international money on the basis of its inability to be fiat money.

Another economist, Charles Kindleberger, who also stressed "the futility of a synthetic, deliberately created international medium of exchange" with the explicit reference to Esperanto, takes a different approach. Since for him the re-enthroning of gold would be analogous to the return to Latin as an international language, he views the elevation of a national currency to international money as the only possibility. Drawing a parallel to the use of English, he says:

> But a common second language is efficient, rather than nationalist or imperialist.
> The power of the dollar and the power of English represent *la force des choses* and not *la force des hommes*. . . .
> The selection of the dollar as the lingua franca of international monetary arrangements, then, is not the work of men but of circumstances. Pointing to its utility involves positive, not normative, economics.[45]

The reasoning here seems to run as follows: since the dollar as world money, as opposed to national money, was not consciously invented by man but generated by the needs of commerce spontaneously, it shares the impartiality inherent in gold.

The problem with this argument is rooted in its failure to give an account of the conditions under which the dollar could become world money, i.e., it could become world money only to the extent that U.S. capitalist hegemony enabled it to act as a surrogate for a world government. Only by assuming the identity of interests on the part of the strongest power with those of imperialism as a whole is Kindleberger able to establish homogeneous interests between the U.S. (i.e., dollar) and the other nations of the capitalist world. This set of identities in part corresponded to reality; to the extent that the dollar was "efficient" Kindleberger is right. But in part that identity of interests did not exist, and as soon as the European countries and Japan became strong enough to assert their interests as separate from those of the U.S., that is to say, as soon as the set of nonidentities began to assert itself over the set of identities, the dollar was no longer "efficient" and the system based on it was doomed to collapse.

What are the objective possibilities for any system such as paper gold; and secondly, how would the existing political struggles shape the particular system which is coming into being?

S states that the new paper gold system "will represent a significant step forward" (727). The question is, forward to what? Although S does not inform us as to what he sees as the end goal, we can surmise that it "would be the establishment of a world central bank that would regulate monetary policies in all countries and, in effect, decide what all currencies would be worth in terms of one another. It's a fact of political life, however, that no government at present appears willing to give up so much of its authority to an international body."[46] Probably not even such a drastic change would suffice: to "regulate monetary policies" presupposes the same ability on the part of this new world organ to intervene presently possessed by the national states. This means that during the "recessionary" phases of the industrial cycle—if such an anachronism will continue to plague our world mixed economy—this supranational body will have to be empowered to take the same coordinating "anticyclical" measures now taken by the national state to restore profitability. And all of this, in turn, would presuppose the existence of one currency—world fiat money—and a tendential average rate of profit unimpeded by any national organs designed to thwart competition.

We contend that unless this blissful state is reached, the present SDR system will be merely another stopgap measure in a long list of delaying tactics. And we also contend that such a state will never exist.

We do not deny that the possibility of certain capitalist states uniting to fight another bloc of capitalist states exists; this may happen in wars or in times of relative peace, as in the Common Market. Unification, if it does occur, would be grounded in the degree of capital interpenetration lacking elsewhere; and more importantly, it would be grounded in an effort to expand at the expense of the U.S. (and more and more of Japan).

Assuming that the world central bank will not to be realized, let us concentrate on the second of the two points we mentioned above: how political forces will shape the limited system now coming into being.

First of all, it must be understood that SDRs are basically an answer to the problems of the dollar within Bretton Woods. Increasingly the EEC countries had to come to the aid of the dollar and the pound sterling. But they wanted to do this within the Group of Ten rather than directly under the authority of the IMC, where the U.S. had greater power. SDRs represent a further compromise along these lines.

One issue at stake, as Birnbaum notes, consisted in the fact that: "From the European point of view—that of countries in chronic surplus—there is no general inadequacy of international liquidity. The Americans, feeling a shortage of liquidity, have had to be 'supplicants' vis-à-vis the Europeans."[47] It appears that originally the U.S. was opposed to such a plan of paper gold. Thus Robert Roosa, Treasury Under Secretary for Monetary Affairs under Kennedy and Johnson and later a partner in Brown Brothers Harriman & Co., took a negative view of the Triffin Plan, one of the first American-authored plans in the 1950s designed to create liquidity along the lines of Keynes' bancor plan defeated at Bretton Woods. The reason for this initial opposition to the supplanting of the dollar lay in the concrete advantages accruing to "the U.S." as a result of the special position of the dollar; but this was a more complicated matter, for although "the U.S." did not want to renounce this power, the Triffin Plan and others embodied certain proposals which would have provided an "American" solution to the problem of the U.S. deficits.

There was a fundamental ambiguity in the U.S. attitude toward such a plan. It would appear that at some point the U.S. realized that if it was fighting a losing battle, it ought to throw its weight behind a plan which would secure it the least unfavorable position: this would entail preserving the role of the dollar for as long as possible as well as reducing the severe U.S. debt as much as possible.

This transition can be observed in the development of the SDRs, which "were originally intended to be in part repayable loans to nations from the I.M.F. rather than a purely monetary reserve."[48] This is where the EEC enters. S mentions (726) that SDR creation is subject to a veto by 15 percent of the voting quotas; but he does not tell us why. Previously major decisions were subject to a 20 percent veto, because the U.S. held more than 20 percent of the votes and thus possessed an effective veto over all important decisions. At the time Roosa was willing to go along with this set-up on the grounds that no new system could be created without EEC cooperation anyway, regardless of whether it had a formal veto. One hypothesis for the turnabout of Roosa et al. would relate to their need to include the EEC in the creation of a new system which would go beyond the short-run goals of the original SDR plan. This expanded plan would seek to relieve the U.S. of the burden of paying off its foreign debt.

The pressure for the European countries to come to terms with the U.S. is mounting because with the growing dollar accumulations the problem is being exacerbated. This increasing pressure on the Europeans to come to a settlement may be the reason for the acceptance by the U.S. of the SDR approach: because it allows the U.S. to combine it with a means of eliminating the huge debt problem.

But contrary to S's view that when the SDR system is paired with a realignment of major currency parities, "we can forget unofficial gold, letting it become the concern of dentists, jewelers, the Mafia, and smugglers" (727), the major realignment of December, 1971, has not eliminated the problem of gold—official or unofficial. At the same time the Bank for International Settlements, an influential "central banker's central bank" has called for the restoration of the convertibility of the dollar into gold lest the capitalist world be divided into currency blocs as a result of the EEC's being forced into creating its own unified currency.

The first possibility, that of a split of the capitalist world into two currency and thus two trading blocs, would signal the outbreak of economic hostilities which would be the practical negation of S's entire book.

The continuing functioning of gold as a guarantee for the SDRs is contradictory. If the SDR system really ever got off the ground, that is, became the credit system it must eventually become if it is to follow the same development traced by the national central banks, gold convertibility is by definition not possible. In other words, there are two possibilities: (1) the non-likelihood of a world capitalist state in which paper money replaces gold; (2) a limited credit system among national capitals with persisting heterogeneous interests. Within this latter system we can again discern two possibilities: either the SDRs remain so limited that gold convertibility is not excluded—in which case merely another delay has been institutionalized which has not dealt with the fundamental problems of the international monetary system; or, the credit system is expanded beyond guaranteed convertibility—in which case another credit pyramid on top of a narrow gold base has been created, but without the homogeneity of interests expressed in a world state which can compel nations to keep or accept SDR's instead of gold. Under this latter system crises could no longer be staved off, and for this reason it is unlikely that SDR's will ever get that far, although "false legislation based on false theories of money" may nevertheless rule the day.

Chapter 27 "Underdevelopment" (S's Chapter 38)

> The word "underdeveloped" I do not understand differently from the words "conquered" or "subjugated," that is, as a participium perfecti passivi.—Günter Anders, "Imperialismus und Kampf dagegen," in *Das Argument*, XI, No. 1-2 (April, 1969), 2, n.1.

This is doubtless the most ahistorical chapter of the book, and as such also the most misleading. It allows S to develop his apologetic powers to the fullest: aside from a few perfunctory remarks concerning the by now widely proclaimed poverty in the "underdeveloped" nations, S furnishes no insight into the depth of the problem or of the hopelessness of any capitalist solution. He promises that "all the economic principles we have learned can now be brought to bear" on this issue (765); however, not only do these "principles" provide no solution to the problem of "underdevelopment," but the reality behind those "principles" created the "problem" itself.

THE CONCEPT OF "UNDERDEVELOPMENT"

This section represents the distillation of the ahistorical approach that permeates the rest of the chapter.

As S we have before us a "formal" definition which does not help explain the phenomenon under review: "Writers used to speak of 'backward' nations, which naturally irritated the people of those lands. To avoid offense the United Nations sometimes uses the roundabout expression 'developing' nation" (8th ed., p. 741; in the 9th ed. "underdeveloped" becomes "less developed" [765]).

Were the "people" "irritated" because: (1) Backward was an incorrect term to apply to their countries? (2) It was correct but they did not like the term because they were ashamed of the reality it characterized? (3) Their nations were at one time more advanced than the present day "forward" nations and the process that made the former "advance" caused the others not only to stagnate, but to fall behind the level of material progress they had once achieved?

Does the UN always try to avoid "offending" people? If the term "developing" is merely a circumlocution, doesn't it mean the same as backward? Don't the "irritated" people realize that the "offense" has not been removed?

Who were the writers who used to speak of backward nations? When did they write? Was there always backwardness? No answers are to be found in S.

S provides us with a two-part definition which he has apparently synthesized from "alternative" ones, a "simple" aspect and an "optimistic" one. According to the first part, underdevelopment means low real per capita income in relation to high per capita income; the second part relates to the ability to raise the level of income.

The definition is unclear on its own grounds: for example, does "capable of substantial improvement in its income level" refer to absolute or relative income level? If it is merely an absolute increase accompanied by an equal or even a greater increase in the countries with higher income levels, then this means that the differential remains constant or even expands. As it turns out, S himself later admits (768 f.) that this differential is widening. Since S's definition provides us with but a single criterion for judging underdevelopment, S would have to admit that the countries in question are not "underdeveloped" in the sense that they do not "seem" to be able make up ground relatively. If on the other hand S merely means an ability to increase income in absolute terms, regardless of the gap between the high- and the low-income nations, then his own definition would condemn these countries to a perpetual state of underdevelopment since their income level would always be lower. In either case, the definition, even on these formal grounds, provides us with no relevant criteria for explaining the origin or development or future of "underdevelopment." Either the country is not underdeveloped but permanently "backward," or it is permanently underdeveloped—not a very enlightening working hypothesis.

In case anyone caught on to this piece of doublethink, S then offers his only historical insight: underdevelopment exists in all countries since perfectibility is impossible: "Even the so-called 'advanced' countries were once underdeveloped by our definition and had to go through *the* process of development" (766 f.—our emphasis). S's radical mockery of the "advanced" nations only serves to divert attention from his underlying ahistorical approach. To begin with: What is the process of development? Were we too harsh in asserting that S has provided us with only one criterion of underdevelopment? Apparently not, since he directs us to table 38-1 which "gives a picture of the relative stages of development of different countries" (766). This table purports to group countries by "level of economic development" (767). What are its classifications? "Highly developed," "intermediate," and "less developed." It does not even present adequate cutoff criteria. All we are told is that all A group countries are above $1,800; the cutoff between B and C is not given. This chart does not show any stages of development whatsoever, let alone *the* process of development. All it presents is a prescientific ordering of some nations according to one statistical criterion. What lends this classification the status of *the* process of development?

If any stages are to be shown, then some time series would have to be used. Let us do this for S. In the eighth edition we find that Bulgaria, Rumania, Yugoslavia, and Cuba all moved up from C (their rank in the seventh edition) to B, and that Czechoslovakia and the USSR moved up from B to A. Thus of a total of ten socialist countries listed, six, or more than half, moved up. Of the eighty-seven capitalist nations listed in B and C in the seventh edition, only four moved up: Lebanon and Libya from C to B, and Japan and Israel from B to A, whereas two other countries, Brazil and Malaysia, moved back from B to C. This would indicate that even according to S's standards, the socialist countries are "developing" quite well, whereas as the capitalist countries are not developing at all.

Let us leave this relatively uninteresting table and return to the underlying ahistorical approach. S claims that "even" the present-day A countries had to go through *the* process of development. What is this supposed to mean? According to the extremely limited standards we have been given, it can only mean that at some time the leading countries, such as U.S., Britain, France, etc., were C-type countries and subsequently made their way to the head of the class. Either this is correct, in which case the former C-type countries must have displaced the then A-type countries, or, this is not correct, in which case they were never underdeveloped in the sense understood by S. If the first is true, then the upward movement of some countries is linked with the downward movement of others, a causal connection which would wreak havoc with the bourgeois conception of harmony. If the latter case turns out to be true, then there is no such thing as *the* process of development and one can draw no analogy between the situation of the so-called underdeveloped countries today and the situation of today's A countries two hundred years ago.

To answer these questions let us examine the findings of Simon Kuznets, who also posed the question of the " 'earlier situation of the more developed countries' with which the present state of the underdeveloped countries should be compared":

> We may then ask whether an earlier comparable situation of the more developed countries, i.e., essentially of Western and Northern Europe and of their offshoots in North America and

Oceania, means a period when they were underdeveloped, i.e., lagged behind the then leading economies; when their backwardness relative to the leaders was as marked as that of the underdeveloped countries today; when their per capita incomes were as low and material deprivation and misery were as widespread as in the latter. . . .

Posed in this fashion, the question has little meaning for the young, relatively "empty" countries peopled by the Western Europeans and their descendants. In the very early history of the United States, Canada, Australia, and New Zealand, the groups involved were small bands of pioneers, voluntary and involuntary; and many of the early settlers may have suffered material deprivation comparable with that in the underdeveloped countries today. But these troubles were the penalty of pioneering, not of economic backwardness; and the comparison is irrelevant. At no time after these early pioneering days had passed and the settled groups had begun to be significantly large did these countries lag much behind the economic leaders.[1]

So then with respect to the younger advanced capitalist nations, at least, this evidence points to the second of the two cases postulated by us above: namely, that they were not underdeveloped in any sense comparable to that status now "enjoyed" by the B and C nations. But we still do not know whether any *causal* connection exists between these concurrent upward and downward movements; that is to say, we do not know whether the blooming of the original advanced capitalist countries was based on or contributed to the decline of the then advanced countries of the East, etc.

This is as far as S's approach can take us—all his quantitative criterion can show is the relative levels of per capita income at any given time. It cannot provide any explanation of why certain countries are moving up while others are moving down; it does not even pose the question of a possible causal connection between the two.

What is the reason for using one, or even several quantitative characteristics to "define" underdevelopment? We are not denying that the fact that France's per capita income is x-times higher than that of the Ivory Coast is significant—on the contrary, this *could* be an important indicator of the material well-being of their respctive inhabitants. But the concentration on such a statistic creates an insurmountable barrier to an understanding of the social and historical causes of this income differential. Such statistics merely point to the symptoms of underdevelopment; and the fact that they are then assigned a central function means in effect that causality is being thrown out the window.

The emphasis on statistics goes hand in hand with the view of underdevelopment as a condition rather than as a historical process. By denying the existence of a process specific to the so-called underdeveloped countries of today, S's theory must also lead to false practical recommendations as to how that "condition" may be abolished.

And finally, S's approach makes it impossible to see any "developmental" difference between socialist and capitalist societies; to imply that the reason for the difference in per capita income in the GDR and Cuba is the same as that of the U.S. and Costa Rica contradicts historical reality.

HISTORICAL ORIGINS OF UNDERDEVELOPMENT

Underdevelopment, as defined quantitatively by bourgeois economists does not have a very long history; it arose with the development of capitalism in Western Europe and the absorption of the non-European areas in the world market, at first by violent means and then by more traditional market procedures.

Although at earlier stages in history differences in the levels of material production attained by various societies or "civilizations" have existed, the point is that by and large these societies had little or no contact with one another— the development of one stood in little relation to the development of the other. This means that the causes of development or lack of development in any of these societies lay within themselves.

METHODOLOGICAL EXCURSUS

Even here we must recognize that undifferentiated talk about development leads nowhere. Although this would seem self-evident for the past, it does not deter S from classifying Nepal and Yemen along with Formosa and Ceylon. If I know that GNP rose by x percent in the first two countries and by y percent in the latter two, have I learned anything significant about their development? One set of countries appears to be an isolated remnant of a direct exploitative society, whereas the other set represents a group of countries with a history of colonial-imperialist exploitation now involved in a process of domestic capitalism. To treat them as undifferentiated in development only serves to mask the essential differences between radically different modes of production.

But more important, this approach blurs the essential distinction between development in capitalist societies and in all other modes of production. Whereas in all previous societies production was oriented at satisfying concrete needs—whether of the immediate producers or of the exploiting master classes, as in slavery or feudalism—and was thus limited by the range of use values desired, in capitalism the bounds of use-value production are broken—production is regulated by the production of value, and more specifically of surplus value. "Development" is now subject to very different laws from those which regulated use-value production in previous societies.

Marxism does not deny the great advance capitalism represents in this respect—that is, that production could now be carried out on a scale inconceivable in any previous mode of production. But the point here is that for the first time "development" meant progress toward creation of something other than the greatest amount of use values consonant with the needs of the whole society and/or of its social classes (constrained of course by the development of the forces of production); for now development was guided and characterized by the accumulation of capital and the production of the greatest amount of value embodied in profit. Increasing GNPs accompanied by declining rates of profit are not a sign of progress in capitalism, although increasing rates of profit accompanied by reductions of output can be.

It becomes clear then that development under capitalism must be understood as a process quite unlike development under feudalism or slavery. One law of development common to capitalism and all preceding modes of production refers to a contradiction involving the impossibility of the continual coexistence of the relations of production and the forces of production; at some point the incompatibility results in the destruction of the mode of production. This does not necessarily lead directly to the formation of a new mode of production—a long period of disintegration, stagnation, and dissolution may ensue. This is not a universal law of contradiction which as it were finds embodiment in empirical cases; but it is a process which has been common to all transitions from one mode of production to another, although the concrete mechanism has been different in each case.

Stagnation, dissolution, etc., cannot be viewed as contrary to or somehow as the absence of development; all it means is that development can no longer take place *within* this particular mode of production—whether and how a transition will take place to a new mode of production depends on historical circumstances which are not inherent in either mode of production.

This line of reasoning leads us back to S's understanding of underdevelopment. In Chapter 37 he had a field day with writers who allegedly "tried to read into economic history a linear progression through inevitable stages" (750); he himself took no stand on the matter at all—he never bothered to inform the reader whether such stages of historical development ever existed, how they came about, etc. But now S himself, in his attempt to measure development by GNP without any explanations, has fallen victim to the "linear progression" thesis. With S progress means only progress toward capitalism ("mixed economy"). Not only does he refuse to comment on the existence of prior modes of production, his whole approach implies that there can be only quantitative differences between societies—the size of their per capita incomes, etc.

Let us resume the discussion of the historical origin of contemporary capitalist "underdevelopment." The decisive turning point here corresponded to the penetration of non-European nations by European merchant capital. This was a transition period in Europe: feudalism was dissolving, trade was developing, peasants were being forced off the land and into the developing cities, small capitalist enterprises were emerging, and capital was beginning to be accumulated by a class of traders. The interest of the merchant capitalists in the non-European areas lay in the huge profits and the cheaper raw materials which could lower production costs of manufactured goods in Europe (this was particularly important for the period in which merchant capital was directing its interest to direct production).

Merchant capital acted as a catalyst in the development of industrial capitalism, for it accompanied the process of the separation of the laborers from their means of production and thus from their means of subsistence; money capital enabled capitalists at this point to reunite the laborers and the means of production by buying them—that is, pay wages and buy machines and raw materials. This process of the separation of the workers from their means of production and subsistence was part of the process of disintegration of feudalism; the accumulation of money in the hands of traders helped accelerate this process of dissolution while the process itself enabled this accumulated money to become capital.[1a]

Under these circumstances the amount of accumulated merchant capital can be crucial to the way in which and the speed with which capitalism may assume control over industrial production. The large accumulation of merchant capital in Western Europe received a critical impetus from its operations abroad.

While all this was taking place the non-European nations were not napping; there too primitive accumulation of capital was taking place. Similar processes could be observed in

India, Japan, China, the Middle East, and Eastern Europe. Although certain factors inhibited the development of capitalism in some of these areas, they were not insuperable.[1b]

In some respects the penetration of Western European merchant capital into the non-European areas was similar to its domestical role: it tended to contribute to the disintegration of the dominant self-sufficient rural communities, thus opening the way to primitive accumulation, separation of the immediate producers from their means of production and subsistence, etc. However, in these countries industrial capitalism did not develop out of this constellation of events. The reason is to be sought in the magnitude of the surplus product (we believe this term to be correct because the societies involved were not capitalist in nature) extracted from the countries as well as in the concrete form forced on the structure of their economies by the invading Western capitalists.

The qualitative structural changes wrought by colonial policy in the non-European areas stemmed in large part from the one-sided interest in contact: the initiative was taken by the European countries in an effort to find raw materials and a market for their manufactures; to this end it sought an "open door" for its exports and a closed door for colonial exports of manufactures.

The influence of colonialism on development in the non-European world has been harshly judged by contemporary left-liberal bourgeois economists. Their line of reasoning is usually embedded in a thesis characterizing foreign investments in the colonies as enclaves, meaning that these parts of the economy were essentially unrelated to the native development, that they were a foreign body which did not initiate the same "spread effects of dynamic growth" known in advanced capitalist countries.

We may accept this thesis insofar as it indicates that an element of capitalism existed in a hypertrophied form in an otherwise weakly developed capitalist country. But as we have seen, it is false to assert that this hypertrophied raw materials and food export sector stood in no organic connection to the rest of the economy; in fact, precisely this penetration caused the inhibition of the incipient elements of capitalism in these countries and forced a permanent structure of so-called underdevelopment upon them.

We may see the germ of truth in the enclave theory in the circumstance that the export sector was oriented at the needs of the development of capitalism in the Western European nations. This can be depicted symbolically with the use of the formulas for the circuit of capital development by Marx.[1c] If we call money capital M; commodity capital C; productive capital P; and money capital and commodity capital containing newly created surplus value M' and C' respectively, then we can formulate capitalist production as follows:

$$M - C \ldots P \ldots C' - M'$$

This means that industrial capital is advanced in the form of money capital in order to buy means of production and labor power; there then follows a period of production during which a surplus value is produced which exists from the process of production in the form of commodity capital and is then sold (realized), leading to the retransformation into money capital—but this time of a greater value. With respect to our subject here, a part of the surplus value from this process is severed from its original self-expanding "flow" and channeled from the advanced capitalist country to the colony. Using lower-case letters here to designate a capital which has been severed from its original process and set into a new circuit of its own, we may describe the circuit of capital in the hypertrophied export branches of the colonies as follows:

$$m - c \ldots p \ldots c'$$

The reader will notice that this circuit is not complete as was the circuit of capital in the metropolis.

> And it cannot be complete. This is grounded in the fact that the c' created in the developing countries with respect both to

its magnitude and to its use value structure is out of all proportion to the internal reproduction process of the developing countries and cannot find here an equivalent, a circumstance which also makes the transformation of c' to m' and hence the process c'-m' impossible. Since however c' is directed to the needs of the metropolises, it can find its equivalent only in the metropolises and must necessarily be realized in the circuit of capital of the metropolises.[2]

We see then that the enclave theory must be taken with a grain of salt, for although it does correctly point to the hypertrophied foreign-dominated export sectors, it does not emphasize the destructive effects which colonial penetration had on the rest of the local economy.[2b]

We have seen that today's "underdeveloped" nations do not conform either to the notions propagated about them by the older theories of backwardness or by the more "modern" theories of "underdevelopment": for as we now know these countries are neither "primitive" economies left behind in the wake of capitalist civilization nor merely "less-developed" capitalist countries on their way to the top. In large part these countries, with certain historical-local modifications, were undergoing the same incipient transformation associated with the rise of merchant capital and primitive accumulation in Western Europe. This process was interrupted by the penetration of foreign capital which foisted upon them a participation in the international division of labor which gave a crucial impetus to Western capitalist development and permanently blocked capitalist industrialization in large parts of the world, and the non-European countries thus thrust onto the world market "found themselves in the twilight of feudalism and capitalism enduring the worst features of both worlds, and the entire impact of imperialist subjugation to boot." "They existed under capitalism, yet there was no accumulation of capital. They lost their time-honored means of livelihood, their arts and crafts, yet there was no modern industry to provide new ones in their place."[3]

Such evidence is ignored only by apologists like S because it directly contradicts his theories of comparative advantage and harmony.³ᵃ

We can now close this brief section on the origins of contemporary "underdevelopment" having learned that present-day conditions in world capitalism are in no sense analogous to those at the beginning of capitalist industrialization in Europe.

The qualitative differences between the possibilities for capitalist industrialization or development then and now may be outlined as follows: Western Europe, in contrast to the countries of the "Third" World today, was not: (1) economically dependent on any other country; (2) characterized by hypertrophied sectors tied to foreign markets and penetrated by foreign capital; (3) subject to stagnation or development in accordance with world market conditions with respect to a single raw material or agricultural commodity; (4) subjected to external financial obligations; (5) confronted with any foreign competition to its nascent industry; (6) dependent on foreign means of production for its expanded reproduction; and (7) economically withered, deformed, or unbalanced, but rather integrated and autocentric.³ᵇ

It is essential to understand these differences, for it is the neglect and intentional masking of these conditions that lie at the base of bourgeois theories of underdevelopment; but even more importantly, these theories of underdevelopment serve as a justification of the various developmental programs which the U.S., other national capitals, and the international organizations like the IMF and IBRD have been trying with varying degrees of success to foist upon the "Third" World countries.

THE ASSUMPTION OF A SOCIETYLESS "THIRD" WORLD

Instead of presenting useful criteria for understanding the process under study, S invents a typical "underdeveloped" person, said to be a farmer or peasant untouched by civilization: "Neither the discipline of markets nor the deliberations of planning commissions mean much to you" (766).

Subjectively speaking this would hold true for almost every capitalist economic agent (including S)—for how many people understand the laws of capitalism? Its only sense then can be objective—that they are not affected by the market since they are not living in a "money economy." This not only contradicts S's imputing to them an "income" in money terms, but more importantly, it distorts the process of underdevelopment as we have seen it, since the peasant economies were influenced (i.e., destroyed) by foreign capitalist penetration.[3c]

Just as in Western Europe, capital had to create a proletariat and a market; this was done in large part by expropriating the land of the peasants who had been only peripherally involved in the sphere of commodity circulation. The methods used could be violent or "peaceful" ones like taxes, rent, interest, construction of railways, etc. Peasants forced to become wage laborers, now had to buy their means of subsistence on the market.

There may of course be some "people"—although hardly in India or Nigeria—in the jungle or desert whom capitalist penetration has passed by, but these are exceptions, and to imply that they are the rule only shows that S himself "knows little of science, but much of folklore" (766).

"THE URGENCY OF THE PROBLEM"—NAMELY, TO PROPAGATE ANTI-COMMUNISM AND TO CARICATURE ANTI-IMPERIALISM

The urgency has to be proved because "there have always been differences between rich and poor" (766), even though the differences that arose are a product of capitalism. That is why S must introduce this factor on an empirical level, having implicitly denied the theoretical reasons for the polarization of wealth and poverty in the "free" world.

The next reason cited for the urgency of the problem is

the "ideological struggle"; finally mention is made of struggle in this best of all possible worlds, but, alas, it seems to be but a struggle for minds and hearts.

With each new edition the motivations of the "free world" become purer and the chances of capitalism's success greater. Thus whereas in the 7th edition the "communists" were still regarding "the underdeveloped regions as our Achilles' heel" (739), by the 8th edition the battle seems to have turned more in "our" favor and "both sides regard the underdeveloped regions as being torn between following the pattern of the mixed economy or following the pattern of socialism" (744—apparently these countries will be privileged insofar as they will be permitted to skip over several hundred years of the premixed economy "pattern.")

On the other hand, the "communists" still seem to be more insistent since they "ceaselessly agitate" and discourse on the polarization of wealth and poverty; but we are not told whether it is as a result of this "agitation" or of self-agitation that people in these countries "are today acutely aware of their poverty and its contrasts with rich lands" (770—perhaps all the people are communists).

Suddenly S realizes that perhaps things are not so bad after all, since extreme poverty may make people incapable of revolution; but, unfortunately this is not foolproof, so "nonetheless, to turn our backs on the problem of development is to court future disaster" (769). Now the intent of this section is becoming somewhat more transparent. If we could get away with letting these countries rot, then they would be okay; unfortunately, however, there is a chance that they might make "communist" revolutions, which for some as yet unelucidated reason would be disastrous for "us."

The thrust of the section is directed against any serious understanding of the worldwide anticolonial and anti-imperialist struggle which has assumed a particularly sharp and successful character since World War II. The reason for the sudden interest in development is not explained; all we hear is that they no longer "accept their relative poverty as the divine will of Allah."

S tells us that "Altruism and political motivation aside, advanced economies have a selfish interest in growth of underdeveloped nations to provide markets for international trade" (5th edition, pp. 779 f.). There then follows a discussion of whether or not growth would increase our exports. Naturally S comes to the conclusion that development would be good for "us." There is a conflict here—a conflict among various capital groups in the advanced capitalist countries. To the extent that growth means a type of industrialization which would eliminate "Third" World dependence on imports of manufactured commodities (i.e., largely consumption items of Department II), this would evoke different responses from different capitals. The exporters of these commodities would of course oppose such "growth"; the producers of the means of production necessary for the production of such commodities would of course support such growth.[3d] But at some point both types of capitals would cease to be interested in such growth once these countries become strong enough to produce their own manufactured items and also begin to invade the markets of the advanced capitalist countries. They would also oppose such growth if it means the end of their direct investment opportunities.

But S is interested in a "more complicated" issue—namely that "we" do not want trade "for the sole purpose of increasing our mere dollar sales"; no, "rational self-interest makes us want other nations to develop so we can *import* from them goods that we can less economically produce at home" (5th ed., p. 780). Of even more interest is S's supplementary explanation: "our main selfish economic reason for wanting development abroad rests on *our desire to have foreign economies grow up which display those differences in comparative advantage that our earlier chapters have shown to be the sole basis for fruitful international exchange*" (ibid.).

This is not an unambiguous statement inasmuch as S made some confusing remarks on this subject earlier (696); there he said that more "benefit" derived from trade with countries of the tropics or Far East whose economies were very different from that of the U.S. than from trade with other advanced capitalist countries with similar economic structures; at the same time, however, he "modified" this dictum to the extent that the underdeveloped nations had so little "purchasing power" that they were really poor customers, whereas most trade took place with the similarly structured economies. So where does that leave us with respect to "growth"? Apparently what S has in mind is the best of both worlds; these countries continue to produce raw materials, but they must somehow get more purchasing power so that they can become better customers.

That this is his motive appears to flow from his closing remark to the effect that "we must admit that the developing countries may not wish to concentrate on the industries that will be of greatest interest to the advanced countries; hence we face a real possible clash of interests" (5th ed., p. 780).[3e]

The next of S's additional points of "urgency" bears the title "Need to avert slump by economic imperialism?" S does not think much of this argument because it emphasizes exports, whereas he has already proved that what "we" want is imports. Nevertheless he summarizes "the Lenin theory of economic imperialism"—as he himself phrases it so precisely—"crudely":

> Wealthy capitalistic nations always face at home a worsening oversaving crisis. To keep their profits from falling and to stave off ever-increasing depression crises, they must dump goods abroad. Solely for this selfish reason do they seem to favor development of backward countries. In actual fact, they will end up enslaving the native peoples in bonds of "colonialism," probably even starting wars among themselves in their rivalry for colonies [5th ed., p. 781].

Commenting on this, S asserts that during the Great Depression "some economists might have been frankly troubled for an answer to the neo-Marxian theory of imperialism," but that with the advent of a modern arsenal of Keynesian programs "there is never any need to create domestic purchasing power by foreign trade" in order to "fight unemployment" (ibid.).

To return to the "crudely" summarized theory: In the first place, it is so crude that it resembles no theory that anyone ever devised. In part it makes no sense whatever, and in part it is taken not from Lenin—but from Keynes. It was Keynes, not Lenin, who spoke of oversaving crises: "the primary evil is a propensity to save in conditions of full employment more than the equivalent of the capital which is required, thus preventing full employment. . . ."[4] Nor did Lenin ever speak of any crises that are "always worsening"; in fact he emphasized that no crisis is impossible to exit from as long as the working class offers no resistance; more important is the fact that the assertion S imputes to Lenin is based on a misunderstanding of Marx's theory of the industrial cycle.

Dumping results from a monopoly position on the home market which allows a capitalist to lower his prices in enemy markets; in "backward" countries dumping would not be necessary because there would be no local competition forcing the foreign capitalists to lower their prices; they would be monopolists there too and could charge the same high prices they do at home. Furthermore, Lenin's theory of imperialism is not concerned with unemployment as a factor of economic crisis which the capitalists must at all costs eliminate. It may turn out to be a political necessity in order to forestall revolution, but a huge reserve army was always a healthy sign.

And, finally, this "crude summary" neglects what Lenin saw as the chief aspect of imperialism—capital export.

None of this bothers S who is sure that "it would be fruitless . . . to study the interplay of political and economic motives and tedious to try to draw up the detailed balance sheet of historical help and harm by advanced nations to underdeveloped ones" (ibid.).

THE ALLEGEDLY NEW CONCEPTS OF BOURGEOIS DEVELOPMENT THEORY

S himself delivers his own judgment when he characterizes this section as "a montage of the most important notions developed in the recent literature" (772). What could be more shabby than to grab a few "notions" that have been floating about for centuries, claim them as achievements of "the recent literature" and impute to them the status of "special features" added to the above growth models? But then again perhaps S is only being consistent, since his emphasis rests on "the economic determinants of production," which do not exist anyway.

"PRECONDITIONS FOR GROWTH"—OR CAPITAL-ACCUMULATION EQUALS DEVELOPMENT

First we are told that "economic development" is "primarily the outcome of the last few centuries of Western history" (722). Now of course all one has to do is define development according to the alleged "six basic trends of economic development" (746) in the advanced capitalist countries and, presto, economic development is restricted to this period. Does S really want to deny the existence of economic development in, say, China prior to the "industrial revolution" in the "West"? This is how S presents the origins of economic development: After "warfare diminished" in some "lucky places" "a surplus over subsistence became possible." Obviously this was a momentous moment in human history, so how does S explain its significance? "And usually wealth was so unequally divided among the aristocratic landowners and the bulk of the populace that the rich were able to abstain from consumption and to funnel savings into capital formation. Economic development could now take place" (772). Finally S makes clear what he has been hinting at all along.

To begin with, he plays fast and loose with chronology, in line with his promise to "abandon strict chronology to stress the important economic principle that the take-off serves to dramatize" (773). The development of a surplus beyond subsistence belongs to the Neolithic age. Then all of a sudden we get "aristocratic landowners," presumably of the "Western" variety since that is where economic development originated a "few centuries" ago.

In point of fact, the creation of reserves, abstaining from their consumption, creating means of production, etc., all preceded the existence of "aristocratic landowners" and capitalism. Thus, the creation of means of production is not the same as capital formation.

At this point, "economic development" could take place. In other words, for S economic development is apparently synonymous with, and/or has as its precondition, capital formation. He may, of course, say this, but if he defines capital formation to mean the making of means of production, then economic development has been taking place for thousands of years in various modes of production. .

There is a rational kernel to S's statement: namely, that with the bursting through of the barriers of use-value-producing modes of production, capitalism did open the way to the qualitatively new kind of development or increase of the forces of production, which S doubtless means. But in that case he would have to specify the characteristics of the capitalist mode of production which made this possible. But S cannot do this, because given his supra historical concept of capital formation he has "aristocratic landowners," presumable feudal lords, "funneling savings [!] into capital formation."[4a]

S asserts that the "notions" mentioned in this section were "developed in the recent literature." The concept of surplus in economic theory first arose among the mercantilists to characterize a positive foreign balance of payments. It was further used by the French physiocrats approximately 150 years later to characterize the unique productivity of agriculture. Smith and Ricardo extended the discussion in part as a polemic against the historically obsolete waste of the feudal mode of production, but also positively as the part of the product which had to accrue to the capitalist in order to produce on an even larger scale.

During the post-Ricardian era, at about the time Marx was writing *Capital,* the concept of surplus began to go out of style, partly because once the battle against feudalism had been won capitalism itself began to create waste on an unprecedented scale, and it had no desire to leave itself open to the criticism of the potentially dangerous concept of surplus. Secondly, with the general rise of subjectivism (marginal utility, etc.) an objective concept like surplus was not likely to find a warm reception and was thus easily replaced by such individual notions as savings and investment; unlike surplus, which the classical bourgeois authors still saw as originating in the process of production, savings and investment, allegedly rooted in personal decision, could conceal their social derivation.[4b]

SOCIAL OVERHEAD CAPITAL

This concept dates back at least to Adam Smith:

> The third and last duty of the sovereign or commonwealth is that of erecting and maintaining those public institutions and those public works, which, though they may be in the highest degree advantageous to a great society, are, however, of such a nature, that the profit could never repay the expence to any individual or small number of individuals, and which it therefore cannot be expected that any individual or small number of individuals should erect or maintain. The performance of this duty requires too very different degrees of expence in the different periods of society.[5]

Let us take a look at the phenomenon of social overhead capital in the context of its alleged creator: Paul Rosenstein-Rodan. He suggested the importance of the phenomenon in the course of offering "an alternative way of industrialization" to that of "the 'Russian model' " for Eastern and Southeastern Europe.[6]

Rosenstein-Rodan sees the main problems with the "Russian model" in its slowness, since it forgoes foreign investment; this leads to "unnecessary sacrifice." But equally important to him is the existence of "appropriate natural resources in the area" which would no longer be available to the international division of labor. Basically his plan recommended building up this part of Europe along lines described by certain current plans: namely "light industires in overpopulated areas," since "even for the purposes of an expanding world economy, the existing heavy industries in the U.S.A., Great Britain, Germany, France and Switzerland could certainly supply all the needs of the international depressed areas."[7] And again, similarly, the exports of these newly industrialized areas will have "to be foreseen and planned in such a way as to minimize the burden of necessary adjustment of economic resources in the creditor countries."[8] Thus in some sense Rosenstein-Rodan is a forerunner of contemporary neocolonial plans. But he goes even further, for he envisions an Eastern European Industrial Trust in which the great imperialist powers would presumably invest, and that their investments would go into social overhead capital or infrastructure, not normally an investment opportunity.

The new aspect of this author's proposal is his adoption of the "Russian model's" approach of planning; for his interest in social overhead capital is directly related to his belief that, "The existing institutions of international and national investment do not take advantage of external economies. There is no incentive within their framework for many investments which are profitable in terms of 'social marginal net product,' but do not appear profitable in terms of 'private marginal net product.' "[9]

It still must be explained under what conditions the individual capitals would have to be interested in investments that are not directly profitable for them. But since Rosenstein-Rodan proceeds from the fiction of a capitalist society dealing only with use values and/or with the satisfaction of consumption, he cannot explain the contradictory relations between the state and the needs of capital's self-expansion.

On the other hand it is not precise to claim, as S does, that external economies benefit everyone and should therefore be financed from taxes: S says for example that "a railroad can benefit all industry" (773). Perhaps, but usually the peasants and small producers in the areas "opened up" by the railroads find their existence destroyed. Perhaps this is historically "progressive" in the U.S. where large-scale industry did eventually arrive; but in cases like India, etc., where these people have been waiting in "disguised unemployment" for more than a hundred years for the social benefits of the railroads, it is pure demagogy even to imply the existence of a "marginal social net product" which is to be "maximized."[9a]

THE POSSIBILITIES FOR CAPITALIST DEVELOPMENT IN THE "THIRD" WORLD

In order to support the thesis that total social planning does not compare to the "mixed economy" and that it is useless to build up industry before agriculture has become dominant, S once again invokes the "law" of comparative advantages: "The whole theory of comparative advantage . . . suggested that growth within a region does *not* best take place in balance" (774). He universalizes a pattern of development that emerged in a *few* countries with *one particular* mode of production at *one particular* time in its history. That this pattern is perhaps not possible for the nonadvanced capitalist nations, or that even if it were it may be inferior to other developmental methods is a possibility S does not even entertain.

The practical consequences of enforcing the "law" of comparative advantage in the past have been outlined by Myrdal:

> Underlying the grand strategy of free international trade, especially in the latter half of the nineteenth century and into the 1920s as well, was the static theory of comparative advantage. Instead of being viewed as exploitation of poor and underdeveloped colonies in the interest of rich countries—which it was in part, though only in part—colonial policy of the laissez-faire variety was rationalized on the ground of mutual advantage. If the South Asian resource endowment made the region peculiarly suitable for plantations and extractive industries, while Europe's resources made it the "natural" center for manufacturing, what could be more mutually advantageous than an exchange of raw materials or agricultural products for manufactured comomodities? Specialization along these lines would seem to make economic sense. Yet it was convenient to ignore

the fact that the expert sectors of the South Asian economies were not run or controlled by or for the local inhabitants and that much of the benefits that should in theory accrue to South Asia went to Europeans.[10]

S, apparently fearing that his advice was a bit too strong, modifies it: "If coffee demand and supply are volatile, and if *future* comparative advantage may lie in certain manufactures, a country like Brazil may be well advised to interfere with the market tendency to specialize in coffee production. But prudent diversification and truly balanced growth are by no means the same" (774). First we get the recommendation, and then this "prudent diversification" concession hedged in with "ifs" and "mays," as if this were a hypothetical situation restricted to a large country with a relatively large industry anyway.

What exacerbates the problem is that such primary products, as opposed to manufactured commodities, are the main generators of money incomes in large parts of the "Third" World; this means that these cash crops must find a market abroad.[10a] Despite its enforced adherence to the "law" of comparative advantages the "Third" World's share of world trade has continued to decline during the post-World War II period, partly because that primary products as a percentage of all world exports have fallen from 54.0 percent in 1953-54 to 41.6 percent in 1965-66.[11] This drop in part reflects the economization on the use of raw materials in the productive processes in the advanced capitalist nations as well as the inroads made by synthetic materials. S of course would like to bring in "the budgetary laws of Engel" to explain this downward movement. But, as the IMF-IBRD study points out, "there is one major exception to this relationship" which focuses on the basis of the problem: "The exception is that very poor consumers and poor countries will normally spend a large proportion of any increase in real income on food rather than on industrial goods and services; and at the extreme, an increase in real income at the lowest level may even lead to a more than proportionate increase in the food component of total expenditure."[12]

S's pooh-poohing of industrialization attempts assumes two forms. On the one hand, he appeals to imperialist antinationalist stereotypes by suggesting that it is "vanity" that causes each country to want its own airline and steel mill (774). The second prong of his attack has a more scientific ring. Here he advises one not to "jump to the conclusion: Industrialization is *cause* rather than *effect* of affluence" (ibid.). And although at one point he admits that regions where agricultural productivity exceeds industrial productivity are the exceptions, a little later he argues that "it simply is not true that the greatest productivity advances of the last century have been in industry rather than agriculture. . ." (775).

No one has claimed that industrialization processes have no prerequisites. Neither has anyone denied that agricultural productivity has increased. The point is to explain why this is so. When S speaks of Holland and Denmark he gives the impression that agriculture and industry are two totally separate spheres. But, in fact, a productive agriculture presupposes a certain level of industrial development.

The fact that smaller capitalist countries like Denmark were able to use their agricultural exports to help build a domestic industry is no proof that this "strategy" is tenable today for the countries of the "Third" World. Although in the abstract it is possible for a "developing" nation to use agricultural exports as a means of involving itself in the international division of labor, and thus of providing itself with the Department I commodities it requires for a program of industrialization, it is precisely the present situation of the capitalist underdeveloped nations, in contrast to, say, that of Denmark in the last century, that obstructs such a strategy.

The absolute level of agricultural productivity is low in most underdeveloped capitalist countries, in large part due to the semifeudal social relations in their agricultural sector. Thus in order to remove this barrier to increased agricultural productivity, some sort of social "revolution" must take place.

What are the possibilities? The common call is for land

reform. Even S speaks of it. The point is the eminently political one of what social forces will support land-reform programs. Certain economists have dealt with the concrete factors at work here, chief among them is Gunnar Myrdal. As he notes, "the power in most underdeveloped countries is monopolized by political elite groups within a tiny upper class whose short-term interests are generally not in line with honestly and effectively carrying out the progressive reforms."[13]

Ruling out an uprising of the masses, Myrdal comes to the following conclusion:

> It would under these conditions seem to be preferable to make a deliberate policy choice in favor of capitalist farming by allowing and encouraging the progressive entrepreneurs among the group of peasant landlords and privileged tenants to reap the full rewards of their strivings. This might encourage more such farmers to act in the same way and, in particular, to give up relying on sharecropping.[14]

But he admits that the prospects are "far from bright" given opposition from above and below; the "rural underclass," is unlikely to be sophisticated enough to see their interest in spreading progressive entrepreneurship among the landowners, particularly since that would imply turning sharecroppers into employed workers, which many of them would consider socially degrading.[15]

S can always turn to land reform; after all, "as the Communists well know, the situation is explosive, and agitation for land reform signifies a ground swell of public sentiment not long to be denied" (778). He fails to explain how these shifty Communists can want both land reform and "collectivization." The consequences of land reform depend on the social forces bringing it about. Paul Baran points out that unless accompanied by capital accumulation and industrialization, agragarian reform (under nonsocialist conditions) is apt to retard rather than advance a country's economic development.[16]

The key issue is industrialization. According to Baran, in the advanced capitalist countries the agrarian revolution was followed by an "agrarian counter-revolution" which capitalized agriculture.[16a] but as we have seen, it is precisely this key factor of industrialization that S wants to deny.

Of course S is willing to admit "the germ of truth in the argument for pushing industrialization in order to speed development" (775). He adds that "fortunately, there is often much 'disguised unemployment' in rural areas," which means that the industrial labor force can rise without causing a drop of output in the agricultural sector (8th ed., p. 750). Obviously S has not understood the problem of industrialization in the "underdeveloped" nations. Even before the penetration by foreign capital, processes of transition from a feudal to a capitalist mode of production had been underway in non-European areas. This penetration on the one hand reinforced this process of transition insofar as it accelerated the dissolution of the villages with their use-value- or small-commodity-production-oriented peasants and artisans. This of course led to the rise of a huge reserve army which could and had to be used by the foreign capitalists in their mines, plantations, railroads, etc.

This, however, was only one side of the development; for on the other hand there were conscious, forceful efforts on the part of the foreign capitalists supported by their governments to prevent the rise of domestic industries. The whole point in destroying an existing system was to gain a labor force and to eliminate local competition. This eventually led to the contradictory economic system known as capitalist underdevelopment. For the foreign capitalists were interested in the destruction of the stagnating old system insofar as it represented competition and barred access to a large "pool" of cheap labor; but they were not interested in its total destruction because this would have undermined their alliance with the domestic ruling class and might have cleared the way for the sort of capitalist revolution experienced in Europe. Thus the foreign capitalists were interested in the preservation of the older system insofar as it continued to stagnate without stimulating the creation of capitalism.[16b]

S does not appear to understand that there were still objective forces at work in these countries "pushing" toward capitalist industrialization despite the successful suppression by the foreign capitalists. Their existence has been testified to repeatedly during periods in which the pressures of foreign control have been relaxed or severed, leading to incipient industrialization on a scale never experienced during the periods of intensive foreign domination.[16c]

Thus at the end of the discussion on industrialization versus agriculture, S has provided no clear answers since he has posed no questions: the "theory" he propounds in Chapters 34 and 35 already informed us that nature has equipped the underdeveloped nations to do what they are presently doing. But since the social forces necessary for a thoroughgoing "classical" capitalist industrial revolution are not present, and since the only forces that could put an end to "underdevelopment" are "ruthless" communist ones, S winds up putting his faith in the "patterns" spontaneously created by "supply and demand . . . in the old days of relatively free enterprise" (774).

CAPITAL ACCUMULATION AND SOCIAL CLASSES

At this point it is necessary to examine the basic concepts of the bourgeois theory of underdevelopment. S opens with the general bourgeois theory of underdevelopment:

> To break out of a vicious circle of poverty and underdevelopment, capital formation is needed. But starving peasants cannot be expected to take much thought of the future. In past ages inequality of landownership probably helped solve the problem of social thrift, but in a ruthless way. Collectivist economies like China, North Korea, and Russia can by fiat impose the same ruthless abstention from current consumption [775].

Let us analyze this passage carefully. Given S's definitions, the first statement is tautological; since he has covertly defined poverty and underdevelopment as characteristic of certain societies trapped in the transition from feudalism to capitalism, it is obvious that what is lacking, at least on the surface, is the main characteristic of capitalism—the production of and accumulation of surplus value. The next sentence consists of two related but separate sociohistorical distortions: i.e., that starving peasants are the relevant social class hindering capital formation, and that whatever class bore this role in the past did so by taking "much thought of the future."

Let us begin with the latter one. Even on the basis of S's "models" and theories, it must be clear that capital formation takes place on the basis of individual decisions by capitalists looking after their own profits.

In fact the whole bourgeois theory of external economies, etc., shows that the "success" of capitalism rested upon the individual capitalist's disregard of both the present as well as the future of the global conditions of capital formation.[16d]

The fact that the state does not take the requisite measures today in the "Third" World is related to the social composition of the societies upon which these states rest; for these states represent the interests of the semifeudal landowners and/or comprador bourgeoisie, the local allies of the foreign capitalists. This coalition is not interested in fostering the growth of "classical" capitalism.[16e]

This leads us to the first of the two misrepresentations in the sentence under question—namely that "starving peasants" are the relevant agents of capital formation. The starving peasants by and large do not own their land; they rent it from landowners. In general, the relation is semifeudal, since the peasants are not capitalist farmers extracting surplus value from their own workers, but rather are running (sub-) subsistence "operations." S confuses things by saying that at some time in the past "inequality of landownership" solved the "problem of thrift," albeit in a "ruthless" manner. We assume this to mean that after expropriations and concentration of landownership the new large landowners assumed the burden of abstaining from current consumption, as it were, since the now "dispossessed" were no longer in a position to do so. This is borne out by S's allegation (772) that the apparently ever-present "aristocratic landowners" could now "funnel savings into capital formation."

But it is not in the nature of feudal lords to abstain from consumption. Not only did they not "funnel savings into capital formation," but they were being worn down by the usurers they had turned to in order to maintain their way of life at a time when the limits of exploiting serfs had already been reached.

Not only does S give this false interpretation, but he also asserts that inequality of landownership is no longer prevalent (772, 775); hence the mass of starving peasants as the main agents of the economy. Although comparable statistics are not very accurate, at least one attempt has been made to estimate the distribution of agricultural land in various countries.[17] It indicates that the degree of inequality is extremely high (higher in general than similar statistics for income distribution) in the "Third" World countries and also very high for many advanced capitalist nations (including the country without a feudal past—the U.S.). So much for S's theory.

Finally we come to S's admission that communist countries apparently are able to foster capital accumulation. (We must deal with this matter as S presents it—that is to say, speak of capital formation in socialist countries. However, that this is not a mere terminological point. The process of capital formation and the process of building the requisite industrial structure in order to create a society directed at satisfying needs are two essentially different social processes. The superficial validity of the theories of convergence which seek to equate the two processes stems from the inability to understand the specific historical conditions under which the socialist societies have arisen.) Here S does not pursue the matter further; but in the final passage of this chapter in the 7th edition, now deleted, he tries his best to prove that socialism is not inevitable for the "backward" countries: "A totalitarian state has certain advantages but also certain disadvantages for a backward country impatient to make progress. Socialism may or may not be desired for its own sake, but there is nothing in the historical experience of development which makes its choice mandatory or necessarily desirable for a nation eager to develop" (755).

After noting that feudal "capital formation" and communist "capital formation" were possible albeit ruthless, he asks: "Why cannot free economies do the same? Why cannot they use the fiscal measures discussed throughout this book to curb consumption and stimulate investment? An important reason lies in the realm of political science. Some of the developed countries are able to impose progressive income taxes and find that the taxes do get paid. In much of the world, this is probably not possible. . . . People simply will not cooperate" (775).

This may well be the most confused ahistorical passage in the entire book; at the same time it shows S's total inability to grasp the real origins of the "mixed" economy.

We know that what S depicts as feudal capital formation was in fact the bloody primitive accumulation process leading to the development of capitalism, the origin of the glorious free economy. The so-called mixed economy is the result of specific features of capitalism in decline: the ability of the working class to win certain economic concessions; the falling rate of profit which necessitates state intervention to redistribute income in favor of the capitalist class; the rise of socialist societies and anti-imperialist struggles.

At this point we must backtrack. S has spoken of a "vicious circle" without having defined it. This theory charges that low per capita income leads to low rates of current investment, which in turn lead to low growth rates; given the common bourgeois notion of Malthusian population growth, all this combines to stagnation. From this flow the policy recommendations of "breaking through the vicious circle" via foreign investment and "aid" along with the fostering of the growth of income inequality domestically to encourage investment.

Our critique must begin at the alleged causal link between low per capita income and low rates of investment. This is based on the fiction of the existence of a starving peasant society and/or the implicit refusal to tax the feudal-mercantile classes.

Paul Baran has contributed to the demolishing of these myths with his theory of potential surplus, which he defines as "the difference between the output that *could* be produced in a given natural and technological environment with the help of employable productive resources, and what might be regarded as essential consumption."[18]

Baran classifies the main categories of potential economic surplus as follows: (1) excess consumption; (2) output lost through the existence of unproductive workers; (3) output lost as a result of irrational and wasteful organization of the productive apparatus; output lost as a result of unemployment caused by the anarchy of capitalist production.[18a]

Applied to the present "underdeveloped" countries, these categories demonstrate that the link between low income and low rates of investment is not a necessary one, but rather is determined by the social relations peculiar to them. In these areas the potential economic surplus is appropriated by landowners, usurers, merchants, foreign capital, and the reactionary states representing these interests.

For the most part these classes do not reinvest this surplus productively; it is either consumed or used to expand unproductive activities or invested in the "First" World. The point of course is how this surplus can be productively used. On the one hand bourgeois economics uses as its point of departure the fiction of little or no "savings"; on the other hand, a certain irony arises when it applies its other axiom, that savings/investment represent abstention from current consumption. The synthesis of these two statements leads to the conclusion that either no investment can take place because the starving peasants are too poor, or that investment can take place only by lowering consumption levels even further. Since the real source of possible investment is concealed, it is then taken for granted that "development" is not possible in a "humane" way without the intervention of foreign capital in its manifold forms.

In a final passage S discovers a third way, as it were, between taxation and coercion: favoring projects which will funnel income to firms and groups *"that can be counted on to do heavy investment"* (775). But this does not solve the problem at hand, for it consists in establishing the preconditions for capitalism, whereas here we are already talking about "projects" without explaining how they are supposed to come into existence. It does not help much that once capitalism has developed, capital accumulation will have its source in "corporations." The problem then reduces to whether there are sufficient capitalist forces within the country to defeat the alliance of reactionary forces.[18b]

To the extent that this "strategy" succeeds, however, the ruling class must be prepared for the inevitable "social unrest"; for this development is nothing but a roundabout way of describing a global increase in the rate of surplus value which expresses itself in a "deteriorating" distribution of income.[18c]

OVERPOPULATION AND UNEMPLOYMENT

The kind of ahistoricism which predominates in this section is the modern resurrection of Malthus: "Indeed, as writers since Malthus have warned, unbridled increase in numbers is likely to invoke the law of diminishing returns. . ." (776). Now as S has already informed us, Malthus is allegedly of value only for the underdeveloped countries (31-32) since he did not see the coming of the industrial revolution and increasing returns (737). But rather than focusing on restraining the universal sexual instinct in the "underdeveloped" countries, S ought to ask why the increasing returns common to "dynamic economic development" have not materialized in these countries (773).

It is again necessary to point out that there is no "correlation" between population density and poverty.[18d] There is no such penomenon as overpopulation in general. Malthus tried to establish both factors, human copulation and plant growth, in his ratio as processes of nature. As long as we are talking about a commodity-producing society with wage labor, it is clear that workers have no immediate relation to the means of subsistence whatsoever; the whole essence of capitalism consists in their being separated from the means of production and hence from the means of subsistence which forces them to work for capitalists in order to be able to maintain a relation at all to the means of subsistence. (The existence of unemployment and the burning of agricultural commodities side by side is only the most striking example.)

What we then have to determine is the "social mediation through which the individual relates to the means to his reproduction and creates them" or, in other words, to the conditions of production.[18e] Bourgeois economists are of course not ignorant of the existence of enormous unemployment in these areas; the type of unemployment they have come to emphasize S calls here the "disguised" variety. S does not define the term, merely referring to people who do "almost nothing" because there is nothing for them to do, and who therefore live with their "kinfolk" until the next "boom" comes "sweeping them into productive city jobs" (777). He also indicates that "the same phenomenon" "is met in advanced countries" (ibid.).

The phenomenon was first developed for "advanced" countries by Joan Robinson during the depression of the 1930s "to describe the adoption of inferior occupations by dismissed workers."[19]

Although the notion of disguised unemployment, even in its "Western setting," remains open to criticism on account of its obvious reliance on marginal productivity, it does point to the undeniably large "service sector" in underdeveloped countries, whereby personal services (in the feudal sense) and state administrative "services" predominate. Given marginal productivity theory's indifference to social relations and thus to modes of production, these "disguised" unemployed are remunerated and, hence, must be productive. However, as one writer expressed it: "Certainly, for a region such as Latin America, an increase in the number of beauty parlors or nightclubs or the size of the police force or activities that come under the heading of services, whatever their contribution to the joy or sorrow of one or another segment of the population may be, cannot represent economic growth."[20]

Connected to this basic failure to understand the peculiar structure of underdevelopment is the bourgeois confusion of the "release," or setting free, of workers in capitalism as the result of increased productivity associated with a rising organic composition of capital and the "excessing" of population in a stagnating economy.

In the latter case there is no economic mechanism to absorb the surplus workers. Here we can see very clearly that "overpopulation" is a relative phenomenon—it can only be related to a specific society at a specific point in its development. The peculiar feature of "overpopulation" in capitalism consists in the fact that for the first time it results from the development of the productive power of labor—an increased productivity which can no longer be utilized within the framework of capitalist productive relations.[20a]

Russia has shown us that one country's overpopulation may be another's underpopulation. Before the Revolution Russia was the textbook example of overpopulation, whereas the socialist development subsequently made it possible to productively utilize an even greater number of workers.[20b]

Notes and References

CHAPTER 10

1. C. Bresciani-Turroni, *The Economics of Inflation. A Study of Currency Depreciation in Post-War Germany*, tr. M. Sayers (London, 1931), pp. 104, 286. Cf. K. Gossweiler, *Ökonomie und Politik in Deutschland 1914-1932* (Berlin, 1971), pp. 143-55.
2. Trakhtenberg, *Sovmenyi kredit i ego organizatsii*, 2nd ed. (Moscow, 1931). See also E. Mandel, *Der Spätkapitalismus* (Frankfurt, 1973), Ch. 13.
3. M. Doff, *Studies in the Development of Capitalism* (London 1963), pp. 236 f.
4. Dobb, op. cit., p. 237-38.
5. Jules Backman et al., *War and Defense Economics* (New York 1952), p. 252.
6. Section 2a; *MEW*, III, p. 119.
7. Ibid., pp. 28-30.
8. Marx, *Contribution. . .*, Ch. 2, Part C; *MEW*, XIII, p. 139.
9. *Capital*, I, pp. 73 f. Cf. above Ch. 2.
10. Hans-Georg Backhaus, "Zur Dialektik der Wertform," in *Beitrage zur marxistischen Erkenntnistheorie*, ed. by A. Schmidt (Frankfurt, 1969), p. 40.
11. Marx, *Grundrisse* pp. 58 f.
12. Ibid., p. 85.
13. G. W. Hegel, *Science of Logic*, Book I, Section 3, Chap. 1.
14. *Capital*, I, p. 127.
15. *Contribution. . ., MEW*, XIII, pp. 72 f.
16. *Grundrisse*, pp. 50-52.
17. E. Varga, *Politico-Economic Problems of Capitalism* (Moscow, 1968), p. 194.

CHAPTER 11

1. R. S. Sayers, *Modern Banking*, 7th ed. (Oxford 1967), p. 1.
2. Ibid.
3. *Capital*, III, Ch. 25; *MEW*, XXV, p. 416.
4. *Capital*, III, Ch. 19.
5. *Business Week*, Sept. 15, 1973, p. 107. For later figures see ibid., Sept. 21, 1974, pp. 60 f.; *Economist*, Dec. 14, 1974, p. 20 of special "Survey."
6. See Ibid., pp. 89-92, 113-15. New York State will, for example, allow statewide banking in 1976 "and the big New York City banks will then be in a position to dominate the whole state." Ibid., p. 92. See ibid., Feb. 23, 1974, pp. 52, 54.
7. Lewis Corey, *The Decline of American Capitalism*, (New York, 1934), p. 401.
8. *Statistical Abstract of the United States*, 1972, p. 447. Cf. the appended chart from *Business Week*, Sept. 15, 1973, p. 88.
9. U.S. Congress, House Committee on Banking and Currency, Subcommittee on Domestic Finance, *Commerical Banks and Their Trust Activities: Emerging Influence on the American Economy*, 90th Cong., 2nd Sess., 1968, Vol. I, p. 79.
10. *Business Week*, July 24, 1971, p. 66 ff.; ibid., Sept. 15, 1973, p. 161.
11. "Gold, Papier und Ware," *Neue Zeit*, 1911-1912, Vol. I, p. 890.
12. R. Guendel, H. Heininger, P. Hess, K. Zieschang, *Zur Theorie des staats-monopolitistichen Kapitalismus* (Berlin, 1967), p. 21.
13. *Capital*, III, Ch. 21; *MEW*, XXV, p. 350 f.
14. *Capital*, II, Ch. 22, p. 381.
15. A. Smith, *Wealth of Nations*, Book II, Ch. 4, Modern Library edition (New York, n. d.), p. 333.
16. Ibid., pp. 334 f.
17. *Capital*, III, Ch. 29; *MEW*, XXV, p. 490.
18. *Capital*, III, p. 457.

CHAPTER 12

1. G. Myers, *History of the Great American Fortunes*, Modern Library ed., p. 621.
2. Myers, op. cit., pp. 602-5.

3. Menshikov, *Millionaires and Managers* (Moscow, 1969), p. 233.
4. Marx, *Capital*, III, Ch. 27; *MEW*, XXV, p. 457.
5. *Statistical Abstract of the United States*, 1972, p. 312.
6. Federal Reserve *Bulletin*, July, 1971, p. 570.
7. S. L. Vygodskiy, *Sovremennyi Kapitalizm* (Moscow 1969), pp. 490 f.
8. Federal Reserve *Bulletin*, July, 1971, Table A64.
9. *Capital*, III, Ch. 29.
10. Thomas Davis, "Bank Holdings of U.S. Government Securities," in Federal Reserve Bank of Kansas City *Monthly Review*, July-August, 1971, pp. 11 f.
11. Federal Reserve *Bulletin*, July, 1971, Table A45.
12. *Statistical Abstract of the United States*, 1972, p. 454; Federal Reserve *Bulletin*, July, 1972, Table A 16.
13. Varga, *Politico-Economics Problems of Capitalism* (Moscow, 1968), p. 187.
14. L. Chandler, *Inflation in the United States 1940-1948* (New York, 1951), p. 241.
15. Board of Governors of the Federal Reserve System, *59th Annual Report*, 1972, pp. 240 f.
16. *Removal of Gold Cover, Hearings Before the Committee on Banking and Currency*, House of Representatives, 90th Cong., 2nd Sess. (Washington, D.C., 1968), p. 42.
17. Nicholas Lash, "What is Money?," in Federal Reserve Bank of Chicago *Business Conditions*, June, 1971, pp. 10 f.
18. *Capital*, II, Ch. 17, Sect. 2.
19. *Capital*, I, Ch. 31; III, Ch. 33.
20. A. Hansen, *Economic Policy and Full Employment* (New York 1947), pp. 263 f.
21. *Capital*, I, p. 782.
22. *Economic Report of the President* (Washington, D.C., 1974), p. 333.
23. Calculated from *Economic Report of the President*, pp. 324, 326 and S (368).
24. Federal Reserve *Bulletin*, July, 1972, Table A 43.
25. P. Mattick, *Marx and Keynes* (Boston, 1969), p. 186.
26. Sources: 1940-1960, *Statistical Abstract*, 1967, p. 403; 1970, Federal Reserve Bank of Kansas City; *Monthly Review*, July-August, 1971, p. 13.
   26a. cf. J. O'Connor, *The Fiscal Crisis of the State*, op. cit., pp. 193ff.
27. "Lord Keynes and the General Theory," in *Econometrica*, July, 1946. Cf. Harold Moulton, *Controlling Factors in Economic Development* (Washington, D.C., 1949), p. 131. See *Economic Report of the President* (Washington, D.C., 1972), p. 55.
   27a. See *Economic Report of the President*, Washington, D.C., 1972, p.55

CHAPTER 13

1. This is taken from Isaak Il'ich Rubin, *Ocherki po marksistkoi Teorii stoimosti* (3rd ed., Moscow-Leningrad, 1928), pp. 233-40.
1a. cf. *Statistical Abstract, 1967*, pp. 88, 644. Sugar is apparently a so-called inferior good.
2. *Economics of Labor* (New York 1941), pp. 317 f.
3. *Capital*, I, op. cit., Ch. 8-10 in Eng. ed.
4. Harry Millis and Royal Montgomery, *Labor's Progress and Some Basic Labor Problems*, Vol. I of *Economics of Labor* (New York, 1938), p. 278.
4a. Op. cit., p. 279.
5. Ibid., p. 280.
6. *Monthly Economic Letter*, Dec., 1971, p. 9.
7. John O'Riley, *Wall Street Journal*, Dec. 27, 1971, p. 1.
8. Source: *Sanierung für wen?*, West Berlin, n.d., pp. 34, 38; cf. B. Jansen, "Wohnungspolitik. Leitfaden durch ein kalkulierten Chaos," *Kursbuch*, No. 27, May, 1972, pp. 12-31.
9. Preben Wilhjelm, *Dansk boligpolitik—forbrydelse eller dumhed?* (Copenhagen, 1971), pp. 14-16, 30-32.
10. Nathaniel Goldfinger, "The Myth of Housing Cost," in *American Federationist*, December, 1969.
11. *Industrialized Housing*. Subcommittee on Urban Affairs of the Joint Economic Committee. Congress of the U.S., 91st Cong., 1st Sess. (Washington, D.C., 1969), pp. 1-8.
12. "Is the Crisis a Catastrophe?," January 1, 1971, p. 39.
13. *Quarterly Journal of Economics*, XLVIII/1, Nov. 1933, p. 140.
14. *Capital*, III, Ch. 36.

CHAPTER 14

1. See *Statistical Abstract of the United States*, 1967, p. 333; *Agricultural Statistics*, 1970, table 677; John A. Schnittker, "Changes Needed in Farm Legislation," U.S. Congress, Joint Economic Committee, *The Economics of Federal Subsidy Programs*, Part 7—"Agricultural Subsidies," Subcommittee on Priorities and Economy in Government, 93rd Cong., 1st Sess., April 30, 1973, p. 858; Federal Reserve Bank of Richmond *Monthly Review*, October 1971, p. 4.
2. B. Ostrolenk, *The Surplus Farmer* (New York, 1932), p. 132.
3. Source: Schnittker, op. cit., pp. 856, 859.

4. T.W. Schultz, *Production and Welfare of Agriculture* (New York 1950), p. 94.
5. W. Blake, *An American Looks at Karl Marx* (New York, 1939), pp. 475 f.
6. *Theorien über den Mehrwert*, I, pp. 382-84.
7. Schultz, op. cit., p. 59.
8. *Statistical Abstract*, 1972, p. 604.
9. *Statistical Abstract*, 1967, p. 617; U.S. Department of Agriculture, *Agricultural Statistics*, 1970, Washington, D.C., 1970, Table 679; *Statistical Abstract of the United States*, 1972, p. 596.
10. Op. cit., pp. 74 f.
11. *Agricultural Statistics*, 1970, Table 671.
12. See John Blair, *Economic Concentration* (New York, 1972), p. 9.
13. Ibid., pp. 20 f., 344-46.
14. Source: *U.S. Census of Agriculture, 1964*, Washington, D.C., 1964, II, 604.
15. Source: Schnittker, op. cit., p. 887.
16. C. E. Harshberger, "Farm Firm Growth: Transition to an Industrialized Agriculture?," Federal Reserve Bank of Kansas City *Monthly Review*, May, 1972, pp. 9 f.
17. See Radoje Nikolitch, U.S. Dept. of Agriculture, Economic Research Service, Agricultural Report No. 175, "Our 31,000 Largest Farms," Washington, D.C., 1970, p. 19.
18. Sources: Nikolitch, op. cit., p. 2; Schnittker, op. cit., p. 887. For the last pre-World War II census, 1939, see T. W. Schultz, *Agriculture in an Unstable Economy* (New York-London), 1945, pp. 200, 234.

CHAPTER 15

1. F. Wieser, *Über den Ursprung und die Hauptgesetze den wirthschaftlichen Werthes* (Vienna, 1884), p. 39.
2. C. Menger, *Grundsätze der Volkswirthschaftslehre*, 2nd ed. (Vienna, 1923), pp. 102 f., 108.
3. *A Critical Dissertation on the Nature, Measures, and Causes of Value: chiefly in reference to Mr. Ricardo and his followers* (London, 1825), pp. 2 f.; cited according to Robert Rauner, *Samuel Bailey and the Classical Theory of Value* (London 1961), p. 5.
4. *A Critical Dissertation...*, pp. 180, 182 f.; according to Rauner, op. cit., p. 67; Marx cites this statement.

5. Marx, *Theories of Surplus Value*, Vol. III, Ch. 20; *MEW*, XXVI: p. 163. This means that the subjective theory of value was in a nutshell already criticized by Marx.
6. A. Marshall, *Principles of Economics* (London, 1969 [1920]), pp. 81 f.
7. Ibid., p. 79.
8. H. H. Gossen, *Entwicklung der Gesetze des menschlichen Verkehrs und der daraus fliessenden Regeln fur menshcliches Handeln* (Braunschweig, 1854 [reprint: Amsterdam. 1967.]). p 12
9. S. Jevons, *Theory of Political Economy* (Harmandsworth, 1970 [1871]), pp. 115 f.
10. "Der Erkenntniswert der funktionellen Preistheorien," in J. Mayer (ed.), *Wirtschaftstheorien der Gegenwart* (Vienna, 1932), II, p. 172.
11. P. Crosser, *Economic Fictions* (New York, 1957).
12. Paul A. Samuelson, "The Empirical Implications of Utility Analysis," in *The Collected Scientific Papers of Paul A. Samuelson*, ed. by Joseph E. Stiglitz (Cambridge, Mass.: M.I.T. Press, 1966), p. 21; originally in *Econometrica* (Oct., 1938).
13. Samuelson, "A Note on the Pure Theory of Consumer's Behavior," in *Collected Scientific Papers*, p. 3; originally in *Economica*, (Feb., 1938).
14. On this matter see James M. Henderson and Richard E. Quandt, *Microeconomic Theory* (New York: McGraw-Hill, 1958), pp. 32-33.
15. Karl Marx and Frederick Engels, *The German Ideology* (Moscow, 1968), pp. 460-61.

CHAPTER 16

1. J. Robinson, *The Economics of Imperfect Competition* (London, 1950 [pub. in 1933]), p. 333.
2. J. M. Clark, *Studies in the Economics of Overhead Costs* (Chicago, 1923), p. 87.
3. J. Schumpeter, *History of Economic Analysis* (New York, 1955), p. 588.
4. P. Sraffa, "The Laws of Return under Competitive Conditions," *Economic Journal*, XXXVI/144 (Dec., 1926), p. 536.
5. W. Eitelman and G. Guthrie, "The Shape of the Average Cost Curve," *AER*, XIII/5 (December, 1952), 836 ff.; Cf. W. Eitelman, "Factors Determining the Location of the Least Cost Point," ibid., XXXVII (Dec., 1947), 910-18; as well as the debate in ibid., XLIII/4 (Sept. 1953), Part I, 621-30, between Eitelman and his critics.

6. J. Bain, *Industrial Organization* (New York, 1959), p. 26.
7. A. Hansen, "The Economics of the Soviet Challenge," in *Economic Record*, XXXVI/73, March, 1960, p. 10.
8. G. Stigler, *The Theory of Price*, 3rd ed. (New York), 1966, p. 6.
9. Samuelson, *Economics*, 3rd ed., p. 408.
10. Ibid., p. 419.
11. Samuelson, *Foundations of Economic Analysis* (Cambridge, Mass., 1971), p. 242.
12. Eitelman and Guthrie, op. cit., p. 832. Cf. R. L. Hall and C. J. Fitch, "Price Theory and Business Behavior," *Oxford Economic Papers*, No. 2, May, 1939; E. Gutenberg, *Grundlagen der Betriebswirtschaftslehre*, Vol. I, 2nd ed.; (West Berlin, 1955), pp. 269-73.
13. *Capital*, III, Ch. 12, Sect. III.
14. All the Jevons quotes are from *The Theory of Political Economy* (Harmondsworth, 1970 [1871]), Ch. 5.
15. H. Lehmann, *Grenznutzentheorie* (Berlin, 1968), pp. 165. Cf. Joan Robinson, *Economic Philosophy* (Garden City, 1964), pp. 92 f., on Keynes' attachment to "the most irremediably metaphysical" of all the concepts in the "neoclassical bag."
    15a. "Sulla relazioni fra costo e quantita prodotta," in *Annali di Economia*, II (1925–1926), 305–307.
16. J. M. Clark, op. cit., p. 448.
17. M. Dobb, *Welfare Economics and the Economics of Socialism* (Cambridge, 1969), p. 11.
18. W. Baumol, *Welfare Economics and the Theory of the State* (London, 1952), p. 58.
19. J. Schumpeter, *Capitalism, Socialism and Democracy* (London, 1966), p. 81.
20. J. Robinson, op. cit., pp. 151 f.

CHAPTER 17

1. See E. Chamberlin, *The Theory of Monopolistic Competition* (Cambridge [Mass.], 1935), pp. 3-4.
2. Bain, op. cit., p. 293.
3. A. D. H. Kaplan, J. Dirlam, R. Lanzillotti, *Pricing in Big Business* (Washington, D.C., 1963), p. 15.
4. A. D. H. Kaplan, *Big Enterprise in a Competitive System* (revised ed.; Washington, D.C., 1964, [1954]), pp. 138, 139.
5. Source: Kaplan, ibid., p. 127.
6. Ellis W. Hawley, *The New Deal and the Problem of Monopoly* (Princeton, 1966), p. 447.

7. Ibid., p. 485.
8. Ibid. pp. 486-488.
9. E. M. Hadley, "Trust-Busting in Japan," in *Harvard Business Review*, XXVI/4 (July, 1948), 427.

CHAPTER 18

1. C. Menger, Grundsatze der Volkswirtschaftslehre (2nd ed.; Vienna-Leipzig, 1923), pp. 154 f.
2. Ibid., p. 41.
3. Much of the above is adapted from Hermann Lehmann, *Grenznutzentheorie* (Berlin, 1968), Chapters 2, 3, and 4.
4. *Capital*, Vol. III, Ch. 14, Sect. I; ibid., p. 243.
5. N. Lenin, The Agrarian Question and the "Critics of Marx," Ch. 1, in *Works*, Vol. 5.
6. J. B. Clark, *The Distribution of Wealth*, (New York, 1965 [1899]), p. 120.
7. L. B. Al'ter, *Burzhuaznaia politicheskaia economiia SShA* (Moscow, 1961), p. 345.
8. J. B. Clark, op. cit., p. 41.
9. Ibid., pp. 45, 46.
10. Ibid., p. 158.
11. E. Preiser, "Erkenntniswert und Grenzen der Grenzproduktivitätstheorie," in *Schweizer Zeitschrift für Volkswirtschaft und Statistik*, LXXXIX/1 (Feb., 1953), 25-54.
12. J. B. Clark, op. cit., p. v.
13. *Capital*, III, Ch. 48, Sect. III; ibid., p. 834.
14. J. B. Clark, op. cit., p. 90.
15. Ibid., p. 84.
16. P. Douglas, *Theory of Wages* (New York, 1934), p. 113.
17. J. B. Clark, op. cit., pp. 113 f.
18. Ibid., pp. 176, 325.

CHAPTER 19

1. Bourgeois newspapers are more realistic. Thus the *Suddeutsche Zeitung*, April 8-9, 1972, p. 8, lamented that land was not being considered as an economic good to be used fruitfully, but rather as a capital asset, so that much land was being "artificially kept out of the play of supply and demand." See a similar report on London: "Britain Moves to Topple Vacant-Building Empire," *New York Times*, June 28, 1972, p. 63. As H. Fassbinder, "Preisbildung, Monopol und Spekulation beim

städtischen Boden," *Probleme des Klassenkampfs*, III/4, 1973, No. 10, pp. 1-32, points out, it is false to try to reduce land prices to speculation.
2. *Theories of Surplus Value*, Vol. II, Ch. 13, Sect. 5; cf. Max Kemper, *Marxismus und Landwirtschaft* (Stuttgart, 1973 [1929]), pp. 26 f.
   2a. For modern confirmation of Marx's description in the penultimate chapter of volume one of *Capital*, see W. Moore, *Industrialization and Labor*, Ithaca, New York, 1951, pp. 51 ff.
   2b. Cf. F. Rinkleff, *Theorien über die Grundrente*, West Berlin, 1974.
   2c. *MEW*, XXVI: 2, 328.
3. D. Ricardo, *The Principles of Political Economy and Taxation*, Everyman edition, p. 38.
4. Ibid., p. 41.
5. *Theories of Surplus Value*, III, Addendum, "Revenue and Its Sources," Sect. 5; *MEW*, XXVI:3, pp. 504 f.
6. *Capital*, III, Ch. 46; *MEW*, XXV, p. 789.

CHAPTER 20

1. *Monthly Labor Review*, May, 1973, p. 90.
2. Ibid., p. 96.
3. *Economic Report of the President* (Washington, D.C., 1973), p. 229.
4. Ibid.; these data refer to a male worker with a wife and two children.
5. *Economic Report of the President* (Washington, D.C., 1974), p. 285.
6. *Monthly Labor Review*, June, 1975, p. 94. Cf. John F. Early, "Factors Affecting Trends in Real Spendable Earnings," ibid., May, 1973, pp. 16-19.
7. Races and Immigrants in America (New York, 1924), p. xxvi; cit. acc. to C. Kindleberger, *Europe's Postwar Growth* (Cambridge [Mass.], 1967), p. 21, n. 13.
8. Paul Douglas, *Real Wages in the United States 1890-1926* (Boston, 1930), p. 445.
9. See R. Boyer and H. Morais, *Labor's Untold Story* (New York, 1970), Ch. 3.
10. Quoted in Galenson and Lipset (eds.), *Labor and Trade Unionism: an Interdisciplinary Reader* (New York, 1960), p. 138.
   10a. Cf. W. S. Woytinsky et al., *Employment and Wages in the United States*, New York, 1953, pp. 322-323.

11. *Capital*, I, Ch. 6 of the Engl. ed.; *MEW*, XXIII, 185.
12. Ibid., p. 666.
13. From 1880 to 1890 average wages for non-agricultural workers rose 12.3 percent while the work week sank from 60 to 58.4 hours. R. Boyer and H. Morais, op. cit., p. 107, n. 2. 107, n. 2.
14. A. Smith, *Wealth of Nations*, Book I, Ch. 10, Modern Library edition (New York, n.d.).
15. *Economic Report of the President*, February, 1970, Tables C-32, C-33. Cf. *Wall Street Journal*, January 26, 1972, p. 1.
16. *Monthly Labor Review*, XCVIII/6 (June, 1975), 82.
17. H. A. Turner and Frank Wilkinson, "Real Net Incomes and the Wage Explosion," in *New Society*, Feb. 25, 1971, pp. 309 f.
18. *Wall Street Journal*, Jan. 21, 1972, p. 30.

CHAPTER 21

1. I. Bliumin, *Sub'ektivnaia shkola v politicheskoi ekonomii* (Moscow, 1928), Vol. I, p. 316.
2. *Theories of Surplus Value*, Vol. I, Addenda, "Productivity of Capital. Productive and Unproductive Labor," Sect. a; *MEW*, 26: 1, pp. 366 f.
3. G. McConnell, *Economics: Principles, Problems and Policies*, 2nd ed. (New York, 1963), p. 567.
4. *Capital*, III, Ch. 21; *MEW*, XXV, p. 351.
5. Keynes, *A Treatise on Money* (New York, 1930), Vol. II, p. 171
6. Ibid., p. 172.
7. Ibid.
8. Keynes, *General Theory*,. . . , p. 27.

CHAPTER 22

1. *Theories of Surplus Value*, Vol. III, Addenda, "Revenue and Its Sources," Part 4; *MEW*, XXVI: 3, pp. 487 f.
2. Jan Pen, *Income Distribution* (New York, 1971), p. 17.

INTRODUCTION TO CHAPTERS 23-27

1. G. Mydral, *The Challenge of World Poverty* (New York, 1970), pp. 297, 301.

2. "Die Juden und Europa" ("The Jews and Europe"), *Zeitschrift für Socialforschung*, Vol. VIII (1939).

CHAPTER 23

1. Marx, *Theories of Surplus Value*, Vol. III, Ch. 21, Sect. lc; *MEW*, XXVI:3, p. 249.
2. *Capital*, I, Ch. 3, Sect. 3c; *MEW*, XXIII, p. 156.
3. Marx, *Grundrisse*, p. 77.
4. *Capital*, I, Ch. 22, pp. 583 f.
5. Ibid., pp. 547.
6. Ibid., p. 584.
7. Ibid.
8. Busch, Schöller, Seelow, *Weltmarkt und Währungskrise* (Bremen, 1971), p. 30.
9. A. A. Mendel'son, *Teoriya i istoriia ekonomicheskikh krizisov i tsiklov* (Theory and History of Economic Crises and Cycles) (Moscow, 1959), II, pp. 526 f.
10. Stephen V. O. Clarke, *Central Bank Cooperation: 1924-31* (New York, 1967), p. 38; this book was published by the New York Federal Reserve Bank.
11. From a letter to Truman in 1946, quoted according to Richard Gardner, *Sterling-Dollar Diplomacy* (Oxford, 1956), p. 76.
12. R. Hilferding, *Das Finanzkapital* (Frankfurt, 1968; [first printed 1910],) p. 442.
13. W. A. Brown, Jr., *The International Gold Standard Reinterpreted, 1914-1934* (New York, 1940), I. p. 147 f.
14. Woytinsky and Woytinsky, *World Commerce and Governments* (New York, 1955), p. 252.
15. Source: Jürgen Kuczynski, *Labor Conditions in Great Britain*, op. cit., p. 95; the figures are probably understated since they refer to skilled workers or workers in a restricted number of industries.
16. Woytinsky and Woytinsky, op. cit., p. 195.
17. Herbert Feis, *Europe the World's Banker, 1870-1914* (New York, 1965 [1930]), p. 29.
18. Robert Heilbroner, *The Economic Problem*, 2nd ed. (Englewood Cliffs, N.J., 1970) p. 639.
19. Angus Maddison, *Economic Growth in the West* (New York, 1967), pp. 28, 30.
20. *Europe's Postwar Growth: The Role of the Labor Supply* (Cambridge, Mass., 1967), p. 30.

21. Jörg Huffschmid, *Die Politik des Kapitals* (Frankfurt, 1971), pp. 14 f.
22. See Ministry of Foreign Affairs, *Factors in Japan's Economic Growth* (Japan, 1962), pp. 10, 12.
23. *Statistical Abstract of the United States,* 1967, p. 814.
24. Altvater, *Weltwährungskrise* (Frankfurt/Main, 1969), pp. 78-119.
25. *Wall Street Journal,* August 30, 1971, p. 1.

CHAPTER 24

1. L. Yeager, *The International Monetary Mechanism* (New York, 1968), p. 3.
2. B. Balassa, *Studies in Trade Liberalization* (Baltimore, 1967), pp. 8 f.
3. C. Kindleberger, *International Economics* (Homewood, 1963), 3rd ed., p. 103; our emphasis.
4. Samuelson, "International Trade and the Equalisation of Factor Prices," *Economic Journal,* LVIII/230 (June, 1948), 182.
5. Ricardo, *Principles...*, Ch. 7, Everyman ed., p. 81.
6. Ibid., p. 83.
7. *A Survey of International Trade Theory,* rev. ed., *Special Papers in International Economics,* No. 1 (Princeton, 1961), p. 7.
8. G. Haberler, *Studies in the Theory of International Trade* (London, 1964 [1937]), p. 437.
9. Ibid., pp. 437 ff.
10. Charles Staley, *International Economics* (Englewood Cliffs, N.J., 1970), pp. 8 f.; our emphasis.
11. C. Staley, *International Economics* (2nd ed.; Englewood Cliffs, N.J., 1967), p. 14; our emphasis.
12. William Branson and Helen Junz, "Trends in U.S. Trade and Comparative Advantage," in *Brookings Papers on Economic Activity,* No. 2/1971, pp. 316 ff.
13. 9.8 percent. Source: First National City Bank *Monthly Economic Letter,* April, 1972, p. 7.
14. Source: U.S. Department of Labor, *Monthly Labor Review,* Sept., 1973, p. 117. For a description of limited value of certain aspects of this industry see "U.S. Textile Industry," in *Progressive Labor,* VIII/1 (Feb., 1971), 55-68; Cf. *Business Week,* Aug. 4, 1973, pp. 22, 24; ibid., Oct. 27, 1973, pp. 122, 124.
15. Samuelson, "Disparity in Postwar Exchange Rates," in S. Harris (ed.), *Foreign Economic Policy for the U.S.* (Cambridge, Mass., 1948), p. 407.
    15a. *Capital,* III, ch. 14, sect. V; German ed., p. 248.

16. W. Leontief, "Domestic Production and Foreign Trade: The American Capital Position Re-Examined," in *Proceedings of the American Philosophical Society*, Vol. 97 (1953); here according to reprint in J. Bhagwati (ed.) *International Trade* (Harmondsworth, 1970), pp. 125 f.
17. For a selected bibliography of similar empirical studies for other countries and their results, see Staley, op. cit., p. 63, n. 16.
18. *An Essay on Trade and Transformation* (New York-Stockholm, 1961), p. 86.
19. See Helmut Hesse, "Die Bedeutung der reinen Theorie des internationalen Handels fur die Erklarung des Aussenhandels in der Nachkriegszeit," in *Zeitschrift fur die gesamt Staatswissenschaft*, CXXII/2 (1966), 221-36.
20. *Business Week*, March 20, 1971, p. 25; it should be noted that "this tidal wave of cheap, but quality, products came largely from Eastern Europe, India and Brazil." Cf. *Neue Zurcher Zeitung*, Oct. 9, 1974, p. 19.
21. *Capital*, III, Ch. 50; German ed., pp. 881 f.
22. Samuelson, "International Trade and the Equalisation of Factor Prices," *Economic Journal*, LVIII/230 (June, 1948), 163-84.
23. "Tinbergen Reassesses Industry 'Rationality,' " *New York Times*, October 5, 1970, pp. 67 f.

CHAPTER 25

1. "The Gains from International Trade Once Again," *Economic Journal*, LXXII (1962), reprinted in J. Bhagwati (ed.), *International Trade*, p. 181.
2. E. H. Carr, *The Twenty Years; Crisis, 1919-1936* (New York, 1964 [1939]), pp. 54 f.
3. *Capital*, III, Ch. 15, Sect. III; German ed., p. 263.
4. Source: *International Financial Statistics, 1972 Supplement*, p. xxix. The reference year for Denmark is 1970.
5. Benjamin Cohen, "Tariff Preferences for the Third World," in *Intereconomics*, No. 9 (1970), p. 286.
6. P. Samuelson, John Coleman, Felicity Skidmore, *Readings in Economics*, 5th ed. (New York, 1967), p. 205.
7. This thesis was developed by S and Wolfgang Stolper in "Protection and Real Wages," in *Review of Economic Studies*, IX (1941), 58-73; reprinted in Bhagwati (ed.), *International Trade*, pp. 245-68.

8. "International Trade and the Equalization of Factor Prices," in *Economic Journal*, LVIII/230 (June, 1948), pp. 176 f.
9. Eleanor Gilpatrick, *Structural Unemployment and Aggregate Demand* (Baltimore, 1966), p. 2.

CHAPTER 26

1. E. Varga, *Die grosse Krise und ihre politischen Folgen*, in Varga, *Die Krise des Kapitalismus;* ed. by Altvater (Frankfurt/Main, 1969), pp. 252-56.
2. J. Roger Wallace, "Business Outlook," *Journal of Commerce*, May 24, 1971, p. 4.
3. See W. S. Woytinsky and E. S. Woytinsky, *World Commerce and Governments* (New York, 1955), pp. 206 f.
4. Ibid., pp. 206-21.
5. Richard Gardner *Sterlin-Dollar Diplomacy* (Oxford, 1956), pp. 61 f.
6. Hugh Seton-Watson, *From Lenin to Khrushchev* (New York, 1962), pp. 300 f.
7. Howard K. Smith, *The State of Europe* New York, 1949), p. 234.
8. H. Parkes, *Partners in Development* (London, 1969), p. 115.
9. This reasoning, as well as the figure of 60 percent on the preceding page, stem from Katja Nehls, *Kapitalexport und Kapitalverflechtung* (Frankfurt, 1970), pp. 28-34.
10. Woytinsky and Woytinsky, op. cit., p. 227.
11. Calculation based on ibid., pp. 229 f.
12. Figure for 1957 taken from F. Hartog, "Trade Arrangements Among Countries: Effects on the Common Market," in Bela Balassa (ed.), *Studies in Trade Liberalization* (Baltimore, 1967), p. 109.
13. V. Grant, "The Multinational Company," in Federal Reserve Bank of Chicago, *The International Monetary System in Transition* (Chicago, 1972), p. 110.
14. Susan B. Foster, "Impact of Direct Investment Abroad by United States "Multinational Companies on the Balance of Payments," in Federal Reserve Board of New York *Monthly Review*, LIV/7 (July, 1972), 172.
15. Nicholas Bruck and Francis Lees, "Foreign Content of U.S. Corporate Activities," in *Financial Analysts Journal*, XXXII/5 (Sept.-Oct., 1966), 127-32.

16. See *Business Week*, Jan. 12, 1974, p. 53; Labor Research Association, *Economic Notes* (June, 1972), p. 6; *IPW Berichte* (Berlin), *Economic Notes*, op. cit.; *Wall Street Journal* (May 26, 1972), p. 28; *Handelsblatt* (March 6, 1974), p. 13.
17. Richard Gardner, op. cit., pp. 11, 295 f.
18. *Policies and Operations: The World Bank, IDA and IFC* (n.p., June, 1971), p. 2.
19. A. Shonfield, *The Attack on World Poverty* (New York, 1962) pp. 140 f. Cf. James O'Connor, "The Meaning of Economic Imperialism," in R. Rhodes (ed.), *Imperialism and Underdevelopment* (New York, 1971), p. 120.
20. N. McKitternick and B. J. Middleton, *The Bankers of the Rich and the Bankers of the Poor: The Role of Export Credit in Development Finance*, Overseas Development Council, Monograph No. 6, Washington, D.C., 1972, p. 22.
21. *Wall Street Journal*, Sept. 28, 1970.
22. Shonfield, op. cit., pp. 156 f.
23. *Policies and Operations* . . . , op cit., pp. 18, 39.
24. Shonfield, op. cit., p. 143
25. *Policies and Operations* . . . , op. cit., p. 64.
26. This analysis is based largely on Harald-Dietrich Kühne, "Imperialistische Interessengegensätze und der neue Abschnitt in der Krise des spätkapitalistischen Währungsystems," in *Wirtschaftswissenschaft*, XVII/2 (Feb., 1969), 237, 243. On London as international banker see Benjamin Cohen, "Measuring the Benefits and Costs of Sterling," in *Euromoney*, I/4 (Sept., 1969), pp. 10-12; I/11 (April, 1970), pp. 39-43; reprinted in *Reprints in International Finance*, No. 15 (Princeton, June, 1970).
27. On this see R. Cooper, *Currency Devaluation in Developing Countries*, Essays in International Finance, No. 86 (Princeton, June, 1971), pp. 13 f.
28. On these latter two points see H. Magdoff, *The Age of Imperialism* (New York, 1969), pp. 91-100.
29. April 23, 1959; cit. acc. Magdoff, op. cit., p. 145.
30. Samuelson, "Disparity in Postwar Exchange Rates," in Seymour Harris (ed.), *Foreign Economic Policy for the U.S.* (Cambridge, Mass., 1948), pp. 411 f.
31. C. Kindleberger, *International Economics* (Homewood, Ill. 1963), p. 320.

32. Peter Kenen, *International Economics*, (Englewood Cliffs, N.J., 1966), p. 42.
33. Outgoing EEC-President S. Manholt in *New York Times*, Jan. 3, 1973, p. 53.
34. J. Viner, *The Customs Union Issue* (New York, 1950), p. 133.
35. S. Dell, *Trade Blocs and Common Markets* (New York, 1963), pp. 40 f.
36. E. Mandel, *Europe vs. America: Contradictions of Imperialism* (New York, 1970), p. 44.
37. Ibid., p. 46.
38. S. Dell, op. cit. pp. 191 f.
39. Ibid., p. 124.
40. Ibid., pp. 108-14.
41. C. Kindleberger, *Europe's Postwar Growth: The Role of the Labor Supply* (Cambridge, Mass., 1967), p. 181.
42. "Noch sind Gastarbeiter nutzlich," *Handelsblatt*, March 14, 1972, p. 1.
43. First National City Bank, *Monthly Economic Letter*, January, 1972, p. 10.
44. Eugene Birnbaum, *Gold and the International Monetary System, Essays in International Finance*, No. 66 (Princeton, April, 1968), pp. 5, 44.
45. C. Kindleberger, *The Politics of International Money and World Language, Essays in International Finance*, No. 61 (Princeton, August, 1967), p. 10.
46. Alfred L. Malabre, Jr., "Is It Really Time for Monetary Cheer?," *Wall Street Journal*, Dec. 2, 1971, p. 18.
47. Birnbaum, op. cit., p. 311
48. Leonard Silk, "The Dollar Overhang," *New York Times*, Oct. 13, 1971, p. 63.

CHAPTER 27

1. "Underdeveloped Countries and the Pre-Industrial Phase in the Advanced Countries: An Attempt at Comparison," in *Proceedings of the World Population Conference, 1954, Papers: Volume V*; here cit. acc. reprint in Agarwala and Singh (eds.) *The Economics of Underdevelopment* (New York, 1963), pp. 137, 138; cf. also S. Kuznetz, *Modern Economic Growth* (New Haven, 1966).

1a.	*Capital*, III, ch. 20; *Grundrisse*, pp. 404 ff.
1b.	Ibid., p. 140, E. Mandel, Der *Spätkapitalismus* (Ffm, 1973), pp. 47-53; *Grundrisse* op cit. pp. 377-83
1c.	*Capital*, II, Chs. 1-4
2.	P. Khalatbari, *Oekonomische Unterentwicklung* (Berlin, 1971), pp. 62 f.
2a.	See e.g. D. Snodgrass, *Ceylon: An Export Economy in Transition* (Homewood, 1966), p. 70
3.	P. Baran, *The Political Economy of Growth* (New York, 1968 (1957), p. 144.
3a.	See the articles by Singer and Myint in The Bibliography.
3b.	C. Bettelheim, *Planification et croissance accélérée* (Paris, 1967 [1964])
3c.	Snodgrass, op cit., pp. 17-19
3d.	Mandel, *Truité.* . . . , op. cit., III, 178-80
3e.	This is a reference to so-called import substitution; see Harry Johnson, "Tariffs and Economic Development, Some Theoretical Aspects," *Journal of Development Studies*, Ill. (Spring, 1965), 26: T. Hurtienne, "Zur Ideologiekritik der Unterentwicklung und Abhángigkeit," in: Probleme des Klassen-Kampfes, 10/3 (1974), 238-239.
4.	J. Keynes, *The General Theory of Employment, Interest and Money* (London 1967 (1936), pp. 367 f.
4a.	Mandel, Traité. . ., op. cit. I Ch. I
4b.	Bettelheim, Planification. . ., op. cit., pp. 61-63
5.	A. Smith, *The Wealth of Nations* (New York, n.d.), p. 68.
6.	P. Rosenstein-Rodan, "Problems of Industrialization of Eastern and South-Eastern Europe," in *Economic Journal* LIII (1943); here cit. acc. reprint in Agarwala and Singh, op. cit., pp. 245-55.
7.	Ibid., p. 247.
8.	Ibid., p. 253
9.	Ibid., p. 250
9a.	A. Hirschman, *The Strategy of Economic Development* (New Haven, 1960), p. 54
10.	G. Myrdal, *Asian Drama* (New York 1968), Vol. I. p. 458 f.
10a.	T. Balogh, *The Economics of Poverty* (London, 1966), p. 115
11.	IMF/IBRD, *The Problems of Stabilization of Prices of Primary Products* (Washington D.C. 1969), p. 12.
12.	Ibid., p. 23
13.	G. Myrdal, *The Challenge of World Poverty* (New York 1970), pp. 262 f.

14.	Ibid., p. 109
15.	Ibid., p. 112
16.	P. Baran, op. cit., p. 168
16a.	Ibid., pp. 168-169
16b.	Mandel, *Der Spätkapitalismus,* op. cit., pp. 53-54
16c.	See the entries in the bibliography by Baer (pp. 96-97); Frank,; Hirschman, "How to Divest. . ."; Ichaltbari, *Ökonomische. . .,* pp. 50-53, 74-77; Hurcienne, op. cit., 234-41, and U.-L. Hiersemantel, *Die Rolle der Exporte in der wirtschaftlichen Entwicklung Brasiliens* (Göttingen, 1974), pp. 69-70, criticize the position presented here.
16d.	Hirschman, *Strategy,* op. cit., pp. 58-59
16e.	Mandel, *Spätkapitalismus,* op. cit., p. 51
17.	Bruce Russett et al., *World Handbook of Political and Social Indicators* (New Haven, 1964), pp. 239 f.
18.	P. Baran, op. cit., p. 23
18a.	Ibid. p. 24
18b.	Baran, op. cit., pp. 201-26
18c.	IBRD President McNamara has dwelt on this theme in recent years.
18d.	Myrdal, *Asian Dilemma,* op. cit. I, 414, 434
18e.	*Grundrisse,* op. cit., p. 501
19.	Joan Robinson, "Disguised Unemployment," in *Economic Journal,* XLVI/182, June 1936, p. 226
20.	Maurice Halperin, "Growth and Crisis in the Latin American Economy," in *Science and Society,* XXV/3, Summer, 1961), pp. 192-228; here quoted acc. reprint in Petras and Zeitlin (eds.), *Latin America: Reform or Revolution?* (New York, 1973), pp. 60 f. See also Frank, *Capitalism and Underdevelopment in Latin America* (New York, 1969), p. 110; *Statistical Abstract, 1967,* p. 868, provides a comparative list of the shares of the non-commodity producing sectors in the gross domestic products of many countries.
20a.	*Grundrisse,* op. cit., pp. 497-98
20b	R. Meek, "Malthus—Yesterday and Today," *Science and Society* XVIII/I (Winter, 1954), 40

Bibliography

Under "I" are listed magazines, newspapers and statistical manuals which appear in footnotes without the name of an author or title of the work cited.
Under "II" are listed all other books and articles cited.

I
African Development
Bank for International Settlements, Annual Reports
Business Week
Chase Manhattan Bank, Business in Brief
Economic Notes
Economist
Frankfurter Allgemeine Zeitung
Frankfurter Allgemeine Zeitung—Blick durch die Wirtschaft
Federal Reserve Bank of Atlanta, Monthly Review
Federal Reserve Bank of Boston, New England Economic Review
Federal Reserve Bank of Chicago, Business Conditions
— International Letter
Federal Reserve Bank of Cleveland, Economic Commentary
— Economic Review
Federal Reserve Bank of Kansas City, Monthly Review
Federal Reserve Bank of New York, Annual Reports
— Monthly Review
Federal Reserve Bank of Philadelphia, Business Review
Federal Reserve Bank of Richmond, Monthly Review
Federal Reserve Bank of St. Louis, Review
— U.S. Balance of Payments Trends
Federal Reserve Bank of San Francisco, Monthly Review
Federal Reserve Bulletin
Federal Reserve System, Annual Reports
Finance and Development
Financial Times
First National City Bank of Chicago, Bond and Money Market Review
— Business and Economic Review
First National City Bank of New York, Monthly Economic Letter
Fortune
Granma
Handelsblatt
IBRD, Directions of Trade
IMF, Annual Reports
— Balance of Payments Yearbook
— International Financial Statistics

IPW Berichte
Jeremiad Quarterly Supplement
Journal of Commerce
Life
Monatshefte der Deutschen Bundesbank
Monthly Labor Review (U.S. Department of Labor)
Neue Zürcher Zeitung
New York Times
Schweizerische Handelszeitung
Spiegel
Stern
Stuttgarter Zeitung
Süddeutsche Zeitung
Survey of Current Business (U.S. Department of Commerce)
Times
US News and World Report
Wall Street Journal
Wirtschaftswoche

II

A. Abboud, "The International Competitiveness of U.S. Banks and the U.S. Economy", in: Federal Reserve Bank of Chicago, *The International Monetary System in Transition*, Chicago 1972

H. Adam, "Statistische Probleme bei Einkommensvergleichen zwischen Selbständigen und abhangig Beschäftigten", in: *WSI Mitteilungen*, XXVI/9 (9/73), pp. 342–47

H. Adam, *Südafrika*, Ffm. 1969

L. Adamic, *Dynamite: The History of Class Violence in America*. Gloucester 1963.

American Economic Association, "The Problem of Economic Instability", in *American Economic Review*, XL/4 (9/50)

Agrarbericht der Bundesregierung, Materialband, Bonn 1973

A. Aguilar, *Latin America and the Alliance for Progress*, NY 1963

R. Ahlheim et al., *Gefesselte Jugend*, Frankfurt/Main 1971

H. Alavi/A. Khusro, "Pakistan: The Burden of U.S. Aid", in: R. Rhodes (ed.), *Imperialism and Underdevelopment*, NY 1971

L. Al'ter, *Burzhuaznaia politicheskaia ekonomiaa SShA*, Moscow 1961

E. Altmann et al., *Wesdeutschland unter den Gesetzen der Reproduktion des Kapitals und die Arbeiterklasse*, Berlin 1960

E. Altvater, *Gesellschaftliche Produktion und ökonomische Rationalität*, Frankfurt/Main 1969

— "Qualifikation der Arbeitskraft und Kompliziertheit der Arbeit—Bemerkungen zum Reduktionsproblem", in: E. Altvater/F. Huisken (eds.), *Materialien zur Politischen Ökonomie des Ausbildungssektors*, Erlangen 1971, pp. 253–302

— *Weltwährungskrise*, Frankfurt/Main 1969

— "Zu einigen Problemen des Staatsinterventionismus", in: *Probleme des Klassenkampfs*, 3, May 1972, pp. 1–53

— "Zur Konjunkturlage der BRD Anfang 1970", in: *Sozialistische Politik*, 5, March 1970

— *Zur Kritik bürgerlicher Konjunkturtheorie*, unpublished manuscript

E. Altvater/F. Huisken, "Produktive und unproduktive Arbeit als

Kampfbegriffe, als Kategorien zur Analyse der Klassenverhaltnisse und der Reproduktionsbedingungen des Kapitals", in: *Sozialistische Politik*, 8, Sept. 1970
A. M. P., Einleitung zu F. Oelssner, *Die Wirtschaftskrisen*, Frankfurt/Main 1971
G. Anders, "Imperialismus und Kampf dagegen oder Philosophisches Wörterbuch heute (II)", in: *Das Argument*, XI/1-2 (4/69)
J. Anderson, "Has Unemployment a Future?", in: *Encounter*, XXXIX/5 (11/72)
J. Andersson, "Politik och paradigma i en ekonomisk läborok," in: *Häften for Kritiska Studier*, 4/1969
V. Andrievskâia, *Osnovnye formy gosudarstvennogo monopolisticheskogo kapitalizma v sel'skom khoziastve SShA*, Moscow 1970
H. Arnaszus, *Spieltheorie und Nutzenbegriff aus marxistischer Sicht*, Frankfurt/Main 1974
H. Arndt, "Stagflation—Was man bisher nicht wußte", in: *Wirtschaftswoche*, 1, July 1, 1971
G. Arrighi, "International Corporations, Labor Aristocracy and Economic Development in Africa", in: R. Rhodes (ed.), *Imperialism and Underdevelopment*, NY 1971
K. Arrow, "Somehow, It Has Overcome", in: *New York Times*, March 26, 1973, p. 39
R. Asher, *Development Assistance in the Seventies*, Washington D. C. 1970
N. Auerbach, *Marx und die Gewerkschaften*, Berlin 1922

F. Baade, *Wettlaufzum Jahre 2000*, Odenburg/Hamburg 1961
G. Bach, *Economics*, Englewood Cliffs 1958
H.-G. Backhaus, "Zur Dialektik der Wertform" in: A. Schmidt (ed.), *Beiträge zur marxistischen Erkenntnistheorie*, Frankfurt/Main 1969
J. Backman et al., *War and Defense Economics*, NY 1952
W. Baer, "Import Substitution and Industrialization in Latin America: Experiences and Interpretations", in: *Latin America Research Review*, VII/I (Spring 1972)
B. Balassa, *Studies in Trade Liberalization*, Baltimore 1967
— "Tariff Protection in Industrial Countries: An Evaluation", in: *Journal of Political Economy*, LXIII/6 (12/65), 573–94
S. Bailey, *Congress Makes a Law*, NY 1965 (1950)
J. Bain, *Barriers to New Competition*, Cambridge 1967 (1956)
— *Industrial Organization*, NY 1959
D. Baldwin, *Economic Development and American Foreign Policy*, Chicago 1966
G. Baldwin, "Braindrain or Overflow", in: *Foreign Affairs*, XLVIII/2 (1/70)
A. Balinky (ed.), *Planning and the Market in the USSR: The 1960's*, New Brunswick 1967
T. Balogh, *The Economics of Poverty*, London 1966
— *Unequal Partners*, Vol. I, Oxford 1963
Bank of Israel, *Annual Report*, Jerusalem 1971
P. Baran, *The Political Economy of Growth*, NY 1968
P. Baran/E. Hobsbawm, "The Stages of Economic Growth", in: *Kyklos*, XIV (1961), 234–42
P. Baran/P. Sweezy, *Monopoly Capital*, NY 1966
A. Bates, "Low Cost Housing in the Soviet Union", in: U.S. Congress, Joint Economic Committee, Subcommittee on Urban Affairs, *Indus-*

trialized Housing, 91. Congress, 1. Session, Washington, D.C. 1969
O. Bauer, "Goldproduktion und Teuerung", in: *Die Neue Zeit,* XXX/2 (1911–12), 4–14, 49–53
W. Baumol, "Acceleration Without Magnification", in: *American Economic Review,* LXVI/3 (1956); 409–12
— *Welfare Economics and the Theory of the State,* London 1952
D. Bechter, "The Retirement Decision: Social Pressures and Economic Trends", in: Federal Reserve Bank of Kansas City *Monthly Review,* Nov. 1972
R. Becker et al., "Fremdarbeiterbeschäftigung im deutschen Kapitalismus", in: *Das Argument,* XIII/9–10 (December 1971)
W. Beckermann/R. Bacon, "The International Distribution of Income", in: P. Streeten (ed.), *Unfashionable Economics: Essays in Honour of Lord Balogh,* London 1970
P. Behrens, *Hermann Heinrich Gossen,* Leipzig 1949
— "Zur Einschätzung der Funktion der gegenwärtigen bürgerlichen Ökonomie und zur Kritik der bürgerlichen Betriebswirtschaftslehre", in: Deutsche Akademie der Wissenschaften zu Berlin, *Schriften des Instituts fur Wirtschaftswissenschaften, 12, Neue Erscheinungen in der modernen bürgerlichen politischen Ökonomie,* Berlin 1961, Vol. 2
D. Belli/J. Freidlin, "United States Direct Investments Abroad in 1970", in: *Survey of Current Business,* Oct. 1971
M. Beloff, *The United States and the Unity of Europe,* Washington, D. C. 1963
R. Bentzel, *Inkomstfördelningen i Sverige,* Uppsala 1953
A. Bergson, *Soviet Economic Planning,* New Haven 1964
— *The Structure of Soviet Wages,* Cambridge 1944
Bericht der Bundesregierung und Materialien zur Lage der Nation 1971
I. Bernstein, *Turbulent Years: A History of the American Worker 1933–41,* Boston 1971
M. Bernstein, *Regulating Business by Independent Commission,* Princeton 1955
V. Gräfin v. Bethusy-Huc, *Das Sozialleistungssystem der Bundesrepublik Deutschland,* Tübingen 1965
C. Bettelheim, *Calcul économique et formes de propriété,* Paris 1970
— *L'économie allemande sous le nazisme,* 2 Vols., Paris 1971 (1945)
— *Planification et croissance accélérée,* Paris 1967
— "Revenue national, épargne et investissement chez Marx et chez Keynes", in: *Revue d'économie politique,* LVIII/2 (March-April 1948), 198–211
W. Beveridge, *Full Employment in a Free Society,* NY 1945
K. Bieda, *The Structure and Operation of the Japanese Economy,* Sydney/NY 1970
E. Birnbaum, "A Cure for Monetary Disorder", in: *Fortune,* LXXXVII/5 (May 1973),
— *Gold and the International Monetary System, Princeton Essays in International Finance,* 66, April 1968
R. Blackburn, "The Unequal Society", in: R. Blackburn/A. Cockburn (eds.), *The Incompatibles: Trade Union Militancy and the Consensus,* Harmondsworth 1967
J. Blair, *Economic Concentration,* NY 1972
W. Blake, *An American Looks at Karl Marx,* NY 1939
E. Blechschmidt, *Löhne, Preise und Gewinne (1967–1973),* Lampertheim 1974

I. Bliumin, *O sovremennoi burzhvaznoi politicheskoi ekonomii*, Moscow 1958
— *Sub'ektivnaia shkola v politicheskoi ekonomii*, 2 Vols., Moscow 1928
A. Bloomfield, *Patterns of Fluctuations in International Investment Before 1914*, Princeton Studies in International Finance, 21, 1968
B. Bluestone, "The Tripartite Economy: Labor Markets and the Working Class", in: *Poverty and Human Resources*, V/4 (July-August 1970)
Board of Governors of the Federal Reserve System, *All-Bank Statistics. United States 1896–1955*, Washington, D.C. 1959
— *Banking and Monetary Statistics*, Washington, D.C. 1943
E. v. Böhm-Bawerk, *Positive Theorie des Kapitals*, Jena 1921
W. Böhning, *The Migration of Workers in the UK and the EEC*, London 1972
M. Bogachevskiy, *Gosudarstvennyi kredit v kapitalisticheskikh stranakh*, Moscow 1966
D. Bok/J. Dunlop, *Labor and the American Community*, NY 1970
E. Boorstein, *The Economic Transformation of Cuba*, NY 1969
H. Boris, "Zur Politischen Ökonomie der Beziehungen zwischen Entwicklungsländern und westlichen Industrieländern", in: *Das Argument*, VIII/3, 38 (June 1966)
S. Borisov, *Zoloto v ekonomike sovremennogo kapitalizma*, Moscow 1968
B. Bosworth, "Phase II: The US Experiment with an Incomes Policy", in: *Brookings Papers on Economic Activity*, 2:1972
W. Bowen, *The Wage-Price Issue*, Princeton 1960
L. Bower, "Unemployment Rate—Recent Trends Follow Movement in GNP Gap", in: Federal Reserve Bank of Dallas *Business Review*, Nov. 1972
S. Bowles, "Unequal Education and the Reproduction of the Hierarchical Division of Labor", in: R. Edwards, M. Reich and T. Weisskopf (ed.), *The Capitalist System*, Englewood Cliffs 1972
M. Bowman, "The Consumer in the History of Economic Doctrine", in: *American Economic Review*, XLI/2 (May 1951), 1–18
R. Boyer/H. Morais, *Labor's Untold Story*, NY 1970
H. Branson/H. Jung, "Trends in U.S. Trade and Comparative Advantage", in: *Brookings Papers on Economic Activity*, 2:1971
B. Brecht, "Schwierige Lage der deutschen Intellektuellen" in: *Gesammelte Werke*, vol. XX, Ffm. 1967
B. Bregel, *Kredit i kreditnaia sistema kapitalizma*, Moscow 1948
C. Bresciani-Turroni, *The Economics of Inflation. A Study of Currency Depreciation in Post-War Germany*, London 1931
P. Brissenden, *The IWW*, NY 1920
J. Brittain, "The Incidence of Social Security Payroll Taxes", in: *American Economic Review*, LXI/1 (March 1971)
— *The Payroll Tax for Social Security*, Washington, D. C. 1972
S. Brittan, "Why the poor need help when we join the Market", in: *Financial Times*, 13.4.1972
T. Brooks, "Job Satisfaction: An Elusive Goal", in: *The American Federationist*, LXXIX/10 (Oct. 1972)
W. Brown Jr., *The International Gold Standard Reinterpreted, 1914–1934*, 2 vols., NY 1940
N. Bruck/F. Lees, "Foreign Content of US Corporate Activities", in: *Financial Analysts Journal*, XXII/5 (Sept.–Oct. 1966)
J. Buchanan/R. Wagner, *Public Debt in a Democratic Society*, Washington, D. C. 1967

N. Bucharin, *Die Politische Ökonomie des Rentners*, Berlin 1926
G. Burck, "The Building Trades versus the People", in: *Fortune*, LXXXII/4 (Nov. 1970)
W. Burke, "Factories on the Border", in: Federal Reserve Bank of San Francisco *Monthly Review*, December 1971
Busch, Schöller and Seelow, *Weltmarkt und Währungskrise*, Bremen 1971
W. Butler/J. Deaver, "Gold and the Dollar", in: *Foreign Affairs*, XLVI/1 (Oct. 1967)

E. Cannan, "Total Utility and Consumers' Surplus", in: *Economica IV* (1924)
P. Capdevielle/A. Neef, "Productivity and unit labor costs in 12 industrial countries", in: *Monthly Labor Review*, Nov. 1973, p. 14–21
F. Cardoso, "Das 'Brasilianische Entwicklungsmodell': Daten und Perspektiven", in: *Probleme des Klassenkampfs*, 6, March 1973, pp. 75–97
E. Carr, *The Twenty Years' Crisis, 1919–1939*, NY 1964 (1939)
S. Castle/G. Kosack, "The Function of Labour Immigration in Western European Capitalism", in: *New Left Review*, 73, May-June 1972
R. Caves (ed.), *Britain's Economic Prospects*, Washington, D.C. 1968
E. Chamberlin, *The Theory of Monopolistic Competition*, Cambridge 1935
L. Chandler, *The Economics of Money and Banking*, NY 1948
— *Inflation in the United States 1940–1948*, NY 1951
P. Cinanni, *Emigration und Imperialismus*, Munich [n.d. 1971]
J. B. Clark, *The Distribution of Wealth*, NY 1965 (1899)
J. M. Clark, "Financing High-Level Employment", in: P. Homan/F. Machlup (ed.), *Financing American Prosperity*, NY 1945
— *Studies in the Economics of Overhead Costs*, Chicago 1923
S. Clarke, *Central Bank Cooperation: 1924–31*, NY 1967
R. Clemens, *The American Livestock and Meat Industry*, NY 1923
G. Cloos, "The Coming Upsurge in Employment", in: Federal Reserve Bank of Chicago *Business Conditions*, Nov. 1971
M. Cogoy, "Werttheorie und Staatsausgaben", in: Braunmühl et al., *Probleme einer materialistischen Staatstheorie*, Frankfurt/Main 1973, pp. 129–198
B. Cohen, *Adjustment Costs and the Distribution of New Reserves*, Princeton Studies in International Finance, 18, 1966
— "Measuring the benefits and costs of sterling", in: *Euromoney*, I/4 (Sept. 1969), 10–12; I/11 (April 1970), 39–43
— "Reparations in the Postwar Period: A Survey", in: Banca Nazionale del Lavoro *Quarterly Review*, 82, Sept. 1967
— "Tariff Preferences for the Third World", in: *Intereconomics*, 9/1970
D. Cohen/M. Lazerson, "Education and the Corporate Order", in: Edwards, Reich and Weisskopf (ed.), *The Capitalist System*, Englewood Cliffs 1972
M. Cohen, "The Direct Effects of Federal Manpower Programs in Reducing Unemployment", in: *Journal of Human Resources*, IV/4 (fall 1969), 491–507
Commercial Office of the Italian Embassy, Italy: *An Economic Profile 1970*, Washington, D.C. 1971
F. Cook, "Hard-hats: The Rampaging Patriots", in: *The Nation*, June 15, 1970, pp. 712–19
S. Coontz, *Productive Labour and Effective Demand*, London 1965

R. Cooper, *Currency Devaluation in Developing Countries*, Princeton Essays in International Finance, 86, June 1971
— "Postscript", in: F. Hirsch, *Money International*, Harmondsworth 1969
D. Cordtz, "Corporate Farming: A Tough Row to Hoe", in: *Fortune*, LXXXVI/2 (Aug. 1972)
L. Corey, *The Decline of American Capitalism*, NY 1934
— *Meat and Man: A Study of Monopoly, Unionism and Food Policy*, NY 1950
CP USA, *The "Productivity" Hoax*, NY 1970
P. Crosser, *Economic Fictions*, NY 1957
— *State Capitalism in the Economy of the United States*, NY 1960
M. Curtis, "Is Money Saving Equal to Investment?", in: *Quarterly Journal of Economics*, LI (1936–37), pp. 604–25

J. Darrell, "The Economic Consequences of Mr. Keynes", in: *Science and Society*, I/2 (Winter 1937)
T. Davis, "Bank Holdings of Municipal Securities", in: Federal Reserve Bank of Kansas City *Monthly Review*, December 1970
— "Bank Holdings of U.S. Government Securities", in: Federal Reserve Bank of Kansas City *Monthly Review*, July-August 1971
E. Deakins, *EEC Problems for British agriculture*. Fabian tract 408, London 1971
P. Deane, *The First Industrial Revolution*, Cambridge 1965
P. Dean/W. Cole, *British Economic Growth*, Cambridge 1967
S. Dell, *Trade Blocs and Common Markets*, NY 1963
H. Denis, *La valeur*, Paris 1950
E. Denison, *Why Growth Rates Differ*, Washington, D. C. 1967
B. Dennis, "Sweden and Foreign Trade", in: Royal Ministry for Foreign Affairs, *Sweden in Europe 1971*, n.d.
H.-U. Deppe, "Zur Morphologie von Unfällen bei der Arbeit", in: *Das Argument*, XIII/11–12 (December 1971)
E. Despres et al., "The Dollar and World Liquidity—A Minority View", in: *Economist*, February 5, 1966, pp. 526–29
W. Deutermann, "Educational Attainments of Workers, March 1973", in: *Monthly Labor Review*, Jan. 1974, pp. 58–62
C. Deutschmann, *Der linke Keynesianismus*, Frankfurt/Main 1973
M. Diab, *The United States Capital Position and the Structure of its Foreign Trade*, Amsterdam 1956
W. Diebold Jr., *The End of the I.T.O.*, in: *Princeton Essays in International Finance*, 16, October 1952
D. Dillard, *The Economics of John Maynard Keynes*, NY 1955
"Discouraged Workers and the Unemployment Rate", in: Federal Reserve Bank of Cleveland, *Economic Commentary*, March 27, 1972
M. Dobb, "A Sceptical View of the Theory of Wages", in: *Economic Journal*, XXXIX (Dec. 1929)
— *Capitalism, Development and Planning*, NY 1970
— *Economic Growth and Underdeveloped Countries*, NY 1967
— *On Economic Theory and Socialism*, London 1955
— *Political Economy and Capitalism*, London 1968 (1937)
— *Soviet Economic Development since 1917*, London 1966
— *Wages*, Cambridge 1966 (1928)
— *Welfare Economics and the Economics of Socialism*, Cambridge 1969
E. Domar, "Full Capacity vs. Full Employment Growth: Comment", in:

Quarterly Journal of Economics, LXVII/4 (Nov. 1953)
R. Dorfman, *Prices and Markets*, Englewood Cliffs 1972²
P. Douglas, "Personnel Problems and the Business Cycle", in: *Administration*, IV (July 1922)
— *Real Wages in the United States 1890-1926*, Boston 1930
— *The Theory of Wages*, NY 1934
A. Downs, *An Economic Theory of Democracy*, NY 1957
J. Duesenberry, *Business Cycles and Economic Growth*, NY 1958
— *Income, Saving and the Theory of the Consumer*, NY 1967 (1949)
S. Dvoilatskiy, *Germaniia v godu 1923*, Moscow 1924

J. Early, "Factors affecting trends in real spendable earnings", in: *Monthly Labor Review*, May 1973, pp. 16-19
O. Eckstein, "Financing the System of Social Insurance", in: W. Bowen (ed.), *The Princeton Symposium on the American System of Social Insurance*, Princeton 1967
Economic Report of the President, Washington D. C. 1950, 1962, 1969-74
R. Edwards, "Who Fares Well in the Welfare State?", in: Edwards, Reich and Weisskopf (eds.), *The Capitalist System*, Englewood Cliffs 1972
L. Eisenstein, *The Ideologies of Taxation*, NY 1961
L. Eisner, *Fremdarbeiterpolitik in Westdeutschland*, Berlin 1970
R. Eisner, "Accelerated Amortization, Growth and Net Profits", in: *Quarterly Journal of Economics*, LXVI/4 (Nov. 1952)
— "Depreciation Allowances, Replacement Requirements and Growth", in: *American Economic Review*, XLII/5 (Dec. 1952)
W. Eitelman/G. Guthrie, "The Shape of the Average Cost Curve", in: *American Economic Review*, XLII/5 (Dec. 1952)
F. Elster, "Bevölkeurungswesen", in: *Handwörterbuch der Staatswissenschaften*, Vol. II, Jena 1899
R. Ely/G. Wehrwein, *Land Economics*, Madison 1964 (1940)
A. Emmanuel, *L'échange inégal*, Paris 1969
F. Engels, "Anteil der Arbeit an der Menschwerdung der Affen", in: *MEW*, XX
— "Der Handelsvertrag mit Frankreich", in: *MEW*, XIX
— Herrn Eugen Dührings Umwälzung der Wissenschaft, in: *MEW*, XX
— Die Lage der arbeitenden Klasse in England, in: *MEW*, II
— "Preface" to the American Edition of Lage der Arbeitenden Klasse in England, in: *MEW*, XXI
— "Der Sozialismus des Herrn Bismarck", in: *MEW*, XIX
— "Umrisse zu einer Kritik der Nationalökonomie", in: *MEW*, I
— Zur Wohnungsfrage, in: *MEW*, XVIII
R. Entov, *Gosudarstvennyi kredit SShA v periode imperializma*, Moscow 1967
R. Erbe, *Die nationalsozialistische Wirtschaftspolitik im Lichte der modernen Theorie*, Zurich 1958
P. Erdós, *Contributions to the Theory of Capitalist Money, Business Fluctuations and Crises*, Budapest 1971
L. Erhard, *Wohlstand für alle*, Düsseldorf 1957
A. Evenitsky, "Marx' Model of Expanded Reproduction", in: *Science and Society*, XXVII/2 (Spring 1963)

A. Fatemi, "The Green Revolution: an appraisal", in: *Monthly Review*, XXIV/2 (June 1972)

Federal Reserve System, *Purposes and Functions*, Washington, D. C. 1963
H. Feis, *Europe The World's Banker, 1870–1914*, NY 1965 (1930)
T. Finegan, "Labor force growth and the return to full employment", in: *Monthly Labor Review*, XCV/2 (February 1972)
Fischer Weltalmanach 1974, Frankfurt/Main 1973
W. Fischer/E. Rondholz, "Revolution und Konterrevolution in Griechenland 1936–1970", in: *Das Argument*, XII/2–3, 57 (May 1970)
A. Fisher, *International Aspects of Full Employment in Great Britain*, London 1946
H. Fisher, *The Portugal Trade*, London 1971
R. Fitch/M. Oppenheimer, "Who Rules the Corporations?", in: *Socialist Revolution*, I/4, 73–107; I/5, 61–114; I/6, 33–94 (July-December 1970)
S. v. Flatov/F. Huisken, "Zum Problem der Ableitung des bürgerlichen Staates", in: *Probleme des Klassenkampfs*, 7, May 1973
D. Fleming, *The Cold War and Its Origins, 1917–1960*, 2. vols., London 1961
P. Foner, *History of the Labor Movement in the United States*, 4 vols., NY 1962ff.
D. Francis, "The Flexible Exchange Rate: Gain or Loss to the United States?", in: *Federal Reserve Bank of St. Louis Review*, Nov. 1971
J. Francis, "Has the Inventory Cycle Lost its Oomph?", in: *Federal Reserve Bank of Philadelphia Business Review*, February 1973, pp. 19–27
A. Frank, *Capitalism and Underdevelopment in Latin America*, NY 1969
— "The Development of Underdevelopment", in: R. Rhodes (ed.), *Imperialism and Underdevelopment*, NY 1971
— *Latin America: Underdevelopment or Revolution*, NY/London 1970
L. Fraser, *Economic Thought and Language*, London 1937
O. Freeman, "Malthus, Marx and the North American Breadbasket", in: *Foreign Affairs*, XLV/4 (July 1967)
M. Friedman, *Capitalism and Freedom*, Chicago 1964
M. Friedman/A. Schwartz, *A Momentary History of the United States, 1867–1960*, Princeton 1963
C. Friedrich (ed.), *Totalitarianism*, NY 1964
H. Friedrich et al., *Frauenarbeit und technischer Wandel*, Frankfurt/Main 1973
I. Friend/S. Schor, "Who Saves?", in: *Review of Economics and Statistics*, XLV/2, part 2 (May 1959)
A. Frumkin, *Modern Theories of International Economic Relations*, Moscow 1969
A. Frumkin/G. Roginskiy, "'Est' li 'ratsional'noe zerno' v burzhuaznoy teorii vneshney torgovlii?", in: *Vneshniaia torgovlia*, 11/1961, pp. 20–31
C. Furtado, *Economic Development of Latin America*, Cambridge 1970

J. Galbraith, *American Capitalism*, Boston 1956
— *The Great Crash*, Boston 1955
— *The New Industrial State*, NY 1968
W. Galenson/H. Leibenstein, "Investment Criteria, Productivity and Economic Development", in: *Quarterly Journal of Economics*, LXIX (Aug. 1955), 343–70
W. Galenson/A. Zeller, "International Comparisons of Unemployment Rates", in: National Bureau of Economic Research, *The Measurement and Behavior of Unemployment*, Princeton 1957
L. Galloway, "Negative Income Tax Rates and the Elimination of Poverty", *National Tax Journal*, XIX/3 (Sept. 1966), p. 298–307

R. Gardner, *Sterling-Dollar Diplomacy,* Ocford 1956
J. Gastwirth, "The Estimation of the Lorenz Curve and the Gini Index", in: *Review of Economics and Statistics,* LIV/3 (Aug. 1972), 306ff.
GATT, *International Trade 1970,* Genf, no year
S. Geiselberger (ed.), *Schwarzbuch: Ausländische Arbeiter,* Frankfurt/Main 1972
A. Gerschenkron, *Economic Backwardness in Perspective,* Cambridge 1966
H. Gerstenberger, *Zur politischen Ökonomie der bürgerlichen Gesellschaft,* Frankfurt/Main 1973
R. Gilbert et al., *An Economic Program for American Democracy,* NY 1938
E. Gilboy, "The Propensity to Consume", in: *Quarterly Journal of Economics,* LIII/1 (Nov. 1938)
— "Reply", in: *Quarterly Journal of Economics,* LIII/4 (Aug. 1939)
J. Gillman, *Prosperity in Crisis,* NY 1965
H. Giersch/R. Richter, *Beiträge zur Multiplikatortheorie,* Berlin (West) 1954
E. Gilpatrick, *Structural Unemployment and Aggregate Demand,* Baltimore 1966
M. Godelier, *Rationalité et irrationalité en économie,* Paris 1966
R. Goldsmith, *The Flow of Capital Funds in the Postwar Economy,* NY 1965
N. Goldfinger, "The Myth of Housing Cost", in: *The American Federationist,* Dec. 1969
L. Goodwin, *Do The Poor Want to Work?,* Washington, D. C. 1972
M. Gordon, "A Case History of U.S. Subersion: Guatemala 1954", in: *Science & Society,* XXXV/2 (Summer 1971), 129–55
A. Gorz, *Stratégie ouvrière et neocapitalisme,* Paris 1964
K. Gossweiler, *Ökonomie und Politik in Deutschland 1914–1932,* Berlin 1971
F. Graham, Exchange, Prices and Production in Hyper-Inflation Germany, 1920–1923, Princeton 1930
V. Grant, "The Multinational Company", in: Federal Reserve Bank of Chicago, *The International Monetary System in Transition,* Chicago 1972
C. Greenwald, "The Changing Composition of the Unemployed", in: Federal Reserve Bank of Boston, *New England Economic Review,* July–Aug. 1971, pp. 2–10
— "Working Mothers: The Need for More Part-Time Jobs", in: Federal Reserve Bank of Boston, *New England Economic Review,* Sept.–Oct. 1972
K. Griffin, *Underdevelopment in Spanish America,* London 1969
H. Großmann, *Das Akkumulations- und Zusammenbruchsgesetz des kapitalistischen Systems,* Leipzig 1929
J. Grunwald, "Foreign Private Investment: The Challenge of Latin American Nationalism", in: *Virginia Journal of International Law,* XI/2 (March 1971)
R. Gündel, "Beziehungen zwischen Außenhandel, Kapitalverwertung und Wachstum" in: G. Kohlmey (ed.), *Außenwirtschaft und Wachstum,* Berlin 1968, p. 46–76
E. Guevara, "The Cuban Economy", in: *Venčeremos! The speeches and Writings of Che Guevara,* edited by J. Gerassi, NY 1968, pp. 349–59
J. Gurley, "Federal Tax Policy", in: *National Tax Journal,* XX/3 (Sept. 1967)
B. Gustafsson, "Fragen der Verstaatlichung in Schweden", in: *Nordeuropa: Jahrbuch für nordische Studien,* 1/1966
— "Rostow, Marx and the Theory of Economic Growth", in: *Science and*

Society, XXV/3 (Summer 1961), 229–44
E. Gutenberg, *Grundlagen der Betriebswirtschaftslehre,* vol. I, Berlin (West) 1961

W. Haber, *Industrial Relations in the Building Industry,* Cambridge 1930
W. Haber/H. Levinson, *Labor Relations and Productivity in the Building Trades,* Ann Arbor 1956
G. von Haberler, "Mr. Keynes Theory of the Multiplier", in: *Zeitschrift für Nationalökonomie,* VII (1936), 299–335
— *Prosperity and Depression,* Geneva 1939
— *A Survey of International Trade Theory,* rev. ed., in: *Princeton Special Papers in International Economics,* 1, 1967
E. Hadley, *Antitrust in Japan,* Princeton 1970
— "Trust-Busting in Japan", in: *Harvard Business Review,* XXXVI/4 (July 1948)
R. Hall, "Why is the Unemployment Rate so High at Full Employment?", in: *Brookings Papers on Economic Activity,* 3:1970, pp. 369–402
R. Hall/C. Fitch, "Price Theory and Business Behavior", in: *Oxford Economic Papers,* 2, May 1939
F. Halliday, "The Ceylonese Insurrection", in: *New Left Review,* 69, Sept.–Oct. 1971
M. Halperin, "Growth and Crisis in the Latin American Economy", in: *Science & Society,* XXV/3 (Summer 1961), 192–228
U. Hampicke, *Zur Kritik der bürgerlichen Agrarökonomie,* Stuttgart 1974
A. Hansen, *Business Cycles and National Income,* NY 1951
— *Economic Policy and Full Employment,* NY/London 1947
— "The Economics of the Soviet Challenge", in: *Economic Record,* XXXVI/73 (March 1960)
— *Fiscal Policy and Business Cycles,* NY 1941
— *A Guide to Keynes,* NY 1953
— "Stability and Expansion", in: P. Homan/F. Machlup (eds.), *Financing American Prosperity,* NY 1945
S. Harris (ed.), *The New Economics,* NY 1948
— *Post-War Economic Problems,* NY 1943
R. Harrod, *The Life of John Maynard Keynes,* London 1951
C. Harshberger, "Farm Firm Growth: Transition to an Industrialized Agriculture?", in: Federal Reserve Bank of Kansas City *Monthly Review,* May 1971
— "The Role of Financial Management in Agriculture", in: Federal Reserve Bank of Kansas City *Monthly Review,* July–Aug. 1972
F. Hartog, "Trade Arrangements Among Countries: Effects on the Common Market", in: B. Balassa (ed.), *Studies in Trade Liberalization,* Baltimore 1967
M. Hauser, "A Survey of Recent Developments in Social Security in The United Kingdom", in: *Social and Economic Administration,* IV/2 (April 1970)
E. Hawley, *The New Deal and the Problem of Monopoly,* Princeton 1966
R. Hawtrey, *The Gold Standard in Theory and Practice,* London/NY 1947[5]
F. Hayek, *The Road to Serfdom,* Chicago 1967
T. Hayter, *Imperialism as Aid,* Harmondsworth 1971
R. Heflebower, "Full Costs, Cost Changes and Prices", in: National

Bureau of Economic Research, *Business Concentration and Price Policy*, Princeton 1955
G. Hegel, *Phänomenologie des Geistes*, in: Werke, vol. II, Frankfurt/Main 1970
— *Wissenschaft der Logik*, in: Werke, vol. V–VI, Frankfurt/Main 1970
H. Hegeland, *The Multiplier Theory*, Lund 1954
R. Heilbroner, *The Economic Problem*, Englewood Cliffs 1970
— *The Making of Economic Society*, Englewood Cliffs 1962
R. Hellmann, *Amerika auf dem Europamarkt*, Baden-Baden 1966
— *The Challenge to US Dominance of the International Corporation*, NY 1970
H. Henderson, *Supply and Demand*, NY 1922
P. Henle, "Exploring the distribution of earned income" in: *Monthly Labor Review*, XCV/12 (Dec. 1972)
E. Hennig, *Thesen zur deutschen Sozial-und Wirtschaftsgeschichte 1933 bis 1938*, Frankfurt/Main 1973
H. Hesse, "Die Bedeutung der reinen Theorie des Außenhandels in der Nachkriegszeit", in: *Zeitschrift für die gesamten Staatswissenschaften*, CXXII/2, 221–36
J. Hickey, "Changes in state unemployment insurance", in: *Monthly Labor Review*, Jan. 1974, pp. 39–46
J. Hicks, *Value and Capital*, Oxford 1965 (1946)^2
— "The Valuation of Social Income", in: *Economica*, New Series, VII/26 (May 1940)
J. Hightower, *Hard Tomatoes, Hard Times: The Failure of the Land Grant Colleges Complex*, Washington, D. C. 1972
R. Hilfderding, *Das Finanzkapital*, Berlin 1947 (1910)
F. Hirsch, *Money International*, Harmondsworth 1969
A. Hirschman, *How to Divest in Latin America and Why*, in: *Princeton Essays in International Finance*, 76, 1969
— *The Strategy of Economic Development*, New Haven 1960
A. Hitler, *Es spricht der Führer*, edited by H. von Kotze/H. Krausnick, Gütersloh 1966
— *Mein Kampf*, Munich 1940
T. Hobbes, *Philosophic Rudiments concerning Government and Society* [1651], in: *The English Works of Thomas Hobbes*, ed. by von Molesworth, Vol. II, London 1841
E. Hobsbawm, *Labouring Men*, Garden City 1967
J. Hodann, "Neue Techniken im Automobilbau—Berichte über die Entwicklung in Schweden", lecture held Nov. 8/9, 1973 in Böblingen, Ms.
J. Hoffmann et al., "Zu einigen Aspekten der Klassenkämpfe in Westeuropa in den 60er Jahren anhand aktueller Untersuchungen", in: *Probleme des Klassenkampfs*, 3, May 1972, pp. 105–27.
W. Hoffmann, "Der Anteil der Verteidigungsausgaben am BSP—ein internationaler und intertemporeller Vergleich", in: *Kyklos*, XXIII (1970), 80–95
M. Horkheimer, *Dämmerung*, Zürich 1934
D. Horowitz, *The Free World Colossus*, NY 1965
H. Houthakler, "The US Balance of Payments—A Look Ahead", in: U.S. Commission on International Trade and Investment Policy, *U.S. International Economic Policy in an Interdependent World*, Washington, D.C. 1971, Vol. I

L. Hubbard, *Soviet Money and Finance*, London 1936
L. Huberman, *The Labor Spy Racket*, NY 1937
M. Hudson, *Super-Imperialism*, NY 1972
H. Hüppauff, "Fordstreik, Anti-Streik-Gesetze und der Mythos der Militanz", in: *Sozialistische Politik*, 3 (October 1969), pp. 14–34
G. Hufbauer/F. Adler, *Overseas Manufacturing Investment and the Balance of Payments*, Washington, D.C. 1968
J. Huffschmid, *Die Politik des Kapitals*, Frankfurt/Main 1971
F. Huisken, *Zur Kritik bürgerlicher Didaktik und Bidungsökonomie*, Munich 1973
I. Hume, "Migrant Workers in Europe", in: *Finance and Development*, X/1 (March 1973), 2–6
T. Humphrey, "Changing Views on Comparative Advantage", in: Federal Reserve Bank of Richmond *Monthly Review*, July 1972
— "Domestic International Sales Corporation", in: Federal Reserve Bank of Richmond *Monthly Review*, June 1972
— "Income Distribution and Its Measurement, Part I", in: Federal Reserve Bank of Richmond *Monthly Review*, Aug. 1971; "Part II", Oct. 1971
E. Hunt/H. Sherman, *Economics*, NY 1972
— *Instructor's Manuel to Accompany "Economics"*, NY 1972
L. Hunt, "Money Stock—Attention to Series Increases As Link to Economy Discussed", in: Federal Reserve Bank of Dallas *Business Review*, Sept. 1972
R. Huntford, *The New Totalitarians*, NY 1972
W. Hutt, *The Theory of Collective Bargaining*, Glencoe 1954 (1930)
S. Hymer, "The Multinational Corporation and the Law of Uneven Development", in: J. Bhagwati (ed.), *Economics and World Order*, NY 1972
S. Hyner/R. Rowthorn, "Multinational Corporations and International Oligopoly: the Non-American Challenge", in: C. Kindleberger (ed.), *The International Corporation*, Cambridge 1970, pp. 57–91
IBRD, *Policies and Operations*, June 1971
International Labour Organisation, *Some Growing Employment Problems in Europe*, Geneva 1973
— *Year Book of Labour Statistics*, Geneva 1971
IMF/IBRD, *The Problem of Stabilization of Prices of Primary Products*, Washington, D.C. 1969
A. Imlah, *Economic Elements in the Pax Britannica*, Cambridge 1958
Imperialismus heute, Berlin 1968
N. Inozemtsev et al., *Politicheskaia ekonomiia sovremennogo monopolisticheskogo kapitalizma*, Moscow 1970, Vol. I

Jahresgutachten 1973 des Sachverständigenrates zur Begutachtung der gesamtwirtschaftlichen Entwicklung, Deutscher Bundestag, 7. Wahlperiode, Drucksache 7/1273
P. Jalée, *L'impérialisme en 1970*, Paris 1970
— *The Pillage of the Third World*, NY 1968
H. Jevons, *Essays on Economics*, London 1905
S. Jevons, *Theory of Political Economy*, Harmondsworth 1970 (1871)
F. Johnson, "Changes in workmen's compensation laws in 1973", in: *Monthly Labor Review*, Jan. 1974, pp. 32–38

H. Johnson, "An Internationalist' Model", in: W. Adams (ed.), *The Brain Drain*, NY 1968, pp. 69–91
— *Comparative Cost and Commercial Policy: Theory for a Developing World Economy*, Stockholm 1968
— "Tariffs and Economic Development. Some Theoretical Issues", in: *Journal of Developmental Studies*, I/1 (Spring 1965)
— "World Trading and Monetary Arrangements", in: J. Bhagwati (ed.), *Economics and World Order*, NY 1972
H. Jung, "Internationale Konzerne heute", in: *Marxistische Blätter*, IX/3 (May–June 1971)
H. Jung/R. Rhomberg, "Prices and Export Performance of Industrial Countries 1953–1963", in: *IMF Staff Papers*, July 1965, pp. 224–71

R. Kahn, "The Relation of Home Investment to Unemployment", in: *Economic Journal*, XLI/162 (June 1931), pp. 173–98
M. Kalecki, "Political Aspects of Full Employment," in: *Selected Essays on the Dynamics of the Capitalist Economy 1933–1970*, Cambridge 1971
— "Three Ways to Full Employment", in: Oxford University Institute of Statistics, *The Economics of Full Employment*, Oxford 1945
S. Kaliski, "Structural Unemployment in Canada: Toward a Definition of the Geographic Dimension", in: *Canadian Journal of Economics*, I/3 (Aug. 1968), 551–65
K. Kapp, *The Social Costs of Private Enterprise*, Cambridge 1950
A. Kaplan, *Big Enterprise in a Competitive System*, Washington, D.C. 1964 (1954)
A. Kaplan et al., *Pricing in Big Business*, Washington, D. C. 1963
S. Katz, *The Case for the Par-Value System, 1972*, in: *Princeton Essays in International Finance*, 92, March 1972
K. Kauffman/H. Stalson, "U.S. Assistance to Less Developed Countries", in: *Foreign Affairs*, XLV/4 (July 1967)
K. Kautsky, *Die Agrarfrage*, Stuttgart 1899
— "Gold, Papier und Ware", in: *Die Neue Zeit*, XXX/1 (1911–12)
— "Goldproduktion und Teuerung", in: *Die Neue Zeit*, XXX/1 (1911–12), 213–30; XXXI/1 (1912–13), 557–63
M. Kawakami, "Relations Between Expanded Reproduction Schema and National Income and Inter-Industry Relations Table", in: The Science Council of Japan, Division of Economics, Commerce and Business Administration, *Economic Series*, Nr. 36, Tokyo, Feb. 1965
K. Kaysen/D. Turner, *Antitrust Policy*, Cambridge 1959
J. Kendrick, *Economic Accounts and Their Uses*, NY 1972
— "Productivity, costs and prices: Concepts and Measures", in: *The American Assembly, Wages, Prices, Profits and Productivity*, NY 1959
P. Kenen, *International Economics*, Englewood Cliffs 1967
— "Nature, Capital and Trade", in: *Journal of Political Economy*, LXXIII/5 (Oct. 1965), 437–60
W. Kennet et al., *Sovereignty and the Multinational Companies*. Fabian tract 409, London 1971
J. Keynes, *The Economic Consequences of the Peace*, NY 1920
— *Essays in Biography*, NY 1963 (1951)
— *Essays in Persuasion*, NY 1932
— *The General Theory of Employment, Interest and Money*, London 1967 (1936)

- "The General Theory of Employment", in: *Quarterly Journal of Economics*, LI/2 (Febr. 1937)
- "National Self-Sufficiency", in: *Yale Review*, XXII/4 (Summer 1933)
- *A Tratise on Money*, 2 vols., NY 1930
J. Keynes/H. Henderson, *Can Lloyd George Do It?*, London 1929
P. Khalatbari, *Ökonomische Unterentwicklung*, Berlin 1971
- *Überbevölkerung in den Entwicklungsländern*, Berlin 1968
K. Kidder, "Wall Street: Before the Fall", in: Federal Reserve Bank of San Francisco *Monthly Review Supplement* 1970
C. Kindleberger, *American Business Abroad*, New Haven/London 1971
- *Europe's Postwar Growth*, Cambridge 1967
- *Foreign Trade and the National Economy*, New Haven 1964
- *International Economics*, Homewood 1963
- *The Politics of International Money and World Language*, Princeton Essays in International Finance, 61, Aug. 1967
A. Kirsanow, *Die USA und Westeuropa*, Berlin 1968
T. Kiss, *International Division of Labor in Open Economies*, Budapest 1971
E. Klee, (ed.), *Gastarbeiter*, Frankfurt/Main 1972
J. Knapp, "Capital Exports and Growth", in: *Economic Journal*, LXVII/267 (Sept. 1957), 432–42
J. Kochan, "The Market for State and Local Government Bonds", in: Federal Reserve Bank of Cleveland *Economic Review*, Aug.–Sept. 1972
K. Kock, *International Trade Policy and the Gatt 1947–1967*, Stockholm 1969
G. Kohlmey, "Karl Marx' Theorie von den internationalen Werten", in: *Probleme der Politischen Ökonomie*, V (1962)
- *Nationale Produktivität—dynamische Produktionen—internationale Arbeitseilung*, Berlin 1966
—"Zum Problem der Weltmarktpreise, besonders der Schere zwischen den Preisen für Primärerzeugnisse und Fertigwaren", in: K. Domdey et al., *Gegenwartsprobleme der internationalen Hendelsbeziehungen*, Berlin 1964, pp. 74–104.
M. Kolganov, *Natsionalniy dokhod*, Moscow 1953
S. Kolm, "La monétisation américaine du capital franąis", in: *Revue économique*, 6, Nov. 1967, pp. 1038–57
G. Kolko, *Wealth and Power in America*, NY 1968
Kommunist, "Die Entwicklung des Kapitals in der BRD und die Lage der Arbeiterklasse, 4/5, Westberlin, Dec. 1971
K. Korsch, *Arbeitsrecht für Betriebsräte*, Frankfurt/Main 1969
G. Kozlov, "Kapitalisticheskaia ekonomika i denezhnoe obrashchenie", in: *Planovoe khoziastvo*, 3, May–June 1947
- *O deystvii zakona stoimosti v usloviiakh sovremennogo kapitalizma*, Moscow 1964
O. Kratsch, "Bürgerliche betriebswirtschaftliche Apologetik zu den aktuellen Abschreibungsproblemen in Westdeutschland", in: *Probleme der Politischen Ökonomie*, III (1961), 210–60
- *Die Wirkungen der Amortisationen auf die Akkumulation des Kapitals im staatsmonopolistischen Kapitalismus*, Berlin 1962
L. Krause, *Sequel to Bretton Woods*, Washington, D. C. 1971
W. Krause, "Keynes und die faschistische Wirtschaftspolitik", in: *Konjunktur und Krise*, X/3 (1966), 239–48
- *Wirtschaftstheorie unter dem Hakenkreuz*, Berlin 1969
I. Kravis, *The Structure of Income*, Philadelphia 1962

W. Krelle, "Grenzproduktivitätstheorie des Lohns", in: *Jahrbuch für Nationalökonomie und Statistik,* CLXII/1 (Jan. 1950)

M. Kriwizki, "Die Lohntheorie der deutschen Sozialdemokratie", in: *Unter dem Banner des Marxismus,* III/3 (June 1929), 381-405

G. Kroll, *Von der Weltwirtschaftskrise zur Staatskonjunktur,* Berlin (West) 1958

J. Kuczynski, *Germany: Economic and Labor Conditions under Fascism,* NY 1945
— *Die Geschichte der Lage der Arbeiter unter dem Kapitalismus,* Berlin 1963 ff., Vol. 7a, 25, 30
— "Kann die wissenschaftlich-technische Revolution unter den Bedingungen des staatsmonopolistischen Kapitalismus durchgeführt werden?", in: *Wirtschaftswissenschaft,* XX/11 (Nov. 1972), 1691-99
— *Labour Conditions in Great Britain: 1750 to the Present,* NY 1946
— "Probleme der Entwicklung einer sozialistischen Landwirtschaft in Kuba", in: *Jahrbuch für Wirtschaftsgeschichte,* 1971/part I
— *Propheten der Wirtschaft,* Berlin 1970
— *A Short History of Labour Conditions Under Industrial Capitalism.* Vol. II. *The United States of America 1789 to the Present,* London 1943

H. Kühne, "Imperialistische Gegensätze und der neue Abschnitt in der Krise des spätkapitalistischen Währungssystems", in: *Wirtschaftswissenschaft,* XVII/2 (Febr. 1969)
— "Die Marxsche Theorie von der Funktion des Geldes als Weltgeld und deren Bedeutung für die Gestaltung und Beurteilung der Außenwirtschaftsprozesse in der Gegenwart", in: Kohlmey (ed.), *Außenwirtschaft und Wachstum,* Vol. III, Berlin 1968

S. Kuznets, "Economic Growth and Income Inequality", in: *American Economic Review,* XLV/1 (March 1955), 1-28
— *Modern Economic Growth,* New Haven 1966
— *National Income,* NY 1946
— *National Product in Wartime,* NY 1945
— "On the Valuation of Social Income—Reflections on Professor Hicks' Article", in: *Economica,* New Series, XV/57 (Febr. 1948)
— "Quantitative Aspects of the Economic Growth of Nations: VIII. Distribution of Income by Size", in: *Economic Development and Cultural Change,* XI (Jan. 1963)
— "Underdeveloped Countries and the Pre-Industrial Phase in the Advanced Countries: an Attempt at Comparison", in: Agarwala/Singh (eds.), *The Economics of Underdevelopment,* London 1969

L. Kyle et al., "Who Controls Agriculture Now?—The Trends Underway", in: *Who Will Control U.S. Agriculture?,* North Central Regional Extension Pub. 21, University of Illinois, College of Agriculture, Special Publication 27, Urbana, Aug. 1972

D. Läpple, *Staat und allgemeine Produktionsbedingungen,* Westberlin 1973

I. Lambi, "The Agrarian-Industrial Front in Bismarckian Politics, 1873–1879", in: *Journal of Central European Affairs,* XX (Jan. 1961), 378-96
— "The Protectionist Interests of the German Iron and Steel Industry, 1873-1879", in: *Journal of Economic History,* XXII (March 1962), 59-70

E. Lande, *Kredit i koniunktur,* Moscow 1930

S. Larsson/K. Sjöström, "Välfärdsmyten i klassamhället—socialpolitik och socialvård i Sverige", in: *Zenit*, Nr. 18, May–June 1970

N. Lash, "What is money?", in: Federal Reserve Bank of Chicago *Business Conditions*, June 1971

F. Lassalle, *Das Arbeiterprogramm*, in: *Gesammelte Reden und Schriften*, edited by E. Bernstein, Vol. II, Berlin 1919

C. Layton, *Trans-Atlantic Investments*, Boulogne-sur-Seine 1968[2]

League of Nations, *International Currency Experience*, 1944

S. Lebergott, "Annual Estimates of Unemployment in the United States 1900–1954", in: National Bureau of Economic Research, *The Measurement and Behavior of Unemployment*, Princeton 1957

F. Lee, *Südafrika vor der Revolution*, n.d. [ca. 1966]

M. Lefkoe, *The Crisis in Construction*, Washington, D. C. 1970

H. Lehmann, *Grenznutzentheorie*, Berlin 1968

R. Lekachman, *The Age of Keynes*, NY 1968

A. Lemnitz/H. Schäfer, *Politische Ökonomie des Kapitalismus—Einführung*, Frankfurt/Main 1972

N. Lenin, "Die Agrarfrage und die "Marx-Kritiker"", in: *Werke*, Vol. V

— *Der Imperialismus als höchstes Stadium des Kapitalismus*, in: *Werke*, Vol. XXII

— *Neue Daten über die Entwicklungsgesetze des Kapitalismus in der Landwirtschaft*, in *Werke*, Vol. XXII

W. Leontief, "Domestic Production and Foreign Trade: The American Capital Position Re-Examined", in: J. Bhagwati (ed.), *International Trade*, Harmondsworth 1970

A. Lerner, "Savings and Investment", in: *Quarterly Journal of Economics*, LII (1937–38)

R. Lester, *The Economics of Labor*, NY 1941

M. Leven et al., *America's Capacity to Consume*, NY 1934

C. Levinson, *Wirtschaftskrise und Multinationale Konzerne*, Reinbeck 1973

C. Lewis, *America's Stake in International Investments*, Washington, D. C. 1938

— *The United States and Foreign Investment Problems*, Washington, D. C. 1948

W. Lewis, "Economic Development with Unlimited Supplies of Labour", in: Agarwala/Singh (eds.) *The Economics of Underdevelopment*, London 1969

R. Lidman, "The Distribution Implications of Agricultural Commodity Programs", in: U.S. Congress, Joint Economic Committee, Subcommittee on Priorities and Economy in Government, *The Economics of Federal Subsidy Programs*, Part 7 — Agricultural Subsidies, 93rd Cong., 1st Sess., April 30, 1973

A. Lindbeck, *The Political Economy of the New Left*, NY 1971

S. Linder, *An Essay on Trade and Transformation*, NY/Stockholm 1961

P. Lindert, *Key Currencies and Gold 1900—1913*, Princeton Studies in International Finance, 24, 1969

G. Lindner, "Die Krise als Steuerungsmittel: Eine Analyse der Bundesbankpolitik in den Jahren 1964–66/67", in: *Leviathan*, I/3 (Aug. 1973), 342–81

S. Lipset, *Political Man*, Garden City 1963

— "The Political Process in Trade Unions: A Theoretical Statement", in: W. Galenson/S. Lipset (eds.), *Labor and Trade Unionism*, NY 1960

R. Lipsey/P. Steiner, *Economics*, NY 1966; NY 1969
I. Little, *A. Critique of Welfare Economics*, Oxford 1965
L. Ljuboshits, *Voprosy marksistsko-leninskoi teorii agrarnykh krizisov*, Moscow 1949
J. Locke, *The Second Treatise of Government*
M. Lorenz, "Methods of Measuring the Concentration of Wealth", in: *Quarterly Publications of the American Statistical Association*, IX (June 1905)
G. Lukács, *Geschichte und Klassenbewußtsein*, Berlin 1923
— *Review of Bucharin, Theorie des historischen Materialismus*, in: *Archiv für die Geschichte des Sozialismus und der Arbeiterbewegung*, XI (1925), 216–24
E. Lundberg, "Sweden's Economy in an International Perspective", in: Skandinaviska Banken *Quarterly Review*, 1968:1
F. Lundberg, *The Rich and the Super-Rich*, NY 1969
C. Luttrell, Research Dept., Federal Reserve Bank of St. Louis, Project for Basic Monetary Studies, Working Paper 2, *Agribusiness*, August 1, 1967
F. Lutz, "The Outcome of the Saving-Investment Discussion", in: *Quarterly Journal of Economics*, LII (Aug. 1938), 588–614
R. Luxemburg, *Die Akkumulation des Kapitals*, Berlin 1923

F. Machlup, *The Book Value of Monetary Gold*, Princeton Essays in International Finance, 91, Dec. 1971
— *Plans for Reform of the International Monetary System*, Princeton Special Papers in International Economics, 3, 1964
— "The Price of Gold", in: *The Banker*, CXVII (Sept. 1968)
A. Maddison, *Economic Growth in the West*, NY 1967
H. Magdoff, *The Age of Imperialism*, NY 1969
S. Mallet, *La nouvelle classe ouvrière*, Paris 1963
T. Malthus, *Principles of Political Economy*, London 1820
E. Mandel, *Die deutsche Wirtschaftskrise*, Frankfurt/Main 1971
— *Die EWG und die Konkurrenz Europa-Amerika*, Frankfurt/Main 1968
— "Die Marxsche Theorie der ursprünglichen Akkumulation und die Industrialisierung der Dritten Welt", in: *Folgen einer Theorie. Essays über das Kapital von Karl Marx*, Frankfurt/Main 1967
— *Der Spätkapitalismus*, Frankfurt/Main 1973
— *Traité d'économie marxiste*, Paris 1969, 4 Vols.
K. Mandelbaum, "An Experiment in Full Employment. Controls in the German Economy, 1933–1938", in: Oxford University Institute of Statistics, *The Economics of Full Employment*, Oxford, 1945, pp. 181–203
A. Mandelstramm, "The Effects of Unions on Efficiency in the Residential Construction Industry: A Case Study", in: *Industrial Labor Relations Review*, XVIII/4 (July 1965), 503–21
Manual del Peronista, Buenos Aires 1948
A. Marshall, *Principles of Economics*, London 1969 (1920)
V. Martynov, *Sel'skoe khoziastvo SShA iego problemy*, Moscow 1971

K. Marx, "Arbeitslohn", in: *MEW*, VI
— "Arbeitslohn und Kapital", in: *MEW*, VI
— "Österreichs Bankrott", in: *MEW*, X
— *Das Elend der Philosophie*, in: *MEW*, IV
— *Grundisse der Kritik der Politischen Ökonomie*, Berlin 1953

- "Instructions for the Delegates of the Provisional Council. The Different Questions", in: Institut of Marxism-Leninism of the Central Committee of the CPSU, *The General Council of the First International 1864–1866,* Moscow, no year
- *Das Kapital, I–III,* in: *MEW,* XXIII–XXV
- "Lohn, Preis Profit", in: *MEW,* XVI
- "Rede über den Freihandel", in: *MEW,* IV
- *Resultate des unmittelbaren Produktionsprozesses,* Frankfurt/Main 1970
- *Theorien über den Mehrwert,* in: *MEW,* XXVI
- "Zur Judenfrage", in: *MEW,* I
- "Zur Kritik der Hegelschen Rechtsphilosophie", in: *MEW,* I
- *Zur Kritik der Politischen Ökonomie,* in: *MEW,* XIII

K. Marx/F. Engels, *Briefe,* in: *MEW,* XXVII–XXXIX
- *Die deutsche Ideologie,* in: *MEW,* III
- *Manifest der Kommunistischen Partei,* in: *MEW,* IV

E. Mason, *Economic Concentration and the Monopoly Problem,* NY 1964
P. Mattick, *Arbeitslosigkeit und Arbeitslosenbewegung in den USA 1929–1935,* Frankfurt/Main 1969
- "Gunnar Myrdal's Dilemma", in: *Science & Society,* XXXII/4 (Herbst 1968), 421–40
- *Marx and Keynes,* Boston 1969

H. Mayer, "Der erkenntnistheoretische Wert funktioneller Preistheorien", in: *Die Wirtschafts theorie der Gegenwart,* Vol. II, Vienna 1932
R. McCloskey, *The American Supreme Court,* Chicago 1967
G. McConnell, *Economics,* NY 1963[2]
B. McCormick, *Wages,* Harmondsworth 1969
J. McCulloch, *The Principles of Political Economy,* Edinburgh 1864
J. McKenna, *The Logic of Price,* Hinsdale 1973
R. McKinnon, *Monetary Theory and Controlled Flexibility in the Foreign Exchanges, Princeton Essays in International Finance,* 84, 1971
N. McKitternick/B. Middleton, *The Bankers of the Rich and the Bankers of the Poor: The Role of Export Credit in Development Finance,* Overseas Development Council, Monograph 6, Washington, D. C. 1972
R. McNamara, "Address to the Board of Governors", in: *IBRD, Summary Proceedings,* Washington, D. C. 1971; 1972; 1973
W. Medvedev, *Obshchestvennoe vosproizdvodstvo i sfera uslug,* Moscow 1968
P. Meek, *Open Market Operations,* Federal Reserve Bank of New York, 1969
R. Meek, "Malthus—Yesterday and Today", in: *Science and Society,* XVIII/1 (Winter 1954)
- "Some Thoughts on Marxism, Scarcity and Gosplan", in: *Oxford Economic Papers, New Series,* VII/3 (Oct. 1955), 281–99

A. Mehnert, *Bedürfnisse—Manipulierung—individuelle Konsumtion in der BRD,* Frankfurt/Main 1973
A. Mendel'son, *Teorii i istoriia ekonomicheskikh krizisov i tsiklov,* Vol. II, Moscow 1959
C. Menger, *Grundzüge der Volkswirtschaftslehre,* Vienna 1923
S. Menshikov, "Comment", in: M. Bronfenbrenner (ed.), *Is the Business Cycle Obsolete?,* NY 1969
- "Mekhanizm sovremennogo tsikla", in: A. Rumiantsev et al., *Sovremennye tsikly i krizisy,* Mowcow 1967
- *Millionaires and Managers,* Moscow 1969
- "Ustarel li ekonomicheskly tsikl?", in: *Mirovaia ekonomika i*

mezhdunarodnye otnosheniia, 8/1967, pp. 89–97
C. Mesa-Lago, "Availability and Reliability of Statistics in Socialist Cuba", in: *Latin America Research Review,* IV/2 (Summer 1969)
L. Meyer, "The Housing Shortage Goes Critical", in: *Fortune,* LXXX/7 (Dec. 1969)
J. St. Mill, *Essays on Some Unsettled Questions of Political Economy,* London 1874
— *Principles of Political Economy,* NY 1909
M. Millenson, "Growth of Government Spending", in: Federal Reserve Bank of Chicago, *Business Conditions,* Febr. 1973, pp. 6–15
H. Miller, *Income Distribution in the United States,* Washington, D. C. 1966
H. Milis/R. Montgomery, *The Economics of Labor,* NY 1938, 2 vols.
C. Mills, *White Collar,* NY 1967
D. Mills, *Industrial Relations and Manpower in Construction,* Cambridge 1972
B. Minhas, "The Homohypallagic Production Function, Factor Intensity Reversals and the Heckscher-Ohlin Theorem", *Journal of Political Economy,* LXX (1962), 138–56
B. Minc, *Zarys teorii kosztów produkcji i cen,* Warsaw 1958
Ministry of Foreign Affairs, *Factors in Japan's Growth,* Japan 1962

W. Mitchell, *Business Cycles,* vol. I: *The Problem and Its Setting,* NY 1927
— *Business Cycles and Their Causes,* Berkeley/Los Angeles 1941
Moody's Industrial Manual, NY 1972
G. Moore, "Comment", in: M. Bronfenbrenner (ed.), *Is the Business Cycle Obsolete?,* NY 1969
W. Moore, *Industrialization and Labor,* Ithaca 1951
T. Morgan, "Distribution of Income in Ceylon, Puerto Rico, United States and United Kingdom", in: *Economic Journal,* LXIII/252 (Dec. 1953)
O. Morgenstern, "Die Macht im Handel der Staaten: Ein Problem der Theorie des internationalen Handels", in: *Jahrbuch für Sozialwissenschaft,* XIV/3 (1963), 48–55
— *On the Accuracy of Economic Observations,* Princeton 1965
H. Morgenthau, *Germany Is Our Problem,* NY/London 1945
S. Morley/G. Smith, "Import Substitution and Foreign Investment in Brazil", in: *Rice University Program of Development Studies, Paper 5,* Spring 1970
J. Morray, The United States and Latin America", in:Petras/Zeitlin (eds.), *Latin America: Reform or Revolution?,* Greenwich 1969
H. Moulton, *Controlling Factors in Economic Development,* Washington D. C. 1949
D. Moynihan, *The Politics of a Guaranteed Income,* NY 1973
A. Müller-Armack, "Sozialpolitik in der sozialen Marktwirtschaft", in: *Wirtschaft, Gesellschaft und Kultur, Festgabe für A. Müller-Armack,* Berlin (West) 1961
— *Zum System sozialer Sicherung,* Cologne 1971
W. Müller, "Die Grenzen der Sozialpolitik in der Marktwirtschaft", in: G. Schäfer/C. Nedelmann (eds.), *Der CDU-Staat,* Munich 1967
W. Müller/C. Neusüß, "Die Sozialstaatsillusion und der Widerspruch von Lohnarbeit und Kapital", in: *Sozialistische Politik,* 6–7, June 1970
B. Muldau, *US-Investitionen in der EWG,* Hamburg 1966
R. Mundell, *The Dollar and the Policy Mix: 1971, Princeton Essays in International Finance,* 85, May 1971

G. Myers, *History of the Great American Fortunes*, NY 1936
H. Myint, "The Classical Theory of International Trade and the Underdeveloped Countries", in: *Economic Journal*, LXVIII/270 (June 1958), 315–37
G. Myers, *History of the Great American Fortunes*, NY 1936 H. Myint, "The Classical Theory of International Trade and the Underdeveloped Countries", in: *Economic Journal*, LXVIII/270 (June 1958), 315–37
— "An Interpretation of Economic Backwardness", in: *Oxford Economic Papers*, June 1954

T. Nakauchi, "Japan's Policy on Multinational Firms", in: *Economic and Business Bulletin*, XXIII/3 (Spring-Summer 1971), 29–36
W. Narr, "Der geplagte Epimetheur", in: *Leviathan*, II/1 (Febr. 1974), 133–55
A. Neef, "Unit labor costs in the United States and 10 other countries", *Monthly Labor Review*, July 1972
K. Nehls, *Kapitalwxport und Kapitalverflechtung*, Frankfurt/Main 1970
D. Netzer, *Economics of the Property Tax*, Washington, D. C. 1966
F. Neumann, *Behemoth*, NY 1966 (1942)
C. Neusüß et al., "Kapitalistischer Weltmarkt und Weltwährungskrise", in: *Probleme des Klassenkampfs*, Nr. 1, Nov. 1971
M. Nikitin, *Teorii stoimosti i ikh evoliutsia*, Moscow 1970
M. Nikolinakos, *Politische Okonomie der Gastarbeiterfrage*, Reinbeck 1973
— "Zur Frage der Auswanderungseffekte in den Emigrationsländern", in *Das Argument*, XIII/9–10 (Dec. 1971), 782–99
R. Nikolitch, U.S. Department of Agriculture, Economic Research Service, Agricultural Economic Report 175, "Our 31,000 Largest Farms", Washington, D. C. 1970
B. Nirumand, *Persien, Modell eines Entwicklungslandes*, Reinbek 1967
R. Nixon, "Asia After Vietnam", in: *Foreign Affairs*, XLVI/1 (Oct. 1967)
T. Noguzi, "Unternehmenskonzentration in Japan aus betriebswirtschaftlicher Sicht", in: H. Arndt (ed.), *Die Konzentration in der Wirtschaft*, Berlin (West) 1971² II, 183–202
W. Nordhaus, "The Worldwide Wage Explosion", in *Brookings Papers on Economic Activity*, 2:1972
E. Nourse, *America's Capacity to Produce*, NY 1934
R. Nurske, *Problems of Capital Formation in Underdeveloped Countries and Patterns of Trade and Development*, NY 1967
V. Nwaneri, "Income Distribution Criteria for the Analysis of Development Projects", in: *Finance and Development*, X/1 (March 1973)

J. O'Connor, "The Meaning of Economic Imperialism", in: R. Rhodes (ed.), *Imperialism and Underdevelopment*, NY 1971
OECD, *The Growth of Output 1960–1980* 1970
— *The Industrial Policy of Japan*, Paris 1972
— *Inflation*, Paris 1970
— *Labour Force Statistics*, Paris 1971
— *Manpower Statistics*, Paris 1965
— *Revenue Statistics of OECD Member Countries, 1968–1970*, Paris 1972
F. Oelssner, *Die Wirtschaftskrisen*, Berlin 1949
B. Ohlin, *Interregional and International Trade*, Cambridge 1935

D. Olatunbosun/S. Ilayide, "Output-Income Effects on Agricultural Export Pricing Strategy in Nigeria: The Case for Cocoa", in: *The Developing Economies,* IX/1 (March 1971)

Iu. Ol'sevich, "O burzhuaznoi konzeptsii 'Neoklassicheskoi Sintese' ", in: I. Dvorkin (ed.) *Kritika teorii sovremennykh burzhuaznykh ekonomistov,* Mowcow 1966

S. Olsson/G. Therborn, "Stuvarstrejk Ådalen 1970", in: *Zenit,* 19/1970

H. Oshima, "A Note on Income Distribution in Developed and Underdeveloped Countries", in: *Economic Journal,* LXVI/266 (March 1956), 155–60

M. Osterland et al., *Materialien zur Lebens- und Arbeitssituation der Industriearbeiter in der BRD,* Frankfurt/Main 1973

B. Ostrolenk, *The Surplus Farmer,* NY 1932

H. Parkes, *Marxism: An Autopsy,* Chicago 1964 (1939)

Partners in Development, London 1969

I. Pearce/S. James, "The Factor–Price Equalisation Myth", in: *Review of Economic Studies,* XIX (1951–52), 111–20

J. Pechman, *Federal Tax Policy,* rev. ed., Washington, DC 1971

— "The rich, the poor and the taxes they pay", in: *Public Interest,* **17,** Fall 1969

J. Pechmann et al., *Social Security,* Washington, D. C. 1968

J. Pechman/B. Okner, "Simulation of the Carter Commission Tax Proposals for the United States", in: *National Tax Journal,* XXII/1 (March 1969)

G. Pehl, *Gegenwartsfragen der öffentlichen Finanzpolitik.* 1967

R. Pelton (pseud.), "Who Rules America?", in: *Progressive Labor,* VII/4 (Febr. 1970)

J. Pen, *Income Distribution,* NY 1972

V. Perlo, *The Unstable Economy,* NY 1973

G. Perry, "Changing Labor Markets and Inflation", in: *Brookings Papers on Economic Activity,* 3:1970, pp. 411–41

— "Real Spendable Weekly Earnings", in: *Brookings Papers on Economic Activity,* 3:1972

— "Unemployment Flows in the United States Labor Market", in: *Brookings Papers on Economic Activity,* 2:1972

G. Persson/L. Berntson, "Svensk arbetsmarknadspolitik: från socialpolitik till liberalism", in: *Zenit,* **17,** March–April 1970

G. Picou, "Government Employment in the US", in: Federal Reserve Bank of Richmond *Monthly Review,* LVIII/4 (April 1972), 2–5

E. Piehl, *Multinationale Konzerne und internationale Gewerkschaftsbewegung,* Frankfurt/Main 1974

A. Pigou, *The Economics of Welfare,* London 1962 (1932)

— *Income,* London 1948

— *The Theory of Unemployment,* London 1933

F. Piven/R. Cloward, *Regulating the Poor,* NY 1971

S. Pizer, "Capital Restraint Programs", in: U.S. Commission on International Trade and Investment Policy, *U.S. International Economic Policy in an Interdependent World,* Washington, D. C. 1971, vol. 1

Politische Ökonomie des Sozialismus und ihre Anwendung der DDR, Berlin 1969

J. Polk, "U.S. Exports in Relation to Trade Abroad", in: B. Balassa (ed.), *Changing Patterns in Foreign Trade and Payments,* NY 1970

J. Polk et al., *US Production Abroad and the Balance of Payments*, NY 1966
R. Prebisch, "Commercial Policy in the Underdeveloped Countries", in: *American Economic Review*, XLIX/2 (May 1959), 251–73
E. Preiser, "Erkenntniswert und Grenzen der Grenzproduktivitätstheorie", in: *Schweizer Zeitschrift für Volkswirtschaft und Statistik*, LXXXIX/1 (Febr. 1953), 25–45
E. Preobrashenskij, *Die neue Ökonomik*, Berlin (West) 1971
Presse und Informationsbüro der Bundesregierung, *Germany Reports*. 1962³
K. Pritzkoleit, *Gott erhält die Mächtigen*, Dusseldorf 1963

J. Quirk/R. Saposnik, *Introduction to General Equilibrium Theory and Welfare Economics*, NY 1968

C. Ramond, "Marketing Science: Stepchild of Economics", in: S. Britt (ed.), *Consumer Behavior and Behavioral Sciences*, NY 1968
V. Rao, "Income, Investment and the Multiplier in an Underdeveloped Country", in: Agarwala/Singh (eds.), *The Economics of Underdevelopment*, London 1969, pp. 205–18
R. Rauner, *Samuel Bailey and the Classical Theory of Value*, London 1961
H. Recktenwald, *Tax Incidence and Income Redistribution*, Detroit 1971
A. Rees, *The Economics of Trade Unions*, Chicago 1963
H. Reichelt, *Zur logischen Struktur des Kapitalbegriffs bei Karl Marx*, Frankfurt/Main 1970
J. Renner, "National Restrictions on International Trade", in U.S. Commission on International Trade and Investment Policy, *U.S. International Economic Policy in an Interdependent World* Washington, D. C. 1971
K. Renner, *Das arbeitende Volk und die Steuern*, Vienna 1909
Report of the President's Committee on Urban Housing, Technical Studies, Washington, D. C. 1968, 2 vols.
— *A Decent Home*, n.d.
D. Ricardo, *Letters*, in: *The Works and Correspondence of David Ricardo*, edited by P. Straffa, Vol. VIII,IX
— *Notes on Malthus*, in: *Works and Correspondence*, London 1966, Vol. II
— *The Principles of Political Economy and Taxation*, London, n.d.
B. Richman, *Industrial Society in Communist China*, NY 1969
D. Ridder/C. Yandle, "Changes in Patterns and Prices in the International Trade in Rice", in: *IMF Staff Papers*, XIX/1 (March 1972)
G. Rimlinger, *Welfare Policy and Industrialization in Europe, America and Russia*, NY 1971
L. Robbins, *An Essay on the Nature and Significance of Economic Science*, London 1940 (1932)
— "The bicentary of David Ricardo", in: *Financial Times*, April 17, 1972, p. 27
M. Rist, *Le Federal Reserve et les difficultés monétaires d'après-guerre 1945–50*, Paris 1952
J. Robinson, "Disguised Unemployment", in: *Economic Journal*, XLVI/182 (June 1936)
— *Economic Philosophy*, Garden City 1964
— *The Economics of Imperfect Competition*, London 1950 (1933)
— *An Essay on Marxian Economics*, London 1967 (1942)

- "International Currency Proposals", in: *Economic Journal*, June–Sept. 1942
- "Marx, Marshall and Keynes", in: *Collected Economic Papers*, vol. II, Oxford 1960
R. Robinson, "Factor Proportions and Comparative Advantages: Part I", in: *Quarterly Journal of Economics*, LXX (May 1956), 169–92
- *Study Guide to Accompany Samuelson, Economics*, NY 1967
D. Rockefeller, "What Private Enterprise Means to Latin America", in: *Foreign Affairs*, XLIV/3 (April 1966)
F. Romig, *Die ideologischen Elemente in der neo-klassischen Theorie: Eine kritische Auseinandersetzung mit Paul A. Samuelson*, Berlin (West) 1971
R. Rosdolsky, *Zur Entstehungsgeschichte des Marxschen "Kapital"*, Frankfurt/Main 1968
S. Rosen, "Keynes Without Gadflies", in: T. Roszak (ed.), *The Dissenting Academy*, NY 1968
F. Rosenstein-Rodan, "Problems of Industrialization of Eastern and South-Eastern Europe", in: *Economic Journal*, LIII (1943)
A. Rosenthal, *The Social Programs of Sweden*, Minneapolis 1967
W. Rostow, *The Process of Economic Growth*, NY 1962
D. Rothman, "Of prisons, asylums and other decaying institutions", in: *The Public Interest*, 26, Winter 1972
J. Rousseau, *Le contrat social*
I. Rubin, "Alfred Amonn und das Objekt der theoretischen Nationalökonomie", in: *Unter dem Banner des Marxismus*, III/1 (Febr. 1929)
- *Ocherki po marksistkoi teorii stoimosti*, Moscow-Leningrad 1928
- *Sovremenny ekonomisty na zapade*, Moscow-Leningrad 1927
P. Rushing, "Cyclical and Structural Change in the US Trade Balance", in: *Federal Reserve Bank of Boston, New England Economic Review*, March–April 1972
B. Russett et al., *World Handbook of Political and Social Indicators*, New Haven 1964
S. Ruttenberg, "Updating the World of Trade", in: *American Federationist*, LXXX/2 (Febr. 1973)

M. Salvati, "Der Ursprung der gegenwärtigen Krise in Italien", in: *Probleme des Klassenkampfs*, Nr. 4, Sept. 1972
H. Samuel, "A New Perspective on World Trade", in: *The American Federationist*, LXXVIII/6 (June 1971), 10–14
P. Samuelson, "At Last, Devaluation", in: *New York Times*, Aug. 18, 1971, p. 37
- "Disparity in Postwar Exchange Rates", in: S. Harris (ed.), *Foreign Economic Policy for the United States*, Cambridge 1948, pp. 397–412
- "Economists and the History of Ideas", in: *American Economic Review*, LII/1 (March 1962), 1–18
- "The Empirical Implications of Utility Analysis", in: *Econometrica*, VI/4 (Oct. 1938), 344–56
- "Foreword", in: R. Poor (ed.), *4 Days 40 Hours*, Cambridge 1970
- *Foundations of Economic Analysis*, Cambridge 1971 (1947)
- "Full Employment After the War", in: S. Harris (ed.), *Postwar Economic Problems*, NY 1943, pp. 27–53

- "Full Employment versus Progress and other Economic Goals", in: M. Millikan (ed.), *Income Stabilization for a Developing Democracy*, New Haven 1953, pp. 547–82
- "The Gains from International Trade Once Again", in: *Economic Journal*, LXXII (Dec. 1962), 820–29
- "Inflation—der Preis des Wohlstands", in: *Der Spiegel*, 35/1971
- *Instructor's Manual to Accompany Samuelson: Economics*, NY 1964
- "International Trade and the Equalisation of Factor Prices", in: *Economic Journal*, LVIII/230 (June 1948), 163–84
- "Lord Keynes and the General Theory", in: *Econometrica*, July 1946
- "Marxian Economics as Economics", in: *American Economic Review*, LVII/2 (May 1967)
- "A Note on the Pure Theory of Consumer's Behavior", in: *Economica*, V/17 (Febr. 1938), 61–71
- *Readings in Economics*, NY 1967
- "Reflections on the Merits and Demerits of Monetarism", in: J. Diamond (ed.), *Issues in Fiscal and Monetary Policy*, DePaul University Press, 1971
- "Social Security", in: *Newsweek*, February 2, 1967, p. 88.
- "Taking Stock of War", in: *New York Times*, March 14, 1973, p. 43
- "The Theory of Pump-Priming Reexamined", in: *American Economic Review*, XXX/3 (Sept. 1940), 492–506
- "Theoretical Notes on Trade Problems", in: *Review of Economics and Statistics*, XLVI/3 (May 1964), 145–54
- "Unemployment Ahead", in: *The New Republic*, Sept. 11, 1944, pp. 297–99; Sept. 18, 1944, pp. 333–35
- "Wages and Interest: A Modern Dissection of Marxian Economic Models", in: *American Economic Review*, XLVII/6 (Dec. 1957), 884–912
- G. Stolper, "Protection and Real Wages", *Review of Economic Studies*, IX/1 (Nov. 1941), 58–73

Sanierung für wen?, Berlin (West), n.d.
J. Say, *A Treatise on Political Economy*, Philadelphia 1832
R. Sayers, *Modern Banking*, Oxford 1967
H. Schäfer, *Imperialismusthesen und Handelsgewinne*, Düsseldorf 1972
G. Schiller, "Die Auswanderung von Arbeitskräften als Problem der wirtschaftlichen Entwicklung", in: *Das Argument*, XIII/9–10 (Dec. 1971), 800–809
H. Schleicher, *Staatshaushalt und Strategie*, Berlin (West) 1971
A. Schlesinger, *Political and Social History of the United States 1829–1925*, NY 1928
E. Schmidt, *Die verhinderte Neuordnung*, Frankfurt/Main 1971
G. Schmölders et al., *John Maynard Keynes als "Psychologe"*, Berlin (West) 1956
J. Schnitker, "Changes Needed in Farm Legislation", in: U.S. Congress, Joint Economic Committee, Subcommittee on Priorities and Economy in Government, *The Economics of Federal Subsidy Programs, Part 7 – Agriculture*, 93rd Congress 1st Session, April 30, 1973
M. Schnitzer, *East and West Germany: A Comparative Economic Analysis*, NY 1972
- *The Economy of Sweden*, NY 1970

G. Schomburg, "Zur Politik der Weltbank, des Weltwährungsfonds und anderer internationaler kapitalistischer Finanzorganiationen

gegenüber den Entwicklungsländern", in: Domdey et al., *Gegenwartsprobleme der Internationalen Handelsbeziehungen*, Berlin 1964
W. Schöller, "Vorbemerkung zum nachfolgenden Aufsatz von F. H. Cardoso", in *Probleme des Klassenkampts*, 6, March 1973
B. Schüngel, "Zur Frage der Abhängigkeit der kapitalistischen Länder von den Rohstoffen der Dritten Welt (1. Teil)", in: *Das Argument*, XI/51 (April 1969)
T. P. Schultz, "Secular Trends and Cyclical Behavior of Income Distribution in the United States: 1944–1965", in: L. Soltow (ed.), *Six Papers on the Size Distribution of Wealth and Income*, NY 1969
T. W. Schultz, "Investment in Human Capital", in: *American Economic Review*, March 1963
— *Agriculture in an Unstable Economy*, NY/London 1945
— *Production and Welfare of Agriculture*, NY 1950
— "Value of US Farm Surpluses to Underdeveloped Countries", in: *Journal of Farm Economics*, XLII (1960), 1019–30
C. Schultze, "Is Economics Obsolete? No Underemployed", in: *Saturday Review*, Jan. 22, 1972
C. Schultze et al., *Setting National Priorities: The 1972 Budget*, Washington, D. C. 1972
G. Schuhmacher, "Public Finance—Its Relation to Full Employment", in: Oxford University Institute of Statistics, *The Economics of Full Employment*, Oxford 1945
J. Schumpeter, *Business Cycles*, NY 1939
— *Capitalism, Socialism and Democracy*, London 1966
— *Economic Doctrine and Method*, NY 1967 (1954)
— *History of Economic Analysis*, NY 1955
— "John Maynard Keynes", in: *American Economic Review*, Sept. 1946
— "On the Concept of Social Value", in: *Quarterly Journal of Economics*, XXIII (1908)
A. Schweitzer, *Big Business in the Third Reich*, Bloomington 1964
W. Semmler/J. Hoffmann, "Kapitalakkumulation, Staatsgeingriffe und Lohnbewegung", in: *Probleme des Klassenkampfs*, 2 (Febr. 1972)
H. Seton-Watson, *From Lenin to Khrushchev*, NY 1962
R. Sheenan, "Proprietors in the World of Big Business", in: *Fortune* LXXV/7 (June 1967), 178–83, 242
H. Sherman, *Profits in the United States*, Ithaca 1968
— *Radical Political Economy*, NY 1972
E. Shershnev, *SShA: Tamozhennyi protektsionizm*, Moscow 1970
A. Shire, "The Industrial Organization of Housing: Its Methods and Costs", in: *The Annals of the American Academy of Political and Social Science*, CXC (March 1937)
A. Shonfield, *The Attack on World Poverty*, NY 1962
— *Modern Capitalism*, London 1969
B. Shoul, "Karl Marx and Say's Law", in: *Quarterly Journal of Economics*, LXXI (1957)
B. Siegel, *Aggregate Economics and Public Policy*, Homewood 1970
H. Singer, "The Distribution of Gains between Investing and Borrowing Countries", in: *American Economic Review*, XL/2 (May 1950)
L. Sirc, *Economic Devolution in Eastern Europe*, NY 1969
G. Siskind, *John Maynard Keynes–ein falscher Prophet*, Berlin 1959

A. Skolnik/S. Dales, "Social Welfare Expenditures", in: *Social Security Bulletin*, XXXV/12 (Dec. 1972)
— "Social Welfare Expenditures, 1972–73", in: *Social Security Bulletin*, Jan. 1974
S. Small, "Statistical effect of work-training programs on the unemployment rate", in: *Monthly Labor Review*, XCV/9 (Sept. 1972), 7–13
A. Smith, *The Wealth of Nations*, NY, n.d.
D. Smith, "The Canadian Full Employment Goal", in: *The Canadian Banker*, LXXI/4 (Winter 1964), 7–13
H. Smith, "An Estimate of the Income of the Very Rich", in: J. Quirk/A. Zarley (eds.), *Papers in Quantitative Economics*, Lawrence 1968
W. Smith, *Macroeconomics*, Homewood 1970
D. Snodgrass, *Ceylon: An Export Economy in Transition*, Homewood 1966
A. Sohn-Rethel, *Geistige und körperliche Arbeit*, Frankfurt/Main 1970
— *Ökonomie und Klassenstruktur des deutschen Faschismus*, Frankfurt/Main 1973
L. Soltow (ed.), *Six Papers on the Size Distribution of Wealth and Income*, NY 1969
W. Sombart, *Warum gibt es in den Vereinigten Staaten keinen Sozialismus?*, Tübingen 1906
R. Sonnemann, *Die Auswirkungen des Schutzzolls auf die Monopolisierung der deutschen Eisen- und Stahlindustrie, 1879–1892*, Berlin 1960
T. Sowell, *Say's Law*, Princeton 1972
P. Sraffa, "The Laws of Return under Competitive Conditions", in: *Economic Journal*, XXXVI/44 (Dec. 1926)
— "Sulla relazioni fra costo e quantita prodotta", in: *Annali di Economia*, II (1925–26)
G. Staley, *International Economics*, Englewood Cliffs 1970
Statistical Abstract of the United States, 1967; 1969; 1972, Washington D. C.
J. Steindl, *Maturity and Stagnation in American Capitalism*, Oxford 1952
— *Small and Big Business*, Oxford 1945
K. Steinhaus, *Zur Theorie des internationalen Klassenkampfs*, Frankfurt/Main 1967
G. Stigler, *The Theory of Price*, NY 1966
S. Stern, "Down and Out in New York", in: *New York Times Magazine*, Oct. 22, 1972
J. Stinson, Jr., "Employment in manufacturing during the '69–'71 Downturn", in: *Monthly Labor Review*, June 1972
J. Stout (ed.), *Economics of the Livestock-Meat Industry*, NY 1964
J. Strachey, *The Coming Sturggle for Power*, NY 1935
P. Sweezy, "John Maynard Keynes", in: *Science & Society*, Fall 1946
— *Monopoly and Competition in the English Coal Trade 1550–1850*, Cambridge 1938
— *The Theory of Capitalist Development*, NY 1968 (1942)
P. Taylor, *The Principles of Scientific Management*, NY 1916
P. Thal, "Zum 200. Geburtstag von David Ricardo: Ricard's Theorie der komparativen Außenhandelsvorteile" in: *Jahrbuch für Wirtschaftsgeschichte*, 1972/part I, pp. 21–39

L. Thurow, *The Impact of Taxes on the American Economy*, NY 1971
V. Timmermann, "Anzeichen für gegenläufiges Verhalten in einzelnen

Branchen—Unternehmerische Entscheidungen unter dem Einfluß der Geld- und Kreditpolitik: Das Beispiel Lieferantenkredit", in: D. Duwendag (ed.), *Macht und Ohnmacht der Bundesbank*, Frankfurt-Main 1973, pp. 97–118

J. Timberger, "Statistical Evidence on the Accelerator Principle", in: *Economica*, V (New Series), May 1938

W. Toal, "Manufacturing Growth, Down South' ", in: Federal Reserve Bank of Atlanta, *Monthly Review*, LVII/8 (Aug. 1972), 130–36

J. Tobin, "On Improving the Economic Status of the Negro", in: *Daedalus*, Fall 1965

A. Tostlebe, *Capital in Agriculture: its Formation and Financing since 1870*, Princeton 1957

I. Trakhtenberg, *Denezhoe obrashchenie kredit v kapitalizme*, Moscow 1962
— *Denezhyne krizisi (1821–1938 gg.)*, Moscow 1963
— *Sovremennyi kredit i ego organizatsiia*, Part I, Moscow 1931

R. Triffin, *The Evolution of the International Monetary System*, in: *Princeton Studies in International Finance*, 12, 1964
— *Gold and the Dollar Crisis*, New Haven 1961

L. Turgeon, *The Contrasting Economies*, Boston 1964

C. Turner, *An Analysis of Soviet Views on John Maynard Keynes*, Durham 1969

H. Turner/F. Wilinson, "Real Net Incomes and the Wage Explosion", in: *New Society*, Feb. 25, 1971

G. Tyler, "Multinationals: A Global Menace", in: *The American Federationist*, LXXIX/7 (July 1972)

L. Ulman/R. Flanagan, *Wage Restraint: A Study of Incomes Policies in Western Europe*, Berkeley 1971

United Nations Economic Commission for Europe, *Incomes in Postwar Europe*, Geneva 1967

United Nations Economic Bulletin for Latin America, "Income Distribution in Latin America", XII/2 (Oct. 1967), 38–60

U.S. *Census of Agriculture, 1964*, Washington, D.C., 1964, Vol. II

U.S. Commission on International Trade and Investment Policy, *US International Economic Policy in an Interdependent World*, Washington D.C. 1971, 2 Vols.

U.S. Congress, House Committee on Banking and Currency, Subcommittee on Domestic Finance, *Commercial Banks and their Trust Activities: Emerging Influence on the American Economy*, 90th Cong., 2nd Sess., 1968, Vol. I

U.S. Congress, Committee on Banking and Currency, *Removal of Gold Cover*, 90th Cong., 2nd Sess., 1968

U.S. Congress, House Committee on Education and Labor, *Construction Safety*, 90th Cong., 1st–2nd Sess., 1968

U.S. Congress, House Committee on the Judiciary, Anti-Trust Subcommittee, *Investigation of Conglomerate Corporations*, 92nd Cong., 1st Sess., June 1, 1971

U.S. Congress, Joint Economic Committee, *Current Labor Market Developments*, Hearings, Part I, Washington, D.C. 1972
— *1962 Supplement to Economic Indicators*, 87th Cong., 2nd Sess., 1962
— *Twentieth Anniversary of the Employment Act of 1946*, 89th Cong., 2nd Sess., Oct. 23, 1966

— Report of the Subcommittee on International Exchange and Payments, *Action Now to Strengthen the Dollar*, 92nd Cong., 2nd Sess., Aug. 1971
— Hearings on HR 16810, *$465 Billion Debt Limit*, 92nd Cong., 2nd Sess., Oct. 11, 1972
— Subcommittee on Fiscal Policy, Studies in Public Welfare, *Paper 2: Economics of Federal Subsidy Programs*, Part 7—Agricultural Subsidies, 93rd Cong., 1st Sess., April 30, 1973
— Subcommittee on Fiscal Policy, Studies in Public Welfare, *Paper Nr. 2: Handbook on Income Transfer Programs*, 92nd Cong., 2nd Sess., Oct. 16, 1972
U.S. Department of Agriculture, *Agricultural Statistics, 1970*, Washington, D.C. 1970
U.S. Department of Labor, Bureau of Labor Statistics, *Bulletin 1656: Compensation in the Construction Industry*, Washington, D.C. 1970
U.S. Senate, Committee on Finance, *Implications of Multinational Firms for World Trade and Investment and for U.S. Trade and Labor*, 93rd Cong., 1st Sess., Febr. 1973
U.S. Senate, Committee on Labor and Public Welfare, Subcommittee on Migrant Labor, *Farmworkers in Rural America, 1971–1972*, 92nd Cong., 1st–2nd Sess., 1972
"U.S. Textile Industry", in: *Progressive Labor*, VII/1 (Febr. 1971), 55–68

E. Varga, *Aufstieg oder Niedergang des Kapitalismus*, Hamburg 1924
— *Die Krise der kapitalistischen Weltwirtschaft*, Hamburg 1921
— *Die Krise des Kapitalismus und ihre politischen Folgen*, ed. by E. Altvater, Frankfurt/Main 1969
— *Die Niedergangsperiode des Kapitalismus*, Hamburg 1922
— "Plans for Post-War Currency Stabilization", in: *The Commercial and Financial Chronicle*, CLIX/4260, March 2, 1944, p. 918
— *Politico-Economic Problems of Capitalism*, Moscow 1968
I. Vasil'chuk, " 'Kapital' K. Marksa i sovremennaia teoriia kapitalisticheskogo pribili i tsen", in: *Mirovaia ekonomika i mezhdunarodnye otnosheniia*, 3/1967, pp. 62–75
R. Vernon, *Sovereignty At Bay*, NY 1971
F. Vilmar (ed.), *Menschenwürde im Betrieb*, Reinbek 1973
— *Rüstung und Abrüstung im Spätkapitalismus*, Frankfurt/Main 1967[3]
J. Viner, *The Customs Union Issue*, NY 1950
— *Studies in the Theory of International Trade*, London 1964 (1937)
I. Vinster, *Angliiskie kapitalovlozheniia za granitseii v periode imperializma*, Moscow 1960
S. Vygodskiy, *Sovremenniy kapitalizm*, Moscow 1969

H. Wagner, "Die zyklischen Überproduktionskrisen der Industrieproduktion in den USA in den ersten beiden Etappen der allgemeinen Krise des Kapitalismus (1914–1958)", in: *Jahrbuch für Wirtschaftsgeschichte*, 1964, part 4, pp. 11–90
M. Ways, "Land: The Boom that Really Hurts", in: *Fortune*, LXXXVIII/1 (July 1973)

M. Weber, "Die Grenznutsenlehre und das 'psychophysische Grundgesetz' ", in: *Archiv für Sozialwissenschaft und Soziapolitik*, XXVII (1908)
— *Wirtschaft und Gesellschaft*, Cologne/Berlin (West) 1964
M. Widenbaum/D. Larkins, *The Federal Budget for 1973*, Washington, D.C. 1972
P. Wicksteed, *The Common Sense of Political Economy*, London 1910
F. Wieser, *Über den Ursprung und die Hauptgesetze des wirthschaftlichen Werthes*, Vienna 1884
R. Wilcock, "The Secondary Labor Force and the Measurement of Unemployment", in: *NBER, The Measurement and Behavior of Unemployment*, Princeton 1957
P. Wiles, *Communist International Economics*, NY 1969
— *The Political Economy of Communism*, NY 1962
— *Prise, Cost and Output*, rev. ed., Oxford 1961
P. Wilhjelm, *Dansk boligpolitik—forbrydelse eller dumhed?* Copenhagen 1971
J. Williams, "Free Enterprise and Full Employment", in: P. Homan/F. Machlup (eds.), *Financing American Prosperity*, NY 1945
J. Williamson, *American Growth and the Balance of Payments*, Chapel Hill 1964
— "Public Expenditure and Revenue: An International Comparison", in: *Manchester School of Economics and Social Studies*, XXIX/1 (May 1961), 43–56
F. Wilson, *Labour in the South African Gold Mines 1911–1969*, London 1972
D. Winchester, "The British Coal Mine Strike of 1972", in: *Monthly Labor Review*, Oct. 1972
W. Wolodin, *Keynes—ein Ideologe des Monopolkapitals*, Berlin 1955
— *Zarabotnaia plata v usloviiakh sovremennogo kapitalizma*, Moscow 1967
W. S. Woytinsky/E. S. Woytinsky, *World Commerce and Governments* NY 1955
— *World Population and Production*, NY 1955

K. Yamamura, "Japanese Anti-Monopoly Policy: 1947–1970", in: H. Arndt (ed.), *Die Konzentration in der Wirtschaft*, West Berlin 1971², Vol. II, pp. 161–82
L. Yeager, *The International Monetary Mechanism*, NY 1968

N. Zaitsev, *Gospodstvo monopolii v sel'skom khoziastve SShA*, Moscow 1966
G. Zenk, *Konzentrationspolitik in Schweden*, Tubingen 1971

OTHER BOOKS OF INTEREST PUBLISHED BY URIZEN

LITERATURE

Ehrenburg, Ilya
The Life of the Automobile, novel, 192 pages
Cloth $8.95 / paper $4.95

Enzensberger, Hans Magnus
Mausoleum, poetry, 132 pages
Cloth $10.00 / paper $4.95

Hamburger, Michael
German Poetry 1910-1975, 576 pages
Cloth $17.50 / paper $6.95

Handke, Peter
Nonsense & Happiness, poetry, 80 pages
Cloth $7.95 / paper $3.95

Hansen, Olaf (Ed.)
The Radical Will, Randolph Bourne (Selected Writings) 1911-1918
500 pages
Cloth $17.50 / paper $7.95

Innerhofer, Franz
Beautiful Days, novel, 228 pages
Cloth $8.95 / paper $4.95

Kroetz, Franz Xaver
Farmyard & Other Plays, 192 pages
Cloth $12.95 / paper $4.95

Montale, Eugenio
Poet in Our Time (essays), 96 pages
Cloth $5.95 / paper $2.95

Shepard, Sam
Angel City, Curse of the Starving Class, & Other Plays, 300 pages
Cloth $15.00 / paper $4.95

FILM

Bresson, Robert
Notes on Cinematography, 132 pages
Cloth $6.95 / paper $2.95

Bresson, Robert
The Complete Screenplays, Vol. I, 400 pages
Cloth $17.50 / paper $6.95

PSYCHOLOGY

Borneman, Ernest (Ed.)
The Psychoanalysis of Money, 420 pages
Cloth $15.00 / paper $5.95

Doerner, Klaus
Madmen and the Bourgeoisie, 384 pages
Cloth $15.00 / paper $5.95

Patrick C. Lee and Robert S. Stewart
Sex Differences, 500 pages
Cloth $17.50 / paper $5.95

Moser, Tilman
Years of Apprenticeship on the Couch, 240 pages / Cloth $10.00

ECONOMICS

De Brunhoff, Suzanne
Marx on Money, 192 pages
Cloth $10.00 / paper $4.95

Linder, Marc
Anti-Samuelson Vol. I, 400 pages
Cloth $15.00 / paper $5.95
Anti-Samuelson, Vol. II, 440 pages
Cloth $15.00 / paper $5.95

SOCIOLOGY

Andrew Arato/Eike Gebhardt (Eds.)
The Essential Frankfurt School Reader, 544 pages / Cloth $17.50 / paper $5.95

Pearce, Frank
Crimes of the Powerful, 176 pages
Paper $4.95

Van Onselen, Charles
Chibaro (African Mine Labor in Southern Rhodesia), 368 pages / Cloth $17.50

Shaw, Martin
Marxism Versus Sociology (A Reading Guide), 120 pages
Cloth $6.95 / paper $2.25

Shaw, Martin
Marxism and Social Science, 125 pages
Paper $2.95

Thönnessen, Werner
The Emancipation of Women, 185 pages
Cloth $10.00 / paper $4.95

Write for a complete catalog to:
Urizen Books, Inc., 66 West Broadway, New York, N.Y. 10007